EASTERN EUROPE

EASTERN EUROPE

An Introduction to the People, Lands, and Culture

VOLUME 1

EDITED BY RICHARD FRUCHT

A B C • C L I O

Santa Barbara, California   •   Denver, Colorado   •   Oxford, England

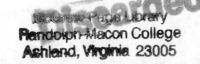

Library of Congress Cataloging-in-Publication Data
Eastern Europe : an introduction to the people, lands, and culture / edited
by Richard Frucht.
    p.   cm.
  Includes bibliographical references and index.
   ISBN 1-57607-800-0 (hardback : alk. paper) — ISBN 1-57607-801-9
(e-book)
   1. Europe, Eastern.   2. Europe, Central.   3.   Balkan Peninsula.
I. Frucht, Richard C., 1951–

DJK9.E25   2005
940'.09717—dc22

                                                        2004022300

This book is also available on the World Wide Web as an eBook. Visit abc-
clio.com for details.

ABC-CLIO, Inc.
130 Cremona Drive, P.O. Box 1911
Santa Barbara, California 93116-1911
This book is printed on acid-free paper.

Manufactured in the United States of America

Contents

Eastern Europe

Volume 1: The Northern Tier

Volume 2: Central Europe

Volume 3: Southeastern Europe

PREFACE

In *The Lexus and the Olive Tree* (Farrar, Straus, and Giroux, 1999) and *Longitudes and Attitudes* (Farrar, Straus, and Giroux, 2002), the award-winning reporter for the *New York Times* Thomas L. Friedman observed that the world has made a remarkable transition during the past quarter century from division to integration. What was once a world of separation, symbolized by the Cold War and "the Wall," evolved, especially with the collapse of the Soviet Union, into a world of globalization and global interconnectedness, symbolized by "the Net." That new reality has led to remarkable changes. Moreover, it is not merely a passing trend; it is a reality that affects every facet of human existence.

Regrettably, however, not everyone has become part of what amounts to a revolution; in some cases, an antimodernism has caused a lag in the developments of the critical trends of democratization and economic change. That gap, epitomized by the difference between the world of the Lexus and that of the olive tree, forms the core of Friedman's analysis of the Middle East, for example. As perceptive as he is of this clash in that region, in many ways Friedman's observations regarding the necessity of seeing the world in a more global and integrated manner are prophetic for many in the West as well. Although Friedman's emphasis is on an antimodernism that creates a gap between the world of the olive tree and the world of the Lexus, preventing interconnectedness from being fully realized, there are other barriers, more subtle perhaps, but no less real, that create gaps in the knowledge of so many areas of the world with which we are so closely linked.

Certainly in the United States, knowledge of other parts of the world is at times regrettably and, some might argue, even dangerously lacking. The events of September 2001 and the actions of a handful of al-Qaeda fanatics are but one example of an inattention to the realities of the post–Cold War world. Despite the fact that the organization of Osama Bin-Laden had long been a sworn enemy of the United States (and others) and his followers had already launched attacks on targets around the globe (including an earlier attempt on New York's World Trade Center), many, if not most, Americans knew very little (if anything) about al-Qaeda, its motives, or its objectives. What is troubling about that limited knowledge is the simple fact that if an organization with such hostile designs on those it opposed could be so overlooked or ignored, what does that say about knowledge of other momentous movements that are not so overtly hostile? In a world that is increasingly global and integrated, such a parochialism is a luxury that one cannot afford.

Although educators have at times been unduly criticized for problems and deficiencies that may be beyond their control, it is legitimate to argue that there are occasions when teaching fails to keep pace with new realities. Language training, for example, hasn't changed much in the United States for decades, even though one can argue that languages critical to the future of commerce and society, such as Japanese, Chinese, or Arabic, are less often taught than other "traditional" languages. Thus the force of tradition outweighs new realities and needs. Such myopia is born out of a curricular process that almost views change as an enemy. Similarly, "Western Civilization" courses, on both the high school and college level, for the most part remain rooted in English and French history, a tunnel-vision approach that not only avoids the developments of globalization or even a global outlook, but also ignores key changes in other parts of Europe as well. Provincialism in a rapidly changing world should only be a style of design or furniture; it cannot afford to be an outlook. In a world of rapid change, curriculum cannot afford to be stagnant.

Such a curriculum, however, especially on the high school level, is often the inevitable by-product of the materials available. When I was asked to direct the Public Education Project for the American Association for the Advancement of Slavic Studies in the early 1990s, I had the opportunity to review countless textbooks, and the regional imbalance (overwhelmingly Eurocentric in presentation, with a continued focus on England and France) present in these books was such that it could lead to a global short-sightedness on the part of students. Despite the fall of the Berlin Wall and the collapse of the Soviet Union, the books usually contained more on obscure French kings that on Kosovo. Educators recognized that, and from their input it was clear that they needed, more than anything else, resources to provide background material so that they could bring to their students some knowledge of changes that only a few years earlier had seemed unimaginable.

This need for general resource works led to the publication of *The Encyclopedia of Eastern Europe: From the Congress of Vienna to the Fall of Communism* (Garland, 2000). Its goal was to provide information on the rich histories of Albania, Bulgaria, Czechoslovakia, Hungary, Poland, Romania, and Yugoslavia. The reception the book received was gratifying, and it has led to this work, which is designed to act in tandem with the information in the *Encyclopedia of Eastern Europe* to offer the general reader a broad-based overview of the entire region running from the Baltic to the Mediterranean. In addition, this book expands the coverage to other areas in the region not addressed in the encyclopedia.

The three volumes of this work cover three groups of countries, each marked by geographical proximity and a general commonality in historical development. The first volume covers the northern tier of states, including Poland and the Baltic states of Lithuania, Estonia, and Latvia. The second volume looks at lands that were once part of the Habsburg Empire: Slovakia, the Czech Republic, Hungary, Slovenia, and Croatia. The third volume examines the Balkan states of Serbia and Montenegro, Bulgaria, Albania, Romania, Macedonia, Bosnia-Hercegovina, and Greece, lands all once dominated by the Ottoman Empire. Each chapter looks at a single country in terms of its geography and people, history, political development, economy, and culture, as well as the challenges it now faces; each also contains short vignettes that bring out the uniqueness of each country specifically and of the area in general. This structure will allow the reader not only to look at the rich developments in each individual nation, but also to compare those developments to others in the region.

As technology makes the world smaller, and as globalization brings humankind closer together, it is critical that regions once overlooked be not only seen but viewed in a different light. The nations of East Central and Southeastern Europe, that is, "Eastern" Europe, are increasingly a vital part of a new Europe and a new world. What during the Cold War seemed incomprehensible to many, namely, the collapse of totalitarianism and the rise of democracy in these countries, is now a reality all should cherish and help nurture; first, though, it has to be understood. It is the hope that this series may bring that understanding to the general reader.

Putting together this work would have been impossible without the scholarship, dedication, professionalism, and patience of the authors. The words are theirs, but the gratitude is all mine. In addition, I would like to thank a number of students and staff at Northwest Missouri State University who helped with the mountain of work (often computer-related) that a project of this size entails. Chief among them is Patricia Headley, the department secretary, who was not only my computer guru but also someone whose consistent good cheer always kept me going. I would also like to thank Laura Pearl, a talented graduate student in English who filled the role of the "general reader" by pointing out what might make sense to a historian but would not make sense to someone without some background in the region. Other students, including Precious Sanders, Jeff Easton, Mitchell Kline, and Krista Kupfer, provided the legwork that is essential to all such projects. And finally, I would like to thank the staff at ABC-CLIO, especially Alicia Merritt, for keeping faith in the project even when delivery of the manuscript did not match initial projections; Anna Kaltenbach, the production editor, for navigating the manuscript through the various stages; the copy editors, Silvine Farnell and Chrisona Schmidt, for their thoughtful and often painstaking work; Bill Nelson, the cartographer; and the photo editor, Giulia Rossi, for creating such a diverse yet balanced presentation.

And finally there are Sue, my wife, and Kristin, my daughter. Words can never express how important they are, but they know.

Richard Frucht
September 2004

Introduction

The use of the term "Eastern Europe" to describe the geographical region covered here is standard, but it is nevertheless something of a misnomer. The problem is that it not only makes a geographical distinction between this area and "Western Europe"; it also implies a distinction in development, one that ignores the similarities between Western and Eastern Europe and instead separates the continent into two distinct entities. It even suggests that Eastern Europe is a monolithic entity, failing to distinguish the states of the Balkans from those of the Baltic region. In short, it is an artificial construct that provides a simplistic division in a continent that is far more diverse, yet at the same time more closely linked together, than such a division implies.

Western Europe evokes images of Big Ben and Parliament in London, the Eiffel Tower and the Louvre in Paris, the Coliseum and the Vatican in Rome, the bulls of Pamplona in Spain. Eastern Europe on the other hand brings to mind little more than the "Iron Curtain," war in Kosovo, ethnic cleansing in Bosnia, orphanages in Romania, and the gray, bleak images of the Cold War and the Soviet Bloc. Just as colors convey certain connotations to people, so too do the concepts of "Western" and "Eastern" Europe convey very different impressions and mental images. The former is viewed as enlightened, cultured, and progressive; the latter is seen as dark, uncivilized, and static. Western Europe is democratic; Eastern Europe is backward and totalitarian, plagued by the kind of lack of fundamental humanity that leads inevitably to the horrors of Srebrenica.

Some of these stereotypes are not without some degree of justification. Foreign domination—whether German, Habsburg, Ottoman, or Russian (later Soviet)—has left parts of the region in an arrested state of development. All the peoples of the region were for much of the last half-millennium the focus and subjects of others rather than masters of their own destinies. Accordingly, trends found in more favored areas were either delayed or stunted. Albanian nationalism, for example, did not take root until a century after the French Revolution. The economic trends of the West as well as the post-1945 democracy movements (notably capitalism and democracy) are still in their infancy.

But labels are often superficial, and they can blind individuals to reality. Certainly, Tirana would never be confused with Paris. Estonia is not England. At the same time, the Polish-Lithuanian state was at its height the largest empire in Europe. Prague stuns visitors with its beauty no less than Paris; in fact, many remark that Prague is their favorite city in Europe. Budapest strikes people in the same way that Vienna does. The Danube may not be blue, but it does run through four European capitals, not just Vienna (Bratislava, Budapest, and Belgrade being the other three). The painted monasteries in Romania are no less intriguing in their design and use of color than some of the grandiose cathedrals in "the West." The Bulgarian Women's Chorus produces a sound no less stunning than that of the Vienna Boys' Choir. In short, to judge by labels and stereotypes in the end produces little more than myopia.

To dismiss Eastern Europe as backward (or worse, barbaric) is to forget that many of the Jews of Europe were saved during the Inquisition by emigrating to Poland or the lands of the Ottoman Empire. To cite the Magna Carta as the foundation of democracy in England, even though in reality it meant little more than protection for the rights of the nobility, is to ignore the fact that first written constitution in Europe was not found in the "West" but rather in the "East" (Poland). And although backwardness and even barbarity certainly can be found in the recent past in the region, no country in Europe is immune from a past that most would rather forget (the Crusades, the Inquisition, religious wars, the gas chambers of World War II, to name but a few). Myths are comfortable, but they can also be destructive. They can ennoble a people to be sure, but they can also blind them to reality and lead to a lack of understanding.

Eastern Europe is not exotic, and an understanding of it is not an exercise in esoterica. Rather the region has been and will continue to be an integral part of Europe. In one sense Europe became a distinct entity when Christianity, the cultural unifier, spread through the last outposts of the continent. In another sense, it has again become a unified continent with the demise of the last great empire that held sway over so many.

When former president Ronald Reagan passed away in June 2004, the media repeatedly recalled perhaps his most memorable line: "Mr. Gorbachev, tear down this wall," a remark made in 1984 as the American president stood in front of the Berlin Wall. In this case the American leader was referring to the concrete and barbed wire barrier behind him erected in the 1960s by the former Soviet Union to seal off its empire from the West. Yet, in many respects, the modern history of Eastern Europe was one of a series of walls, some physical (as in the case of the Iron Curtain), others geographical (all of the nations in the region were under the domination of regional great powers), and, one could argue, even psychological (the at times destructive influence of nationalism that created disruption and violence and has been a plague in the lands of the former Yugoslavia on numerous occasions in the past century). These walls have often determined not only the fate of the nations of the region but the lives of the inhabitants as well.

The past is the DNA that tells us who we are and who we can be. It is the owners' manual for every country and every people. Without that past there would be no nation and no nationalism. It is that past that provides the markers and lessons for nations and peoples. It gives direction to the present. It provides a bedrock upon which we build our societies. Whether it leads to myths that embody virtues or myths that cover up what we don't wish to acknowledge, it is the shadow that we can never lose. Thus, when each of the nations of East Central and Southeastern Europe was reborn in the nineteenth or twentieth centuries (in some cases twice reborn), the past was the compass directing them to the future.

Nations are a modern concept, but peoples are not. Poland, for example, once a great and influential European state in the Middle Ages, was partitioned in the late eighteenth century, only to rise again, like a phoenix, in 1918. And even when it again fell prey to the domination of outside influences following World War II, it was the people, embodied in Solidarity, the workers' union, who toppled the communist regime. Despite the fact that at one time or another all of the peoples and nations addressed in these volumes were under the rule or direction of a neighboring great power, the force of nationalism never abated.

Nothing is more powerful than an idea. It can inspire, unify, give direction and purpose; it can almost take on a life of its own, even though it may lie dormant for centuries. In his *Ideen zur Philosophie der Geschichte der Menschheit* (Ideas on the Philosophy of the History of Mankind), the eighteenth-century German philosopher Johann Herder captured the essence of nationalism in his analysis of the *Volk* (the people). Herder emphasized that a spirit of the nation (which Georg Hegel, the nineteenth-century German philosopher most noted for his development of the concept of the dialectic of history, later termed the *Volkgeist,* or "spirit of the people") existed that transcended politics. From the point of view of Herder and the other German idealist philosophers, peoples developed distinct characteristics based upon time and place (reflecting the *Zeitgeist,* the "spirit of the time"). Societies were therefore organic, and thus each had to be viewed in terms of its own culture and development. Accordingly, each culture not only was distinct but should recognize the distinctiveness of others, as characteristics of one culture would not necessarily be found in another. To ignore that uniqueness, which gives to each Volk a sense of nobility, would be to ignore reality.

For the peoples of Eastern Europe, language, culture, and a shared past (even if that past was mythologized, or in some cases even fabricated), exactly that spirit of the Volk that Herder, Hegel, and others saw as the essence of society, proved to be more powerful and more lasting than any occupying army or dynastic overlordship. And when modern nationalism spread throughout Europe and for that matter the world in the nineteenth and twentieth centuries, culture became the genesis of national revivals.

For centuries, Eastern Europe served as a crossroads, both in terms of trade and in the migrations (and in some cases invasions) of peoples. The former brought prosperity to some parts of the region, notably the northern and central parts of the belt between the Baltic and Mediterranean seas, while the latter left many areas a mosaic of peoples, who in the age of nationalism came to struggle as much with each other for national dominance as they did with their neighbors who dominated them politically. As the great medieval states in the region, from the Serbian Empire of Stefan Dušan to the First and Second Bulgarian Empires, to the Hungarian and Polish-Lithuanian states, fell to stronger neighbors or to internal difficulties, no peoples were left untouched by outsiders. Greece may have been able to remain outside the Soviet orbit in the 1940s, but for centuries it was a key possession of the Ottoman Empire. Poland may have been the largest state of its time, but it fell prey to its avaricious neighbors, the Russians, Prussians, and Austrians. Yet, despite centuries of occupation, in each case the Volk remained.

One of the dominant elements in modernization has been the establishment of modern nations. While the rise of the modern nation-state was late arriving in Eastern Europe, and some in Eastern Europe had failed to experience in the same manner some of the movements, such as the Renaissance or the rise of capitalism, that shaped Western Europe, it was no less affected by the rise of modern nationalism than its Western neighbors. Despite the divergent and, in some cases, the retarded development of the region in regard to many of the trends in the West, the nations of Eastern Europe in the early twenty-first century are again independent members of a suddenly larger Europe.

The story of Eastern Europe, while often written or at least directed by outsiders, is more than a mere tale of struggle. It is also a story of enormous human complexity, one of great achievement as well as great sorrow, one in which the spirit of the Volk has triumphed (even though, admittedly, it has at times, as in the former Yugoslavia, failed to respect the uniqueness of other peoples and cultures). It is a rich story, which will continue to unfold as Eastern Europe becomes more and more an integral part of Europe as a whole (a fact evident in the expansion of the European Union and NATO into areas of the former Soviet Empire). And in order to understand the story of that whole, one must begin with the parts.

CONTRIBUTORS

VOLUME 1

Terry D. Clark is a professor of political science and the director of the graduate program in international relations at Creighton University. He received his Ph.D. from the University of Illinois at Urbana-Champaign in 1992. A specialist in comparative politics and international relations, he was instrumental in developing Creighton University's exchange program with universities in Eastern Europe. He has published three books and numerous articles devoted to the study of postcommunist Europe. His research interests include the development of democratic institutions and the evolution of public opinion supporting such institutions in Lithuania and Russia.

Mel Huang is a freelance analyst on the Baltic states and is also a research associate with the Conflict Studies Research Centre (CSRC) at the Royal Military Academy, Sandhurst. He previously worked as the primary Baltics analyst for the analytical department of Radio Free Europe/Radio Liberty and served as the Baltics editor of the award-winning online journal Central Europe Review.

Aldis Purs received his Ph.D. in history from the University of Toronto in 1998. He has taught at Vidzeme University College, Wayne State University, and Eastern Michigan University. He is a coauthor of *Latvia: The Challenges of Change* (Routledge, 2001) and *The Baltic States: Estonia, Latvia, and Lithuania* (Routledge 2002) and a contributor to the University of Manchester research project "Population Displacement, State Building, and Social Identity in the Lands of the Former Russian Empire, 1917–1930."

Piotr Wróbel holds the Konstanty Reynert Chair of Polish Studies at the University of Toronto. He received his Ph.D. from the University of Warsaw in 1984. He has been a visiting scholar at the Institute of European History in Mainz, at Humboldt University in Berlin, at the Institute of Polish-Jewish Studies at Oxford, and at the United States Holocaust Memorial Museum in Washington, D.C. He has authored or coauthored some fifty articles and nine books, including *The Historical Dictionary of Poland, 1945–1996* (Greenwood, 1998). He currently serves on the advisory board of *Polin: A Journal of Polish-Jewish Studies,* on the board of directors of the Polish-Jewish Heritage Foundation of Canada, and on the governing council of the American Association for Polish-Jewish Studies.

VOLUME 2

June Granatir Alexander is a member of the faculty of the Russian and East European Studies Program at the University of Cincinnati. In addition to numerous scholarly articles, reviews, and encyclopedia entries, she is the author of two books: *The Immigrant Church and Community: Pittsburgh's Slovak Catholics and Lutherans, 1880–1915* (Pittsburgh, 1987) and *Ethnic Pride, American Patriotism: Slovaks and Other New Immigrants in the Interwar Era* (Temple University Press, 2004).

Mark Biondich is an analyst with the Crimes against Humanities and War Crimes Section of the Department of Justice of Canada. He received his Ph.D. in history from the University of Toronto in 1997 and is the author of *Stjepan Radić, the Croat Peasant Party and the Politics of Mass Mobilization, 1904–1928* (Toronto, 2000), as well as a number of articles and reviews concerning Croatian, Yugoslav, and Balkan history.

András A. Boros-Kazai was raised in a proletarian district in Budapest before coming to the United States, where he studied at Kent State University and the University of Pittsburgh. He earned his Ph.D. in history from Indiana University in 1982. He is currently a freelance translator, a researcher-consultant, and an adjunct member of the faculty at Beloit College.

Brigit Farley received her Ph.D. from Indiana University. She is an associate professor of history at Washington State University. A specialist on twentieth-century Russian and European cultural history, and the author of a number of articles, reviews, and encyclopedia entries, she is currently working on the life and death of a Moscow church.

Daniel Miller received his Ph.D. from the University of Pittsburgh, and is a professor of history at the University of West Florida in Pensacola. His research involves Czech and Slovak history, especially between the two world wars, and focuses largely on agrarian political history. He is the author of several chapters and articles along with *Forging Political Compromise: Antonín Švehla and the Czechoslovak Republican Party, 1918–1933* (Pittsburgh, 1999), which has been translated into Czech. He is also one of the coauthors of a volume in Czech on the history of the Slovak and Czech agrarian movement. In the preparation of his chapter, he would like to acknowledge the contributions and suggestions of Gregory X. Ference of Salisbury University, Lenka Kocková and Pavel Kocek (on several aspects of Czech culture and history), Alex Švamberk (on Czech popular music), and Ivan Lalák (on modern architecture).

VOLUME 3

Robert Austin is a lecturer and project coordinator with the Centre for Russian and East European Studies at the University of Toronto. He is also a project manager with Intermedia Survey Institute in Washington, D.C. His current research focuses on interwar Albania and media trends in contemporary Albania. He was aided in the preparation of his chapter by Brigitte Le Normand, who received her M.A. from the University of Toronto and is currently pursuing her Ph.D. in history at UCLA.

Richard Frucht is a professor of history and chair of the Department of History, Humanities, Philosophy, and Political Science at Northwest Missouri State University. He received his Ph.D. from Indiana University in 1980. The author of a number of books and articles on Eastern Europe, most recently he was the editor of *The Encyclopedia of Eastern Europe: From the Congress of Vienna to the Fall of Communism* (Garland, 2000).

Alexandros K. Kyrou is an associate professor of History and the director of the Program in East European Studies at Salem State College. He received his Ph.D. from Indiana University and was a Hanaah Seeger Davis Visiting Research Fellow in Hellenic Studies at Princeton University, a senior research fellow of the Kokkalis Program on Southeastern and East Central Europe at the John F. Kennedy School of Government at Harvard University, and a research scholar at the Institute on Religion and World Affairs at

Boston University. He is also the associate editor of the *Journal of Modern Hellenism*.

Katherine McCarthy teaches history at Bradley University and is a research associate in the Russian and East European Center at the University of Illinois, Urbana-Champaign. She completed her Ph.D. in East European history at the University of Pittsburgh in 1996 and has written on peasant issues in the former Yugoslavia.

Nicholas Miller is an associate professor at Boise State University. He has written extensively on the Serbian community in Croatia, Serbian nationalism, and Serbia since 1945, including *Between Nation and State: Serbian Politics in Croatia, 1903–1914* (Pittsburgh, 1997). He is currently completing a manuscript on an intellectual circle in Serbia during the communist era.

James P. Niessen is World History Librarian at Rutgers University in New Brunswick, New Jersey, and Vice President for Research and Publications of H-Net: Humanities and Social Sciences OnLine. He earned a Ph.D. in East European history from Indiana University and taught history at several universities before pursuing a library career since 1994. His published works include more than fifteen studies on modern Romanian and Hungarian history, libraries, and archives.

Aleksandar Panev teaches history and philosophy at Appleby College in Oakville, Canada. He received his B.A. and M.A. degrees from the University of Belgrade and his Ph.D. from the University of Toronto. He is also an associate of the Centre for Russian and East European Studies at the Munk Centre for International Studies at the University of Toronto and has served as a faculty research associate at Arizona State University and the University of Skopje.

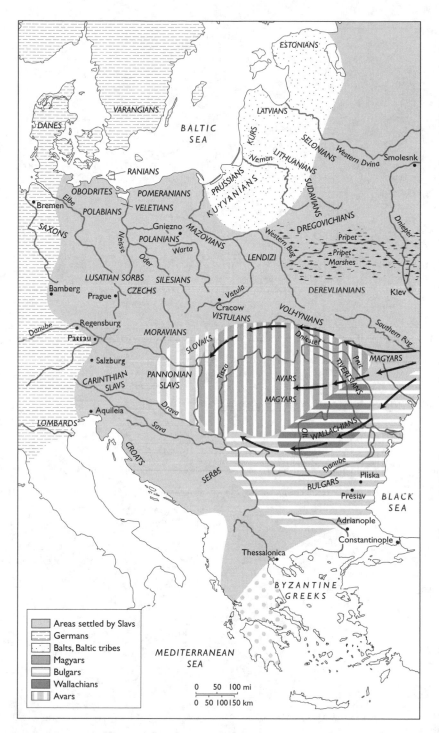

The peoples of Eastern Europe in the ninth century.

Territorial divisions in Eastern Europe in the thirteenth century (at the time of the Mongols).

Eastern Europe in the late sixteenth century.

Eastern Europe after the Congress of Vienna (1815).

Eastern Europe in 1914.

Eastern Europe between the World Wars.

Eastern Europe after World War II.

Eastern Europe in 2004.

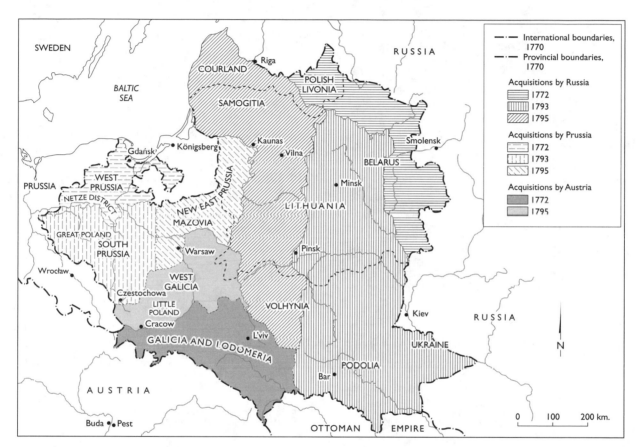

The Partitions of Poland, 1772–1795.

POLAND

PIOTR WRÓBEL

LAND AND PEOPLE

Poland (Polish: Polska), the ninth biggest state of Europe (after Russia, Ukraine, France, Germany, Spain, Sweden, Finland, and Norway), is located in the center of the continent on the North European Plain, approximately between forty degrees and fifty-five degrees north latitude and fourteen and twenty-four degrees east longitude (the geometrical middle point of Europe is near Warsaw). The territory of Poland (of a roughly circular shape) extends 649 kilometers from south to north and 689 kilometers from west to east and comprises a total of 311,904 square kilometers (including inland waters but excluding the 8,682 square kilometers of Poland's territorial sea).

The frontiers of Poland measure 3,495 kilometers. In the north, the frontier runs along the Baltic Sea coast (1,281 kilometers) and further eastwards across the flat Baltic Sea littoral along the border with Russia's Kaliningrad District (210 kilometers). The frontier then turns to the south and runs along the borders with Lithuania (for a distance of 103 kilometers), with Belarus (416 kilometers), and, partially along the Bug River, with Ukraine (for 529 kilometers). From Poland's southernmost point by Mount Opołonek in the Bieszczady Mountains, the frontier of Poland moves to the northwest along the borders with Slovakia (541 kilometers), following the watershed of the Carpathian Mountains, and with the Czech Republic (790 kilometers), following the watershed of the Sudety Mountains. When the border reaches the Neisse River (Polish: Nysa), it turns to the north and runs along this river and the Oder (Odra) River to the Baltic Sea, bordering Germany (a distance of 467 kilometers).

Poland is a mostly lowland country, open to the east, but in its landscape more akin to Western Europe. More than 70 percent of Poland's territory lies below 200 meters above sea level, and only about 3 percent rises above 500 meters. A narrow strip called the Coastal Lowlands runs along the Baltic shore. An elevated cliff comes close to the sea in several places but, in the regions of the deltas of the Oder and the Vistula Rivers (Wisła), the Central Lowlands extend deeper into the land. Farther to the south, an elevated landscape forms a belt of postglacial morainic ravines and ridges, rising to over 300 meters above sea level in several places. This area, made up of what are referred to as the Pomeranian and Masurian Lakelands, is divided by the broad valley of the Vistula River; it is abundant in picturesque lakes of various origins and sizes. South of the hilly lake region, the Central Lowlands

1

The Podhale region in the Carpathian Mountains. (Courtesy of Piotr Wróbel)

stretch from the Oder to Poland's eastern border. Ice Age glaciers flattened this part of the country completely, and the elevation rarely exceeds 45 meters above sea level. This zone is the Polish heartland and the principal site of agriculture.

The three belts—the Coastal Lowlands, the Lakelands, and the Central Lowlands—belong to the Great European Plain. South of the Great European Plain, the terrain ascends, forming a strip of old mountains and plateaus (or uplands) cut by the Oder and Vistula Rivers into three sections: ranges of mountains called the Sudety, together with their foothills, located west of the Oder; the Silesian, Cracow-Częstochowa, and Little Poland Uplands, situated between the Oder and the Vistula; and the Lublin Plateau and Roztocze Hills, between the Vistula and the River Bug. The Sudety, a part of the larger Bohemian Massif, rise steeply from the foothills and stretches from the western border of Poland to the Moravian Gate in the east. The Sudety are diversified and divided into smaller ridges. The highest of them, the Karkonosze (German: Riesengebirge), rises to 1,602 meters at Mount Śnieżka. The plateaus situated between the Oder and the Vistula form several separate units framed to the north by the slightly higher but old and eroded Góry Świętokrzyskie (Holy Cross Mountains), reaching 612 meters at Łysica Mountain. The Lublin

Plateau, limited by the Bug River to the east and the steep Roztocze escarpment to the south, forms a tableland cut by numerous deep ravines.

The next geomorphic region, situated south from the uplands, is called the Subcarpathian Basin. Located between the old mountains and plateaus and the Carpathian Mountains, like a large valley, it stretches from the eastern border of Poland to its southern border in the region of the Moravian Gate. These fertile basins, divided by higher terrain but connected by gates, are linked to the Coastal Lowlands through the outlet of the Vistula valley. To the south, the basins are framed by the arch of the Carpathian Mountains and their foothills. These rugged young mountains rise to an elevation of 2,499 meters at Mount Rysy (the highest point of Poland); they are difficult to cross, and they form the natural southern border of Poland.

In general, Poland's relief, shaped by the actions of Ice Age glaciers, is divided into several parallel east–west zones. The average elevation of the whole country is 173 meters. Located in the middle of the Great North European Plain, Poland is thus widely open to both the east and the west, a fact that has affected her entire history.

Geologically speaking, Poland is located on an important tectonic border dividing Europe into two halves. The border runs diagonally from the northwestern to the southeastern corners of Poland. The country's northeastern part lies on the East European (or Russian) platform, built from old rocks with a thin cover of later sedimentary rocks. The western and southern parts of Poland belong to West European geological formations, with young Alpine folds, including the Carpathians and the Subcarpathian region. These geological conditions are barely visible in the relief of Poland; nevertheless, it is due to them that the more valuable mineral resources lie very deep in the north, whereas in the Sudety and the Uplands these resources are more accessible and have been exploited since the early Middle Ages. Most Polish mineral deposits are located in three regions: Upper Silesia, the southern part of Lower Silesia, and the Świętokrzyskie Mountains area.

For a long time, Poland's most important mineral was black coal of high quality. The Upper Silesian Coal Basin, the Central Sudety region near the town of Wałbrzych, and coal beds on the River Wieprz in Eastern Poland (discovered in 1955) were among the richest black coal deposits in the world. In 1980 Poland was the fourth biggest world black coal producer, with 172 million tons of coal mined in that year alone. Later, black coal mining became less profitable, and now some of the Polish deposits are exhausted. In addition, Poland has less important deposits of brown coal, exploited mostly in the central and the southwestern parts of the country near the towns of Konin and Turoszów, respectively. Poland also has major reserves of peat.

Poland's oil resources are small. Exploited for over a hundred years in the Krosno-Jasło fields in the Carpathians, they are now almost exhausted. New pools have been found on the Baltic coast and in western Poland, but their exploitation is still of a limited and experimental character. The natural gas deposits, mostly in the Subcarpathian Basin, are only slightly richer than the Polish oil fields.

Poland has rich deposits of metal ores, particularly copper (in the Legnica-Głogów Basin) and zinc (in the neighborhood of Bytom, Chrzanów, and Olkusz). Also, lead and nickel are mined in Silesia. Iron ore, exploited chiefly in the regions of Częstochowa and Łęczyca, is inadequate and of poor quality. Sources of other metals offer only insignificant amounts. Poland has large quantities of sulfur, in the region of Tarnobrzeg and Staszów, and of rock salt, mined since the Middle Ages near the towns of Bochnia and Wieliczka and in new centers located in Pomerania and Central Poland. Also, potassium, phosphate rock, and barite are mined in several locations. The Lower Silesian low-grade uranium pitchblende deposits were of great importance during the Cold War in the production of munitions. Large amounts of granite are quarried for the needs of the building industry, mostly in the Sudety Foothills, and smaller amounts of basalt, porphyry, limestone, sandstone, cretaceous marls, hard quartzite, gypsum, magnesite, kaolin, gravel, sand, and clay are obtained in many locations. Several Polish spas offer mineral springs and warm medicinal waters.

Polish soils form a mosaic without clearly marked distinct zones. Over 70 percent of Poland's surface is covered by light-colored, relatively infertile podzol and pseudopodzol, typical of colder climates, and by light sandy glacial soils. Richer brown earth soils and rendzina are concentrated primarily in southern Poland and in the eastern part of the Coastal Lowlands. The fertile loess is located on the banks of most rivers and in the Vistula Delta. The best soils, the chernozems, are to be found only in upland regions in southern and southeastern Poland. Yet, with good management, even the mediocre Polish soils give good yields.

Poland lies nearer to the North Pole than to the Equator, within the cool temperate zone of southern Canada, southern England, Belgium, and Holland. Due to the lack of sizable landform barriers, various masses of air meet over the Polish territories during different seasons: oceanic polar air from the North Atlantic, subtropical air from the Azores area, polar-continental air from Eastern Europe, and warm and dry subtropical continental air from the southeast. As a consequence, Polish weather varies greatly, sometimes from day to day, and the climate ranges from oceanic to continental. Polish winters are either humid and warm, especially in the western part of the country, or clear and frosty, especially in the east. There are six seasons in Poland: snowy winter (one to three months); early spring, alternating wintry and spring weather (one to two months); sunny spring (one to two months); warm summer (two to three months); sunny and dry fall (one to two months); and misty and humid late fall or early winter (one to two months). Mean annual temperatures vary between 6 degrees and 8.5 degrees Celsius. Mean monthly temperatures range from 16.5 degrees and 19 degrees Celsius in July and from 0 degrees to minus 4.5 degrees Celsius in January.

The warmest part of Poland is in its southwestern corner, the coldest, in the region of Suwałki in the northeast. Days with frost range from about 30 in the western lowlands to over 100 in the mountains; snow cover lasts from 40 to 90 days, depending on the region. Recently, however, there have been several winters with barely any snow. The growing period varies from 160 to 220 days per year. The Polish climate is becoming dryer, and the mean precipitation is about 600 millimeters. Climatologists distinguish twenty-one agricultural-climatic regions in Poland; however, it is easier to notice seven climatic belts: Baltic, Lakeland, Central Lowlands, Central Uplands, Carpathian foothills, mountains, and the continental climate along the eastern border of the country.

About 99.7 percent of Poland's territory lies in the catchment basin of the Baltic Sea (53.9 percent of this area belongs to the Vistula drainage basin, 34 percent to the Oder, 11 percent to the direct Baltic basin, and 11 percent to the Niemen River basin). The Vistula and the Oder are the two largest and longest rivers of Poland (1,047 kilometers and 854 kilometers respectively) and, like most other important Polish rivers, rise in the southern mountains. Polish rivers usually have two high waters during the year: in the spring, when the snow melts, and in late June or early July, when it rains in the mountains. Since most Polish rivers are not regulated, catastrophic floods are not uncommon. In the fall, waters are low and, in the winter, they usually freeze. In the Oder drainage basin, the ice lasts usually about one month, in the Bug (a right tributary of the Vistula) drainage area—between sixty and eighty days (from mid-December to mid-March). Rivers in Poland are swollen with storm floods or blocked by ice dams relatively frequently.

There are 9,300 lakes (larger than 2.5 acres, or one hectare) in Poland. They cover about 3,200 square kilometers, which constitutes 1 percent of the total area of the country. Peat bogs cover an additional 13,000 square kilometers, or about 4 percent of Poland. Most Polish lakes are located in the Pomeranian and Masurian Lakelands. At no great distance beneath the plains there are layers of underground water, which can be reached easily by dug wells. Polish territorial sea amounts to 8,682 square kilometers and includes two big bays: the Pomeranian and the Gdańsk.

Poland's organic world belongs to the temperate belt of the northern hemisphere and is not very rich in species. The northeastern limits of the European beech, the silver fir, and the brown oak run across Poland. Pine, oak, beech, and fir are the most common trees in Poland. During the Middle Ages, Poland was a country of forests and swamps, but now woodlands cover only about 27 percent of the country's area. Most Polish forests are divided into four kinds: coniferous, mixed deciduous, alder swamps, and humid woods in river valleys. Mountain, steppe, rock, high–mountain, marsh, and water forests form only small islands. There are twenty-three national parks in Poland with an overall surface of 305,675.5 hectares, almost 1 percent of the country's territory, and 1,354 reserves, covering 141,225 hectares. In zoo-geographic terms, Poland belongs to the European–West Siberian province, with 83 species of mammals, 211 of nesting birds, 55 of fish, 17 of amphibians, and 8 species of reptiles. Roe deer, stags, and wild pigs still live in most Polish forests. In the north, some elk can be found, and in the mountain forests of the Tatra and Bieszczady Mountains, brown bears, lynx, and wildcats still appear occasionally. The European bison, wolves, otters, beavers, and other rare animals live mostly in the reserves and national parks. Altogether about 390 species are protected.

Human economic activities have changed the physical characteristics of Poland. Industrialization has threatened the Polish natural environment, and there is severe pollution in several regions, especially in the densely populated Upper Silesian, Łódź, Warsaw, and (to some extent) Mielec-Sandomierz and Sudety areas. These areas constitute an advanced and long-established industrial part of Poland. The regions of Cracow, Częstochowa, Opole, Gdańsk, Szczecin, and Wrocław belong to the newly developed zone, which is seriously polluted because of sulfur dioxide emissions from the coal-fired power plants. Kujavia, Białystok, Lublin, and the Świętokrzyskie Mountains region offer some tradition and potential for industrial growth. The rest of the country, especially the northeastern Białystok and Olsztyn provinces, the central part of the Pomeranian Lakeland, and the districts located along the Belarusian and Ukrainian borders

Pollution in Warsaw. (PhotoDisc)

belong to what is called Poland B, an underdeveloped, backward, and poor region with no prospects for quick improvement. Since the 1999 administrative reform, Poland has been divided into sixteen provinces (województwa), which consist of counties (powiaty), which in turn are divided into urban and rural districts (gminy). There are 308 counties and 2,489 districts in Poland.

In 2003 Poland had 38,622,000 citizens and was the eighth most populous nation in Europe. Poles constitute 5.3 percent of all Europeans and 0.65 percent of the world's population. In the year 2001 the official estimates of Poland's population numbered 38,634,000 people (broken down by age: 0–14 years, 18.39 percent; between 15 and 64 years, 69.17 percent; and over 65 years, 12.44 percent). Females made up 51.4 percent of Poland's population, males, 48.6 percent. In 1995 Poland had 38,620,000 citizens. If the demographic trends and the population growth rate (–0.02 percent in 2002) do not change, Poland will have 33 million citizens in 2050.

During the twentieth century, the population of Poland underwent major changes. According to the 1931 census, Poland's population in its prewar borders numbered 32,107,000. The 1938 estimates gave a figure of 34,849,000, and the estimates of mid-1939 a total of 35,100,000. In addition, about 1.5 million ethnic Poles lived in the states bordering on Poland. During World War II, Poland suffered the largest relative casualties in Europe. The census of 1946 showed 23,930,000 people living within the new borders of Poland. This difference of almost eleven million included the killed, the deported, and those who found themselves beyond the new borders of the state. The official death toll was 6,028,000, which included 644,000 killed during military operations (123,000 soldiers and 521,000 civilians) and 5,384,000 people who lost their lives as a result of the Nazi terror. The data, announced by the communist Polish authorities, did not include the people who died under the Soviets and applied only to the territories within the new Polish borders. The density of population diminished from 83 per square kilometer in 1931 to 77 in 1946. In addition, the territories gained by Poland from Germany in 1945 were inhabited by about 8,900,000 people in 1939. Most of them fled or were killed by the end of the war; about two million were expelled by the Polish communist authorities between 1945 and 1948, and about 1.5 million were classified as autochthonous Poles. Also about 500,000 Ukrainians and Belarusians were transferred to the Soviet Union.

In the late 1940s about two million people were repatriated from the Soviet Union to Poland, mostly from prewar Polish territories and from Germany. The second wave of repatriation took place in 1957–1958, when about 200,000 Poles arrived from the Soviet Union. After the war, the Polish birthrate started growing rapidly and reached 1.9 percent in 1953. Later, the birthrate averaged 1.7 percent from 1955 to 1960, but diminished to 0.9 percent in 1965. In the early 1980s Poland's birthrate of 1.0 percent put Poland behind only Albania, Ireland, and Iceland among European countries. In the late 1990s the birthrate declined again. In 2001 it was estimated to reach 10.2 births per 1,000 population and, with a relatively high death rate, the population

Polonia

About one third of the Polish nation lives outside Poland. This phenomenon, known as Polonia, or the Polish Diaspora, appeared as a consequence of emigration and changes to the country's borders. Polonia includes all the people who consider themselves Polish, regardless of their place of birth and language.

Emigration from Poland started as early as the seventeenth century. After the partitions of Poland in the late 1700s, a large part of the nation's territory was incorporated into Russia. Most of these lands were never returned to Poland, and the Polish population was forced to live in Russia. A similar situation appeared after 1939 and 1945, when the Soviet Union annexed almost one-half of the prewar Polish state. Economic emigrants, mostly peasants and workers, constantly flowed to both Americas and Western Europe. They were followed by political refugees. The United States attracted the largest group of Poles. The first of them landed in Jamestown in 1608. By the end of World War II, about 6 million Polish people lived in America.

Presently, between 14 and 17 million Poles live outside Poland, in over two dozen countries. The largest Polish population outside of the nation itself resides in the United States and is concentrated in major metropolitan areas such as New York, Detroit, and Chicago. Nearly a million Poles reside in France and Brazil, while Germany is home to 1.5 million. Canada, Belarus, Ukraine, Lithuania, Great Britain, Australia, and Argentina also boast sizable Polish populations. Usually, they establish various Polonia organizations and contribute greatly to the development of their new countries. Frequently, they stay in touch with Polish economic, political, and cultural life. Sometimes, they re-emigrate back to Poland.

growth rate became negative (–0.03 percent). This, in turn, was caused by a relatively low life expectancy (69.26 years for men and 77.82 for women), by a relatively high infant mortality rate (9.39 deaths for 1,000 live births), and by a low total fertility rate (1.37 children born per woman). In 1950 Poland's population reached 25,008,000 (80 persons per square kilometer), in 1960, 29,776,000 (95 per square kilometer), and, in 1970, 32,642,000 (104 per square kilometer). Only in 1978 did Poland return to its prewar population level.

In 1995 the density of population in Poland reached 124 persons per one square kilometer, still lower than in the most developed Western European countries (Belgium, 334; France, 107; Holland, 378; Germany, 230). Some 61.6 percent of all inhabitants of Poland (23,777,000) lived in towns and cities, and 38.4 percent (14.843,000) in the countryside. In 1931 about 72.6 percent of Poland's population was classified as rural. This shows that the most important postwar demographic change was intense urbanization, prompted by central economic planning and the modernization of Poland. In the early 1950s about 250,000 persons were migrating from rural communities to cities and towns every year. Many cities extended their administrative borders and included suburban communities. In the 1970s about 2 million people moved from the countryside to the towns and, in the 1980s about 1.3 million. In 2002 about 61.8 percent of Poles lived in urban areas and 38.2 percent in the countryside.

Most Polish towns are small or medium-sized. Forty-three cities have populations of more than 100,000 people. Warsaw, the capital and the largest city of Poland, has about 1.7 million inhabitants. The other big cities are Łódź (790,197), Cracow (741,841), Wrocław (633,887), Poznań (573,814), and Gdańsk (456,284).

The catastrophe of World War II changed the social structure of Poland. The Nazis and the Soviets killed or eliminated several ethnic and social groups, such as Jews, landowners, and bourgeoisie. In addition, the occupiers tried to annihilate the Polish elites and decimated the intelligentsia, a class of people with higher education, retaining the ethos of the Polish nobility and a belief in their special responsibility towards Poland, which constituted the core of the most important professions. Those who survived emigrated or lost their social status under the communist authorities, which had two priorities: to create a big working class and to recruit a new intelligentsia from among the peasants and workers that would be obedient to the ruling party. A "new class" of loyal government functionaries was built. The civic society and the autonomy of political and social organizations were destroyed. This social engineering did not bring the expected results. Most members of the new classes rejected the communist ideology. Extended families, circles of friends, and independent networks helped individuals to survive everyday difficulties and to outmaneuver the state apparatus. Many Poles assumed a cynical attitude toward the state, viewed direct and indirect stealing from it as an acceptable behavior, separated "us" (the people) from "them" (the authorities), and, eventually, forced the corrupt and hypocritical communist establishment to abdicate. Nevertheless, a big working class, over two times larger than before World War II, has been formed. Most workers of communist Poland were employed in large state enterprises, heavy industry and mining, usually inefficient and heavily subsidized. Around 1980, about 40 percent of

Gdańsk, Poland. (PhotoDisc)

Poland's working people were employed in industry, 30 percent in agriculture, and 39 percent in the service sector. Most younger workers had some education, and the phenomenon of illiteracy disappeared. Still, after the fall of communism, many Poles did not abandon their pre-1989 skepticism of the elite and their pretensions.

During the communist period, many peasants and workers were recruited into managerial posts, into the state and party apparatus, the army, and the professions. The wartime losses of the intelligentsia were made up, but the intelligentsia partially changed its character. Before 1945, the Polish intelligentsia played a leading role in Poland's fight for independence and for preserving national consciousness. Many members of the intelligentsia maintained the aristocratic values of their ancestors, but at the same time introduced new and progressive ideas to Polish society. After 1945, the communists diversified the class basis of the intelligentsia, promoting peasants and workers and creating for them special preferences in education. In the 1970s and the 1980s the educational preferences became less efficient, and the mobility from the working classes to the intelligentsia slowed. The intelligentsia returned to the traditional pre-1945 values and resumed the role of protector of Polish national identity and sovereignty. In 2000 the labor force in Poland amounted to 17.6 million people, 22.1 percent of them in industry, 27.5 percent in agriculture, and 50.4 percent in services.

Poland is one of the most homogenous countries in Europe, even though before World War II Poland was a typical Central European multinational state and the nation's national minorities constituted about 31 percent of the entire population. The Nazi and Soviet extermination policies and the moving of Polish borders in 1945 changed this completely. Moreover, the Polish communist authorities tried to Polonize the minorities. Today about 97 percent of Polish citizens are ethnically Polish; however, there are still sizable non-Polish ethnic communities in the country. Some German sources estimate the non-Polish population at 2.5 million, or 8 percent of the population.

The largest national minority is probably (Polish national censuses do not ask about nationality) constituted by the Germans. Many people in the former German territories hid their German identity to avoid deportation to destroyed Germany in the late 1940s. Later, however, many Silesians and autochthonous inhabitants of the Masurian Lakeland were bitter over communist policies and changed their national identity. Others declared themselves German to receive help and preferential treatment from the German government. Before 1989, the communist authorities claimed that there were only about 4,000 Germans in Poland. Today, estimates reach 500,000 people, with most living in the Opole region, Upper Silesia, and the northern provinces of the country. After 1989, numerous German organizations, schools, libraries, and political parties appeared in these regions. Special ties with Germany made the Opole region one of the most prosperous areas in Poland. The lifestyle of some Silesian communities is closer to that of Germany than to that of Poland. The German minority has representation in the Polish parliament (the *Sejm*).

The Polish Language

Polish is the official language of Poland and a vernacular of most citizens. Together with Czech and Slovak, it belongs to the West Slavic subgroup of the Slavonic languages, which in turn belongs to the Indo-European languages. Polish began to form in the tenth century, when its development was stimulated by the establishment of the Polish state. The first documents written in Polish come from the fourteenth century, even though Latin remained the language of the state chancery for the next several centuries. In the twentieth century the migrations, moving borders, state-controlled education and mass media homogenized the language, but several local dialects still survive, and some of them, like Kashubian, for example, are sometimes classified as separate languages. Most members of the national minorities in Poland have been bilingual. Polish is an inflected language with seven cases, two numbers, three genders in the singular and two in the plural. Verbs are conjugated by person, tense, mood, voice, and aspect. Unlike other Slavonic languages, Polish has nasal vowels. Polish grammar abounds in rules, and the rules have numerous exceptions. The language is considered difficult to learn.

The Ukrainians, the second largest minority, made up about 14 percent of Poland's population (about 5.5 million people) before World War II, but most of them found themselves in the territories taken by the Soviets in 1945. In addition, thousands of Ukrainians living within the new Polish borders were deported to the Soviet Union in 1945 and 1946, and in 1947 the Polish communist authorities deported most of the remaining Ukrainians from their native Rzeszów and Lublin regions to the former German territories in the north and in the west. Many deportees were widely dispersed and assimilated. After 1989, the Ukrainian minority began rebuilding its social organizations, political parties, schools, and cultural institutions. It received parliamentary representation, recovered a part of the former property of the Ukrainian Catholic Church, and revived its activities in the southeastern corner of Poland. Contemporary estimates of the Ukrainian population range from 200,000 to 700,000. Most probably, this community is not larger than 400,000.

Belorussians were also numerous in Poland before the war (about three million in 1939), but most of them lived in the territories taken by the Soviets in 1945. Less assertive of their national identity than the Ukrainians, the Belarusians, to use the current spelling, now mostly live in the eastern part of the Białystok region on the Belarusian border, one of the poorest Polish areas and sparsely populated by peasants. After 1989, the Belarusians also revived their national and political activities. Their community is probably made up of about 300,000 members, but their spokespersons claim as many as 500,000.

The Jewish minority, 3.3 million before 1939, was exterminated during World War II. Only about 300,000 Polish Jews survived the war, mostly in the Soviet Union, but almost all of them left Poland, tormented by memories of the Holocaust and persecuted or harassed by anti-Semites and the communist authorities. About 3,000 people belong to the Jewish religious communities now, and about 30,000 claim Jewish ancestry. In the early 1980s interest in and even fascination with Jewish history and culture appeared among some educated Poles. On the other hand, according to several surveys, many Poles believe that the Jews constitute a threat to Poland and exert too much influence. The Jews have contributed greatly to Polish cultural and political life.

In addition to these four groups, there are several smaller national minorities in Poland: Slovaks (about 25,000), Roma (Gypsies, between 15,000 and 50,000), Lithuanians (about 30,000), Russians (about 10,000), Greeks and Macedonians (about 10,000), and other small communities. In the 1980s Poland became a transit route for illegal migration from the former Soviet Union and Southeastern Europe to the west.

For centuries, Poland has been a predominantly Roman Catholic country, and for most Poles identity is a unique combination of national and religious beliefs. During the era of foreign oppression, the Catholic Church remained for the Poles the primary source of moral values and the last bulwark in the fight for independence and national survival. The establishment of communist power had little effect on the religious practices and feelings of most Poles. The communist authorities did not manage to subjugate the Catholic Church, which preserved its autonomy, became the most powerful independent Polish national organization, and in the 1970s assumed the role of mediator between the regime and the rebellious population. The 1978 election of Cardinal Karol Wojtyła as Pope John Paul II contributed greatly to the fall of communism in Poland and all over the world.

According to official Polish statistics, 34,609,000 persons, about 96 percent of the entire population of Poland, belonged to the Roman Catholic Church in 2000. Over 80 percent of them declare that they attend mass regularly. Over 5 million people listen to and support an ultranationalist and conservative radio broadcasting station and propaganda institution called Radio Maryja. The remaining 4 million non–Roman Catholic Poles profess no religion or belong to over forty denominations. The largest among them are the Orthodox Church (numbering about 554,000 people), the Jehovah's Witnesses (123,000), the Ukrainian Catholic Church (110,000), the Evangelical Church of the Augsburg Confession (87,000), and the Old Catholic Churches (50,000). The other Protestant, Muslim, Judaic, and Far Eastern religions have far fewer members. The Christian Churches of Poland cooperate through the Polish Ecumenical Council, founded in 1946 and extended in the late 1970s.

Interior of a church in Lublin, Poland. (Corel Corporation)

HISTORY

Situated on Europe's major east-west passageway, Poland has had a stormy history, and its borders have repeatedly changed. In the mid-sixteenth century the Polish-Lithuanian Commonwealth (a federation with neighboring Lithuania) was the largest state of Europe. In the nineteenth and the early twentieth centuries Poland did not exist at all; between 1939 and 1989, the country was occupied or controlled by the Third Reich and the Soviet Union; and after 1989, Poland became completely free again. The partitions of Poland (1772–1795) constitute the most important turning point in Polish history: a change from a mostly successful state to foreign occupation and fighting for survival.

PREHISTORY

The Polish state was established gradually in the ninth and tenth centuries, but the prehistory of Poland began when the first human beings appeared between the Vistula and the Oder Rivers about 100,000 years ago. A permanent settlement started there between 8000 and 5500 years B.C.E. The corridor between the Carpathians and the Baltic Sea, a part of an open plain stretching from Central Asia to the Northern Sea, served as a passage through which numerous tribes went west and east. The local people defended themselves, building strongholds surrounded by palisades and earth walls. The best preserved of these was constructed by a tribe belonging to the Lusatian Culture near Biskupin in Greater Poland (the traditional name of an area in west-central Poland). Around 400 B.C.E., Scythians and Sarmatians, coming from Asia, destroyed the culture. Simultaneously, Celts were attacking from the west and, at the beginning of our era, Germanic tribes migrated from Scandinavia through today's Poland to the southeastern European steppes. In the fifth century C.E. the Germanic tribes were pushed back across the borders of the Roman Empire by the Huns, who established a state in Central Europe.

The state of the Huns, however, disintegrated quickly, and Central Europe became dominated by the Slavic people. From their original habitat in today's eastern Poland, the Slavs started an unprecedented expansion. Around 500 C.E., they crossed the Danube. In contrast to their Asian enemies, they were not nomads but agrarian people, permanently settling in the newly colonized regions. By the seventh century, the area between today's eastern Germany and Russia proper, and between the Baltic, Black, and Adriatic Seas was Slavicized. Initially, all the Slavs shared the same language and culture, but later local differences developed. In the mid-sixth century, the Slavs were conquered by Asian Avars, who created an Avaro-Slavic empire so powerful that it almost took Constantinople. A Slavic rebellion against the Avars destroyed their empire in the mid-seventh century. A mysterious individual named Samo established the first, short-lived Slavic state, with its center in today's Bohemia. Samo controlled some regions north of the Carpathians. At the beginning of the ninth century, the Greater Moravian Reich was formed. It included today's Bohemia, Moravia, Slovakia, Hungary, Silesia, Little Poland (one of the historical regions of Poland, located in the south around the city of Cracow), and possibly western Ukraine. All these invasions brought to Central Europe new cultural influences and political stimuli.

Numerous Slavic tribes lived north of Greater Moravia. Less influenced by western and southern European cultures and attacked by the Vikings, they developed slowly, were still pagan, and lived in small tribal semi-state organizations. One such organization was established by the Polanie tribe in the Poznań region (Polanie means, in Polish, people living on fields or in wood clearings). In the ninth century the Polanie were checked by Greater Moravia, and their state expanded slowly. About 900, however, the Moravian Reich was destroyed by Hungarian forces coming from the southeast. During the resulting short period in which a power vacuum existed north of the Carpathians, better conditions for expansion appeared for the Polanie. Their state started growing faster, even though the Czechs reintegrated most of the former Moravian lands.

PIAST POLAND: TENTH TO FOURTEENTH CENTURY

The first major written source about Poland was recorded in 965 by a Jewish merchant from Spain, Ibrahim-ibn-Jaqub. He visited Central Europe and wrote about a powerful state, ruled by a man called Mieszko. Mieszko's name appeared later in many documents, but all that is known about his predecessors comes from oral tradition. Some legends indicate that Mieszko's ancestors took over power in the mid-ninth century. Later, Poland's ruling family was called the Piast dynasty. The Polish verb piastować means "to cradle in one's arms," and scholars suspect that, as in the Frankish empire, Mieszko's great-grandfather was a court official who rebelled against a tribal chieftain.

Born around 922, Mieszko came to power in 960. Operating from his domain, Wielkopolska (Greater Poland), he conquered Kujavia, Mazovia, and Pomerania. Flanked by Kievan Rus in the east and by the Czech kingdom in the south, he tried to expand westwards, planning to subjugate the territories of the Obodrites, the Slavic tribes living between the Oder and the Elbe Rivers. Both the Holy Roman Empire of the German Nation and the Czechs shared the same plan. In 937 the Saxons crossed the Elbe and founded the city of Magdeburg. In 961 Emperor Otto I obtained papal support for raising the see of Magdeburg as a missionary bishopric throughout the Slavic lands, including Poland. Christianization from the Holy Roman Empire would mean German political domination and possibly extinction, the eventual fate of the Obodrites and the Baltic Prussians.

Mieszko broke the link between Christianization and Germanization. He forged a political alliance with the Czech king Boleslav and married his daughter Dobrava. She came to Poland with a Christian mission, and in 966 Mieszko accepted Christianity from Bohemia, which had been baptized over a century earlier. The bishopric of Poznań was established directly from Rome and placed outside the Magdeburg jurisdiction. Poland's decision to accept baptism became one of the most important decisions in the nation's entire history.

Poland now joined the family of Latin Christian nations, and accepted their legal, administrative, and cultural patterns. A group of educated foreigners came to Poland. The acceptance of one God eliminated various tribal gods and integrated the country. The new religion was much more sophisticated than the old one; it opened new intellectual horizons to the Poles, offered an ideological support derived from God to the power of princes, and sanctioned a new social structure and a new ruling class. Christianity also offered a more rational view of the world, deeper religious experience, international prestige, and a religious sanction for the conquest of pagan lands.

Mieszko changed his policies by the end of his reign. He took Silesia and Małopolska (Little Poland) from the Czechs. After his death in 992, his son, Bolesław the Brave (Chrobry), was considered a powerful ruler and a major partner of Emperor Otto III, who wanted to unite Europe. Yet after Otto's death, a new German dynasty started a war against Poland. Between 1002 and 1018, Bolesław defended his country and conquered new provinces. In 1018 he invaded Kiev and put his man on its throne. In 1025, shortly before his death, Bolesław was crowned the first king of Poland.

However, Poland was not yet fully integrated. Bolesław's successor, King Mieszko II, was overthrown by a rebellion of the "aborted" tribal chieftains and an anti-Christian pagan reaction. Poland was attacked by its neighbors, divided, and devastated. A German emperor, fearful that chaos could destabilize the entire region, helped to rebuild order and put his vassal, a Piast prince, Casimir the Restorer *(Odnowiciel),* on the throne of the shrunken state. Casimir moved the capital of Poland from the ruined city of Poznań to Cracow and reunited most of the lost provinces. When he died in 1058, his successor, Bolesław the Bold *(Śmiały),* threw off German control and crowned himself king. However, his bold policies provoked an opposition. When he accused the bishop of Cracow, Stanisław, of treason and killed him, an antiroyal rebellion forced Bolesław to leave Poland in 1079. He was replaced by his brother Władysław Herman. Constantly challenged by the magnates, Władysław had to divide the state between himself and his two sons. One of them, Bolesław the Wrymouthed (Krzywousty), proved to be an outstanding and ruthless ruler. He killed his stepbrother Zbigniew after their father's death in 1102, regained Pomerania and Christianized it in 1124–1128, and secured peace along the borders of Poland.

In 1138 Bolesław died, leaving a testament that divided the state between his five sons. The oldest of them received, in addition to his principality, a large territory stretching across Poland and including Cracow. This "seniorial" province was supposed to go to the senior princes in the future and to support their authority over junior rulers. Bolesław tried to prevent civil wars among his heirs, but he turned Poland from a relatively strong state into a conglomeration of weak principalities. The seniorial province was soon divided, and the principle of seniorat was abandoned; the number of principalities was growing, their rulers were involved in fraternal wars, and Poland's neighbors seized some provinces.

Competition between the princes, while politically unfortunate, stimulated the economy. Under Bolesław the Wrymouthed, Poland was about 225,000 square kilometers in size and had about one million subjects, almost five persons per square kilometer. In comparison to Germany (with ten inhabitants per square kilometer) and France (fifteen inhabitants), Poland was an underpopulated and underdeveloped country. Substantial demographic growth and stagnating food production in Western Europe triggered mass migration to the east. Polish princes welcomed new settlers, who brought with them new technology and modes of life, reorganized and developed Polish towns and a market economy, and established new branches of manufacturing. Jewish immigrants especially revitalized trade with foreign countries. Colonization on the basis of German law changed Poland. After 966, individual immigrants—clerics, knights, and merchants—reshaped Polish elites. The German colonization, about 250,000 people strong, brought to Poland large groups of peasants and artisans and changed the entire society.

A strong market, developing culture, growing Polish identity, and one ecclesiastical organization helped to reunite Poland. At the same time, outside threats from the Mongols, the Czechs, the Brandenburgians, and the Teutonic Order (which settled in Prussia in 1226), pushed Poland toward unification. Several local and foreign rulers tried to unite the Polish lands, but Władysław the Elbow-Short (Łokietek) succeeded in doing so. Operating from his tiny principality in Southern Kujavia, Władysław reunited the two principal Polish provinces—Greater and Little Poland—and was crowned king of Poland in 1320. When he died in 1333, nobody questioned the integrity of Poland and the right of Władysław's son, Casimir, to the Polish crown.

Casimir, later called the Great (Wielki), established good relations with several neighbors of Poland, and under his rule Cracow became an important diplomatic center. Casimir won a case against the Teutonic Order at a papal court, recovered some provinces, and signed a peace treaty with the German knights. Cooperating with his cousin, the king of Hungary, Casimir captured the Ruthenian principalities of Galicia and Volhynia. He also codified the law, modernized the administration, built numerous fortifications, and established the University of Cracow in 1364. There was a popular saying that Casimir inherited a Poland made out of wood and bequeathed a nation made of stone. At the same time, when Western Europe was decimated by the Black Death, Poland developed quickly and reached Western levels in its economy and culture.

JAGIELLONIAN POLAND: FOURTEENTH TO SIXTEENTH CENTURY

Casimir had no acceptable heir, and due to a dynastic agreement, following his death the crown of Poland went to Louis d'Anjou, the king of Hungary. Louis rarely visited Poland and neglected it. Moreover, it appeared that Louis would not have a male successor either. To placate the Polish opposition and to assure the Polish throne for one of his daughters, Louis gave the gentry privileges, issued in Košice in 1374. The nobles had to keep their castles in repair and were required to perform unpaid military service for defense within the frontiers of Poland, but the land tax was reduced to a symbolic sum of two pence per acre, and only locals could receive official posts in their provinces. The Polish lords fulfilled their part of the deal. After Louis's death in 1382, his daughter Jadwiga was crowned the king (*sic*) of Poland in 1384. Intelligent, well educated, and beautiful, she became very popular. The lords, however, did not accept Jadwiga's fiancé, Wilhelm von Habsburg, as their future comonarch. Neither did they intend to continue the Polish-Hungarian personal union. Instead, they planned a union with Lithuania, which would terminate Lithuanian raids against Poland and would create a power able to stop the expansion of the Teutonic Order. The Poles also hoped that by Christianizing Lithuania, the last pagan state in Europe, they would dominate this large country politically.

The ruler of Lithuania, Jogaila, accepted the Polish offer. He expected the Poles to support him against the Teutonic Knights, Muscovy, and his cousin Vytautas (Witold), who wanted the Lithuanian throne for himself. In 1385 the Polish-Lithuanian personal union was signed. Lithuania accepted Christianity from Poland, and the Lithuanian gentry received Polish coats of arms and the privileges of the Polish nobility. Jogaila was baptized, received a Christian name, and became known as Władysław Jagiełło. In 1386 he married Jadwiga and was crowned king of Poland.

Poland-Lithuania became a great power. In 1410 its armies annihilated the forces of the Teutonic Order at the battle of Grünwald. Jagiełło's son and successor, Władysław of Varna (Warneńczyk, 1434–1444), was also elected king of Hungary, but he was subsequently killed during a war against the Ottoman Empire. His brother and heir, Casimir Jagiellon (Kazimierz Jagiellończyk, 1447–1492), incorporated Gdańsk, Pomerania, and the bishopric of Warmia into Poland after a great victory in the Thirteen Years' War (1454–1466) against the Teutonic Knights. The remaining lands of the Teutonic Order, later called Ducal Prussia, became a vassal state of Poland. Casimir's eldest son, Władysław, became king of Bohemia in 1471 and later of Hungary (in 1490). His brothers, John Albert (Jan Olbracht), Alexander Jagiellon (Jagiellończyk), and Sigismund the Old (Zygmunt Stary), were Casimir's successors on the Polish throne (1492–1501, 1501–1506, and 1506–1548, respectively).

Poland-Lithuania was a loose federation. Not only did the two partner states have different official languages and separate armies, laws, and judicial and administrative systems, but the Lithuanian nobles strongly protected their separateness. They did not accept automatically new Polish kings as their grand dukes but elected their own monarchs within the Jagiellonian family. In 1434, when Władysław of Varna succeeded to the Polish throne, the Lithuanians put his brother Casimir Jagiellon on the throne in their capital, Wilno (Vilnius in Lithuanian). Finally, in 1447, after the death of Władysław and a long interregnum, Casimir became the ruler of both federated entities. A similar situation happened in 1492. John Albert became king of Poland, but Alexander took the Lithuanian crown. The latter acquired the Polish throne after the death of his older brother in 1501.

The Polish-Lithuanian state was a complex phenomenon. Polonization of Lithuania progressed slowly, contrary to the belief of most Poles, and in fact was never complete. Populated by many ethnic groups and by adherents of several religions, and located between three growing powers (the Habsburg Empire, Muscovy, and the Ottoman Empire), Poland-Lithuania had to form its own original and efficient political system. It emerged gradually. The Polish nobles received privileges that made their status attractive and allowed them to dominate their state. In the fourteenth century a territorial self-government appeared in Poland. Noblemen established a provincial Council of Landlords, transformed later into dietines (sejmiki), to decide about local matters. Beginning in the early fifteenth century, King's Councils met to consult representatives of the dietines. In 1463 a two-chamber parliament was formed, composed of the Senate (upper chamber) and the Sejm (lower chamber), whose deputies represented the dietines. The senators were appointed by the monarch from among the highest state officers. They expressed opinions on legislation in the Sejm and discussed foreign policy. The constitution of 1505, known as Nihil novi (Nothing new), guaranteed the chamber of deputies that "no new laws shall be made by us [the king] or our successors, without the consent of the councilors and territorial deputies" (Jędruch 391). This law, stipulating that the king had no right to legislate without the approval of the Sejm and the Senate, formally recognized the existence of the two-chamber parliament.

The nobility, which constituted about 8 percent of the entire Polish-Lithuanian population, was the only estate that fully participated in politics. Representatives of towns lost their right to representation in the Sejm in 1505. From that time, only Vilna and Cracow were represented; even they, however, did not have voting rights. Only the upper echelons of the clergy participated in politics. The peasants were degraded to the status of slaves. Poland developed mass production and export of grain and became the breadbasket of Western Europe. The landowners needed cheap labor and reversed a progressing emancipation of peasantry. Most peasants became the property of feudal lords. In the sixteenth century the corvée rose to six or more days a week, and the peasants were subjected to the landowners' jurisdiction.

The power of the gentry was not absolute, however. Kings still preserved significant powers, and the nobility was divided. During the Reformation, many nobles left the Catholic Church and joined Protestant denominations. In the sixteenth century rich nobles grew into an oligarchy, and the middle nobility initiated a political campaign against it, known as the "execution-of-the-law" movement. It asked for equality among the nobles and demanded that the state take back the estates illegally held by magnates whose ancestors had received land in exchange for services that were no longer performed. The nobility also demanded more privileges and insisted on the free election of the king. The execution movement did not, however, reach its goals. The magnates saved their position. Sigismund the Old (1506–1548) was alive when he crowned his son Sigismund II Augustus (Zygmunt August, 1548–1572) king of Poland.

After succeeding to the throne following his father's death, Sigismund II Augustus cautiously supported the "execution movement" and favored religious tolerance. Simultaneously, he was strengthening the state. In 1569 he managed to arrange the Union of Lublin, which replaced a personal union between Poland and Lithuania with a real interstate federal union, the Polish-Lithuanian Commonwealth, based on common institutions. Even though the legal systems and administrations remained separate, kings were supposed to be elected jointly, the parliaments were held jointly on Polish territory, and the Commonwealth acted as a single entity in external affairs.

A part of Lithuanian gentry opposed the new union. To break their resistance, the King transferred the Ukrainian provinces from the Grand Duchy of Lithuania to Poland, accelerating the process of closer integration of these states. Three years later, Sigismund Augustus died.

THE FIRST ROYAL ELECTIONS: THE SIXTEENTH AND SEVENTEENTH CENTURIES
After the death of Sigismund Augustus, the Commonwealth faced a challenge. The Jagiellonian dynasty was extinct. The

nobility had to elect a monarch for the first time in completely free elections. This required new procedures, which were now formed ad hoc. The power was taken by an interrex, as the person who took the place of the ruler after the death of the ruler was called. After a short disagreement with Protestant magnates, the archbishop of Gniezno and the primate of Poland took the office. This became a fixed political custom: a primate always performed the function of interrex. The next steps also became a part of the Commonwealth's political system. In the provinces, power was taken by special dietines. In January 1573 the Convocation Sejm gathered to prepare the elections. The deputies decided that every noble would have the right to participate in the elections and would have one vote. Among several candidates to the Polish throne, Henri de Valois (Henryk Walezy), a brother of the King of France, was the most popular. Unfortunately, he had been involved in the massacre of French Protestants on Saint Bartholomew's Day in 1572. As a result, Polish Protestants objected and arranged the so-called Warsaw Confederation to protest. Their objections were overcome when the Catholic deputies agreed to adopt a charter that guaranteed absolute religious freedom.

In April 1573 about 50,000 noblemen gathered near Warsaw and elected Henri king of Poland. Before the coronation, he had to sign two sets of documents; these were later endorsed by everyone who came to the throne. The first set, which were accepted every time without alteration and called the Henrician Articles, summarized all the gentry's privileges and stipulated that the king would convene the Sejm every two years, would not name a successor nor marry without Parliament's consent, and would have limited legislative powers and limited authority over *levée-en-masse* (the organization of armed forces based on the principle that each nobleman was obliged to participate in his monarch's war operations), and that sixteen senators would accompany him as permanent advisers. The second set, called Pacta Conventa, contained specific conditions for each king who signed them. Henri promised the nobility an alliance with France and a trade agreement advantageous to Poland. He pledged to build a fleet to stop Russian navigation on the Baltic Sea, to send the Gascon infantry to Poland in a case of war, to pay the debts of Sigismund Augustus, to refill the treasury, and to finance the education of one hundred Polish noblemen in France

Jan II Kazimierz. (Historical Picture Archive/Corbis)

and the invitation of foreign scholars to Poland. Henri accepted the conditions in Paris, arrived in Poland, and was crowned in Cracow. A Coronation Sejm closed all the electoral procedures.

Henri spent only four months in Poland, leaving the country secretly to claim the throne of his deceased brother; he did not return. After some confusion, the electoral procedure was repeated in 1575; the nobility split and elected two kings: Stephen Batory, the prince of Transylvania, and Maximilian Habsburg, the German emperor. Eventually Batory, whose party proved to be stronger, won the competition. He had a master plan. In order to liberate his Hungarian fatherland from the Turkish yoke, he intended to establish a great coalition, including the Commonwealth and Muscovy. Polish-Russian relations were poor, though. Moscow wanted to gather all the lands of Kievan Rus, and a state of almost perpetual war was waged on the Lithuanian-Muscovite border for centuries. Batory decided to force Moscow to cooperate. He reformed the Commonwealth army, settled internal problems such as the rebellious policies of Gdańsk, and led three victorious expeditions against Muscovy. The borders of the Commonwealth were pushed to the east, but Batory died in 1586.

After a stormy interregnum and a short civil war (a part of the gentry elected Archduke Maximilian Habsburg), Sigismund Vasa, a son of King John III of Sweden, became king of Poland in 1587. A pious Catholic educated in Germany, Sigismund met with opposition from Polish dissidents (non-Catholic Christians). Moreover, he was pressed by his father to return to Sweden to fight against the Reformation and to take the Swedish throne. Sigismund considered this option and secretly negotiated with the Habsburgs, who were supposed to receive some Polish lands in exchange for their support against the Swedish Lutherans. The scheme failed, and Sigismund faced a humiliating Inquisition Sejm, which exposed the secret negotiations and forbade the king to leave Poland without the permission of Parliament. In 1594 Sigismund was crowned king of Sweden, but he refused to guarantee religious freedom to the Lutheran majority, which then elevated its own leader to the throne in Stockholm. Sigismund tried to recover the throne and, during a civil war, to intimidate the opposition in Sweden into aiding him, ceded some Swedish possessions to Poland. This initiated a long series of Polish-Swedish conflicts in the seventeenth century.

Sigismund's uncompromising Catholicism shaped his policies. Most people in the eastern parts of the Commonwealth were of the Orthodox faith and considered the patriarch of Moscow to be their spiritual leader. Sigismund wanted to change this unfortunate situation. He was personally interested in the reunification of Christianity. Accordingly, the 1596 Union of Brest-Litovsk liquidated the Orthodox Church in Poland. Its leaders, the metropolitan of Kiev and several bishops from the eastern provinces, petitioned Rome for reunion. It was agreed that the Uniates, later called Greek Catholics, could preserve their old Slavonic rites and ceremonies, being obliged only to acknowledge dogmas from Rome and the supremacy of the pope. The union, which was supposed to spread into Rus-

sia and the Balkans, took as its pattern the decisions of the Council of Florence, which, for some time, settled the differences between Eastern and Western Christians in 1493. Not all the Orthodox Christians of the Commonwealth accepted the Union, and soon the Orthodox Church reorganized itself.

Regardless of the unhappy commencement of Sigismund's reign, the Commonwealth was still a great power. At the beginning of the seventeenth century, Polish grain exports to to Western Europe reached their peak. Central Poland did not witness a war for almost three centuries. Culture and scholarship thrived. The Commonwealth became a refuge for political and religious exiles from other countries. The Poles placed a friendly *hospodar* (prince) on the Moldavian throne in 1595, stopped a Swedish invasion with a sensational victory at Kircholm in 1605, and intervened several times in Muscovy. After the extinction of the Rurikid dynasty, the Poles put two usurpers on the throne in Moscow and occupied it for some time. In 1610 Sigismund rejected a compromise Muscovite offer that his son Władysław should convert to Orthodoxy and take the throne in Moscow. After several years of wars in which Muscovy defended itself and its new dynasty, the Romanovs, it signed a truce with the Commonwealth, which was now involved in wars against Sweden.

When Sigismund died in 1632, the nobility unanimously elected his son Władysław. The new king wanted to recover the crown of Sweden as well as reclaim the throne of Muscovy, and fought with both of them with varying degrees of success. His favorite project, however, was a great war with the Turks and the recovery of Southeastern Europe. He began military preparations and reached an agreement with the Cossacks. These rebellious and warrior-like free settlers established a form of self-government on the depopulated steppe between Muscovy, the Commonwealth, and the Turkish possessions north of the Black Sea. Polish nobility, colonizing these areas, tried to abolish Cossack semiautonomy. The Commonwealth registered a small and changing number of Cossacks and paid them for the defense of the southern borders. This attempt to tame the Cossacks led to conflict, and Cossack uprisings broke out every several years. Władysław promised the Cossacks privileges and new lands after a victorious war against the Ottoman Empire. The enthusiasm first felt among the Cossacks at this offer soon turned, however, to disappointment and anger, when the king became ill; the Sejm opposed the war, and various concessions given to the Cossacks were reversed. A personal conflict between a Polish official and one of the Cossack leaders, Bohdan Khmelnytsky, triggered the outbreak of a new uprising in 1648.

The beginning of the Khmelnytsky uprising coincided with the next royal election in Poland. In 1648 Władysław died, and the nobles elected his brother, John Casimir (Jan Kazimierz) king of Poland and grand duke of Lithuania. The new monarch tried to reach an agreement with Khmelnytsky, who won several battles against the Poles and established a large Cossack state. When the negotiations failed, John Casimir organized two successful campaigns against the Cossacks.

The king also tried to strengthen royal power, but he faced new challenges. In 1652 a Sejm deputy used the power known as the *liberum veto* for the first time. According to Polish tradition, all nobles were politically equal, and every parliamentary bill had to be passed unanimously. Initially, however, the liberum veto right had been understood differently; after 1652, used more and more frequently, it paralyzed the Polish political system. In 1654 the Cossacks turned to Muscovy for help and signed the Pereiaslav Treaty, which created an autonomous Cossack state as a protectorate of the Muscovite tsar. This, in turn, provoked a new Polish-Russian war. While the Polish army was fighting in the east, the Swedes invaded Poland, starting what was called the Swedish Deluge in 1655. The king, abandoned by most magnates (who now switched their allegiance to Sweden), fled abroad, and the Swedes occupied most of Poland and Lithuania proper.

The abusive Swedish attitude toward the Polish Catholic tradition provoked spontaneous popular resistance. The Swedes were ejected from Poland, and the war was concluded with the Treaty of Oliva in 1660, when John Casimir renounced his rights to the Swedish throne and Northern Livonia (today's Latvia). In the meantime, Poland had to force back a Transylvanian aggression and recognized the full sovereignty of Ducal Prussia in return for its support against Sweden. The long Russian war was concluded in 1667. To accelerate the recovery of the country, the king tried to introduce reforms, but his efforts met with opposition from the magnates. One of them started a mutiny, which defeated the royal army. The king, tired and depressed after the death of the queen, abdicated in 1668 and left for France, where he served as a titular abbot of a monastery until his death.

Portrait of Tadeusz Kościuszko, veteran of the America Revolution and leader of the Polish National Insurrection in 1794. (National Archives)

DECLINE AND PARTITION IN THE SEVENTEENTH AND EIGHTEENTH CENTURIES

After the wars of the mid-seventeenth century, the Commonwealth was exhausted. Its population had fallen from 10 million in 1648 to 6 million in 1668. Its economy and towns were in ruin. People did not migrate to the Commonwealth any longer. Groups such as the Jews and several non-Catholic denominations in fact began to leave. The brutalities of the wars and the fact that the aggressors were not Catholic destroyed the previous sense of religious tolerance. The Commonwealth became a confederation of territories controlled by the magnates. In the xenophobic atmosphere dominating the Commonwealth, the nobility did not want to have another foreigner on the throne, and they elected Michał Korybut Wiśniowiecki in 1669. The nobles hoped that the new king, a son of a famous conqueror of the Cossacks, Jarema Wiśniowiecki, would be as brave as his father. Unfortunately, Michał Korybut proved to be completely incompetent. In 1672 the Commonwealth was defeated by the Turks, lost three provinces, and had to pay the sultan a yearly tribute. If the king had not died in 1673, the humiliated nobility would probably have forced him to abdicate.

In 1674, after a divided election, one of the best Polish military commanders, Jan Sobieski, was elevated to the throne. He rebuilt the army, signed a treaty with France, and planned to subjugate Prussia and to strengthen the Polish position in the Baltic region. The magnates, however, were more interested in Ukraine. The Commonwealth returned to an anti-Turkish alliance with the Habsburgs. In 1683 a military expedition led by Jan III Sobieski saved Vienna, which had been besieged by the Ottomans. As a result of this new war with the Turks, Poland recovered its three lost southern provinces in 1699. The king, however, died in 1696, disliked by the nobles, who opposed the royal family's plans to introduce a hereditary monarchy in Poland.

Not only was the 1697 royal election divided, but for the first time a candidate from a clear minority became king. Most nobles voted for Prince Conti of France, but the Elector of Saxony, Augustus II Friedrich Wettin, supported by a smaller group of nobility, came to Poland with his army and took power. Saxony was blossoming under his government, and he impressed the Polish nobles by converting from Lutheranism to Catholicism. He had ambitious plans and intended to realize them using Poland as a springboard. Augustus wanted to strengthen royal power in the Commonwealth and to gain Livonia and Courland for his family as a hereditary property. He promised several monarchs various Polish territories in exchange for their support. In 1700 Saxony joined a Russian-Danish anti-Swedish coalition to recover Livonia, taken from Poland by Sweden in the seventeenth century. Formally, the Commonwealth did not participate in the Great Northern War of 1700–1721, but most of its operations took place on Polish territories and devastated them. In 1704 Charles XII of Sweden ejected Augustus from Poland and put the palatine of Poznań, Stanisław Leszczyński, on the Polish throne. In 1706 Augustus, defeated in Saxony, renounced all claims to the throne, but his supporters in the Commonwealth fought together with Russian armies against the Polish supporters of the Swedes and Leszczyński. In 1709 Charles XII suffered a major defeat at Poltava in Ukraine. The Swedes were subsequently driven from the Commonwealth, controlled now by the Russians.

Augustus returned to Poland and tried to ensure his absolute power, which led to a conflict with the nobility. Russia's tsar, Peter the Great, mediated the dispute, dictated a settlement, and forced both sides to accept it in 1717 during the so-called Silence Sejm, when none of its members dared to utter a word. Augustus renounced his absolutist aspirations and sent his Saxon troops back to Saxony; the army of Lithuania was reduced to 6,000 men and that of Poland to 18,000. The nobility was guaranteed its former privileges, including the *liberum veto*. Although Russia took Livonia, its troops stayed in the Commonwealth, which now became a Russian protectorate.

During the Great Northern War, Poland's territories were devastated by the Russian, Swedish, and Saxon armies, which lived off the land. Poor harvests in 1706–1708 and the Great Plague, which raged until 1711, completed the destruction. Lithuania alone lost about one-third of its population.

In 1733 Augustus II was succeeded on the Polish throne by his son, Augustus III. Russian armies intervened against the candidacies of Portuguese Prince Emanuel and Stanisław Leszczyński, and won the War of Polish Succession. The new king rarely visited the Commonwealth, left it in the hands of his favorites, and subordinated Polish interests to the Wettin dynastic interests. Russia, supported by Prussia, in turn guaranteed what was called the Golden Freedom of the Polish nobility.

Growing anarchy and decline marked the Saxon times. The first signs of economic and cultural recovery, however, emerged by the end of this era. After the death of Augustus III in 1763, Tsarina Catherine the Great put Stanisław August Poniatowski on the throne of Poland in 1764. The new king, linked to a powerful *Familia* (magnate faction) gathered around the enlightened and patriotic Czartoryski family, initiated new reforms. These reforms, however, were perceived by the nobility as an attack on its liberties executed by a Russian puppet. After the Russian ambassador to Warsaw kidnapped Polish senators opposing Russian control, conservative and patriotic nobility started an uprising in 1768. Known as the Bar Confederation, since it originated in the small town of Bar in Podolia, it fought against the reforms and foreign interference in Polish internal af-

fairs. At the same time, a popular uprising, the so-called Koliivshchyna rebellion, took place in Polish Ukraine. Taking advantage of the chaos caused by the Bar Confederation, the Ukrainian revolt, and the Turkish-Russian war, Austria incorporated some Polish territories in 1770, a harbinger of what was to follow.

Two years later, on the initiative of Frederick the Great, Prussia, Russia, and Austria organized the first partition of Poland. According to the anti-Polish coalition, the partition was necessary to save the international balance of power, order, and the harmony threatened by "Polish anarchy." Russia annexed poor eastern provinces beyond the Rivers Dvina and Dnepr, altogether comprising 92,000 square kilometers, inhabited by 1.3 million Belarusians. Austria's share was more valuable: a territory known later as Galicia (83,000 square kilometers, populated by 2.65 million people, mostly Poles and Ukrainians). The most precious was the Prussian acquisition: West Prussia (Gdańsk Pomerania), with the Bishopric of Warmia (Ermland). Even though the region was only 36,500 square kilometers and had only 580,000 inhabitants, and the Prussians did not receive the city of Gdańsk, their gain constituted one of the most developed regions of Poland, and its occupation united the two biggest but previously isolated provinces of Prussia: Brandenburg and East Prussia. As a result of the partition, the Commonwealth lost 30 percent of its territory, 37 percent of its population, many important resources, access to the Baltic, and its natural southern border, the Carpathians.

The exhausted Commonwealth could not resist. Most of its inhabitants passively accepted the catastrophe. The political elites, however, saw the partition as a humiliation and a warning. The king and his collaborators managed to transform the Permanent Council, forced upon the monarch by the Russians to limit his power, into an effective and stable government. Slowly and patiently, the government introduced positive changes. In 1773 the Commission of National Education, the first European education ministry, was established, and the entire school system was reformed and modernized. Thanks to royal support, an unprecedented cultural revival took place in the 1770s. All the cautious preparations of the postpartition era bore fruit after 1787, when Russia became involved in another war with Turkey and Poland regained her sovereignty for a short time. The Sejm that gathered in Warsaw in 1788 constituted itself into a Confederation, which eliminated the threat of liberum veto and initiated a period of unprecedented rule by parliament. In 1789 the French Revolution, which stimulated political activities, especially among the Polish burghers, inspired the Sejm. In 1790, in order to complete unfinished legislative projects, the Sejm doubled the number of the deputies after an additional election. On 3 May 1791, after long and meticulous preparations, in a legitimist coup d'état, the Sejm accepted a new constitution, widely regarded as a symbol of hope and an effort to preserve the existence of the Commonwealth.

This first modern European constitution (and the second one in the world, preceded only by the document drawn up in 1787 in the United States) reflected the lessons of the Enlightenment and the French and American Revolutions.

It replaced the elective monarchy with a hereditary constitutional one and offered the throne, surprisingly, to the Wettin dynasty. It eliminated the liberum veto; checked the liberties of the nobility; recognized the sovereignty of the people as the source of all law; guaranteed religious freedom; divided the government into three distinct branches, legislative, executive, and judicial; established a modern government responsible before Parliament; and decided to rebuild the army. This constitution completed the union with Lithuania, creating one government, one administration system, one army, and one treasury for the two parts of the Commonwealth. The townsmen received a number of rights that previously had been enjoyed only by the nobility, such as (limited) rights of participation in the Sejm. On the other hand, the constitution did not give a proper consideration to the Jews and peasants, who were offered only vague promises of the state's legal protection.

The constitution was received enthusiastically in Western Europe, but it alarmed Poland's neighbors. Russia signed a peace treaty with Turkey in May 1792 and sent over 90,000 troops to punish its disobedient vassal. Prussia broke its defensive alliance with Poland and joined the Russian aggression. In a Ukrainian border village of Targowica, a group of Polish conservative pro-Russian magnates organized a confederacy in defense of the Golden Freedom. The untrained Polish army could not stop the Russian troops, which gave the power in Poland to the Targowica people. Those magnates reversed all the changes initiated by the 3 May constitution but were unable to establish a functioning government, and the monarchs of Russia and Prussia decided to partition the Commonwealth again, using as a pretext the theory that the "deadly Revolution that has occurred in France" (Israel 415) had spread into Poland and threatened their countries.

The second partition in 1793 left only a little Polish buffer state of 215,000 square kilometers and 4 million inhabitants. Russia took a huge territory of 250,000 square kilometers and 3 million people. Prussia's acquisition had only 58,000 square kilometers and 1.1 million people, but it linked Prussian Silesia with previously occupied Western Prussia. Poland was in turmoil, ruled by the Targowica magnates, who concentrated on self-enrichment and settling scores with their enemies. Many political refugees escaped abroad, mainly to Saxony and France. The rump Commonwealth remained under the occupation of the Russians, who arrested Polish patriots and started demobilizing the Polish army. In March 1794 one of the regiments resisted. The news about the rebellion triggered successful uprisings in Cracow, Warsaw, and Vilna. General Tadeusz Kościuszko, a celebrated veteran of the American Revolution, was chosen the chief (*Naczelnik*) of the insurrection and defeated a Russian army unit at Racławice on 4 April 1794. Kościuszko tried to start an American style national uprising, but the nobility was against the social changes that would follow it and especially opposed liberation of the peasants. In October 1794, Kościuszko was defeated and imprisoned. In November the Russians took Warsaw, killing about 10,000 civilians during the siege of the city. In January 1795, Prussia, Russia, and Austria, which also sent troops across the Polish border, signed the treaty that decreed the third partition of Poland. Russia again took the largest share, but Prussia occupied central Poland, including Warsaw, which became a dilapidated border town. In November 1795, Stanisław August Poniatowski, who desperately had tried to save his country, abdicated, and in 1798 he died in St. Petersburg. The partitioning powers signed an agreement about "the need to abolish everything, which can recall the memory of the existence of the kingdom of Poland" (Lukowski and Zawadzki 105).

As a consequence of the partitions, the fourth most populous country of Europe (after France, the Holy Roman Empire of the German Nation, and Russia) disappeared from the map. For the first time since the fall of Byzantium, a major European state was annihilated completely. Russia took 62 percent of its area and 45 percent of the population, Prussia 20 percent of the land and 23 percent of the people, and Austria 18 percent of the land and 32 percent of the population. The newly drawn borders did not correspond to any old divisions and divided a mostly agricultural country. Only about 17 percent of its population lived in towns, and there was only one city there: Warsaw, with almost 200,000 inhabitants in 1795. Most peasants were serfs owned by their landlords. The former Commonwealth was a home to the largest Jewish community in the world. About 750,000 Jews constituted almost 10 percent of the entire society and over 75 percent of European Jewry. The most important part of the Polish heritage, however, was the nobility. It also made up about 10 percent of the population and was uniquely diversified: from peasant-like petty noblemen, who owned small farms or had virtually nothing, to powerful magnates, whose estates were larger than some European states. Of different ethnic and religious backgrounds, they were united by a common identity as Polish noblemen who looked down on those primitive Muscovites, greedy Prussian nouveaux riches, and treacherous Austrians.

THE NINETEENTH CENTURY

While the partitioning powers were dividing the Commonwealth, Polish émigrés in Western Europe started building organizations that were supposed to represent Poland and to prepare the groundwork for its revival. Despite quarreling and fighting each other, they established a network of conspiracies in the country and asked the Western powers, especially revolutionary France, for help.

In 1796 French authorities established a Polish legion to fight against Austria. The march of the legion began with the words "Poland is not yet lost as long as we live"; it later became the Polish national anthem. In 1799 two Polish legions were formed. Altogether, over 25,000 soldiers, mostly peasants and townsmen, served in the legions, which became venues for political education.

At the same time, many Polish nobles had a vision of a reconstructed Polish state in union with Russia. Prince Adam Czartoryski, a personal friend of Tsar Alexander I and the Russian minister of foreign affairs, best represented this orientation.

In 1806 a successful Polish uprising in western Poland followed a spectacular French victory over Prussia, which was forced to sue for peace. Napoleon came to Warsaw and, in 1807, defeated the Russians, who were trying to defend the old international system in Europe. In July 1807 Napoleon met Alexander I and the King of Prussia at Tilsit (on the Niemen River). They established a new order in Eastern Europe. The lands taken by Prussia in the second and the third partitions were now transformed into the Duchy of Warsaw, a small state of 102,000 square kilometers and 2.6 million people. In 1809, after a French victory over Austria, the duchy received the territories grabbed by the Habsburgs during the third partition as well, growing to 155,000 square kilometers and 4.3 million inhabitants. The throne of the duchy was given to King Frederick August of Saxony, who was instated as a hereditary prince. The state received a constitution written by Napoleon, which stipulated that "all citizens are equal before the law." The constitution liberated the peasants but did not give them the right to their land, which, de facto, preserved serfdom. Although Jews received full rights, those guarantees were soon suspended for ten years. In addition, the Napoleonic Civic Code was introduced in the duchy.

In practice, however, the old socioeconomic order was preserved; the duchy was little more than a French vassal state and a military bridgehead in Eastern Europe. Controlled by French generals and residents, the duchy spent two-thirds of its budget on the army, which fought for Napoleon on many fronts, not necessarily "For Your and Our Freedom," as a nineteenth-century slogan of Polish revolutionaries announced. About 100,000 Polish soldiers participated in Napoleon's Russian invasion in 1812. Most of them perished together with the French army. In February 1813 the Russians took Warsaw and established a provisional regime headed by a Russian senator. Polish dreams of a revived Commonwealth disappeared.

The fate of Poland was decided during the Congress of Vienna in 1814–1815. After some disagreement within the victorious anti-Napoleonic coalition, the Duchy of Warsaw was divided into three parts. A tiny strip of land near Cracow (1,164 square kilometers) populated by 140,000 inhabitants was transformed into the Republic of Cracow. Supposedly "free, independent, and neutral" but "under the protection" of the partitioning powers, it survived until 1846, when it was incorporated into Austria. The western part of the Duchy of Warsaw (29,000 square kilometers with 1.3 million people) went to Prussia as an autonomous Grand Duchy of Poznań (Posen). It had its own currency and parliament; Polish was an official language in administration and schools. The king of Prussia took the title of Grand Duke of Poznań and was represented there by a Polish vice-regent, Prince Antoni Radziwiłł. The duchy became the breadbasket of Prussia and started developing quickly. Its peasantry was included in the land reforms that had been initiated in Prussia in 1808; the peasants were liberated, but they had to pay for the land given to them during the reform. Consequently, only the richest farmers survived and formed a strong Polish-speaking class. The poor had to migrate to urban centers, which also strengthened the future Polish national movement in the eastern provinces of Prussia.

Most territories of the Duchy of Warsaw were reorganized as the Congress Kingdom of Poland, a small state of 128,000 square kilometers and 3.3 million inhabitants. The kingdom, theoretically independent, was linked by personal union with Russia. Alexander I became its first king, and its constitution was one of the most liberal in Europe, even though serfdom was not abolished. Polish was the only official language. Alexander's brother, Grand Duke Constantine, became the commander in chief of the kingdom's army and the troops in Lithuania. This joint appointment was considered the first step toward the reunification of the Commonwealth under Russian rule. In 1816 Warsaw University was opened, and a modern educational system continued the work of the Commission of National Education. After an initial economic crisis, the authorities in Warsaw started a relatively successful industrialization of the kingdom.

On the other hand, Grand Duke Constantine dominated the imperial lieutenant governor, General Józef Zajączek, and governed the kingdom as a despot. Censorship was introduced, people were imprisoned without trial, the sessions of the Sejm were "delayed," the constitution was disregarded, and a secret police was organized. The Poles argued that the Congress of Vienna gave them certain freedoms that the partitioning powers were not observing and that other states that had signed the Vienna agreements should intervene on behalf of Poland. When this did not happen and a legal opposition was paralyzed, clandestine organizations appeared. One of them, the Cadet Corps in Warsaw, initiated a revolt in November 1830, alarmed by a rumor that Polish troops would be sent to suppress the revolution in Belgium and would be replaced in Poland by the Russian Army. The political establishment of the kingdom was completely surprised by (and unprepared for) the uprising. Moderate leaders, who assumed power, started negotiating with the tsar instead of organizing an offensive against the Russians. The divided national government did not pass reforms to win the support of the peasantry and did not gain any foreign aid. This allowed the Russian army to gain needed time to regroup and crush the insurrection, even though the Poles offered strong resistance at several battles.

The defeat of the November Insurrection of 1830–1831 was followed by severe reprisals. The Polish army, the Sejm and Senate, the University of Warsaw, and many other national institutions were dissolved. Russification began, and the Polish administration came to be controlled centrally from St. Petersburg. Thousands of Polish soldiers were conscripted into the Russian Army, and thousands of people were deported to Siberia. About ten thousand officers, politicians, artists, and professionals, in a movement called the Great Emigration, left Poland for the West, mostly ending up in France, and continued intensive political and cultural activities there. The kingdom was ruled, and terrorized, until 1856 by the man called the prince of Erevan and Warsaw, the commander in chief of the Russian occupying forces, General Ivan Paskevich. His government was so oppressive that even the events of the 1848–1849

Springtime of Nations (commonly known as the revolutions of 1848) did not spread to Russian Poland.

The first positive changes appeared in the Congress Kingdom after Russia lost the Crimean War of 1853–1856 and the "policeman of Europe," Nicholas I, died and was replaced by a new "tsar-reformer," Alexander II, in 1855. Facing numerous international challenges and starting an ambitious reform program, Russian authorities wanted to pacify Poland and sought a modus vivendi with the Poles. After the death of Paskevich, a new plenipotentiary of the tsar, Prince Mikhail Gorchakov, introduced a new, milder government in Poland. Political amnesty was decreed, censorship was relaxed, the archepiscopal seat in Warsaw, vacant for years, was filled, Poles were readmitted to the administration in the western Russian provinces, and a Medical-Surgical Academy and a School of Fine Arts were established in Warsaw.

In 1857 an Agricultural Society was created in Warsaw. It gathered about four thousand members—rich landowners and the heads of the most prominent Polish gentry families. Soon, it became a substitute diet. Chaired by popular aristocrat Andrzej Zamoyski, it debated on the issues most important for the Congress Kingdom, which had changed tremendously by the mid-nineteenth century.

A slow process of industrialization and recovery after the disaster of partitions and the Napoleonic era had already started in the 1820s. In 1851 the Russian-Polish tariff border was abolished. This led to new opportunities for Polish industry, which recaptured the Russian markets. The railroad network was developed, the textile and light industries were modernized, and new iron works and mines were opened. The Crimean War had created a demand for grain, and mass sugar production began. The kingdom's population grew from 4.1 million in 1830 to 4.8 million people in 1860. Warsaw, with 180,000 inhabitants in 1830, grew to a size of 230,000 in 1860. Emancipation and assimilation of the Jews started. Over 50 percent of peasants paid rents and were free of serfdom.

In 1859 the Russians asked the Agricultural Society to prepare a land reform project for the Congress Kingdom. This initiative helped to revive political life in Poland. Public opinion was electrified with the news of the outbreak of war in 1859 between France and Austria and of the unification of Italy. Beginning in 1858, a series of patriotic demonstrations took place in Warsaw. Polish political émigrés abroad intensified their activities and sent their envoys to Poland, where underground organizations appeared. In early 1861, when a plan of agricultural reform in Russia proper was already known, meetings of the Agricultural Society were backed up by huge demonstrations demanding more autonomy for Poland. On 27 February 1861, Russian troops opened fire on the crowds and killed several people, including two members of the Agricultural Society. Its leaders called upon the people to start "moral resistance" and "moral revolution."

In response, the Russians opened negotiations with Count Alexander Wielopolski. A conservative and conciliatory aristocrat who opposed conspiracy and resistance, Wielopolski competed politically with the popular Zamoyski, believing that loyalty toward Russia would be rewarded with autonomy and cultural freedom for the Congress Kingdom. He was appointed a member and later the head of the reestablished Administrative Council of the kingdom. He dissolved the Agricultural Society, tried to diminish the growing tension between Polish society and the Russian occupational apparatus (during a demonstration in April 1862 the Russian troops killed approximately one hundred civilians in Warsaw), and continued his reforms, aimed at the emancipation of the Jews, Polonization of the kingdom's administration, and modernization of its educational system. When the Russians once again introduced military conscription in Congress Poland, he decided to use the draft to smash the conspiracy, especially in Warsaw.

Yet, a day before the levy was to take place, young men escaped from the city to the surrounding woods, and a week later, on 22 January 1863, an underground National Central Committee issued a manifesto. It called the people of Poland, Lithuania, and Ruthenia to arms, announced the establishment of a national government, promised freedom and equality to all the citizens irrespective of religion, proclaimed the peasants to be full owners of the land they cultivated, and offered indemnities to the landlords. During the night of 22/23 January, 6,000 badly armed insurgents attacked eighteen Russian garrisons (holding nearly 100,000 troops). Intensive guerrilla fighting started in the entire kingdom and in the formerly Polish "western gubernias" of Russia (Lithuania, Belorussia, and Ukraine). An underground state was created with its own postal services, finances, secret police, and diplomatic representatives.

France, Austria, and Great Britain sent diplomatic notes to St. Petersburg regarding the situation in Poland. A "Polish Meeting," a large demonstration of support for Poland in July 1863 in London, became a starting point for the organization of the First Working Men International. Unfortunately, the Western powers limited themselves to written protests. The insurgents took no major town, and the National Government could not act openly. The Russians, pressed by the Prussians to crush the uprising as quickly as possible, sent a regular army of 300,000 men to Poland and began a brutal crackdown on the insurgents and the population in general.

The Polish underground was divided; the "Reds" and the "Whites" competed politically and had different plans for the uprising. Initially, there was no supreme command and no coordinated strategy. In the fall of 1863 the Lithuanian insurrection was crushed by the "hangman of Vilna," the governor Mikhail Muravyov. Russian-introduced emancipation of the peasants prompted them to abandon the rebels. In October 1863 a retired professional officer of the Russian Army, Romuald Traugutt, took over the national government as a dictator and revived the uprising, but he was arrested in April 1864 and executed in Warsaw. In May 1864 General Fedor Berg, the commander in chief of the Russian army in Poland and the newly appointed viceroy, announced the end of the campaign, even though the last skirmishes continued until the spring of 1865.

The failure of the January Uprising was followed by harsh retributions. About four hundred insurgents were executed after trials; an unknown number were shot or hanged by the Russian army, and thousands were deported to Siberia. About 1,600 estates in the Congress Poland and 1,800 estates in the western gubernias were confiscated and given to tsarist officials. A contribution of 20 million rubles was forced upon the landowners of the Congress Kingdom of Poland. The name of the kingdom was changed to Vistula Land, which was reduced to a tsarist province; it lost all autonomy and separate administrative institutions. Even the Bank of Poland was transformed into a subsidiary branch of the Imperial Bank. No municipal government existed, no justices were elected, and trials by jury were not permitted. Intensive Russification began. The Warsaw Main School was reshaped into a Russian university. The Uniate Church was abolished completely, the Catholic clergy was harassed, and by 1870 not a single Polish bishopric had a bishop. Anti-Polish feelings were fostered in Russia; Lithuanian and Ukrainian nationalism in turn awakened on the territories of the former Polish-Lithuanian Commonwealth.

The land reform of 19 February (2 March) 1864 was supposed to widen an abyss between the gentry and the peasants. The latter received the land they used. All their obligations toward the landlords were liquidated. The villagers enjoyed self-government and were allowed to gather wood for burning from landlords' forests and to use manorial pastures. Landlords were paid compensation in the form of forty-two year amortization bonds, which quickly depreciated. To pay the compensation, the Russian authorities introduced a new land tax on farmers.

The reform was very profitable to the regime, but it simultaneously triggered significant social changes. In the countryside, the peasants, formerly exploited by the gentry, came to be oppressed by the Russian state apparatus. The great latifundia (landed estates) were virtually unaffected, but the middle and petty gentry were ruined. Thousands of noblemen moved to the towns and cities, but there their opportunities were limited. Administrative positions were reserved for Russians, and trade and industry were in the hands of the Jews and Christian bourgeoisie. In addition, a mass of landless peasants moved to the cities, becoming part of a growing proletariat. A new class of intelligentsia also formed, hostile toward the magnates, the peasants, the bourgeoisie, the Jews, and the Russians.

The changes triggered by the land reform contributed to the rapid industrialization that took place in the former Congress Kingdom in the 1870s and 1880s. Russian protectionist policies stimulated the development of textile and metallurgical industries. Railroad construction created a new demand for iron and coal. The value of production grew from 30 million rubles in 1864 to 190 million in 1885, while the number of workers expanded from 80,000 to 150,000. The output of coal grew from 312,000 tons in 1870 to over 3 million tons in 1890. By 1890, industrial production exceeded agricultural production, and foreign investments reached about 39 percent of capital. Warsaw, with 600,000 people in 1890, became one of the largest cities of the empire, and Vistula Land its most advanced part. Its socioeconomic conditions, however, still did not meet Western standards and, in 1897, over 68 percent of the people in the former Congress Kingdom still lived in the countryside.

The failure of the January Uprising and its socioeconomic consequences strongly affected public life. Political pessimism prevailed in Poland. Conspiracy and armed struggle were considered suicidal folly. Positivism became the leading political trend. A reaction against romanticism in literature and politics, it propagated the "heroism of a reasonable life" and a program of "organic work" that was supposed to preserve cultural and material aspects of Polish life through universal education, technological progress, industrial development, and modernization. Positivists fought against the remaining elements of feudalism and supported the emancipation of women, Jews, burghers, and peasants. They praised economic entrepreneurship and emphasized that every citizen of Poland, regardless of his or her national, religious, or social background, could contribute to the development of the country.

Positivists assumed a critical, realistic, practical, and "apolitical" attitude. This stance was exploited by the supporters of Triple Loyalism, a collaboration program with the authorities of Russia, Prussia, and Austria. After a quarter of a century, however, positivism lost its popularity. It did not bring any political results and was rejected by many political émigrés still active in the West and by the young people who had not experienced the January Uprising. In the late 1880s a secret Association of Polish Youth, Zet, was established. Both socialist and nationalist, Zet returned to the idea of freedom fighting, rejected positivism, and maintained that ordinary people better preserved the national tradition than did the upper classes. In 1887 one of the organizers of Zet, Zygmunt Miłkowski, published a booklet "About Active Defense and National Treasury," which argued against passive resistance and supported preparation for active struggle against the occupiers of Poland. That same year, he established the Polish League in Switzerland. The league anticipated a conflict between the great powers, formulated a program of reconstruction for a Polish state within the prepartition borders, stood against social revolution and international socialism, and condemned positivists and conservatives for their loyalty to the powers occupying Poland.

In 1893 the Polish League was transformed into a more active National League, a clandestine organization, led by Roman Dmowski, that penetrated various Polish political camps. The National League also criticized the loyalists, condemned tsarist oppression, called for pressure on Russian authorities, and organized political demonstrations in Warsaw. Dmowski, who had just graduated from the Biology Department of the Russian Warsaw University, published several political writings and soon became an intellectual leader of the Polish nationalistic movement. In 1897 the league was reorganized as the National Democratic Party (Endecja, or Endeks). It established branches in Prussian Poland in 1904 and, in 1905, in Galicia. It published several periodicals, and its program, based on social solidarity, anti-Semitism, and hostility to socialism, was increasingly popular.

At the same time, modern political parties were also established on the political left in the former Congress Kingdom of Poland. In 1881 a young member of the intelligentsia, Ludwik Waryński, organized the first Polish workers' party, Proletariat. Destroyed by the tsarist police two years later, it was succeeded by the Second Proletariat in 1888. Some of its members joined the Polish Socialist Party (PPS) in 1892. Founded in Paris by the Congress of Polish Socialists, it called for Polish independence and establishment of a democratic republic. In 1893 the first PPS groups were organized in Russia and Prussia. A former political deportee to Siberia, Józef Piłsudski, became one of the most important PPS leaders. In the same year, Marxist radical activists, who opposed the pro-independence stand of the PPS program, formed a party known later as the Social Democracy of the Kingdom of Poland and Lithuania. Other ethnic groups of Russian-occupied Poland also created their first parties by the end of the nineteenth century. Bund, the General Jewish Workers' Union in Lithuania, Poland, and Russia, was established in 1897 and propagated a radical Marxist and anti-Zionist program.

The development of the Polish nation followed different lines in the Prussian- and Austrian-occupied territories of the former Polish-Lithuanian Commonwealth in the nineteenth century. The king of Prussia, Frederick William III, kept in mind the two Polish uprisings of 1794 and 1806 and guaranteed Poles the maintenance of the Catholic religion and the Polish national character of the Grand Duchy of Poznań (Posen), which had been attached to his state during the Congress of Vienna. A Polish aristocrat, Prince Antoni Radziwiłł, represented the king in the duchy as its viceroy. The duchy minted its own small coins, and Polish was its official language. In 1823 an agrarian reform was implemented, but only big holdings were enfranchised. Smallholders commonly moved to the towns, strengthening their Polish character. The well-organized, relatively wealthy Polish peasantry became a strong supporter of Polish national ideas. The Prussian bureaucracy, at the same time, opposed the king's Polish policy of compromise and planned to Germanize the duchy.

In 1830 Polish public opinion in the duchy enthusiastically welcomed the outbreak of the November Insurrection, and contingents of Poznań volunteers participated in the uprising. After the revolt, however, Radziwiłł was removed from his position, and a new program of Germanization began. A local insurrection, begun in 1846, failed. The outbreak of the revolutions of 1848 brought a plan for national reorganization of the duchy, but it failed too. Moreover, the 1863 January Insurrection in the Congress Kingdom resulted in close Russian-Prussian cooperation against the Poles. Prussian authorities changed the name of the duchy to the Posen Provinz and incorporated it into the general Prussian administrative system. In 1871 the Poles protested against the incorporation of their lands into united Germany. Bismarck's anti-Polish policy became a part of the *Kulturkampf* (the struggle to subject the Roman Catholic Church, national minorities, and semi-autonomous provinces to strict state control). As a result, the Polish language was gradually withdrawn from schools and administration, and the Polish press and Polish organizations in general were harassed. In 1886 a colonization commission was created to buy Polish lands for German settlers, and several German private and governmental organizations tried to Germanize the Polish provinces completely. The Poles, however, reacted with well-organized economic and cultural activities, which slowly started to turn the tide, shaping the future national character of the Prussian-occupied Polish territories. In this struggle, the National Democratic Party became a dominating Polish political force in Prussian-occupied Poland.

In Austria, the modernization of Polish society progressed at a much slower pace. In 1815 the Habsburgs did not recover all the Polish territories they had taken during the partitions of Poland. They kept the lands incorporated into their empire after the first partition of 1772 and officially called them the Kingdom of Galicia and Lodomeria. Cut off from its Polish hinterland by an artificial border and isolated from the old Habsburg lands by the Carpathian Mountains, Galicia stagnated economically, becoming one of the poorest regions in Europe. The monarchs of Austria exploited Galicia economically and treated it as a reservoir of manpower for their army. In 1846, after a failed uprising and a peasant antigentry jacquerie, the Republic of Cracow was incorporated into Galicia. Two years later, during the revolutions of 1848, serfdom was abolished in Galicia, but its semifeudal social structure did not change quickly. To overcome a deep crisis in the Habsburg monarchy in the mid-nineteenth century, Vienna made a Compromise (*Ausgleich*) with the Hungarians that reshaped the structure of the empire in 1867. Under its provisions, Galicia received a broad autonomy. Polish became its official language, and the Polish gentry controlled its government. The province now became a center of Polish culture. The Galician population was about 8 million people at the beginning of the twentieth century and consisted mostly of Poles (45 percent), Ukrainians (45 percent), and Jews (6 percent).

Autonomy led to the creation of a thriving political life in Galicia. Initially, the most influential people were conservative loyalists, but by the end of the nineteenth century, they were losing ground to the Polish Peasant Party (established in 1895), the Polish Social Democratic Party (formed in 1892), and numerous other national minorities' parties. In 1905 a Galician branch of the National Democratic Party was also established in the province and soon dominated local political life.

At the beginning of the twentieth century, therefore, the Poles had no state and were second-class citizens in Germany and Russia. They populated mostly underdeveloped, poor, agrarian territories. The illiteracy rate was high and the countryside overpopulated. The Poles were divided into several antagonistic social classes and were burdened with the memory of the collapse of the Polish-Lithuanian Commonwealth at the end of the eighteenth century as well as the failed national uprisings of the nineteenth century. Nevertheless, the Poles constituted a relatively large nation of over 30 million people spread across the former Congress Kingdom (12 million), Galicia (8 million), the former Grand Duchy of Poznań (8 million), Pomerania (almost 2 million), Upper Silesia (almost 2 million), East Prussia, Lithuania, Belorussia, and Ukraine (several million). Their demographic growth, 1.3 percent a year, was among the

Józef Piłsudski

Considered by many historians to be the most outstanding Polish politician of the twentieth century, Piłsudski was one of the most important contributors to the reestablishment of the Polish state in 1918. Born in 1867 in a noble family northeast of Vilna, he was raised in the patriotic tradition of the Polish–Lithuanian Commonwealth. In 1887 he was arrested by the tsarist police for his contacts with Russian *Narodnik*s (Populists) and sent to Siberia. In 1892 he returned to Vilna and joined the newly established Polish Socialist Party (PPS). Soon, he became one of its most important leaders and the editor-in-chief of the party organ *Robotnik* (The Worker). He commanded the party underground activities during the 1905 revolution in Russia, and after the end of the revolution, in 1908, he moved to Austrian-controlled Galicia. Anticipating the outbreak of World War I, he created there, first secretly and then legally with the support of the Austrian authorities, several paramilitary organizations. After the beginning of the war, they took part in the anti-Russian offensive and were reformed into the Polish Legions.

In 1916, when Germany and Austria established a Polish puppet state, Piłsudski joined its government, but after the March 1917 revolution in Russia, he reversed his strategy, opposed any cooperation with Berlin and Vienna, and was imprisoned by the Germans in the fortress of Magdeburg. Released after the outbreak of the German revolution in early November 1918, he returned to Warsaw, accepted the position of chief of state and commander in chief of the Polish Army, and managed to build a compromise between various political forces fighting for power in Poland.

In 1918–1921 he led the Polish Army during several border wars and managed to finish them in a manner favorable to Poland. In March 1920, during the war against Soviet Russia, Piłsudski became the marshal of Poland. In late 1922 he transmitted his power to the newly elected president, Gabriel Narutowicz. In 1923 he resigned from his last official position of chief of the Polish General Staff and retired from politics.

Soon, however, he gathered around him many political and military leaders who opposed the excesses of the "Parliamentocracy" and criticized chaos and corruption in Poland. On 12 May 1926, Piłsudski started a military coup d'état and after several days of bloody struggle, he established a dictatorship known as *Sanacja*. Initially, the marshal tolerated the opposition, but in 1930 its leadership was arrested, and the regime slid into an unscrupulous authoritarianism. Piłsudski decided personally about all the most important governmental decisions. Disillusioned with the policies of the Western powers towards Germany and East Central Europe, he accepted a principle of equilibrium in the foreign strategy of Poland. It should engage on neither the German nor the Soviet side but should balance between those two powers.

In April 1935 the Sejm, controlled by Sanacja, accepted a new constitution that sanctioned a strong presidential system, de facto a dictatorial political system, in Poland. A month later, Piłsudski died. His political camp partially disintegrated and moved to the right. Despite all his mistakes and shortcomings, Marshal Piłsudski was one of the most charismatic leaders in the entire history of Poland, and his positive contribution to its liberation and development cannot be denied.

---

highest in Europe. They had developed a sophisticated national elite and a fascinating culture. Several modern political parties mobilized thousands of Poles and coordinated their activities. Polish national consciousness was relatively strong. At the beginning of the twentieth century, it was already obvious that German and Russian attempts to denationalize and assimilate the Poles had failed. Several countries in the West, particularly France and the United States, hosted large groups of immigrants from Poland and active Polish political centers that influenced the situation in the country.

Moreover, the Poles had their national Piedmont in autonomous Galicia. Not only did Polish political and cultural life flourish there, but Galicia also became a refuge for Poles escaping from Germany and Russia as well as the center of

the Polish national freedom movement. Stimulated by international events, the movement was growing faster at the beginning of the twentieth century than before.

Russia's defeat in the 1904 war with Japan triggered a revolution in the tsarist empire in January 1905. The former Congress Kingdom, one of the most industrialized parts of Russia, became an important center of that revolution. The Polish Socialist Party (PPS), an important co-organizer of the antitsarist resistance, transformed it partly into a national uprising. After the collapse of the revolution and the restoration of tsarist control, thousands of its veterans escaped to Galicia. Piłsudski was one of the most stubborn fighters, but in 1908 he also followed them. Anticipating the outbreak of World War I, he helped to establish in Galicia the nucleus of a future Polish army, the

Rifleman Association and the Union of Armed Struggle. In 1912 the Piłsudskiite wing of the PPS helped to form, and became an activating force in, the Temporary Committee of [Polish] Confederated Independence Parties.

Despite their dreams of a future independent state, most Poles of Russia, Austria, and Germany did not expect to recover their state soon and did not participate in the freedom movement. Of the many nations living within the borders of these three empires, however, Poles were among the best prepared to create and rebuild their state.

WORLD WAR I

The outbreak of World War I brought both misfortune and hope to the Poles. In 1914 and 1915 heavy fighting took place on the Polish territories. The Russians occupied most of Galicia and defended the former Congress Kingdom. Hundreds of thousands of Poles were mobilized into the Austrian, Russian, and German armies. The Polish economy was paralyzed, and Polish territories were devastated and exploited economically. As part of their own war efforts, the partitioning powers tried to gain Polish support. Many Poles realized that the situation, one in which Berlin, Vienna, and St. Petersburg were engaged on opposite sides of the front, created new opportunities for the Polish national cause. In August 1914 Polish politicians active in Austria formed the Supreme National Committee. It continued Galician prewar paramilitary preparations and formed the Polish Legions that fought on the side of the Austrian army. In addition, Piłsudski created an underground Polish Military Organization, which fought for an independent Poland. Another group of Polish politicians in Russia believed that only this power would be able to unite all the Polish territories into one autonomous unit. Led by Roman Dmowski, this pro-Russian orientation established the Polish National Committee in November 1914 and tried to form Polish military units within the tsarist army. Only in Germany were there no significant signs of Polish support.

In mid-1915 the Germans and the Austrians pushed the Russians from the Polish territories. The tsarist armies evacuated the most important industrial facilities and a part of the population, which added to the wartime destruction. The German-occupied region was now reorganized as the General Government Warsaw. The Austrians established the General Government Lublin in the southern part of the former Congress Kingdom. Both occupiers mercilessly exploited their territories, removing from Poland everything useful for their own war industries. Poland was supposed to be a part of *Mitteleuropa* (Central Europe), a German-controlled agricultural semi-colony, buying the products of German industry and delivering cheap labor and food. The Germans, however, overestimated their military potential and started experiencing serious problems in 1916. A shortage of "cannon fodder" (troops) was especially pressing, and the Berlin leadership began looking for new soldiers in their occupied territories. German intelligence discovered quickly that the Russian mobilization in the Polish provinces was shallow and that approximately one million soldiers could be taken from these territories. International

Portrait of Józef Piłsudski, one of the most outstanding Polish political leaders. (Library of Congress)

law, however, prohibited conscription in occupied lands. It was also obvious that men enlisted by force would not be good soldiers. The German and the Austrian authorities nevertheless decided to encourage the Poles to volunteer.

On 5 November 1916, the emperors of Germany and Austria proclaimed the establishment of a Kingdom of Poland. It was to be formed on the territories of the former Congress Kingdom; its exact borders were to be determined in the future. An army of this "hereditary and constitutional Monarchy" was to be organized under the joint control of the German and Austrian governors-general of occupied Poland. A Polish Provisional Council of State was formed to help the German and Austrian authorities form the *Polnische Wehrmacht* (Polish Armed Forces).

The concept of the kingdom was so vague and the German-Austrian intentions were so clear that a large section of the Polish public opinion ignored the Declaration of 5 November. Yet the so-called activists, coming mainly from Piłsudski's wing of the PPS, the National Union of Workers, the National Union of Peasants, and the landowners' milieus, decided to use this opportunity to start building a Polish state apparatus under Austro-German supervision. The University of Warsaw reopened, and Polish educational network and central state institutions were formed. Piłsudski worked at the Military Department, and his Legionnaires were to be reorganized into new units. The Declaration of 5 November thus destroyed the past solidarity of the partitioning powers with regard to the Polish question. In December 1916 the tsar himself mentioned the idea of a future free Poland in his order to the army.

In the spring of 1917 the Piłsudski political camp started redesigning its strategy. The February Revolution in Russia, which toppled the Romanov dynasty, had changed the international situation. The Provisional Government in St. Petersburg now supported a plan for a sovereign Polish state allied with Russia. The Petrograd Soviet also recognized Poland's right to independence. Poles in Russia started organizing themselves. A Polish Liquidation Committee began to reshape the old tsarist occupational apparatus for Poland into the nucleus of a new administration. A newly established Supreme Polish Military Committee helped to form the First Polish Corps, with over 30 thousand soldiers. Later, the Second and the Third Corps were formed. After the Russian declarations, the Western powers were not bound by any commitments, thus freeing them to form their own Polish policies. The Polish National Committee, which organized in 1914 in Warsaw and moved to St. Petersburg in 1915, was reestablished in Lausanne, Switzerland, after the February Revolution and, in the fall of 1917, it settled in Paris. It was recognized by the Western powers as an official representation of Poland, a de facto Polish government, and political leaders of the Polish Army in France (a force composed of volunteers from America as well as Polish POWs from the German and Austrian armies; it reached about seventy thousand soldiers in 1919).

The Russian Revolution soon turned into a civil war. Piłsudski realized that Russia had ceased to be Poland's main enemy and that there was no need anymore to concentrate on fighting against it. In addition, the United States joined the Entente in April 1917. Collaboration with Germany and Austria became needless and awkward, especially since the Central Powers were implementing the stipulations of the 5 November Declaration very slowly. Piłsudski now convinced the Legionnaires to reject the oath of allegiance to the two emperors. This boycott of the Polnische Wehrmacht irritated the Germans, who interned most Piłsudskiite soldiers. Those who were Austrian citizens were incorporated into the Austrian army. Piłsudski, imprisoned by the Germans, thus became the first Polish leader who fought against all the three partitioning powers during World War I. As a consequence, his legend grew quickly, while his men concentrated on the development of the Polish Military Organization.

The Germans tried to stop the disintegration of the pro–Central Powers political "orientation," and in September 1917 they appointed a Regency Council. It was supposed to exercise power in the half-fictitious Kingdom of Poland and consisted of three conservative politicians: Prince Zdzisław Lubomirski, a philanthropic mayor of Warsaw, Aleksander Kakowski, the archbishop of Warsaw, and Count Józef Os-

trowski, a rich landowner. Accompanied by a new Council of State as a semi-parliament and controlled by the German governor-general of Warsaw, Hans von Beseler, the regents limited their activities to education, administration, and justice.

In early 1918 the German Reich signed a peace treaty with Bolshevik Russia and Ukraine (the Treaty of Brest-Litovsk). Ukraine, a German puppet state occupied by the German army, became the breadbasket of the Reich. To strengthen the German-Ukrainian "friendship," Berlin gave Kiev the Chełm Region, a part of the former Congress Kingdom of Poland located on the western side of the River Bug. This triggered a storm among the Poles. The pro-Austrian "orientation" disintegrated, and the Council of State of the Kingdom of Poland proclaimed on 5 November 1916 resigned. A Polish Auxiliary Corps, which had still remained on the Austrian side, mutinied, crossed the front, joined the Polish Second Corps in Russia, and now fought against the Germans. The Polish Military Organization also intensified its activities.

Meanwhile, Poles were encouraged by a series of pronouncements issued by the Entente states declaring an independent Poland to be a part of their wartime goals. In January 1918 President Woodrow Wilson of America devoted to Poland the thirteenth of his famous Fourteen Points: "An independent Polish state should be erected which should include the territories inhabited by indisputably Polish populations, which should be assured a free and secure access to the sea, and whose political and economic independence and territorial integrity should be guaranteed by international covenant" (cited Macmillan 496).

After the last unsuccessful German military offensive in the west in the summer of 1918, the Central Powers asked President Wilson for peace on 5 October 1918. Several weeks later, the Habsburg monarchy disintegrated, and a revolution erupted in Germany and within the ranks of its armies in the east. German soldiers did not want to fight for the empire any longer and started returning home. In several Polish towns and cities, including Warsaw, local populations disarmed the German units. On 11 November 1918, a delegation of the new republican German government signed the armistice in Compiègne, northeast of Paris.

INTERWAR POLAND

The rebuilding of the Polish state after World War I was a complicated process. For over 120 years, the Polish lands had been divided into several units with different administrative, judicial, and economic systems. Some parts of Poland had developed considerably, while others were among the most backward regions of Europe. In November 1918 only a small fragment of Polish lands was controlled by the Poles, who themselves were deeply divided. Moreover, there were several centers of Polish authorities in different places competing against each other for power in the still-to-be-organized state.

The Warsaw-based Regency Council, the provisional supreme authority of the German-established Kingdom of Poland, proclaimed the independence of Poland on 7 October 1918. Even though Warsaw was still in the hands of a

German garrison, the regents took over control of the Polnische Wehrmacht, organized a government, and by the beginning of November tried to extend their power outside Warsaw and its region. A National Democratic prime minister, appointed by the regents, established contact with Dmowski's National Committee in Paris, intending to be a diplomatic representative of the Kingdom of Poland. The committee, however, did not recognize the regents and considered itself a Polish government-in-exile.

In Cracow, the Polish members of the Austrian parliament formed a Polish Liquidation Committee. Supported by most Polish parties in Galicia, it became a local government, took over the power from the Habsburg administration, and sent back to Warsaw an official delegated by the regents to govern in Galicia. Yet the Liquidation Committee controlled only the western part of this region. On 1 November 1918, representatives of the Ukrainian parties proclaimed the establishment of the Western Ukrainian Peoples' Republic with a capital in Lvov. Ukrainian soldiers from the Austrian army and from local paramilitary organizations took over the city as well as most towns in eastern Galicia. This triggered a Polish uprising in Lvov, where Ukrainians constituted only about 20 percent of the entire population, an action that led to the 1918–1919 Polish-Ukrainian War. In addition, radical Polish peasants in northern Galicia did not recognize the Liquidation Committee and briefly established the Tarnobrzeg Republic in early November.

In Poznań, which was still a part of the German Reich, the Polish members of the Reichstag and the Prussian Diet met in mid-November. They formed a Supreme Popular Council, which was elected in December. The council established its agencies in Silesia and Gdańsk (Danzig), also held by the Germans. In the mining regions of the former Congress Kingdom, across the border from Silesia, communists attempted to initiate a Bolshevik-like revolution. In the Cieszyn (Teschen) region, the Polish National Council took over power. During the night of 6 November 1918, supporters of Piłsudski and several left-wing parties established a Provisional People's Government of the Republic of Poland in Lublin. Led by an experienced Galician politician, Ignacy Daszyński, it did not recognize other Polish governments and issued a radical manifesto presenting its socialist program. The population of Poland, an impoverished and ruined country, plagued by speculation, disorder, and inflation, was confused and divided.

Many people believe that the situation was saved by Piłsudski. Released from a German prison, he came to Warsaw on November 10. The Lublin Government and the Regency Council subordinated themselves to him. Piłsudski appointed a new central government and declared himself chief of state. He was recognized by the Entente and reached a compromise with the political Right and Dmowski's Committee in Paris. In January 1919 a new compromise government was established, headed by Ignacy Paderewski, a famous musician and a friend of President Wilson. In the same month, a Constituent Assembly was elected through a democratic election organized in all the territories held by the Poles. In February, the assembly accepted a "Small Constitution" that defined the Polish political system and kept Piłsudski as chief of state.

The basic elements of the new state structure were established. Now, Poland had to settle her borders, a difficult task. During the Paris peace conference that began in January 1919, only France supported Poland's territorial claims. To establish those claims, Poland went through a series of devastating wars with most of her neighbors. These local conflicts and a war for survival against Soviet Russia dominated the period from 1918 to 1921. Between November 1918 and July 1919, Poland fought against the Western Ukrainian Peoples' Republic, defeated it, and took over the ethnically mixed territories of Eastern Galicia. On 28 December 1918, a Polish uprising erupted in the German-held but predominantly Polish Poznań region. Within several weeks, the insurgents pushed out the Germans, who continued to resist until February 1919, when, under pressure from the Entente, an armistice was signed. As a result, the region of Poznań remained in Polish hands, even though legally it still belonged to Germany until the Treaty of Versailles of 28 June 1919 handed it officially to Poland. In January 1919 Czechoslovak forces attacked the Cieszyn region and took its western part. In August 1919 an unsuccessful Polish rising started in Silesia.

The most dangerous threat, however, came from the east. The Bolshevik leadership in Russia dreamed of a world revolution and intended to export their revolution to Western Europe. When the Germans started evacuating their armies from the east in November 1918, the Bolsheviks declared the Brest-Litovsk Treaty null and void, and the Red Army followed the Germans in their march westward. In early January 1919 the Soviets took Vilna and declared the establishment of a Soviet Socialist Lithuanian-Belorussian Republic. At the same time, the Poles started their march eastward, taking over the eastern territories of the former Polish-Lithuanian Commonwealth that had been evacuated by the Germans. As a result of these two opposing movements, the Polish and Soviet units met south of Vilna in February 1919. Initially, both the Soviets and the Poles concentrated on their other wars, but soon these first skirmishes evolved into a major confrontation. In April 1919 Piłsudski organized a military expedition and removed the Red Army from his native Vilna. In the summer of 1919 the Poles took most of Belorussia, and in May 1920 the Polish army entered Kiev.

It appeared that Marshal Piłsudski had realized his great plan. He believed that small national states had no chance of survival sandwiched between Russia and Germany. Raised in the tradition of the Polish-Lithuanian Commonwealth, he wanted to form a similar federation, which would be able to resist foreign pressure. Yet such a federation program had many opponents. Polish landlords from the eastern borderlands rejected any idea of Belorussian, Lithuanian, and Ukrainian autonomy and wanted their estates, which had been divided by local peasants during the revolution, returned to them. To most Poles, the capturing of a territory by the Polish army meant an automatic incorporation of this territory into the Polish state. A majority of Lithuanian and Ukrainian politicians were also against the idea of any ties with Poland.

In June 1920 the Red Army regrouped and started a major offensive. In early August 1920, the Soviet forces appeared at the gates of Warsaw, formed a Provisional Revolutionary Committee of Poland, and pronounced the establishment of the Polish Socialist Soviet Republic. The Poles answered with a total mobilization of all forces. A coalition Government of National Unity was formed in Warsaw. Volunteers rushed to the army, which grew to almost one million soldiers. France delivered significant military help. During the crucial battle of Warsaw in mid-August 1920, the Soviet front was broken and pushed back. In September the Poles won another major battle on the River Niemen. On 12 October 1920, both sides accepted a cease-fire, and on 18 March 1921 the Riga Peace Treaty was signed in the capital of Latvia. The longest border of interwar Poland was settled by a compromise: significant Polish ethnic islands remained on the non-Polish side of the frontier, and significant non-Polish ethnic islands on the Polish side.

The "Bolshevik War" (also known as the Polish-Soviet War) had several negative international repercussions. The Soviets handed Vilna to Lithuania in the summer of 1920, and a long and bitter conflict between Poland and Lithuania began when the Poles seized the city in October. The near catastrophe of Polish forces in the summer of 1920 encouraged the Germans to initiate strong anti-Polish tactics in Silesia. The Poles answered with a second uprising in August 1920. An Inter-Allied Commission and Western military units were sent to Silesia to maintain order and to prepare a plebiscite (which took place in March 1921). The Germans brought between 100,000 and 200,000 voters by special trains from the interior of Germany, won the plebiscite, and refused to divide Upper Silesia. The Poles answered with the Third Silesian Uprising in May 1921. Eventually, the province was divided between Poland and Germany. Another plebiscite, held in Polish-speaking territories in East Prussia, was lost by the Poles in 1920, and only several small communities were transferred to Poland. The last contestable fragments of the nation's borders were finally accepted by an Ambassadors' Conference arranged by the League of Nations in March 1923.

Poland, with an area of 388,600 square kilometers, became the sixth largest country of Europe. According to the 1921 census, it was populated by 27.2 million people. As in most East Central European states, sizable national minorities lived in Poland. Poles constituted about 69.2 percent of the entire population, "Ruthenians" (mostly Ukrainians) 14.3 percent, Jews 7.8 percent, Belorussians 3.9 percent, Germans 3.9 percent, and "others" 0.8 percent. Most inhabitants of Poland were Roman Catholics (63.8 percent). Greek Catholics constituted 11.2 percent, Orthodox Christians 10.5 percent, Protestant 3.7 percent, Jewish 10.5 percent, and "others" 0.3 percent. Most Polish citizens, over 63 percent, worked in agriculture. Only six cities had more than 100,000 inhabitants: Warsaw 937,000, Łódź 452,000, Lvov 219,000, Cracow 184,000, Poznań 169,000, and Vilna 129,000.

Like most European states, Poland accepted a democratic political system after 1918. The Constitution of 17 March 1921, one of the most democratic supreme laws at the time, proclaimed a republic with a parliamentary-cabinet system of government. A bicameral parliament, elected in universal, secret, direct, equal, and proportional elections, represented the people and dominated the political scene.

Nevertheless, there were problems. The political Right, afraid that Piłsudski would be elected president, managed to limit the powers of this office. Critics of the constitution claimed that it gave too much power to the legislature and too little to the executive. In addition, most citizens of Poland did not have any political experience, and over 33 percent of them were illiterate. Political parties were numerous, small, and not ready to compromise. Badly treated national minorities strengthened the opposition; and the economy was in a bad shape.

Subsequent governments introduced several reforms. They established a strong Polish currency, balanced the budget, prepared an agricultural reform, and started developing an industrial infrastructure. In the mid-1920s, the economy recovered, but the overall situation was still difficult. Strikes and even local worker rebellions destabilized political life, and governments changed frequently. Internationally, the situation worsened. In 1922 the Soviets and the Germans signed a Cooperation Treaty; in 1925 the Western powers guaranteed the western borders of Germany but neglected to issue any such guarantees for its eastern frontier. Also in 1925, Germany started a tariff war with Poland.

Initially, the Polish political scene was balanced between the Right (the National Democracy), the Center (the Polish Peasant Party Piast, the Christian Democracy, and the National Workers' Party), the Left (the Polish Socialist Party, the Polish Peasant Party Liberation), and the national minorities' parties. Gradually, however, the political Right grew stronger. In 1922 radical National Democratic propaganda led to the assassination of the first elected president, Gabriel Narutowicz. The land reform, although accepted by the parliament, was not fully introduced. People became tired of the chaos in administration and corruption in politics. During 1924–1925, the democratic system was becoming increasingly unpopular among a majority of Poles. A popular conviction held that the chaotic situation in Poland needed a strong leader to run the show.

On 12 May 1926, several army regiments, led by generals sympathizing with Piłsudski, entered Warsaw and took control of the city after two days of fighting (in which over three hundred people were killed) with government units. The coup enjoyed strong support from the political Left. On 14 May, the president and the government resigned. The presidency, according to the constitution, passed to the speaker of the parliament, who appointed a temporary premier. New presidential elections were scheduled. Even though the National Assembly did not change after the coup, Piłsudski was elected president. He recognized this as a legal consecration of his intervention, but, to the public's general astonishment, he did not accept the presidency but recommended his friend, a former socialist and a prominent scientist, Ignacy Mościcki, for the post. The National Assembly elected Mościcki.

The Piłsudski coup ended the conflicts that had existed between the Left and the Right and eased the social tensions that had marked the first years of the Second Republic. Similar phenomena were seen in other interwar European states, but in Poland authoritarian goals and tactics were put into effect by the Left rather than the Right. Piłsudski did not intend to become a Polish Mussolini. He meant to tolerate the Sejm, considered himself a democrat, and wanted to return to the chief of state formula of 1918. With his modesty, martial appearance, and ability to combine political realism with dedication to a romantically conceived cause, Piłsudski remained very popular. Some historians call the political system of 1926–1930 a "guided democracy." From 1926 to 1930, the Sejm continued its work, even though Piłsudski himself appointed all the cabinets. They had no majority in the parliament, and the latter, at least initially, did not try to abolish them. The marshal emphasized that he did not plan any revolutionary changes. He intended to strengthen the executive, restore Poland's "moral health," and eliminate corruption, incompetence, administrative disorder, and partisan greed. His regime now took the name of Sanacja (moral sanitation).

The first Sanacja governments eliminated much of the chaos of the previous administrations and achieved some continuity and stability. Also, a large part of the national minorities accepted the coup, hoping that the new authorities would change their attitude toward the non-Polish population. Yet Sanacja did not manage to ease ethnic tensions. Moreover, even though the economy improved, Piłsudski abandoned social reforms, arguing that Poland could not afford them. As a consequence, he lost the support of the Left. Constitutional amendments that eased legislative action and increased the authority of the executive were supported by the Right. In November 1926 a decree was issued restricting the liberty of the press. Brought to power by the Left, Piłsudski was now building support on the Right. He did not have a clear program, and the concept of Sanacja had no real content. Overwhelmed by too many assignments, Piłsudski did not have time to attend to several important matters, such as the economy and the army. He regarded military discipline and order as the highest civic virtues and approached politics from the point of view of military tactics and strategy.

After the coup, the Piłsudskiites began assuming leading positions in Poland's governmental system. Frequently, they lacked administrative competence, had no experience running a complex state mechanism, and suffered from many other shortcomings. Imbued with a conspiracy mentality and accustomed to approaching problems from a military point of view, the Piłsudskiite veterans formed an informal and closed ruling group, which initiated a process of militarizing the state.

Piłsudski formally respected the prerogatives of the Sejm, but he planned to reshape the Polish political system and to change the constitution. He intended to do this in a semidemocratic way, and thus needed a majority in the parliament. Piłsudski needed a new political party, one that would unite all his supporters and would win the parliamentary elections. In 1927 several small parties, professional, social, and cultural associations, and numerous opportunists were merged into an umbrella organization called the Non-Party Bloc of Cooperation with the Government (BBWR). The Bloc propagated the slogan of Sanacja and emphasized the "interests of the state" but, in the 1928 elections, it garnered only 28 percent of votes, and thus was unable to achieve a majority in the parliament and to control the legislative process. This failure made the political atmosphere even tenser. The conflict between the Sejm and the marshal worsened. The opposition grew. In December 1926, in an effort to revitalize the Right, Dmowski established a radical Camp for a Greater Poland (OWP). It organized fighting squads and propagandized with authoritarian slogans, borrowing frequently from the Italian fascists' model. In 1928 the OWP helped to reshape the National Democracy into the National Party (SN).

In the fall of 1929 a powerful left-of-center coalition was formed. Called Centrolew, it intended to replace the Piłsudski regime with a democratic government. It capitalized on the growing frustration of the working classes, struggling under the effects of the Great Depression, particularly severe and long lasting in Poland. In 1930 Centrolew organized a Congress for the Defense of the Law and the Freedom of the People and issued an appeal to organize similar demonstrations. They were dispersed by the police. About ninety Centrolew leaders and approximately five thousand people from various parties and opposition organizations were arrested and detained in the fortress of Brest-Litovsk. In the atmosphere of intimidation, parliamentary elections were organized, and the BBWR gained 56 percent of votes. Sanacja was able to implement its laws but could not change the constitution.

The Brest-Litovsk action, the elections of 1930, and the trial of the arrested opposition leaders brought a definitive end to democracy in interwar Poland. A large part of Polish public opinion was outraged by police terror and electoral forgeries, and the support for Sanacja diminished visibly. The opposition, paralyzed in the Sejm, continued its activities elsewhere. Piłsudski abandoned "guided democracy" and ruled in a ruthless way, brutally imposing his will on the nation. In the Sejm, the BBWR passed a far-reaching Enabling Act, making it possible for the government to rule by decree. Limitations of basic freedoms were implemented, and citizens felt more like subjects than partners of the authorities. For his part, Piłsudski focused on the preparation of a new constitution. It went into effect on 23 April 1935. Its introduction violated some provisions of the 1921 constitution, as well as procedural regulations. The new constitution abandoned the liberalism of the Polish constitutional tradition and assumed an elitist, antidemocratic, antiparliamentarian, and authoritarian character.

The new constitution was tailor-made for Piłsudski. However, he died on 12 May 1935, and his premature death constituted another turning point in interwar Polish history. The Piłsudski charisma, which had veiled a hardened and arbitrary authoritarian regime, as well as corruption and governmental malpractice, was gone. The Piłsudski camp now disintegrated into several ambitious cliques, each competing against the other and all moving toward stricter autocracy. Some historians believe that political life in post-1935

Poland occasionally resembled practices to be found in contemporary totalitarian societies. In May 1936 the last inter-war Polish government was appointed. Headed by General Felicjan Sławoj-Składkowski, a blind follower of Piłsudski and his minister of the interior from 1926 to 1931, it included two generals and three colonels, and in many ways resembled an army junta. In February 1937 the regime tried to rebuild a government party, the Camp of National Unity (OZN). It was intended to be a hierarchically organized totalitarian movement. OZN stressed the importance of the army and military-like discipline, used Italian fascist slogans and elements of National Democratic programs. Propagating a vision of Poland as a state of Polish Catholics who would "defend their culture," it also emphasized "economic self-sufficiency," excluding Jews and other national minorities.

The continuing economic crisis made the general situation in Poland even worse. The regime met with growing opposition from the Left and the Center. The Peasant Party introduced a new political weapon—the peasant strike. The PPS increased its activities. In 1936 General Władysław Sikorski and Ignacy Paderewski initiated a new movement, the Front Morges, named after Paderewski's Swiss residence. The Front Morges attempted to consolidate the opposition by voicing harsh criticism of Sanacja's authoritarian regime and its risky foreign policy of nonalignment and attempted balance between Nazi Germany and the Soviet Union. In 1932 a Polish-Soviet Non-Aggression Pact was signed. In 1934 a Polish-German Declaration on the Non-Use of Violence followed and, in the same year, the Polish-Soviet Pact was extended for another ten years. In 1934 Poland rejected a French project of an Eastern Pact, in which France, Germany, the USSR, Poland, and Czechoslovakia would guarantee East European borders.

The "balanced policy" pursued by Poland worked in the early 1930s, when Soviet-German relations were poor, but collapsed by the end of the decade, when Berlin and Moscow started cooperating. In addition, Polish neutrality was perceived in Europe as a pro-German position, especially in 1938 when Poland participated in the partition of Czechoslovakia (after the Munich conference).

The reign of Sanacja was not, however, entirely negative. It realized several useful goals, especially in terms of economic development. After 1936, a brilliant deputy premier responsible for the economy, Eugeniusz Kwiatkowski, introduced some elements of American, German, and Italian economic policies and managed to start an economic boom. Sanacja helped to integrate the country and to strengthen Polish identity. Poland's population grew from 27.2 million in 1921 to 35.1 million in 1939, a growth rate much faster than the European average. During the interwar period, a new generation of young Poles appeared. Educated in Polish schools and highly patriotic, they considered the existence of a Polish state playing an important part in the European international system as an indisputable fact.

WORLD WAR II

By the late 1930s, Germany and Russia had recovered their strength and began to reconstruct their empires. On 23 Au-gust 1939, their foreign ministers, Joachim von Ribbentrop and Vyacheslav Molotov, signed a pact that divided East Central Europe and Poland into two spheres of influence. Stalin and Hitler decided that Poland should cease to exist once and for all. Thus, on 1 September 1939, Germany invaded Poland, and seventeen days later the Soviet Union followed suit. Unfortunately, a shortsighted selfishness prevailed in France and Great Britain. They accepted Poland's deadly struggle as a "useful diversion providing breathing space" (Bethell 117) and failed to deliver promised help. The Polish army surrendered after thirty-five days of bloody fighting.

Poland was now partitioned again. Almost 50 percent of its territory was taken by the Soviet Union, 48.4 percent by Nazi Germany, and 1.6 percent by Lithuania. The occupation of Poland by the Germans lasted longer than in any other country (leaving aside a milder occupation of Bohemia) and was the most severe. The Poles were ranked by the Nazis as the second lowest racial group in Europe next to the Jews and the Gypsies. Over 6 million Polish citizens, 3 million Christians and 3 million Jews, were killed during the war, which constituted the largest casualty rate among European states. Millions more were deported to Germany and Russia or left in the territories taken by the Soviet Union after the war. In 1939 Poland had 35.1 million inhabitants; by 1945 only about 23 million remained.

It was not only the Germans who killed Poland's citizens. In fact, the Soviet occupation in 1939 resembled German rule in many respects. The Soviets and the Germans cooperated against the Poles and followed the rule of *divide et impera* (divide and conquer). The first element of this division was the territorial fragmentation of Poland. The Germans partitioned their booty into two segments. The entire

German troops parade through Warsaw, Poland, in September 1939. (National Archives)

northwestern part of Poland (as well as a portion of central Poland) was incorporated directly into the Third Reich, becoming an integral part of it. The rest of central and southern Poland was transformed into a colony-like General Government (Generalgouvernement; GG). The Soviets divided their spoils between Soviet Belorussia and Ukraine. A region of Vilna was given to Lithuania, free in 1939 but occupied by the Soviets in 1940.

The population of Poland was divided into several categories on both sides of the Molotov-Ribbentrop line. Both the Soviets and the Germans did their best to deepen the ethnic conflicts in the former Polish territories. The most savage and devastating attack was organized by the invaders against the elite of Polish society. Both the Germans and the Soviets were determined to kill the best and the brightest, and, to a large extent, they succeeded. During World War II, the Polish nation was decapitated: the most promising youth, the most patriotic intelligentsia, and the most outstanding intellectuals perished. During the Katyn massacre in April and May 1940, the Soviets killed 21 university professors, 300 physicians, and hundreds of lawyers, teachers, and engineers. Altogether, during World War II, Poland lost 45 percent of its physicians and dentists (both Christian and Jewish), 57 percent of its lawyers, over 15 percent of its teachers, 40 percent of its university professors, and over 18 percent of its clergy.

The occupiers waged war on Polish culture and did their best to lower the intellectual and moral level of Polish society, to corrupt and demoralize it, and to promote drunkenness and collaboration. Mass deportations were the most efficient Soviet method of de-Polonizing the territories incorporated into the USSR. The deportations started immediately after September 1939 and lasted until the very day of the German attack on the Soviet Union (22 June 1941). Altogether, the Soviets deported over 300,000 people to remote Soviet provinces. Probably about 30 percent of the deportees died in the Soviet Union. A portion of those who survived did not manage to return to Poland or to escape abroad.

A similar deportation and de-Polonization plan was implemented by the Germans. In the winter of 1939–1940 about one million Poles were deported from the territories incorporated into the Reich to the General Government. Thousands of the deportees died during the transportation or immediately after they arrived in the GG. Moreover, the Nazi authorities deported local populations from several attractive regions in the GG, such as the Zamość region, and tried to colonize them with German settlers. More than 200,000 Polish children were kidnapped and taken to the Reich for Germanization.

Both the Germans and the Soviets terrorized Polish society. Prior to 25 October 1939, when the Polish territories

Entrance to the Nazi Auschwitz camp. (Corel Corporation)

were still under the administration of the German Army, the Wehrmacht executed over 16,000 Poles. The German air-force, participating in the September campaign, deliberately bombed civilian targets and civilians escaping from the burning towns and cities. As early as November 1939, street roundups started in Poland. During the next years, the Germans established in Poland over three hundred labor, concentration, and extermination camps. In April 1940 Heinrich Himmler ordered the establishment of a large concentration camp near Oświęcim, which had been previously incorporated into the Reich and renamed Auschwitz. In June 1940 the first transport of Polish political prisoners was brought to the camp. Soon, Auschwitz acquired its reputation as the harshest camp, where tortures and executions of prisoners defined daily routine. In August 1942 a systematic killing of the Jews began in the gas chambers of the Birkenau section of Auschwitz, making it the main Nazi center of mass extermination of the Jews.

The Soviets also initiated a policy of terror. Frequently, the Red Army shot prisoners of war on the spot. People's militias, established by the new authorities, initiated random retribution against Polish officers, policemen, local officials, judges, and any other employees of the Polish state apparatus. In October 1939 the NKVD forced the local population to "elect" "People's Assemblies" in Western Ukraine and Western Belorussia. Their representatives were sent to Moscow, where they asked the Supreme Soviet to incorporate the eastern Polish provinces into the Soviet Union. From over 6 million Polish citizens (both Jews and Christians) killed during the war, almost 5.4 million died as a direct result of German and Soviet mass terror.

Both the Germans and the Soviets started systematic economic exploitation of the conquered Polish territories. Between 1939 and 1944, the Germans deported about 2 million Poles to the Reich to work in agriculture and industry.

There was one striking difference between the Soviet and the German occupation in Poland: different policies toward the Jews. From the beginning of the war, the Germans started an extermination campaign against the Jews. The first ghettos were organized in October 1939. In November 1940 the large ghetto of Warsaw was sealed. The Jews were tortured, robbed, and starved to death. The Germans encouraged Polish anti-Semites, who participated in various activities directed against the Jews.

In June 1941 the Germans invaded the Soviet Union and occupied all the territories of the prewar Polish state. Now, Poland was divided between the Reich (30.8 percent), the General Government (38.8 percent), and the so-called *Reichskommissariats* (30.3 percent). After their initial victory in Russia, the Germans undertook even crueler policies toward the population of Poland. In 1942 and 1943 most Polish Jews were killed, mostly in Auschwitz, Treblinka, Majdanek, Chełmno, Sobibór, Bełżec, and other extermination camps. Altogether, the Germans exterminated approximately 3 million Jewish citizens of Poland and 3 million Jews brought to occupied Poland from abroad.

In September 1939 most Poles believed that the war was not yet finished, that only the first campaign had been lost. A Polish government in exile was established abroad. Thou-sands of Polish soldiers escaped from occupied Poland. Polish army units were organized in France and in the Middle East. In 1940 Polish soldiers fought the Germans in Norway, France, and in the skies over England. In 1944 Polish troops took part in the Allied invasion of France. The Second Polish Corps took the German stronghold on Monte Cassino that opened the way to Rome in May 1944. The First Polish Army, organized by the Soviets in 1943, went with the Red Army to Berlin. The Second Polish Army, established by the communists in 1944, stopped the relief of Berlin during the Battle of Bautzen in April 1945. By the end of World War II, the Polish Armed Forces were the fourth largest among the Allies, following the armies of the Soviet Union, America, and the British Commonwealth.

As early as September 1939, the Poles started organizing their underground state and anti-German resistance. Communication between the Polish government in exile and the underground in Poland was established. Polish clandestine political parties, operating under the German occupation, began a process of uniting the armed underground. In 1943 most of it merged into the Home Army (AK). Only a few clandestine military organizations boycotted the unification: National Armed Forces (NSZ) on the radical Right and the People's Guard (GL, later People's Army—AL), representing the Polish Workers' Party (PPR) established underground by communist messengers sent from Moscow. The Home Army numbered 380,000 organized and sworn resistance fighters, the largest anti-German underground army in occupied Europe. The Polish underground state also included a clandestine civilian administration, secret educational institutions, and a justice system. Some of the accomplishments of the Polish resistance made, as General Dwight Eisenhower, the supreme Allied commander in the west, said, a "decisive contribution to the Allied war efforts" (Keegan 111).

After the Nazi invasion of the Soviet Union in June 1941, the Polish government in exile and the Soviets signed a mutual assistance and nonaggression pact on 30 July 1941. Despite this outward show of unity, establishing cordial Polish-Soviet relations was not possible. Even though an "amnesty" was offered to the Polish people in the Gulag (the Soviet prison system) and a Polish army was organized in Russia, not all the Polish prisoners were released, and not all of those who were released could join the army. The treaty did result in saving tens of thousands of Polish lives, however, and Poland maintained its status as an ally, allowing the government in exile to continue its activities. Nevertheless, Stalin's government announced with increasing frequency that it was going to deal with "ethnic Poland" only. The Curzon Line, practically identical to the Molotov-Ribbentrop line, appeared more and more often in official Soviet statements as the legal western border of the USSR. A conflict over the Polish army in Russia ended with the evacuation of the Polish troops to Persia, and Soviet-Polish relations deteriorated even further.

On 13 April 1943, Berlin radio announced the discovery of mass graves at Katyn. Moscow called the report a "fabrication by Goebbels' slanderers" (Wróbel 24), but there were so many indications that the officers were indeed executed

The Warsaw Ghetto

Ghettoization of the Jews constituted one of the crucial phases of the Nazi policy aimed at the extermination of European Jewry. Most Jewish ghettos established by the Germans during World War II were located in Polish, Ukrainian, Belorussian, and Lithuanian territories occupied by the Third Reich. The largest European ghetto was formed in Warsaw, where over 370,000 Jews lived before the war (nearly 30 percent of the city's population).

The Germans occupied Warsaw in September 1939, immediately initiated anti-Jewish persecutions, and, in early 1940, began to organize a ghetto in the city. Between April and August 1940, a 3.5 meter wall was built around the so-called *Jüdische Wohnbezirk* (Jewish residential quarter), the northeastern district of Warsaw where much of the prewar Jewish population resided. In November 1940, after an exchange of population between the "Jewish" and "non-Jewish" parts of Warsaw, the ghetto was sealed off. This small area of 73 streets (out of a total of 1,800 streets in the city) became a home to 396,000 Jews, over 30 percent of the city's population. Soon, the Germans started moving Jews from Western Europe to Poland and from the smaller ghettos to the larger ones. In March 1941 over 445,000 Jews lived in the Warsaw Ghetto. The conditions in this densely crowded district worsened. In October 1941 Hans Frank, the German governor general of occupied Poland, decreed that every Jew found outside the ghetto without permission would be executed. The Germans exploited the ghetto population economically and established a daily caloric quota that led to starvation. By mid-1942, over 100,000 people had died in the ghettos of Warsaw and Łódź alone, even though numerous members of the *Judenräte* (Jewish Councils), established by the Germans to administer the ghettos, tried to make ghetto life bearable. In the summer of 1942 most residents of the Warsaw Ghetto were sent to the Treblinka extermination camp and gassed to death.

The Jews answered the Nazi oppression with organized resistance. Among the approximately 60,000 Jews who remained in the ghetto, several underground organizations sprang up. When the Germans attempted to kill the rest of the ghetto's population in January 1943, the Jewish Fighting Organization (ŻOB) and the Jewish Military Union (ŻZW) answered with armed resistance and stopped the German operation. The Germans prepared a new offensive and entered the ghetto on 19 April 1943. The Jewish fighters, some 500 strong, started an insurrection. Street fighting lasted until 24 April. The Germans then withdrew from the Warsaw Ghetto, regrouped, and began to burn and systematically demolish one city block after another. On 8 May, the Germans took the bunker that served as the ŻOB headquarters. Eight days later, SS Major General Jürgen Stroop dynamited the Great Synagogue of Warsaw and declared an end to the uprising. However, small Jewish groups continued to fight in the ruins of the ghetto until mid-August 1943. The last of the groups survived in the ruins until the 1944 Warsaw Uprising.

by the NKVD that the Polish government in exile asked the International Red Cross to investigate. Moscow used this move by the London exiles as a pretext to break its relations with the Polish government. Relations were never resumed. In January 1944 the Red Army crossed the Polish interwar borders and in July 1944 entered Polish ethnic territories west of the Curzon Line. Along with the Soviet military, a Soviet-controlled Polish Committee of National Liberation (PKWN) was established as a de facto government and started administering the Polish communist Piedmont, the Lublin area taken by the Soviets in the summer of 1944.

By the end of 1943, the Polish government in exile and the leaders of the Polish underground state in occupied Poland realized that the question of Poland's eastern borders was beyond their control. They also understood that Poland's postwar independence was in jeopardy. Everywhere in the Soviet-controlled "liberated" territories, Soviet authorities used methods and implemented policies well known to the Polish people from the period 1939–1941.

Polish leaders desperately sought a solution and decided to organize a local uprising behind the German front in order to assist the Soviet offensives. Polish resistance soldiers were to cooperate with the Red Army, help it to break the German lines, and establish a Polish temporary administration. This operation received the cryptonym Tempest; it began in March and April 1944 in former eastern Poland. In July the Polish underground armed forces attacked Vilna, and participated in the capture of Lvov and Lublin. In all these cases, the Soviets cooperated with the Home Army during the fighting. Immediately after the fighting, however, NKVD units disarmed the Poles, merged the soldiers into the Polish communist army or into the Red Army, and arrested the officers. Many of them were executed, and the majority were deported to the Gulag. A Polish underground administration simply could not be tolerated by the Soviets anywhere.

The original plan of Tempest did not foresee any fighting in large cities. It was feared that casualties would be too large. On 29 July 1944, however, Soviet units appeared in

Warsaw's eastern suburbs. The Germans panicked and started evacuating their governing apparatus in Warsaw. The Home Army Command knew about the attempt on Hitler's life earlier that month. The Soviet-sponsored Polish Radio in Moscow constantly called upon the population of Warsaw to fight the Germans alongside the Red Army. The capture of the Polish capital seemed imminent, even though the Germans had managed to recover from the panic and ordered the mobilization of 100,000 young people for work on Warsaw's fortifications. The Wehrmacht was going to reshape the city into a stronghold, which was to stop the Soviet offensive. Therefore, the Home Army commanders believed it was necessary to take Warsaw before a siege could commence. At the same time, the Polish government in exile believed that it was the last opportunity to establish Polish independent authorities in Warsaw.

On 1 August 1944, Warsaw's units of the Home Army attacked the Germans and gained control of most of the city within three days. Only 10 percent of the Polish fighters were armed. The Red Army deliberately stopped its offensive and remained idle. The Soviet Air Force, so active over Warsaw before, disappeared, allowing the Germans to bomb the city without restraint. The Red Army also stopped and disarmed detachments of the Home Army marching to Warsaw, and the Soviet government refused to allow the Western Allies to use Soviet air bases to airlift supplies for the fighting Poles. For their part, the Germans sent fresh units to Warsaw, swelling their forces to 17,000 well-armed men plus artillery, tanks, and planes. On October 2, after sixty-three days of desperate fighting, the Poles surrendered.

The Home Army Command and about 12,000 insurgents were taken as prisoners of war. The Germans deported the remainder of the city's population to various camps and almost completely gutted the city. Over 200,000 civilians died; about 18,000 Home Army soldiers were killed, and another 7,000 were wounded. The main body of the Home Army was eliminated. The best representatives of the Polish youth of Warsaw, almost the entire generation, perished. When the Red Army took the Polish capital in January 1945, it was a gigantic ruin. Over 80 percent of the city's buildings were destroyed. The defeat of the uprising weakened organized resistance in Poland and helped the Soviets establish their political domination over the country.

The disastrous fate of Poland was confirmed during the Yalta conference in February 1945. The conference was the culmination and a catastrophic consummation of wartime strategic decisions of American and British leaders and their policies toward Moscow. In the Polish political vocabulary, the name of Yalta became a symbol of treason and betrayal, and the Yalta conference is considered to be a close copy of the Munich conference. The American president, Franklin Delano Roosevelt, accepted the loss of East Central Europe in exchange for a Soviet agreement on his United Nations plan and a Soviet promise to participate in the final stage of anti-Japanese operations. The Western Allies lost Poland and the entire region of East Central Europe—the key to the western parts of the Old Continent and to international stabilization during the postwar era.

The Nazi totalitarian occupation of Poland was now replaced by Soviet totalitarian control. After 1945, the Polish people continued to be deported to the Soviet camps and exterminated. The new oppressors drastically changed the borders of Poland, which lost 20 percent of its prewar area and two major centers of Polish national culture, Vilna and Lvov. The Soviets continued the economic exploitation of Poland and the extermination of the Polish elites.

COMMUNIST PERIOD

According to the official Marxist historiography of the former People's Republic of Poland (PRL), this state was established on 22 July 1944 in Lublin, which had been recently liberated by the Soviets. On that day, the Polish Committee of National Liberation (PKWN), formed on 20 July in the nearby town of Chełm, issued a manifesto announcing that the Polish government in exile was illegal and promising social reforms. In fact, however, the PKWN was organized earlier in Moscow, where the manifesto had already been prepared. The PKWN, frequently called the Lublin Committee, was the de facto government of Poland established by the Soviets to counterbalance the émigré "London government." Most members of the committee had belonged earlier to the Union of Polish Patriots in the USSR and the Central Bureau of the Polish Communists in the USSR. Some came from the Homeland National Council (KRN), a semi-parliament formed by the Polish Workers' Party (PPR) underground in occupied Poland. The PKWN administered the provinces of Rzeszów, Białystok, Lublin, and parts of Warsaw and Kielce, where it introduced land reform and the first communist changes.

The Western powers did not recognize the Lublin Committee and asked the Soviets specifically not to proclaim it the government of Poland. Yet, on 1 January 1945, the committee was transformed into the Provisional Government of the Republic of Poland. Beginning in February 1945, it resided in Warsaw and took over administration of the provinces liberated by the Red Army after January 1945. On 28 June 1945, on the basis of the Yalta agreement, the Provisional Government accepted several Polish émigré politicians from London and the London-oriented underground and was reorganized into the Provisional Government of National Unity (TRJN). It consisted of twenty-one persons, eighteen of whom belonged to communist or communist-controlled organizations. Stanisław Mikołajczyk, the prime minister of the Polish government in exile in the years 1943–1944, was appointed deputy premier of the TRJN. The Western powers recognized the new government and, simultaneously, withdrew their recognition of the government in exile. The latter protested to the Allied governments and continued its activities.

The TRJN, supported by the Soviets, following the decisions of the Potsdam Conference of July–August 1945, took over the former German territories east of the Oder and Neisse (Nysa) Rivers. About four million German inhabitants of these regions were deported to Germany between 1945 and 1947. The Provisional Government of National Unity continued land reform and nationalization

Portrait of Władysław Gomułka, 20th century Polish communist leader. (Library of Congress)

of economic enterprises in Poland. Over one million estate workers and peasants received 6 million hectares of arable land. In 1949 peasants owned 86 percent of it, and the state farms used 9 percent. Large private agricultural enterprises, held before the war mostly by former gentry, disappeared, later causing problems with the food supply. Even though the PKWN manifesto did not mention nationalization, the authorities, through a series of decrees, administrative procedures, and the Industry Nationalization Act of 3 January 1946, took over an absolute majority of all the industrial enterprises. In 1947 most cooperatives were closed, and the government became virtually the only employer outside the agricultural sector. The new authorities were aiming at the elimination of the free market and the introduction of a centrally planned economy. The noncommunist members of the government were increasingly marginalized and intimidated.

The Sovietization of Poland provoked resistance. Many guerrilla units remained in the woods and continued military operations against the new occupation. Out of about 80,000 former Home Army soldiers who continued fighting, about 30,000 belonged to the Freedom and Independence (WiN) organization established in September 1945 in Warsaw. In 1946 guerrilla activities intensified, and many Polish provinces plunged back into war. Simultaneously, noncommunist politicians tried to reestablish their political parties. The largest of them, the Polish Peasant Party (PSL), reached a membership of 800,000 in May 1946. It received

only three portfolios in the provisional government but aimed at quick elections, hoping to gain a majority vote.

The communist-controlled authorities and their Soviet supervisors answered these challenges with terror. Between 1945 and 1947, about half a million Soviet troops were stationed in Poland (later about 150,000 and, after 1955, about 80,000). They helped the NKVD, the Polish communist-controlled armed forces, the newly organized Citizens' Militia (MO), and the Ministry of Public Security (MBP) to introduce mass repression. Before December 1945, the regime organized 1,576 punitive operations and killed about 3,000 people. Thousands were put into prisons and concentration camps or deported to Siberia. Many veterans of the Home Army and returnees from the West were imprisoned or executed. Already in June 1945, concurrently with the Moscow Conference that established the TRJN, the Soviets arranged a show trial of sixteen leaders of the Polish World War II underground state, kidnapped from Poland to Moscow. Altogether, during the period from 1945 to 1948, about 150,000 Poles were imprisoned by the Soviet authorities.

The communists knew that they would not win the democratic and free parliamentary elections that, according to the Yalta Agreement, were supposed to take place in Poland as soon as possible after the war. Therefore, the regime harassed the opposition, postponed the elections, and staged their rehearsal. On 30 June 1946, a referendum was held. People answered three questions concerning the abolition of the Senate, changes in the economic system, and the new western border of Poland. The regime announced that the referendum results confirmed popular support for the new government. The real outcome, however, validated the worst worries of the regime; it could count on less than one-third of Poland's population. Consequently, the authorities intensified the repression; the elections of 19 January 1946 were held in an atmosphere of terror, and their results were completely falsified. The communist-controlled parties received a great majority of the seats in the new Sejm; the PSL was removed from the government and destroyed. Mikołajczyk and a group of noncommunist leaders escaped abroad, but the underground was exhausted, and the communists achieved hegemony.

The Sovietization of Poland was further accelerated by the development of the Cold War. In 1948 the Three-Year Reconstruction Plan was reformulated, and investments were reallocated to heavy industry. Warsaw was not allowed to participate in the Marshall Plan, which provided American assistance to rebuild Europe.

Poland became a one-party state, and almost all aspects of its life were controlled by the ruling Polish United Workers' Party (PZPR; often referred to as "the Party"), which was purged of what were described as right-wing nationalistic tendencies. Its membership amounted to nearly 10 percent of the entire adult population. Intimidation of the Catholic Church intensified. In 1950 the *nomenklatura* system was introduced—only PZPR members could occupy important administration positions. The Polish Army officer corps was purged and staffed with Soviet citizens. Konstantin Rokossowski, a Soviet marshal, became the marshal of Poland, a

Polish minister of defense, the PZPR Politburo member, and later a deputy premier of Poland. Close economic ties were established between the USSR and Poland, which joined the Council of Mutual Economic Assistance (COMECON) in 1949. In 1954 one-third of the Polish adult population was registered on special secret police lists as "criminals and suspects." In 1952 a new constitution, a copy of the 1936 Soviet constitution, was adopted. Poland became a totalitarian state controlled by Moscow.

At the same time, however, the Stalinist system started eroding. The regime did not manage to collectivize agriculture. The Catholic Church survived police pressure. After the death of Stalin in March 1953, a crisis appeared within the leadership of PZPR. A large working class, created by economic changes, was frustrated by its falling standard of living. Inflation and permanent shortages of goods were eliminated by such tricks as an unexpected change of monetary system or the drastic increase of prices. A walkout of the workers of Poznań on 28 June 1956 turned into a mass armed revolt crushed only by a military operation. Władysław Gomułka, the secretary general of the Polish Worker's Party in 1943–1948, arrested for "nationalist deviations," was rehabilitated and appointed first secretary of the Party. Approved by the Soviet leader Nikita Khrushchev, he restored stability in Poland. To achieve this, he approved the dissolution of most collective farms, reached a modus vivendi with the Catholic Church, tolerated more freedom in culture and private life, and made several compromises with Poland's traditions (which seemed antithetical to the communist doctrine of internationalism). Most Soviet "advisers," including Marshal Rokossowski, were sent back to their country, and the economic ties to the Soviet Union were made less unfair to Poland. Many Poles were enthusiastic about the new leader and believed that a new, happier era had begun.

Initial enthusiasm was soon replaced with disappointment. Gomułka, an unsophisticated, ascetic, and traditional communist, did not change essential elements of the system and suppressed "revisionists." No major economic and political reforms were undertaken. Censorship and total police control were quickly rebuilt. The conflict with the Catholic Church returned. The standard of living fell once again, and prospects for the people were grim.

Members of the intelligentsia and professionals began to voice complaints. At the same time, Party factions fought for power and plotted against Gomułka. A nationalistic-communist group within the authorities provoked the March events of 1968—student demonstrations followed by a major crackdown on intellectual opposition and vitriolic anti-Semitic campaigns and purges. Gomułka nevertheless held on to his position. He joined the Soviet invasion of Czechoslovakia in August 1968 to put down the liberal "Prague Spring" that so frightened the Party hierarchy, and in 1970 normalized relations with the West German government, which accepted the post-1945 Oder-Neisse border. Gomułka considered this his life achievement, but at home he continued to lose credibility, by virtue of his inability to halt the decline of Poland's economy. Shortly before Christmas 1970, his government announced drastic increases in food prices. This announcement triggered riots in the Baltic ports, which were crushed by police and the army. In an atmosphere of a near civil war, Gomułka had a heart attack and was replaced by Edward Gierek, a Party secretary of Silesia and the leader of a "technocratic" Party faction.

Gierek, who had spent his youth in France and Belgium as an immigrant miner from Polish Silesia, represented a different kind of personality than Gomułka had. The first secretary of the Katowice provincial Party organization after 1957, he was considered one of the most powerful and most popular politicians in the country. He believed that Poland needed a Western-oriented modernization program, and he promised to improve the material situation of the people and to reevaluate governmental economic policies. His regime received large loans from the West, and the first years of his decade in power became the most successful period in the entire history of communist Poland. Gierek liberalized cultural policies and opened the borders for most people who wanted to travel or to work abroad. To many of these "tourists," these months or years abroad proved to be very educational, as it opened their eyes to the reality of the world outside the propaganda of the authorities.

Gierek did not change the essential elements of the communist system. As had happened under Gomułka, resources allocated initially to the light and food industries to appease the population returned to heavy industry when the regime felt safe again (thus continuing to adhere to the ideological line). The government tried to regain control over the economy and introduced painful price increases. The workers answered with the rebellion of 1976, suppressed quickly by the regime. The 1975 administrative reform that replaced sixteen big provinces with forty-nine small units weakened the state apparatus. The 1976 amendments to the constitution that defined Poland as a socialist state and the Party as the leading political and social force responsible for the strengthening of Poland's friendship with the USSR proved to be highly unpopular. The intelligentsia, outraged by the regime's incompetence and by brutalities directed against innocent people, began to form various organizations in order to help the persecuted workers and defend Polish cultural achievements. Some of them, such as the Workers' Defense Committee (KOR), became very active and influential. A secret publishing and cultural "second circulation" appeared. In 1978 Cardinal Karol Wojtyła was elected pope and became unquestionably the highest spiritual authority for most Poles. The Gierek government wasted the foreign loans received from the West, and debts began to increase dramatically. The regime was unable to change the course of the economy and was soon almost crushed by the Solidarity revolt of 1980.

Like previous revolts, the national uprising of 1980 was triggered by a rise in the price of food. In August about 80,000 workers were on strike. At the Gdańsk Shipyard, a long time center of antiregime opposition, the striking employees, led by Lech Wałęsa, formulated economic and political demands, and together with representatives from other enterprises, established the Inter-Factory Striking Committee. Advised by a group of intellectuals who came

Lech Wałęsa carried on shoulders by a crowd in front of the Supreme Court after the "yes" sentence in the registration of Peasant Solidarity was declared, ca. 1980. (Bettmann/Corbis)

primarily from Warsaw, it coordinated protests in northeastern Poland. Similar committees appeared in Szczecin and in Silesian Jestrzębie Zdrój. They demanded the legitimization of independent trade unions, the lifting of censorship, the release of political prisoners, the strengthening of the position of the Catholic Church, and changes in government priorities in social welfare.

The regime, going through a crisis after the fall of Gierek, could not resist, and it accepted most of the strikers' demands. On 31 August 1980, the Gdańsk Agreements were signed. They sanctioned the right to strike and to form free trade unions, and several other freedoms previously limited by the regime. Similar agreements were signed in Szczecin and Silesia. In September the Independent Self-Governing Trade Union, Solidarity, the first free labor organization in any communist state, was formed and named Wałęsa as its chairperson. In December a separate union, called Rural Solidarity, was established. By the spring of 1981, Solidarity had 10 million members, most adult citizens of Poland, and was the largest trade union in Europe. Soon, it was radicalized and became a national antitotalitarian independence

movement, attracting all Poles who held to a noncommunist worldview. Yet, in contrast to all the previous revolts in communist Poland, Solidarity strictly adhered to a nonviolent strategy, making the situation of the regime even more difficult.

From the start, the government did not have a sincere attitude toward Solidarity; it harassed Solidarity, sought conflicts with it, and tried to stop its development. In the fall of 1980, Soviet troops massed on the border with Poland, and Moscow sent several warning letters to Warsaw embodying the basic principle of the Brezhnev Doctrine (which stated that the Soviet Union had the right to intervene in any state in which "socialism" seemed to be threatened). In 1981 the conflict intensified, even though Solidarity tried to restrain itself. In February 1981 General Wojciech Jaruzelski became the premier, and, in October, he replaced Stanisław Kania as the first secretary of the PZPR Central Committee.

Jaruzelski, a professional military man who had joined the communist-controlled Polish Army in the USSR in 1943 and who had served as the minister of defense after 1968, became the most powerful person in Poland. An ambitious, strong follower of the communist regime (but also an intelligent person), he was not able to ease the confrontation with Solidarity, and he began losing control over radical factions in the Party hostile to the democratic opposition. The political conflict faced by Warsaw was paralleled by a deepening economic crisis that made everyday life difficult, a situation that only radicalized the masses even further.

Solidarity aroused enormous enthusiasm among the Poles. They believed that it was a real turning point, that this time, without a war or a bloody uprising, Poland would be able to change at least partially the inflexible, dilapidated, and corrupt system imposed on the country by Stalinist Russia. However, their enthusiasm, hopes, and overwhelming dedication were soon defeated. On 13 December 1981, Jaruzelski announced the imposition of martial law. Normal life was paralyzed, and democratic freedoms were suspended; the army patrolled the streets of Polish towns and cities. About ten thousand people linked to the opposition or simply disliked by local Party leaders were imprisoned or interned in special camps. Universities, schools, live theaters, and movie theaters were temporarily closed. Polish television discontinued its normal programming, and even the telephones ceased to function. People were not allowed to travel freely, and a curfew was introduced. In many factories, workers tried to start occupational strikes, but the army broke their resistance. At the Wujek coal mine in Katowice, the riot police (ZOMO) shot to death nine miners. Jaruzelski became the chief of the junta-like Military Council of National Salvation (WRON). Solidarity, first suspended and then declared illegal, went underground and formed secret structures, headed by the leaders who managed to escape the police.

The regime believed that it had reintroduced "normalization." As a result, martial law was suspended on 13 December 1982 and lifted on 22 July 1983. In November 1982 Wałęsa was released from prison. The underground Solidarity was divided and lost strength during the following years.

In 1985 the coming to power of Mikhail Gorbachev in the USSR widened the Polish regime's margin of maneuver, since the hard-line faction within the Party lost Soviet support. In September 1986 almost all the political prisoners were freed. In December 1986 the Prime Minister's Consultation Council, including non-communist experts, intellectuals, and public figures, was formed.

Normal life in the country was, however, still frozen, and the Jaruzelski regime, like its predecessors, was unable to solve the economic problems. The standard of living in Poland deteriorated visibly; food stores were getting emptier, and the lines in front of them much longer. In March 1987 the authorities raised food prices by 10 percent and fuel prices by 40 percent. During the 1 May celebrations, antigovernment demonstrations and clashes with the police took place in many places in Poland. In November 1987 a regime-organized referendum on "Further Reformation of the State and National Economy" failed as a result of a Solidarity-led boycott.

In 1988 price increases caused a new wave of strikes. Some members of the opposition and the authorities came to the conclusion that neither side would be able to win and that their conflict might destroy Poland. The Catholic Church also urged a compromise. On 31 August 1988, Lech Wałęsa met the communist minister of interior, General Czesław Kiszczak. They initiated talks that led to the Round Table Negotiations. Opposed by radical members of the opposition and hard-line communists, the negotiations commenced in February 1989. On April 5, an agreement was signed. It provided for the relegalization of Solidarity and freedom of association. It also stipulated that partially free parliamentary elections would be organized in June 1989.

The communists did not intend to give up power. They hoped that the opposition would not be able to organize an effective electoral campaign during the two months that were left before the elections. The Party further hoped that Solidarity would assume much of the responsibility for the situation in Poland without significant participation in the government. The communists, however, miscalculated. According to the Round Table Agreement, only 35 percent of seats in the Sejm were to be contested during the elections. The Polish United Workers' Party and its allies, the United Peasant Party and the Democratic Party, were to take 65 percent of the uncontested seats, plus whatever portion they won of the contested 35 percent. In addition, the names of thirty-five politicians backed by the communists were placed on an uncontested national list. Finally, a hundred-member Senate was to be established in completely free elections.

The elections of 4 and 18 June 1989 dealt a mortal blow to communist power in Poland. Solidarity took all the contested seats in the Sejm and ninety nine seats in the Senate, leaving one seat to a rich businessman with a fancy to start a political career who bought most of the votes in his electoral district. Out of the thirty-five candidates on the uncontested national list, thirty-three failed to gain the required 50 percent of the votes and were replaced ad hoc by less well-known candidates. In the aftershock caused by this landslide, Wałęsa managed to convince the Peasant and the Democratic Parties that they should abandon the defeated communist party. As a result of their shift in allegiance, the Party unexpectedly became a minority in the parliament, holding only 38 percent of the seats.

POSTCOMMUNIST POLAND

Since Mikhail Gorbachev had no intention of intervening, the communists could not threaten Polish society with Soviet aggression, and the electoral victory was spectacular. Nevertheless, the democratic opposition played it safe. In August 1989 a Catholic journalist, Tadeusz Mazowiecki, became the first noncommunist prime minister since 1945, but his government included three communists. Moreover, General Jaruzelski was accepted by Solidarity as the president of Poland. In June 1990, when the situation had stabilized, the communist ministers were replaced by Solidarity politicians, and in the fall of 1990 General Jaruzelski resigned under public pressure.

Portrait of Aleksander Kwaśniewski, president of Poland (1995–).
(Embassy of the Republic of Poland)

Initially, the Mazowiecki government enjoyed overwhelming support. Soon, however, serious problems arose. The new government inherited an economic catastrophe. Politicians and economists disagreed about the direction of economic transformation. It was not clear whether the new authorities should reform the economy slowly, supporting the poorest sectors of society and subsidizing some branches of industry and agriculture, or whether they should move quickly, changing as much as possible during the initial period of broad social support. Some politicians began to talk about a "third way" between communism and capitalism. Mazowiecki's deputy prime minister and finance minister, Leszek Balcerowicz, wanted to move quickly.

No communist economic system had ever been dismantled before, and Balcerowicz's "shock therapy" included a series of high-risk changes. The population began to feel their effects, as the recession in Poland became even worse. The inflation rate became staggering, and massive unemployment appeared. Mazowiecki's policies were quickly criticized. Especially controversial was his "thick line" policy, which suggested that an individual's communist involvement should be disregarded in the new Poland and that everybody, no matter what his or her position in the communist apparatus had been, should be allowed to participate in political and public life.

In 1990 Mazowiecki decided to participate in the presidential election. His decision contributed to the so-called war at the top, which divided Solidarity. Already in the spring of 1990, a center-right political party, the Center Alliance *(Porozumienie Centrum)* was formed. It supported Wałęsa against the allegedly too liberal Mazowiecki, whose supporters established the Citizens' Movement for Democratic Action (ROAD) and the Forum of Democratic Right (FPD). During the presidential elections held in November 1990, Mazowiecki came in third, with 18 percent of the vote. An émigré entrepreneur, Stanisław Tymiński, took second with 23 percent. Wałęsa received 40 percent of the vote and a week later gained a landslide victory of 74 percent in the second round of elections. Humiliated, Mazowiecki resigned as premier and was replaced by a liberal economist, Jan Krzysztof Bielecki. Solidarity, which had largely been responsible for the victory over communism not only in Poland but (as a symbol) throughout East Central Europe as well, was now divided. Mazowiecki's supporters united and formed the Democratic Union. By January 1991, about forty political parties were registered in Poland.

Bielecki continued Mazowiecki's policies and held the office of premier until December 1991, when he resigned after the first truly democratic and completely free parliamentary elections in October of that year. The elections were necessary. The Polish United Workers' Party had ceased to exist in 1990, and most Poles believed that the Sejm elected in June 1989 was not representative and that the Round Table compromise was no longer binding. The October 1991 elections produced a severely fragmented Sejm comprising twenty-nine parties, including the Democratic Left Alliance (Sojusz Lewicy Demokratycznej—SLD), a successor of the communist party. No single party received more than 13 percent of the total vote. A shaky coalition of several center and rightist parties formed the next government under Jan Olszewski, a former opposition activist. The government collapsed after five months of chaotic performance.

The next premier, Hanna Suchocka, a member of Solidarity, after a conflict with a Solidarity trade union, was overthrown by a no-confidence vote in May 1993. President Wałęsa, hoping to save the government, dissolved the parliament, and called for new elections. Held in September 1993, they brought the Solidarity era to an end. Most Polish voters were frustrated with the hardships of the postcommunist transition. As a result, the newly elected parliament was dominated by the political Left (the Democratic Left Alliance and the Polish Peasant Party). They formed the first non-Solidarity government since 1989, led by peasant leader Waldemar Pawlak, and later succeeded by postcommunist politicians Józef Oleksy and Włodziemierz Cimoszewicz. The divided political Right lost its parliamentary representation. In addition, a postcommunist candidate and a former minister in the last pre-1989 government, Aleksander Kwaśniewski, won the presidential elections in November 1995, defeating Wałęsa by a narrow margin (51.7 percent to 48.3 percent).

Poland was ruled once again by the people who had lost power in 1989. They had returned to government legally and democratically, but they neither were able nor wanted to restore the pre-1989 system. The Soviet Union no longer existed, Poland was independent, and there was no outside pressure. Polish hard-line communists, disappointed and confused, retired and did not participate in the new administration. The ruling postcommunists styled themselves European social democrats, and true supporters of pluralism and democracy. They had an efficient party apparatus, inherited from the PZPR, and a political team better prepared for political life than the amateurs who had come to power in 1989. They subsidized agriculture and heavy industry and initially enjoyed widespread social support.

Nevertheless, the postcommunists had no new economic program and became hostage to the same problems that had plagued the country since the collapse of the Soviet empire. They did not deliver on their electoral promises and were unable to make the transition any less painful. They slowed down privatization and reforms, which only served to make the situation worse. The Polish Peasant Party was unable to solve the problems of Polish agriculture. Social polarization continued to grow. The old Party apparatus, working now for the postcommunist governments, included thousands of cynical apparatchiks who used old ruling methods and, at the same time, had no sense of measure and displayed no shame in enriching themselves.

In 1996 one of the postcommunist premiers, Oleksy, was accused of being a Russian intelligence agent. The charge was difficult to prove, but a large segment of Polish public opinion was alarmed. The political pendulum swung back. Solidarity overcame its internal crisis and became the nucleus of a right-center coalition—the Solidarity Electoral Alliance (AWS). It included about thirty political parties and cooperated with the Catholic Church. The Democratic Union, renamed the Freedom Union, also gathered some small political groups; it was strengthened and redirected toward a more conservative path by its new leader Balcerowicz. The AWS won the 1997 parliamentary elections, formed a coalition with the Freedom Union, and established a new government led by a Solidarity activist, Professor Jerzy Buzek.

The elections stabilized the political situation in Poland. A new constitution was adopted in 1997. More importantly, the economic situation improved. The shock therapy so hated and derided earlier in the decade had eventually created a basis for steady economic development. Poland's trade had reoriented itself toward the West. Foreign debts were mostly cancelled. The communist economy was dismantled, and the vigorous private sector became the engine of economic expansion.

Encouraged by this success, the new government initiated several reforms. They introduced a new administrative division of the country and new systems of health insurance, old age pensions, and education. Implementation of all these reforms, however, proved to be much more difficult than the government expected. It was also difficult to keep together the forty political parties constituting the Solidarity Electoral Alliance. Some of these parties had mixed feelings about plans to enter into the European Union (EU). Most of the Polish clergy was afraid that integration with

Western Europe would threaten the Christian character of Polish society. A radical and xenophobic anti-European and antimodernization Catholic broadcasting station, Radio Maryja, with about 5 million listeners, propagated a theory of an anti-Polish world conspiracy, and created an atmosphere of threat and insecurity.

The conservative and populist leaders in and out of the Solidarity Electoral Alliance frequently attacked Balcerowicz, now the deputy premier and the finance minister. They claimed that he dominated the cabinet and controlled the economy. The opposition charged that the government had been taken over by the Freedom Union in spite of the fact that it was the Solidarity Electoral Alliance that had won significantly more parliamentary seats than the Union. Balcerowicz's economic policy was too radical for the main component of the coalition, the trade union Solidarity. Some of its Sejm representatives voted against governmental reforms. After months of quarreling, the ruling coalition came apart in June 2000. Balcerowicz, the brilliant minister of foreign affairs Bronisław Geremek, and several other Freedom Union ministers left the cabinet. With 186 deputies in the 460-seat Sejm, the Buzek cabinet now became a minority government. It was badly hurt by growing unemployment, other economic problems, and charges of corruption.

The parliamentary elections of September 2001 created a new political situation. The postcommunist Democratic Left Alliance, the Polish Peasant Party, and the Labor Party formed a majority coalition of 256 seats, and Leszek Miller established a new government. The AWS, with only 5.6 percent of the vote, failed to win any seats in the Sejm. Since Aleksander Kwaśniewski was reelected president of Poland in 2000, the Left had returned to power once again.

When Miller became the new premier, Poland's overall situation was complex. On the one hand, in March 1999 Poland had joined NATO (the North Atlantic Treaty Organization), considerably improving the country's international situation. Germany, which had already recognized the western borders of Poland in 1990, became the principal sponsor of Poland's entry into European Union. In 1992 Poland applied for full membership of the EU. In 1996 it was admitted to the Organization for Economic Cooperation and Development. In 1998 negotiations with the EU commenced. Poland had dramatically transformed its economy since the fall of communism and after 1994 was among the fastest growing countries in Europe. A new positive image of Poland appeared in the West. In December 2002 Poland concluded the "accession" negotiations regarding its entry into the EU during a conference in Copenhagen. In April 2003 Poland, together with fourteen other candidates, signed the Accession Treaty in Athens. The president of Poland ratified the treaty, after, in June 2003, over 77 percent of Poles said yes to joining the EU in a referendum (with a 59 percent turnout). Poland joined the European Union on 1 May 2004, a symbol of its reincorporation into the mainstream of Europe.

On the other hand, there are still serious problems, especially in the areas of subsidized agriculture, coal mining, and heavy industry. The differences between the private and state sectors contribute to the fact that Poland's trade balance is negative. To some extent, this situation is caused by continued chilly relations with Russia. The political atmosphere in Poland has been additionally poisoned by the screening of the most important politicians and state officials in order to verify whether they cooperated with the secret police before the fall of communism. In addition, economic conditions continued to worsen after 2001, with unemployment reaching 18 percent in 2003. By the end of 2002, the Polish economy was in its worst shape since the early 1990s. In January 2003 Poland was confronted with the "Rywingate," a corruption scandal (so named after the main suspect, a film producer, Lew Rywin) that tainted the premier. In March 2003 disagreements over governmental policies prompted the Peasant Party to leave the coalition. As a result, the Miller cabinet became a minority government, and public opinion polls showed that the government had the support of less than one-quarter of the people.

In the wake of the turmoil of the decade following the collapse of communism, political life has become increasingly less relevant to Polish citizens. Some who have become very rich and many who live better now than before 1989 do not care about elections and the parliament. The poorest have lost any hope they had for the future. Intellectuals and the intelligentsia, disgusted with political scandals and corruption, have withdrawn from politics. Without outstanding leaders and moral role models, most Poles are confused. To many, capitalism—with its eternal fight for a paycheck—is simply boring. Some former pre-1989 opposition activists are bitter; the new Poland is not only different from the communist Polish People's Republic, but also very different from the Poland of their old dreams.

POLITICAL DEVELOPMENTS

Poland is a democratic multiparty republic with a bicameral parliament. The Constitution of the Republic of Poland of 2 April 1997, ratified in a popular referendum on 25 May 1997, forms the legal foundation of the Polish political order and defines its basic rules. The nation is the supreme authority in Poland, which is a sovereign and independent state. Its citizens, who must be eighteen years of age or older, elect their representatives to the Sejm and Senate (the two houses of the parliament) during free and universal elections. Parliament makes decisions for the people, who also elect local governments and participate in a public life based on the principle of political pluralism and freedom of association of social organizations. State power is divided between the legislative, the executive, and the judiciary.

The power of legislation is exercised by the bicameral parliament. Its lower chamber, the Sejm, consists of 460 members chosen in universal, equal, secret, and direct ballot for four years (two seats are assigned to ethnic minority parties). The 1997 constitution and the reformed administrative division of 1999 required a revision of the electoral law. Passed in April 2001, the revised electoral law replaced a system in which some deputies were elected nationally with one in which all deputies are elected by voters in their constituencies, and it changed the method of proportional representation used to determine how many deputies would be elected from each party, eliminating the premium for the largest parties.

The new electoral ordinance also stipulated that with the exception of small ethnic parties, only parties receiving at least 5 percent of the total votes and political coalitions receiving at least 8 percent of the total votes can enter the parliament. The Sejm adopts bills, inspects activities of governmental organizations, appoints members of several constitutional bodies, helps to create the government, and can take votes of no confidence in the cabinet or its individual ministers. The Sejm is independent of the Senate and acts in a transparent and permanent way. There is no break between the terms of the out-going and the new Sejm; however, the latter is not obliged to continue the legislative initiatives of its predecessor. The Sejm can introduce martial law.

The upper chamber, the Senate, consists of one hundred senators elected for four years by universal, direct, and secret ballot. The Senate can review, correct, or reject bills adopted by the Sejm. Such bills return to the Sejm and are accepted if an outright majority does not reject them. The Senate approves the appointment or dismissal of several important state officials.

Executive power is carried out by the Council of Ministers, which thus constitutes what is traditionally called the Government, and the president. The latter is the highest representative of the Republic of Poland and the supreme commander of its armed forces, and sustains the observance of the constitution and the security and sovereignty of the state. The president can initiate legislation, issue regulations and orders, dissolve the Sejm, and veto a bill. Elected for five years by universal, equal, direct, and secret ballot, the president can serve a maximum of two terms and is answerable only to the State Tribunal. The office of the president, recreated in 1989, has been occupied by Wojciech Jaruzelski (19 July 1989–22 December 1990), Lech Wałęsa (22 December 1990–22 December 1995), and Aleksander Kwaśniewski (since 22 December 1995).

The Government, formed and headed by the prime minister and endorsed by the president and the Sejm, conducts domestic and foreign policies. The Council of Ministers can initiate legislation and can issue regulations. It is obliged to ensure the implementation of the laws, to prepare the state budget, and to execute it. The Government leads and controls the activities of all administrative institutions and is responsible before the Sejm. Individual ministers and the premier are answerable to the State Tribunal. After 1989, the post of the prime minister was occupied by the following politicians: Tadeusz Mazowiecki (24 August 1989–14 December 1990), Jan Krzysztof Bielecki (1 January 1991–5 December 1991), Jan Olszewski (6 December 1991–4 June 1992), Waldemar Pawlak (5 June 1992–8 July 1992), Hanna Suchocka (10 July 1992–18 October 1993), Waldemar Pawlak (18 October 1993–21 March 1995), Józef Oleksy (25 March 1995–1 February 1996), Włodzimierz Cimoszewicz (16 February 1996–17 October 1997), Jerzy Buzek (17 October 1997–19 October 2001), and Leszek Miller (since 19 October 2001).

Judicial authority is executed by the courts (district, provincial, military, administrative, and appeal courts), supervised by the Supreme Court, as well as by the Constitutional Tribunal and the State Tribunal. The Supreme Court, the last resort of appeal, clarifies legal provisions and resolves disputable legal questions. The president of Poland appoints the judges and the first president of the Supreme Court. They are previously selected by the National Judicial Council and the Supreme Court Justice General Assembly. The Constitutional Tribunal, a fully independent body of fifteen judges chosen by the Sejm for nine years, supervises the compatibility of governmental activities and newly accepted laws, decrees, and regulations with the Constitution and international agreements. The State Tribunal examines constitutional liability and criminal cases involving the holders of the highest state offices, such as president of the republic, Government members, the president of the Supreme Court, and heads of central administrative offices. In addition to the Supreme Court and the two tribunals, the rights and freedoms of citizens are protected by the Commissioner for Civil Rights Protection, an office established in 1987. The Supreme Chamber of Control (NIK) audits the activities of governmental institutions. All the court decisions can be appealed to the European Court of Justice in Strasbourg.

In 1990 local self-governments were revived, and the 1997 constitution endorsed them as one of the most important principles of the Polish political system. Adult citizens elect these local governments in universal, equal, secret, and direct ballot on all the three levels of the administrative structure: councils in urban municipalities and rural communes, *sejmiki* (little parliaments) in districts and provinces. These assemblies set local by-laws, pass budgets and inspect their execution, set local taxes and fees, and appoint local officials.

Poland has been governed by a coalition cabinet headed by Leszek Miller, the leader of the center-left Democratic Left Alliance (SLD) since the election of September 2001, when a block of the SLD and the Labor Party (UP) received 216 of 460 seats in the Sejm. Led by younger leadership members of the former Polish United Workers' Party (PZPR) and consisting mostly of the former PZPR members, the SLD is seen by many people as a postcommunist organization partially responsible for the activities of the 1945–1989 communist regime. In 2001 the SLD-UP coalition was 15 parliamentary seats short of having a majority in the Sejm. Therefore, to strengthen their position, the SLD and the UP, led by Marek Pol (the infrastructure minister), formed a coalition with the Polish Peasant Party (PSL), headed by Jarosław Kalinowski (the deputy premier and agriculture minister) and controlling 42 seats. After the October 2001 elections (with a turnout of 46.3 percent), the opposition was divided into several parliamentary clubs. The Citizens' Platform (PO) had 65 MPs, Self-Defense (Samoobrona) 53 MPs, Law and Justice (PiS) 44 MPs, the League of Polish Families (LPR) 38 MPs, and the German minority 2 MPs.

In March 2003 the Peasant Party (PSL) left the governing coalition, and Poland was led by a minority cabinet. Also, most parties lost some MPs and the (December 2003) division of the Sejm members into parliamentary clubs and groups was slightly different than in 2001: the Democratic Left Alliance (SLD) had 191 MPs, the Citizens' Platform (PO) 56, Law and Justice (PiS) 43, the Polish Peasant Party (PSL) 37, Self-Defense 31, the League of Polish Families (LPR) 29, the Labor Party (UP) 16, the Democratic People's Party (PLD) 10, the Conservative-Popular Party (SKL) 8, the Polish People's Bloc (PBL) 6, the Polish Reasons of State (PRS) 5, the Catholic National Movement (RKN) 5, the Polish Alliance (PP) 3, and the Movement for the Reconstruction of Poland (ROP) 3; seventeen are unaffiliated deputies.

Poland maintains an army of about 175,000 troops. The government intends to limit these forces to 150,000 in 2006. The army relies on general conscription. All adult men are subject to a twelve-month long service. The priorities of the military authorities are modernization of equipment and a further integration with NATO, which plans to move some of its bases to Poland. The Polish Army has participated in several peacekeeping operations, most recently in Iraq, Kosovo, and Lebanon.

Church and state are separate in Poland. The Catholic Church's role in politics is modest, even though, in the first years after the fall of communism, the church was quite visible in public life. This engagement caused some problems, and after the experiences of the 1993 and 1997 electoral campaigns, when the clergy was really involved in political struggle, the church no longer interferes directly in politics.

The establishment of the current political system in Poland followed the fall of communism and the disintegration of the Soviet Union. The Round Table Agreement of 1989 started systemic changes in Poland. The office of president was reintroduced. Since, as a part of the compromise between the regime and the democratic opposition, General Wojciech Jaruzelski became the head of state, the presidential power came to be limited and curbed by the parliament. The Senate was restored, and the idea of partially free elections was accepted by the regime. After the electoral victory of Solidarity in June 1989, the complete transformation of the system began. The Little Constitution, accepted by the Sejm on 1 August 1991 and ratified in October 1992, defined new roles for the president, the premier, and the parliament.

Lech Wałęsa, a dominating personality and the dynamic leader of Solidarity, elected president by direct elections in 1990, did not want to accept the 1989 presidential limitations. In addition, a strong president was necessary to push reforms through the parliament. The Little Constitution increased the authority of the president to such an extent that some deputies were afraid that the head of state would be able to dominate the government. According to the new principles, the president could submit a candidate for premier to the Sejm, and he approved the premier's choice of ministers, approved all the important military and national security appointments, and helped to select the ministers of defense, foreign affairs, and internal affairs. To accelerate the reforms, the Little Constitution gave special powers to the government, which could issue decrees with the force of law if the cabinet had the support of an absolute majority

Lech Wałęsa

One of the most important founders of Solidarity and the president of Poland from 1990 to 1995, Wałęsa became a symbol of the changes that started in 1980 and led to the redemocratization of Poland after 1989. Born to a poor peasant family in north central Poland in 1943, he graduated from a secondary vocational school and worked as an electrician for a state agriculture machinery center. In 1967 he moved to Gdańsk and was hired at the Lenin Shipyard. He participated in the December 1970 uprising of the Gdańsk and Gdynia workers and was elected chairman of a workshop strike committee. Dismissed from work in 1976 and involved in an underground free trade movement, he changed jobs frequently or was unemployed and harassed by the police.

In early August 1980 the workers striking in the Gdańsk Shipyard demanded the reinstatement of Wałęsa. He joined the strike and became its leader. He managed to convince his colleagues to form the Inter-Factory Strike Committee and to fight for trade union pluralism and the political rights of the workers. On 31 August 1980, after several days of negotiations between the communist authorities and the Strike Committee led by Wałęsa, the latter signed the Gdańsk Agreement with the government. The workers received the right to strike and to form independent trade unions. Wałęsa became the hero of the hour and was elected chairman of the National Coordinating Commission of the newly founded Solidarity trade union.

Wałęsa developed Solidarity's national organization, which soon gathered 10 million members, and his prestige as a symbolic leader of the democratic opposition grew. After the imposition of martial law in December 1981, Wałęsa was interned and remained imprisoned until November 1982. In October 1983 he received the Nobel Peace Prize. He maintained contacts with the underground Solidarity and in 1988 reemerged as one of the most important politicians in Poland. In 1989 he was a dominating figure during the Round Table Negotiations and formed a noncommunist majority in the Sejm after the June 1989 elections. Wałęsa's closest adviser, Tadeusz Mazowiecki, became the first noncommunist prime minister in Poland since 1945. However, a disagreement between Wałęsa and Mazowiecki triggered a war at the top and the disintegration of Solidarity. In 1990 Wałęsa won the presidential elections in Poland against Mazowiecki and a maverick candidate, Stanisław Tymiński.

Wałęsa's presidency was not perfect. He became involved in several conflicts with the Sejm and the leading politicians. Before the 1993 parliamentary elections, Wałęsa established a new party, the Non-Party Bloc for Supporting the Reforms (BBWR). The Bloc received only sixteen seats in the Sejm and two seats in the Senate. The elections were won by a postcommunist coalition. During the 1995 presidential elections, Wałęsa was defeated by a former communist minister, Aleksander Kwaśniewski. In 1997 Wałęsa established the Christian Democratic Party of the Third Republic, which did not manage to play an important role in Polish politics. In the 2000 presidential elections, Wałęsa won only about 1 percent of the popular vote. Although he had become politically marginalized, his previous contribution to the redemocratization of Poland is undeniable, and Wałęsa remains a historical and political figure of the highest importance.

of the Sejm. Only elections, constitutional amendments, the state budget, and civil and political liberties were protected from the force of decree.

The Little Constitution was a step forward, but the functions of the president and the premier were still not completely clear, and both of them tried to extend their power. The president especially argued that the Sejm held too much power and dominated the political system. In fact, the parliament was rather slow, devoting much time to secondary matters, while urgent and fundamental issues, such as privatization, electoral law, the role of the prosecutor general, and financial and penal law were still unsolved. This was caused, among other things, by the limited political qualifications of the deputies, most of whom did not have any political experience; out of 460 MPs, only 16 were economists, and only 22 were lawyers. In addition, the Sejm was divided into many parliamentary clubs, and Polish party geography was changing quickly.

Between 1989 and 2001, three parliamentary and three presidential elections took place in Poland. The Poles elected their presidents in 1990 (Lech Wałęsa), 1995 (Aleksander Kwaśniewski), and 2000 (Aleksander Kwaśniewski), and the Sejms in 1991, 1993, and 1997. Among the 29 parties that entered the Sejm after the elections of 1991 (with a 43 percent turnout), the following parties had the largest representations: the Democratic Union (UD) 62 MPs, the Democratic Left Alliance (SLD) 60, the Confederation of Independent Poland (KPN) 51, the Catholic Electoral Action (KAW) 50, the Polish Peasant Party (PSL) 50, the Center Alliance (PC) 44, the People's Democratic Congress (KLD) 37, the Peasant Movement 28, Solidarity 27, and the Polish Party of Beer Lovers 16. Before the 1993 parliamentary elections (which had a 51 percent turnout), a new electoral law introduced a 5 percent threshold for the participating parties. As a consequence, only six of them received parliamentary seats: the Democratic Left Alliance (SLD) 171 seats, the Peasant Party (PSL) 132, the Democratic Union (UD) 74, the Labor Party (UP) 41, the Confederation of Independent Poland (KPN) 22, and the Non-Party Block for Support of the Reforms (BBWR) 16. Two seats went to the German minority, and four to independent politicians. This division facilitated the comeback of the postcommunist government that ruled until 1997.

The parliamentary elections of 1997 brought dramatic changes, even though the turnout was again low (48 percent). Solidarity Electoral Action (AWS) received 201 seats, the Democratic Left Alliance (SLD) 164, the Polish Peasant Party (PSL) 27, the Freedom Union (UW) 60, the Movement for the Reconstruction of Poland (ROP) 6, and the German minority 2.

The electoral results reflected a pendulum effect in Polish politics after 1989: the Solidarity era of 1989–1993 was followed by the return of the postcommunist Democratic Left Alliance (SLD) to power in 1993, followed by a Solidarity period of 1997–2001 and then another SLD comeback in 2001. It is also striking that the role of the intelligentsia and intellectuals in politics and in public life has been gradually diminishing. Some sociologists claim that the Polish intelligentsia is disappearing. The powerful Democratic Union (later, after mergers with other similar but smaller parties, renamed the Union of Freedom and supported primarily by the intelligentsia) dominated the political scene in the early 1990s but did not manage to enter parliament in 2001. Also Solidarity, divided and compromised, ceased to be an important political factor, and several representatives of political "folklore," such as the Polish Party of Beer Lovers, disappeared completely in the new environment of a stabilized democratic system.

POLITICAL SYSTEMS IN POLAND BEFORE 1989

Before the fall of communism, Poland was a Soviet satellite, and the country's political system reflected this situation. In theory, the 1952 constitution, patterned directly on the Soviet constitution and amended in 1976, guaranteed democratic freedoms, named the people of Poland the sovereign source of power, and established a system that, allegedly, expressed "the interests and the will of the working people." The Polish People's Republic (Polska Rzeczpospolita Ludowa—PRL), according to the 1952 constitution, was a "People's Democracy," a transition form from "bourgeois democracy" to the Soviet form of communism. In practice, however, the Polish United Workers' Party (Polska Zjednoczona Partia Robotnicza—PZPR) acted as the directing force, and its leadership, supervised by the Soviet government, constituted the policy-making center of the state. The parliament was arranged in such a way that it had to rubber-stamp PZPR decisions and to give ex post facto approval of governmental measures. The goal of these measures was to build a new social system and to eliminate those classes of society that were seen as living by exploiting workers and peasants. During some periods, the Sejm was allowed a greater scope for debate and activity, but it never received power to make policy.

The Polish governmental structure was also modeled on the Soviet system. The structure was highly centralized and controlled by the PZPR Politburo. Its decisions were executed by the Council of State and the Council of Ministers. The Council of State (a collective head of state) was elected by the Sejm from among its members and included not only Party functionaries but also the highest governmental officers who did not belong to the PZPR. The council issued decrees during the intervals between the sessions of the Sejm and controlled local provincial, city, district, and communal councils. The council called elections to the Sejm and convoked it, appointed several civilian and military officials, ratified international treaties, could declare war or martial law, and performed other functions of a head of state. Frequently, especially in the 1950s and 1960s, Sejm sessions were very brief; the Council acted as the main legislative body, and its decrees were automatically approved by the parliament.

The Council of Ministers, subordinated to and controlled by the Party leadership, was the decision-making and ruling center of the administration. It coordinated the activities of particular ministries and state institutions, prepared economic plans, and supervised local people's councils. According to the constitution, the government was elected by the Sejm, or by the Council of State when the parliament was not in session. In practice, however, the ministers and the premier were appointed by the Party leadership, which had special organs duplicating and paralleling the state institutions. The 1976 constitution amendments stipulated that Poland was a socialist state and that the PZPR was the leading political force in the construction of socialism. Another amendment declared a perpetual Polish-Soviet alliance, which made any action to abandon the alliance illegal and any Soviet intervention to preserve the alliance constitutional.

The PZPR structure was highly centralized and undemocratic; the Party leadership was formed not during free elections by Party members, even though this was the official theory, but by appointments and selections. This led to serious succession problems when particular First or General Secretaries died or were unable to work. The central organs of the Party—the Political Bureau, the Party Secretariat, and the Central Committee—supervised the work of provincial, city, and local PZPR committees. The nomenklatura system, which, as described above, meant that only PZPR members could occupy important administration positions, guaranteed PZPR control over all important offices and appointments, establishing a list of positions that could be occupied only by trusted PZPR members. Also the entire judicial system, the Central Planning Commission, the regional administration, and the command of the armed forces were parts of the nomenklatura.

Strict censorship, various other forms of diffusion and control of public information, and extensive security services—the secret political police, the so-called Citizens' Militia (Milicja Obywatelska—MO), the Motorized Detachments of the Citizens' Militia (ZOMO), and several other organs of the Ministry of Interior—assured the internal security of the Polish one-party state.

POLITICAL SYSTEMS IN POLAND BEFORE 1945

During World War II, Poland was occupied by Nazi Germany and the Soviet Union. The occupiers destroyed most of the prewar political institutions. Some of them were reconstructed underground. The legal continuation of the interwar Polish Second Republic was executed by the government in exile and the National Council (Rada Narodowa) established in 1939 in France (and later re-formed in London after the fall of France in 1940) and recognized by most states of the anti-Nazi coalition.

Before World War II, Poland was formally a parliamentary democracy. The Constitution of March 1921, one of the most progressive constitutions of the interwar period, gave Poland a democratic representative government. According to the 1922 electoral law, members of the Sejm were elected by universal franchise on the basis of proportional representation. In addition, a special national list guaranteed parliamentary representation to small parties. Nevertheless, the reality of the situation after World War I was that the newly rebuilt Polish state consisted of several regions that had belonged to three different empires before 1918, and the political scene was fragmented and chaotic. It was difficult to form a ruling majority; and the governments changed frequently. With no political experience among most citizens, a weak president, and a stalemate in the Sejm, the political system did not function properly. The 1926 military coup d'état of Marshal Józef Piłsudski introduced an authoritarian dictatorship in Poland. Initially, the dictator tolerated the parliament and tried to preserve a façade of democracy, but after 1930 even the so-called controlled democracy disappeared, and the entire power was solely in the hands of Piłsudski and his assistants. They imposed a new constitution in 1935, which guaranteed an authoritarian system. After the death of Piłsudski in 1935, his successors went even further to the right and experimented with elements of totalitarianism.

CULTURAL DEVELOPMENT

Poland is located in the heart of Europe, and as a consequence Polish culture has been nurtured by many different traditions. German, French, and Italian influences have been particularly strong and Poland, unlike its eastern neighbors, was deeply immersed in the most important European spiritual movements, such as Renaissance humanism, the Reformation, the Counter-Reformation, the Enlightenment, and romanticism. Therefore, even before the partitions of Poland at the end of the eighteenth century, Polish cultural identity had been strong, and in the nineteenth century it helped the Poles to survive an era of foreign occupation and denationalization. Moreover, even though Poland is located on the periphery of European Latin culture, Polish contributions to Western civilization have been significant. Poland has been a home to many artists, scholars, writers, musicians, and entertainers of the highest international caliber. Some of them initiated new artistic trends and schools of thought, or created patterns exported to other countries; some even became so well known around the world (for example, Nicolaus Copernicus, the opera singer Ada Sari, Artur Rubinstein, and Fryderyk Chopin) that many people do not identify them as Polish—and indeed Chopin is usually referred to by the French version of his first name (Frédéric) and even called a French composer, though at his death Polish soil was strewn on his grave.

Long before the establishment of the Polish state in the tenth century, the territories of the future Poland were populated by innovative and creative people. It appears that eastern Poland constituted the cradle of the Slavic ethnic group, a place where it was formed and started developing an original Slavic culture of earth and timber strongholds and a distinctive religion. Nevertheless, the common Slavic elements, existing mostly in language, literature, and folklore, are rather weak in Polish culture, which was transformed by the adoption of Roman Catholic Christianity. As early as the tenth and the eleventh centuries, after the baptism of Poland in 966, the first Romanesque buildings were erected there. Beginning in the twelfth century, *palatia* and churches were decorated with stone sculptures in Poland. Two columns in the monastic church of the Norbertine nuns in Strzelno, covered with rich relief, and the cast bronze door from the Gniezno Cathedral are outstanding examples of Romanesque art.

After Poland became a part of Western civilization, Latin was accepted as the language of state administration and was used in Polish literature until the sixteenth century. In the early Middle Ages, when Latin was the only Polish literary language, monks and priests produced a number of saint's lives, annals, and chronicles. *Chronicon,* written in about 1115 by a Benedictine monk known only as Gallus Anonymous, and the *Annales seu cronicae inclyti Regni Poloniae* (Yearbooks of the Famous Kingdom of Poland), finished in 1480 by Bishop Jan Długosz, introduced Polish history to Europe. The earliest example of Polish prose was *Kazania świętokrzyskie* (Sermons of the Holy Cross), written at the end of the thirteenth century. The oldest surviving Polish text of poetry is a song called "Bogurodzica" (Mother of God), composed in the fourteenth century and accepted as a medieval equivalent of a national anthem.

In the thirteenth century Gothic became the dominant artistic style in Poland, and the face of Polish towns was altered by the influx of settlers coming from Western Europe. One of them, Veit Stoss from Nuremberg, known in Poland as Wit Stwosz (1447–1533), spent about twenty years in Cracow and created there many sculptures. His wooden altar in the spectacular Gothic Church of Holy Mary ranks as one of the most outstanding objects of that kind in Europe. Between the thirteenth and the sixteenth centuries, thousands of Gothic buildings were constructed in Poland (and many of them have survived). Most of them were churches, but some, such as Collegium Maius in Cracow, tenement houses in the "old towns" of Poland, and military structures of the Teutonic Order in Pomerania and former East Prussia, are reminders of the atmosphere of medieval

Redbrick walls of Malbork Castle. (Corel Corporation)

lay life. The redbrick castle of Malbork, the former head-quarters of the Teutonic Knights, is one of the most impressive objects of its kind in Europe. Many Gothic buildings were decorated with stone and wooden sculptures as well as paintings. The union with the Grand Duchy of Lithuania in turn brought eastern influences into Poland. Gothic chapels with Byzantine decoration inside in Cracow and Lublin belong to the most unusual masterpieces of medieval art.

By the end of the Gothic era, the first works of secular literature appeared in Poland. In 1551 Marcin Bielski completed the first general history in Polish, *Kronika wszystkiego świata* (Chronicle of the Whole World). Jędrzej Gałka (fl. ca. 1449), a follower of Jan Hus and John Wycliffe, wrote a song called *Pieśń o Wiklefie* (Wycliffe Song) and *Rozmowa mistrza Polikarpa ze śmiercią* (Dialogue between Master Polycarp and Death), a poem criticizing the papacy. Students of the University of Cracow, established in 1364 and later called the Jagiellonian University, wrote love letters and fictional stories, such as *Powiastki polsko-włoskie* (Polish-Italian Stories). Also, poems depicting customs, such as *Pieśń o chlebowym stole* (Song about a Plentiful Table), recording political events, such as *Wiersz o zabiciu Andrzeja Tęczyńskiego* (A Poem on the Assassination of Andrzej Tęczyński), or satirical pieces, such as *Satyra na leniwych chłopów* (Satire on the Lazy Peasants), appeared. A growing number of religious writings were

published, including *Raj duszny* (Paradise of the Soul) written in Polish by Biernat of Lublin (1465–1530), one of the founding fathers of literature in the Polish language.

In the first years of the sixteenth century the Renaissance in its Tuscan Italian form appeared in Poland. The arcaded galleries of the Royal Wawel Castle and the Sigismund Chapel in Cracow, built for Sigismund the Old (1467–1548), belong to the most outstanding masterpieces of Renaissance art north of the Alps. Also Cracow's Sukiennice (Cloth Hall), burghers' houses in Gdańsk and Kazimierz on the Vistula, and many tombs, town halls, and other objects represent the Renaissance style, frequently overlapping with Gothic. In the 1580s Jan Zamoyski, the chancellor of Poland and one of the richest men in Europe, built for himself the entire town of Zamość, an exquisite Italian masterpiece of urban planning.

The Renaissance also initiated the golden age of Polish literature. New literary trends were brought to Poland by diplomats representing foreign courts, Poles who studied abroad, and Western humanists, such as Fillipo Buonaccorsi, known in Poland as Kallimach (1437–1496), and Conrad Celtis (1459–1508), who settled in Poland. Initially, the new tendencies and the medieval literary tradition overlapped, and the resulting cultural heterogeneity was accepted as one of the characteristic features of the Renaissance. The fast development of printing made books popular and accessible.

Wawel Castle

This large conglomeration of historical buildings, located on a hill overlooking the Vistula River, is considered by most Poles their national shrine and a symbol of the Polish statehood. The first stronghold on the Wawel Hill was built in the ninth century by the Vistulians (Wiślanie) tribe. The fort became a capital of their state, which was incorporated into the Greater Moravian Reich, the Czech Kingdom, and, in the 990s, into Poland. In 1000 Wawel, together with the borough that rose around it, was called Kraków (Cracow) and became the see of a bishopric. In the 1040s the capital of Poland was moved to Cracow, and Wawel was developed as the residence and the coronation place of the Polish monarchs.

Cracow became the most important cultural center in Poland, and Wawel was extended and rebuilt many times. It is the largest and oldest conglomeration of pre-Romanesque and Romanesque stone structures in Poland. King Casimir the Great (Kazimierz Wielki) erected several new Gothic structures and strong fortifications on the hill in the fourteenth century, and King Sigismund the Old (Zygmunt Stary) rearranged his royal residence in the Renaissance style at the beginning of the sixteenth century. Starting with the early seventeenth century, when the capital of Poland was moved to Warsaw, Wawel began to decline. It was partially destroyed and looted during the Swedish invasion of 1655 and the 1700–1721 Great Northern War. After the third partition of Poland, Cracow was occupied by the Austrians, who looted Wawel and turned it into military barracks. Reconstructed after World War I, Wawel became a residence of the Nazi governor general of occupied Poland, Hans Frank, during World War II. The Germans looted a large part of Wawel's treasures.

After 1945, Wawel was restored again and belongs now among the most impressive European historical objects north of the Carpathians. For centuries, the old Wawel Cathedral has been a burial place of Polish kings and outstanding leaders such as Tadeusz Kościuszko, Adam Mickiewicz, and Marshal Józef Piłsudski.

Several Poles participated in the Renaissance cult of ancient Roman poetry. Others started translating and adapting foreign works. Some authors took part in the intellectual debate triggered by the Reformation and the Counter-Reformation. But the most important phenomenon for the development of Polish literature was the appearance of a group of poets writing in Polish. The most outstanding representative of their first generation was Mikołaj Rej (1505–1569), a courtier, a politician, and a Protestant activist. He wrote light verse and little jokes, but also serious works. His satirical *Krótka rozprawa między Panem, Wójtem a Plebanem* (Short Conversation between a Squire, a Bailiff, and a Parson) included a critique of the king and supported the political demands of the middle gentry. Rej adapted The Psalms of David and wrote dramas, philosophical treaties, epigrams, polemics, and didactic works in rich Polish.

Jan Kochanowski (1530–1584), probably the most outstanding Polish poet of the pre-Partition period, represented the second generation of Polish Renaissance humanists. Extensively educated in Poland and Italy, he served as one of the royal secretaries in Cracow and then became a wealthy landowner. Although he started by writing Latin poetry in Italy, he became a master of the Polish language. He was also active as a translator and playwright and influenced generations of Polish writers and poets. After Rej and Kochanowski, Polish literature became a national literature, reflecting all aspects of Polish life.

The cultural interchange between Poland and Italy resulted in the appearance of the greatest of Polish scholars: Mikołaj Kopernik (Nicolaus Copernicus). Educated in Cracow, Bologna, and Padua, Kopernik returned to Poland in 1503 and was active as a physician, administrator, economist, and translator of the Greek Byzantine poetry. His real pas-

Portrait of sixteenth-century Polish astronomer Nicolaus Copernicus. (Library of Congress)

sion, however, was astronomy, and his discoveries in this field became a watershed in our knowledge of the universe. His *De revolutionibus orbium coelestium* (On the Revolutions of the Celestial Spheres) challenged the entire medieval worldview. No longer could the Earth be considered the center of the universe; together with other planets, it moves around the sun.

The Renaissance triggered an unprecedented development in Polish music. Like other segments of Polish culture, the original Slavic tunes were transformed by the arrival of Christianity. By the end of the fourteenth century, music was taught at the Cracow Academy, and Poles were used to organ music played in churches; however, there are few traces of original music written in Poland in the Middle Ages. During the sixteenth century, several outstanding Polish musicians appeared, such as Marcin Leopolita, a court composer of Sigismund the Old, and Mikołaj Gomułka. Polish composers, influenced primarily by Italian music, wrote both sacral and secular music, introduced new instruments, and achieved renown throughout Europe.

In the last years of the sixteenth century, the baroque style appeared in the Polish-Lithuanian Commonwealth. Soon baroque became so popular that it was considered a Polish national style, neatly fitting in the gentry's Sarmatian (so-called) culture (Polish nobles believed that, unlike the Slavic peasants, they were of Iranian Sarmatian origin, and their ancestors had come from Asia and subjugated the local population). Sarmatian culture borrowed many elements from Turkey and the Orthodox East. Many older objects were rebuilt in the baroque style, which was sponsored by the new Counter-Reformation order, the Jesuits.

The construction of the first Polish baroque church, the Church of Saints Peter and Paul in Cracow, started in 1597, only fourteen years after the completion of the first baroque building, the Il Gesu Church in Rome, which served as a prototype for further baroque ecclesiastical projects throughout Europe. This fact reflects the position Poland occupied on the cultural map of Europe in the early modern era. A number of Polish magnates constructed spectacular baroque residences, such as the buildings of the same type as the Lubomirskis' *palazzo in fortezza* found in Łańcut and Wiśnicz, the Koniecpolski Palace in Warsaw, or the palace of the Cracow bishop in Kielce. Tylman of Gameren (1632–1706), one of the most outstanding architects of his era, although originally from Holland, built late-baroque palaces for the Lubomirskis and the Krasińskis, important noble families, in Warsaw. Also, middle and petty gentry built their manors in the baroque style. All these residences and churches were richly decorated. Several uniquely Polish types of baroque art were developed, such as the coffin portrait used to represent the dead person during the funeral.

The baroque, so congenial to the Polish gentry's spirit, also influenced the development of Polish literature. The metaphysical religious poetry of Mikołaj Sęp Szarzyński (1550–1581) expressed the search for the meaning of the human existence. Jan Andrzej Morsztyn (1621–1693), the greatest representative of baroque poetry in Poland and an outstanding translator from French and Latin, wrote about the richness and beauty of the world and praised love as the

Copernicus

Mikołaj Kopernik, known in the West as Nicolaus Copernicus, the most outstanding Polish astronomer, was born in 1473 in the town of Frombork (in German, Frauenburg), east of Gdańsk. Educated in Cracow, Bologna, Padua, and Ferrara, he returned to Poland in 1503 and served his uncle, the bishop of Warmia, Lucas Watzenrode, as secretary and physician. In 1510 Kopernik settled as a canon in Frombork. During the 1520–1521 wars with the Teutonic Order, Kopernik led a defense of the Polish-held Olsztyn castle.

In Frombork, where he spent most of his life, Kopernik conducted his astronomical observations and wrote his main works, including a summary of his theory that the earth revolved around its axis and, together with the other planets, around the sun. Due to the revolutionary character of this theory, which conflicted with the official teaching of the Catholic Church, Kopernik, a priest, did not dare to publish his work, and it circulated in a manuscript. Kopernik also translated Greek poetry and studied economics, authored a currency reform, and formulated an economic law, later known as Gresham's law, based on the observation that coins of less intrinsic value will displace coins of greater intrinsic value.

Eventually, encouraged by other scholars, he published an extract of his work on astronomy. The complete version was published in 1543 by a German scholar, Georg Joachim von Lauchen, in Nuremberg, as *De revolutionibus orbium coelestium* (On the Revolutions of the Celestial Spheres). Kopernik's heliocentric theory caused a revolution in human thought, marking a major step in human knowledge of the universe. The earth ceased to be considered the center of the universe and the focal point of creation. It is believed that, under attack by other scholars and church authorities, Kopernik was presented with the Nuremberg edition of his work on the last day of his life.

highest value. Krzysztof Opaliński (1609–1655) composed political satires, and Wespazjan Kochowski (1633–1700) wrote about the wars with the Turks. Other poets specialized in pastorals, romances, love songs, and above all, religious poetry. Many noblemen, among them Jan Chryzostom Pasek (1636–1701), wrote diaries and memoirs. Anonymous playwrights authored numerous satiric comedies, commenting on contemporary events and popular cultural trends.

Polish music also achieved the highest level of mastery during the baroque era, participating in and reflecting the changes in European music. Moreover, beginning in the seventeenth century, Poland was invaded by English traveling theaters, playing mostly Shakespeare, and by Italian commedia dell'arte companies. Both invasions strongly influenced the development of the Polish theater, which previously had been limited mostly to religious performances. In the 1630s the first permanent theaters appeared in Poland and became an important component of Polish culture. Even toward the end of the seventeenth century and at the beginning of the eighteenth century, when literary production declined, the theater still developed, sponsored by the new Saxon dynasty and the rich magnates.

The first Saxon monarch on the Polish throne, Augustus II, tried to reform the Polish political system in the spirit of enlightened absolutism, following the examples set by other great monarchs of Europe. Groups of Italian and Saxon architects and artists now became active in Poland. They erected a spectacular Saxon Palace and the Saxon Axis in Warsaw. During the reign of Augustus III in the mid-eighteenth century, architects and artists moved into a rococo phase. Many residences and churches were rebuilt and received new French rococo decoration after 1730. Several huge axial park-and-palace complexes were built for the magnates. These rich patrons also supported a number of painters, who produced mostly portraits and religious scenes. Some of them specialized in church interiors. The late baroque and rococo eras also saw a blossoming of timber architecture. Many wooden churches, imitating earlier brick structures, were built in Poland, and wooden synagogues and mosques became a uniquely Polish-Lithuanian phenomenon.

The fine arts and culture in general revived in Poland after 1764 under the patronage of a new king, Stanisław August Poniatowski. He invited artists from abroad and began organizing such modern institutions as the National Museum and the Academy of Art. The baroque style was gradually replaced by classical tendencies. The king rebuilt his residences in Warsaw, the Royal Castle and the Łazienki Palace. "Picturesque" landscape parks, a style adopted from England, became popular in Poland. Among several outstanding painters active in the Polish-Lithuanian Commonwealth at that time, there were three special artists. Marcello Bacciarelli (1731–1818), an Italian who had become a Polish citizen, who painted many portraits of the king and prominent Poles, became the director of royal buildings and, after the opening of Warsaw University in 1816, the first dean of the Fine Arts Department. Bernardo Bellotto, called Canaletto (1721–1780), another Italian sponsored by the king, painted numerous Warsaw landscapes and scenes of everyday life; his paintings are an excellent source of historical information, and they made possible the reconstruction of the Old Town in Warsaw after 1945 as it was in the eighteenth century. Thirdly, Jean-Pierre Norblin (1745–1830), a French painter, draftsman, engraver, and a court artist of the Czartoryski family, depicted the world of the Polish gentry.

The results of the royal sponsorship and encouragement were especially visible in literature and related branches of culture. In 1765 the National Theater was founded in Warsaw. This stimulated further development of drama. Several playwrights, such as Franciszek Bohomolec (1720–1784), Wojciech Bogusławski (1757–1829), and Franciszek Zabłocki (1752–1821), wrote comic operas, political dramas, and adaptations of Western plays. These theatrical performances constituted a part of the royal program of "Enlightenment of Sarmatians" and reflected political life in the country, especially during the Great Sejm of 1788–1792 (which attempted to deal with the disintegration of the Polish state). A generation of outstanding actors appeared in Poland. Many magnates' theaters were active in this movement, and the first public theaters were established in Lublin (1778), Lvov (1780), Cracow (1781), Poznań (1783), and Vilna (1785).

The royal cultural campaign was supported by a number of outstanding writers. Bishop Adam Naruszewicz (1733–1796), a personal friend of King Stanisław August, helped him to organize the so-called Thursday dinners, which gathered the top intellectuals at the royal court. Naruszewicz published articles in the newly established and numerous Polish periodicals and taught in the newly organized schools, such as the Collegium Nobilium and the Knights School. He wrote poetry, translated foreign and classical authors and, encouraged by the king, authored a monumental *History of the Polish Nation from the Times of Its Conversion to Christianity*. Bishop Ignacy Krasicki (1735–1801), another associate of the monarch, established an official press organ called *Monitor*, wrote satirical poems commenting on contemporary political life, edited an encyclopedia, and published the first Polish modern novel, *Przypadki Mikołaja Doświadczyńskiego* (The Adventures of Nicholas Tryall).

The 1780s brought the European fashion of sentimentalism to Poland and saw the blossoming of political writing. Journalism became a separate profession. Poets devoted their works to revolutionary ideas. A Commission of National Education, the first European ministry of education, established in 1773, founded a network of modern schools with a new educational program. Graduates of these schools participated in the rapidly growing and modernizing public and cultural life.

The loss of Polish independence at the end of the eighteenth century brought a halt to this impressive growth of Polish culture and introduced important changes into it. The sponsorship previously offered by Polish state institutions disappeared. The territories occupied by Russia, Prussia, and Austria were exposed to the artistic tendencies of these powers (which tried to change the cultural profiles of their newly acquired territories). In response, Polish artists were obliged by Polish society to sustain a patriotic awareness and, if possible, resistance against foreign domination. Before the 1863 January Uprising, Polish cultural life was dominated by romanticism, even though in the visual arts classical forms survived until the mid-nineteenth century, when, in architecture, they were gradually replaced by historical styles (neo-Renaissance, neo-Gothic, and neo-baroque). Around the year 1900, Polish architecture developed under the influence of technical inventions, such as steel constructions and prefabricated elements, even though numerous artists tried to create a national style. Simultaneously, Secession, also known as Art Nouveau or Jugendstil, became very popular, especially in Cracow and Lvov, which became the main centers of Polish cultural and artistic life.

The romantic period is considered the greatest in Polish literature. Romanticism replaced Polish late classicism, which lacked freshness and authenticity. The "youngs" (romantics) opposed the "olds" (classicists) and rejected the spirit of conciliation, post-Enlightenment conformism, and rationalism. Instead, the romantics propagated exaltation, patriotism, unconstrained creative imagination, heroism, and a return to old traditions. Their works, frequently pessimistic and bitter, were saturated with tragedy, mystical faith, symbols, hidden truths, and references to ancient beliefs, spirits, and superstitions. They were strongly influenced by Western romanticism, but they added the strength of their faith in the possibility of restoring Poland and continued the patriotic trend initiated by émigré soldier-poets in the Polish Legions of the Napoleonic army. One of them, Józef Wybicki (1747–1822), a politician, publicist, and playwright, wrote the famous "Dąbrowski's Mazurka" ("Mazurek Dąbrowskiego"), which later became the Polish national anthem.

Romanticism produced a galaxy of Polish poets and writers, but the most outstanding of them was Adam Mickiewicz (1798–1855), considered by most Poles their national prophet. His *Ballady i romance* (Ballads and Romances), published in 1822, heralded the era of romanticism in Poland by drawing on Polish and Lithuanian folklore and history. His greatest achievement, *Pan Tadeusz* (1834), is revered as a national epic; it became a bible for Polish émigrés.

After the defeat of the 1830–1831 November Uprising, the most outstanding Polish poets and writers were active in exile. Three of them especially inspired the next several generations of Polish poets. Juliusz Słowacki (1809–1849), a playwright and symbolist poet, reached beyond the borders of romanticism, developing his own mystical doctrine, a visionary interpretation of history, and technical virtuosity especially visible in his lyrical poems, considered by many the finest Polish lyrical poetry. His plays, still staged in Poland, laid the foundations of the Polish tragic drama. They deal with Polish history and contemporary discussions led by the members of the Great Emigration, discussed above. Zygmunt Krasiński (1812–1859) wrote novels modeled on those of Walter Scott and influenced by George Gordon Byron's narrative poems, as well as dramas. One of his works, *Nieboska Komedia* (Undivine Comedy), presented a dark, gloomy picture of the future European revolution, a conflict between the aristocracy and the disinherited masses. Cyprian Kamil Norwid (1821–1883), who was a poet, painter, and sculptor, wrote lyrical and epic

Adam Mickiewicz

One of the most outstanding Polish poets and the founder of Polish romanticism, Mickiewicz is considered by most Poles their national prophet and sage. He made major contributions to the development of Polish language, culture, and national consciousness. Born in 1798 into an impoverished Polish noble family in the eastern part of the former Polish-Lithuanian Commonwealth, he studied at the University of Vilna, the most important Polish institution of higher learning at his time. After 1819, he taught in a high school in Kaunas (Kowno). Arrested in 1823 for a participation in a secret student organization, he was deported to Russia. He lived in Moscow, St. Petersburg, and Odessa, and befriended the most outstanding Russian writers and intellectuals.

In 1829 he left Russia and, after an unsuccessful attempt to join the 1830–1831 uprising in Poland against the Russians, he settled in Paris, the main center of Polish political life in the mid-nineteenth century. He taught Latin literature at the College of Lausanne and held the first chair of Slavic literatures at the Collège de France. In 1848 he organized a Polish Legion in Italy to fight against Austria. Later, he edited an international socialist paper, *La Tribune des Peuples*. He died in 1855 in Constantinople, where he was trying to establish Polish and Jewish Legions to fight against Russia during the Crimean War. He was buried in Paris, but in 1890 his body was transferred to the Royal Crypt of the Wawel Castle in Cracow, the Polish national shrine.

Mickiewicz opened the era of romanticism in Poland with his first book of poetry, *Ballads and Romances,* in 1822. A year later, this debut was followed by the second volume, which contained a historical poem *Grażyna: A Lithuanian Tale* and two parts of *Forefathers' Eve (Dziady),* a drama based on Lithuanian folklore. Mickiewicz continued publishing in Russia and in Paris, where he wrote numerous political articles and a mystical interpretation of Polish history in Biblical prose, *Books of the Polish Nation and of the Polish Pilgrims.* His greatest achievement, however, was a sentimental novel in verse, *Master Thaddeus (Pan Tadeusz).* Completed in 1834, it recalled historical events in Lithuania in 1811–1812 and portrayed the unique culture of Polish gentry society. *Pan Tadeusz* became a bible of all Polish émigrés and is revered as the Polish national epic. Other works of Mickiewicz as well constitute a source of artistic and spiritual inspiration for Polish writers, politicians, and intellectuals.

poetry, politically involved, deeply philosophical, and probably the most original among the romantic poets.

The torch of national spirit was also carried by romantic prose writers. Zygmunt Miłkowski (1824–1915), also known as Teodor Tomasz Jeż, and Józef Kraszewski (1812–1887) wrote historical novels, Maurycy Mochnacki (1803–1834) specialized in literary criticism and political pamphlets, and Joachim Lelewel (1786–1861) became one of the fathers of modern Polish historiography. Some romantics used Belorussian and Ukrainian folklore motifs and contributed to the development of literatures of these nations. Others concentrated on radical revolutionary ideas. Aleksander Fredro (1793–1876), one of the most outstanding Polish comic playwrights and author of over thirty comedies, rejected romanticism even though he was active during the romantic era. He reached back to the eighteenth-century Enlightenment tradition, and the Nobel Prize–winning poet Czesław Miłosz in his *History of Polish Literature* called him "the last writer of the old *Respublica*" (Miłosz 250).

The classicists also lost the war against the romantics in painting. The new artistic current concentrated on the country's past and nature, monuments, and folklore. Inspired by the French romantics, Polish painters gave an unprecedented prominence to national and historic themes and appealed to national consciousness; Artur Grottger (1837–1867), for example, painted two great series, *Polonia* (1863) and *Lithuania* (1865), devoted to the 1863 January Insurrection and depicting the fight for Polish freedom and its martyrs. Later, this trend reached its zenith in the painting of Cracow's artist Jan Matejko (1838–1893), whose realistic historical iconography presented an interpretation of the entire history of Poland. The revolutionary and national tones also sounded in Polish romantic music. Stanisław Moniuszko (1819–1872), the most representative opera and song composer of the Polish nineteenth-century national school, composed several operas devoted to popular romantic subjects.

Yet nothing that Polish composers produced in this period could compare to the unique work and genius of Fryderyk Chopin (1810–1849). Involved with the avant-garde of European romanticism, he represented the clearest example of this trend in music. Polish folk music belonged among the most important sources of his inspiration. Chopin was the greatest composer that Poland ever produced and, together with Beethoven, revolutionized Western music.

The defeat of the 1863 January Uprising, the last outburst of political romanticism in Poland, triggered profound changes in Polish culture. Positivism, one of the main European philosophical currents initiated in the 1840s, played a role in Poland rather in literary and sociopolitical movements than in scholarly and philosophical activities. It took shape as a reaction against romanticism, emphasizing the cultivation of a critical, realistic, and practical attitude, and on the economic and educational foundations of political programs. Positivists rejected the ideology of national uprisings and advocated the development of economic, educational, and cultural activities, similar to the "organic work"

Portrait of nineteenth-century Polish composer Fryderyk Chopin. (Library of Congress)

initiated in Prussian-occupied Poland that had already taken place in the first half of the nineteenth century. Positivism fought against the remaining elements of feudalism, propagating activities that would help to overcome the backwardness of the Polish nation, and supporting the emancipation of women, Jews, burghers, and peasants. Thus positivist literature, realistic and at the same time tendentious, created a new kind of protagonist, a bearer of the banner of civilization and a social worker.

The best representative of this program was Eliza Orzeszkowa (1841–1910), a publisher, bookseller, publicist, and writer. Most of her novels, devoted to women's emancipation, the peasant question, and the Jewish problem, had a strongly didactic character. Bolesław Prus (1847–1912) represented a more sophisticated version of positivism, and his *Lalka* (A Doll) is frequently considered one of the best Polish novels. Also his *Faraon* (The Pharaoh), based on ancient Egyptian history and discussing timeless problems of political power, belongs among the most interesting products of the Polish literature. For twenty years, Prus wrote regular essays for the Warsaw newspapers and periodicals. Other writers also worked as journalists, and periodicals became a popular and important means of disseminating and discussing new ideas. Some of the most famous Polish novels were printed in installments in the press. The *Trilogy* of Henryk Sienkiewicz (1846–1916), one of the most popular

Fryderyk Chopin

The most outstanding Polish composer and a renowned pianist, Fryderyk Chopin has become a symbol of Polish music. Born in 1810 in Żelazowa Wola near Warsaw in the family of a French tutor who settled in Poland during the Napoleonic period and married a Polish wife, Chopin was a child prodigy, composing and performing from his early childhood. He studied music in the Warsaw Main School of Music. In 1830 he left Warsaw and settled in Paris a year later. In 1837 he became the friend and lover of the French writer and feminist George Sand and produced his best works at her residence in Nohant. From his early years Chopin suffered from the tuberculosis that led to his death in 1849 in Paris. He is buried in the Père Lachaise Cemetery in Paris, but his heart is enshrined in the Holy Cross Church in Warsaw.

As a young man, Chopin became familiar with the folk music in his native region of Mazovia in Central Poland, an influence that was reflected later in his music. Before 1830, he composed under the influence of early romantic music. In Western Europe, Chopin kept in touch with the most outstanding musicians, writers, and artists and became involved with the avant-garde of romanticism. His works, composed mostly for the piano, displayed national and romantic characteristics. After, 1839, in his late period, Chopin introduced elements of the postromantic style to his music, which was emotional and pure in form, and combined the tradition of European piano music with Polish folk and national music. Chopin's genius greatly influenced the further development of music.

nominated by the tsar, censored its repertoire, and many Western authors, including Shakespeare, were banned.

The situation improved in the late 1860s, and several great stars, such as Helena Modrzejewska (1840–1909), appeared on the stages of the WGT. Still, its repertoire and the quality of production did not match the artistic level of the actors. Permanent theaters were also active in other cities, and, particularly in autonomous Austrian-controlled Galicia, in Lvov and Cracow, the theatrical life was much more interesting than in Russian-occupied Poland.

Tsarist oppression also slowed the development of Polish academic life in Russian-occupied Poland. Many scholars moved to Galicia or to Western Europe. Some of them, such as Maria Curie-Skłodowska (1867–1934), a physicist and the 1911 recipient of the Nobel Prize for Chemistry, made spectacular careers there.

Galicia, administered by Poles and enjoying many freedoms, including the right to use Polish as the official language, became a source of a new trend in Polish culture. Sometimes called Young Poland, it was a form of modernism, or neoromanticism, and it transformed all branches of Polish culture. The adherents of the new trend wanted to liberate art and literature from the constraints of social and national service, defended the independence of art, and propagated the idea of art for art's sake. Like other cultural movements of this era, such as Young Germany, Young Scandinavia, or Young Belgium, Young Poland reached back to romanticism, rejected positivism and realism, despised bourgeois values and the bourgeois way of life, and moved toward aestheticism and decadentism, emphasizing intuition and the vital forces of life. Polish writers and artists were particularly influenced by German culture. The works of Arthur Schopenhauer, Frederick Nietzsche, Gerhart Hauptmann, and others were translated into Polish and published in many copies. Some Polish writers, such as Stanisław Przybyszewski (1868–1927), were popular both in Poland and Germany.

Polish music also caught up with Europe in the first decade of the twentieth century, when the Young Polish Composers Publishing Company was established in Berlin and the Warsaw Philharmonic Orchestra was organized. Europe venerated the great pianist Ignacy Paderewski (1860–1941) and the greatest harpsichordist of her time, Wanda Landowska (1879–1959). Several outstanding composers, such as Karol Szymanowski (1882–1937), Mieczysław Karłowicz (1876–1909), Ludomir Różycki (1884–1935), and Grzegorz Fitelberg (1879–1953), who were active at that time made important contributions to the history of Polish and European music.

In the arts, the Young Poles developed new techniques, such as lithography or typography. It was in literature, however, that the new trend was most successful. Kazimierz Tetmajer (1865–1940) wrote nostalgic poems and other works devoted to his native Tatra Mountains region. Jan Kasprowicz (1860–1926) authored religious works and composed poetry depicting the world of Polish peasants. Tadeusz Miciński (1873–1918) became a forerunner of expressionism and surrealism. Władysław Reymont (1867–1925) published essays, short stories, and historical novels. In 1924 he re-

Polish writers, was first published as a newspaper series. In 1905 Sienkiewicz received the Nobel Prize for literature for his *Quo Vadis?* a novel on early Christianity under Nero; it was his most popular work abroad. Positivism also produced two important poets: a reflective lyricist, Adam Asnyk (1838–1897), and Maria Konopnicka (1842–1910), an author of lyric poems and short stories devoted to the life of the poor and oppressed people.

Many Polish writers of the second half of the nineteenth century wrote for theaters. The Warsaw National Theater played an important political role after the partitions of Poland. After the failure of the 1830–1831 November Uprising, the word "National" was removed from its name and, in the 1850s, it was merged with other theaters active in the capital of Poland into a state-controlled institution called the Warsaw Governmental Theaters (WGT). Its president,

Portrait of Maria Curie-Skłodowska, Polish physicist who discovered radioactivity around the turn of the twentieth century. (Library of Congress)

ceived a Nobel Prize in literature for his huge novel *Chłopi* (The Peasants), written in 1904–1908. Stefan Żeromski (1864–1925) became one of the most popular Polish writers; Stanisław Brzozowski (1878–1911) distinguished himself as a literary critic, and Stanisław Wyspiański (1869–1907) was a great visionary playwright, a gifted poet, and an outstanding painter.

In 1914 the development of Polish culture was interrupted again. World War I is remembered in Poland with mixed feelings. On the one hand, it brought unprecedented destruction, suffering, and casualties. In four years, hundreds of thousands of Poles fought in the armies of Austria, Germany, and Russia, and the Muses were mostly silent. On the other hand, however, the war resulted in the restoration of an independent Polish state. After a long foreign domination, the regained freedom stimulated an eruption of cultural life. In literature, the first postwar decade was dominated by lyric poetry. The tone was set by the young group of "Skamander" poets, such as Jarosław Iwaszkiewicz (1894–1980), Julian Lechoń (1899–1956), Antoni Słonimski (1895–1976), Julian

Tuwin (1894–1953), and Kazimierz Wierzyński (1894–1969). They published their own monthly and contributed to numerous periodicals, but they did not have a common theoretical program beyond the desire to reflect contemporary life and to emphasize its fullness and vitality. They abandoned national "martyrology" and combined lyrical expression with satire, irony, and absurd humor. Other interwar poets represented a variety of trends. The so-called avant-garde group, including Tadeusz Peiper (1891–1969), Czesław Miłosz (b. 1911), Julian Przyboś (1901–1970), and Jalu Kurek (1904–1983), was influenced by such movements as futurism, expressionism, and surrealism.

In the second decade of the interwar period, the novel and other prose forms moved to the foreground, with such outstanding authors as Zofia Nałkowska (1884–1954), Julian Kaden-Bandrowski (1885–1944), Zofia Kossak-Szczucka (1890–1968), Maria Dąbrowska (1889–1965), Teodor Parnicki (1908–1988), Stanisław Witkiewicz (1885–1939), and Bruno Szulz (1892–1942). Their rich work represented a galaxy of motifs and genres, from the historical novel, through drama, literary criticism, realistic tendencies, modernism and anti-modernism, to experiments and multiform vanguard trends. They belonged to various literary groups and writers' professional organizations and contributed to numerous periodicals.

Interwar Polish musical, theatrical, and artistic activities were equally extensive. National artistic institutions were revived and supported by the state. National minorities contributed widely to Poland's cultural life. Close contacts with foreign writers and artists were established. The most current French influences were felt, especially in painting and architecture. Polish universities developed the arts and sciences. A cinema industry appeared in Poland and developed quickly; cabaret theaters and operettas became very popular; Polish bookstores were full of books translated from foreign languages. It seemed that Polish culture was trying to make full use of the opportunities created by freedom.

Unfortunately, this creative period lasted barely twenty years. World War II surpassed all the tragic experiences of the Poles and was not just a simple interruption in the cultural development of the country. According to the Bureau of War Reparations, Poland lost 38 percent of its assets, as compared with the 1.5 percent and 0.8 percent lost by France and Great Britain respectively. Two great cultural centers, Lvov and Vilna, were incorporated into the Soviet Union and de-Polonized. The Soviets and the Nazis tried to exterminate the elites of the Polish nation, and indeed the casualties of Polish culture were enormous. The Grand Theater in Warsaw, for example, destroyed during the war, was not reopened until 1965.

After 1945, gradually but quickly, the cultural profile of the country was changed by the communists and their Soviet sponsors. In 1948 the Communist Party introduced the new literature and art of socialist realism. Many writers and artists accepted Marxist-Leninist theories; however, some ceased writing and painting altogether or emigrated, like Miłosz, who won the Nobel Prize in Literature in 1980. Even musicians had to abandon their artistic integrity and visions, labeled now by the authorities as formalistic, decadent, and alien to the great socialist era.

After 1956, thanks to the thaw that followed the death of Stalin, cultural life started to recover. Writers began to settle accounts with Stalinism and, frequently, their own fascination with communism. Some émigré writers, such as Witold Gombrowicz (1904–1969), were allowed to publish in Poland or, like Melchior Wańkowicz (1892–1974) and Stanisław Cat-Mackiewicz (1896–1966), returned to Poland. Censorship was relaxed, and new literary forms appeared at the hand of writers such as Stanisław Lem (b. 1921), an outstanding science fiction writer, and Leszek Kołakowski (b. 1927), a master of philosophical essays. Poetry blossomed with such poets as Zbigniew Herbert (1924–1998) and Wisława Szymborska (b. 1923), the winner of the 1996 Nobel Prize in Literature. The early 1960s brought the golden age of Polish drama, developed by Sławomir Mrożek (b. 1930), Stanisław Grochowiak (1939–1976), and Tadeusz Różewicz (b. 1921), among others. The late 1960s and the 1970s, however, were not good to the literature. Censorship once again became oppressive. The crackdown that followed the student demonstrations of 1968 decimated the literary milieu, and afterwards many authors published their works through underground publications. The imposition of martial law divided literary society; it started recovering in the late 1980s, but faced new challenges after the fall of communism. During the economic transformation there was no money to subsidize the writers, and most citizens of Poland could not afford to buy books.

The post-Stalinist relaxation and the collapse of the Stalinist system of artistic control brought a dramatic change in music and the fine arts as well. Outstanding new composers, such as Krzysztof Penderecki (b. 1933) and Henryk Górecki (1933–2003), appeared and soon gained worldwide fame. Visual artists, who had found a narrow margin of freedom under Stalin initiating the Polish school of poster art, broke their isolation from the West and caught up with its contemporary artistic tendencies. Władysław Hasior (b. 1928) formed his first provocative and poetic assemblages in 1957. Tadeusz Kantor (1915–1990) arranged his first exhibition in 1965.

Today, Polish artists are still shaking off the legacy of communism and are looking for a new place in a free market democracy. Yet, with two laureates of the Nobel Prize for Literature, many outstanding artists active in the country and abroad, and with a vibrant artistic life in Poland, contemporary Polish culture is certainly an interesting phenomenon.

ECONOMIC DEVELOPMENT

In 2000, Poland's economic transformation after the end of communism seemed an unqualified success, earning it only praise for its thorough reforms. *The Economist,* for example, usually moderate and cautious in its approach, spoke glowingly in its 29 April 2000 issue:

The Chicago-sized skyscrapers punching skyward along John Paul Avenue confirm Warsaw's place as the undisputed business capital of Central and Eastern Europe. This city is now the continent's second-largest building site after Berlin, yet, back in 1990, its dominance seemed unlikely. . . . Foreign and local bankers say that investors in Warsaw can get their money back, and more, in seven years or so. Put it into Paris or Berlin and it could take 20 years. The Poles' rollicking economy, which has grown by nearly a third in the past five years, is now almost four times as big as Ukraine's, over three times Hungary's and nearly three times the Czech Republic's. And the prospect of early entry into the European Union should tempt more foreign businessmen to set up shop in Poland—with the advantage of much lower costs, especially of labor, than elsewhere in the Union. According to a poll of international businessmen conducted by A. T. Kearney, an American consulting company, Poland may, in the next three years, become the world's fifth largest recipient of foreign direct investment—after the United States, Britain, China, and Brazil. Poland's foreign investment agency says it expects some $12 billion to flow in this year, compared with last year's estimated record of $8 billion. That, according to UN figures, would give Poland roughly 40 percent of last year's total foreign direct investment in the entire swathe of Europe, including Russia itself, that was once controlled by the Soviet Union. More buildings seem destined to sweep the sky in Warsaw. (49)

Unfortunately, in 2000, the Polish economy began to regress. The growth in GDP (gross domestic product), still high in 1998 and 1999 (over 6 percent), fell to 4.1 percent in 2000, 1.1 percent in 2001, and 1.5 percent in 2002. Poland's agriculture remains inefficient. It is handicapped by structural problems, lack of investments, and a surplus of labor. The government is closing subsidized state-owned enterprises, such as coal mines and steel mills. In the overpopulated industrial regions, where these companies are located, there are no new jobs for heavy industry workers, and in January 2003 the unemployment rate in Poland reached 18.7 percent. Foreign investments are concentrated in the richest parts of Poland, while underdeveloped provinces have stagnated. Mass social protests and the policies of the ruling Democratic Left Alliance, dominated by the post-communist Social Democratic Party, have slowed down the privatization and restructuring process of Polish industry. In 2001, the private sector produced over 75 percent of the GDP and employed over 70 percent of working Poles. It is expected that by 2005 the ownership structure of the Polish economy will resemble the Economic Union structure, with public ownership limited to about 15 percent.

Bottlenecks also exist in fiscal and monetary policies. The budget deficit, at 2 percent in 1999, amounted to about 4.1 percent of the GDP in 2002 and is expected to rise to over 5 percent in 2004. There has been a tension between the government, which has demanded that the interest rates be cut sharply, and the Monetary Policy Council, which resists pressures for a relaxation in the monetary policy. Reforms in health care, education, the pension system, and the state administration, initiated in 1999, proved to be very expensive and caused serious fiscal pressures.

The overall picture is not, however, entirely dark. The weakening of the Polish economy has been part of a world trend: the average world GDP growth sank to 3.4 percent in 2000, 1.5 percent in 2001, and 1.5 percent in 2002. In Germany, one of the strongest economies of the world, the GDP growth is even slower: 3 percent in 2000, 0.6 percent in 2001, and 1.2 percent in 2002. Despite these facts, consumer spending in Poland was still growing by over 2 percent in 2001. The Polish currency—the zloty—has been relatively strong (3.8 zloty per U.S. dollar in December 2003, 3.98 in December 2002, 4.01 in December 2001, and 3.47 in 1998), and net exports have been rising. Consumer price inflation has fallen faster than expected, to 1.6 percent in July 2002 and below 1 percent four months later.

Poland is an attractive country for foreign investment. By the end of 2000, over 850 companies from 35 countries had started activities in Poland. In 2000 the value of investments from the European Union reached 67 percent of the Union's total investments in the former communist bloc (compared with 47 percent in 1993). Between 1990 and 2000, foreign investments in Poland increased from 100 million to almost 40 billion dollars, which represents about a third of the total for Central and Eastern Europe. Among the investors are such well-known companies as Isuzu, Toyota, Estée Lauder, and Flextronics. Moreover, entry into the European Union constitutes a stimulating economic factor and a great opportunity for Poland. The country has adjusted its laws and institutions to the European Union regulations, and the EU is the main trade partner of Poland (70 percent of its exports and 60 percent of its imports in 2002). Poland has become the largest eastern trade partner of Germany and managed to escape the consequences of the collapse of the Russian economy in 1998, mostly due to the fact that Polish exchange with the countries of the former Soviet Union had been reduced to only about 7 percent of Poland's international trade.

The Polish government plans to return to 5 percent annual GDP growth in 2004, to activate the labor market, and to increase employment. Using European funds, the authorities are developing and modernizing infrastructure, especially communication, roads, and the rail network. Investments in the construction industry should ease housing problems. The government continues to work on the restructuring of brown coal mining, as well as the energy, steel, chemical, and defense sectors. Radical reforms are necessary in agriculture to improve its profitability, to strengthen its competitiveness, to energize economic activities in rural areas, and to adapt Polish agriculture to EU standards. The government's positive expectations are based, among other things, on the fact that Polish firms and managers now have the skills and instincts of their Western counterparts. The Polish sense of strong individualism and respect for entrepreneurship, the spirit of free enterprise and private initiative, subdued under the communist system, survived, and thus it could be reactivated under better conditions.

THE POLISH ECONOMY BEFORE WORLD WAR II

The economic strategy imposed on Poland by the Soviets failed for numerous reasons, such as the destruction of World War II and the fact that Poland was a relatively poor and mostly underdeveloped country before 1939. This, in turn, was a legacy of the nineteenth century, when Polish territories were divided among Russia, Austria, and Prussia and belonged to several administrative units. While most European countries were building modern economies and infrastructures, the Polish provinces were integrated into several different political and economic systems, exploited, and deliberately kept underdeveloped, or were destroyed during national uprisings.

Galicia, Austrian-occupied southern Poland, was in the worst shape. It stagnated long before the partitions. Initially, after the partitions, the Austrian authorities did not intend to keep Galicia and wanted to exchange it for another territory somewhere in Central Europe. Therefore, Vienna did not invest in Galicia but overtaxed it, exploiting it and overburdening it with a monstrous bureaucracy and large bor-

The Handlowy Bank in Warsaw. (Frank Ossenbrink/Corbis Sygma)

der garrisons. Cut off from its hinterland in central Poland, this poverty-stricken region was isolated from other Habsburg lands by the Carpathian Mountains. As late as 1890, over 77 percent of the Galician population worked in agriculture and only 9 percent in industry. In 1867–1871 Galicia enjoyed autonomy, but power remained in the hands of the gentry, who owned over 42 percent of the arable land and 90.5 percent of the forests.

In 1880 about 77 percent of the Galician population were illiterate. The province constituted 26.1 percent of the entire territory of the Austrian part of the Habsburg Empire and was inhabited by 26.9 percent of its population. Simultaneously, however, Galicia had only 9.2 percent of Austrian industrial enterprises. According to the famous book *Galician Misery in Numbers,* published by Stanisław Szczepanowski in 1888, the food consumption of an average Galicianer constituted about 50 percent of an average European's diet, and his work capacity about 25 percent. Approximately 50,000 people died annually of starvation in Galicia. At the beginning of the twentieth century, poverty in Galicia became less severe, primarily due to the exploitation of coal, salt, and oil. Coal mining also developed in the Grand Duchy of Cieszyn Silesia, which constituted a separate province, smaller but much richer than Galicia.

The economic situation in Russian Poland was even more complex. Initially, the Congress Kingdom of Poland was underdeveloped and predominantly agricultural. The army took 50 percent of its revenue, and the kingdom almost went bankrupt when its grain market collapsed after 1815. In the 1820s new taxes, monopolies, and economic institutions, such as the Bank of Poland and the Land Credit Society, were introduced. The government sold state estates and received foreign loans. A slow process of industrialization began, and the kingdom recovered from the disasters of the partitions and the Napoleonic period. The 1830–1831 uprising stopped these changes and brought negative economic consequences. Recovery returned in the 1850s, when Poland recaptured Russian markets, started developing railroads, opened new iron works and coal mines, modernized the textile and light industries, and initiated mass sugar production.

In the 1860s there were 75,000 industrial workers among the 4.8 million inhabitants of the kingdom. Urbanization and industrialization accelerated after 1863, even though the failure of the January Uprising was followed by severe anti-Polish persecutions, and the kingdom was abolished and the area incorporated directly into Russia. After the emancipation of the peasants in 1864, a significant portion of the population moved to the towns and cities of Poland. In the 1870s and the 1880s an industrial revolution took place there. Between 1882 and 1914, Warsaw, the third biggest city of the Russian Empire, grew from 382,000 to 884,000 inhabitants. New industrial centers appeared, such as the Łódź textile region, the metallurgical center in Warsaw, and the Dąbrowa coal basin. The value of production grew from 30 million rubles in 1864 to 228 million in 1890. Investments from Western Europe grew rapidly, and the former Congress Kingdom became the most advanced part of the Russian Empire.

This picture contrasted sharply with the situation in what were called the western *gubernias,* the eastern provinces of the former Polish-Lithuanian Commonwealth, which were incorporated directly into Russia after the partitions of Poland in the late eighteenth century. They remained almost exclusively agricultural. Industry existed only in Białystok and Vilna. In some parts of the western gubernias, poverty and backwardness were worse than in Galicia.

Prussian-occupied Poland developed more evenly. Greater Poland (Wielkopolska) became the breadbasket of Northern Prussia and Berlin. In contrast with the situation in the areas controlled by Russia and Austria, emancipation of the peasants in Prussia did not create small inefficient farms. The land ownership structure was optimal: medium-sized gentry estates and relatively large and economically strong peasant holdings. Smallholders commonly moved to the towns, where small local industry developed. A similar situation was found in Gdańsk Pomerania, while Silesia (which did not belong to the Polish-Lithuanian Commonwealth but was predominantly Polish) became one of the most industrialized regions of Europe.

After 1918, the government of the reborn Polish state faced the enormous task of integrating all of these regions into one economy. New currency, banking, communication, and transportation systems had to be established. The damages of World War I and the 1919–1921 Polish-Soviet War had to be repaired. In 1919 Poland's industrial production reached 30 percent of the 1913 level. Over 65 percent of Poland's citizens still worked in agriculture. Most farms in the south and the east were unproductive dwarf holdings. Industry was poorly distributed, private investment capital was small, the level of literacy low, and the demographic growth high.

In spite of all these handicaps, the government succeeded in several fields. The Baltic port and city of Gdynia was built; the Central Industrial Region, involving a fifth of Polish area and population, was created; a modern armament industry was built from scratch; and Warsaw became a center of new high-technology production. At the same time, however, agriculture still lagged behind. The Polish economy was hard hit by the Great Depression, and several branches of the industry had not achieved the 1913 level of production by 1939.

THE COMMUNIST ECONOMY

The post-1989 economic situation of Poland is difficult to understand without basic information about the communist era. As Jerzy Lukowski and Hubert Zawadzki put it in their *Concise History of Poland,* "The forty-five-year period of communist rule in Poland cannot be simply dismissed as one in which nothing constructive or beneficial was achieved" (280). Most scholars agree, however, that the Polish economy was mismanaged and misdeveloped by the communist regime. It imposed on Poland a utopian economic strategy in a time of deep postwar crisis. During World War II, most Polish towns were damaged or destroyed, with destruction reaching over 80 percent. About

42 percent of all Polish farms were also destroyed, and most farmers lost at least part of their livestock. Banks and finances did not exist. The Polish population was reduced from 35 to 24 million and did not return to prewar levels until 1975. Both the Germans and the Soviets deliberately exterminated Polish elites and professional classes. The newly acquired western territories were initially treated by the Red Army as occupied areas and were heavily looted. Poland was among the most damaged territories of postwar Europe. In addition, unlike the Western countries, the nation received only very limited help, and that was far outweighed by the Soviet exploitation of the country after 1945.

The Polish economic system during the communist seizure of power in 1945–1948 resembled the Soviet New Economic Policy of 1921–1928. In January 1946 a radical nationalization bill was passed. In 1947 the private sector of industry was reduced to 20 percent of production and 10 percent of labor, and a Three-Year Plan for postwar reconstruction was introduced. Within a year, industrial production reached 70 percent of the prewar level. In 1944 and 1945 land reform was introduced. Large farms and land estates were divided into small lots and redistributed among masses of peasants. Agriculture recovered quickly, and by 1948 Poland was able to export foodstuffs. In 1949 agricultural production reached 91 percent of prewar levels.

However, these more benign economic policies were changed during the Stalinist period after 1948. Collectivization of agriculture was initiated. As a result, serious problems with food supplies started, and Poland ceased to export foodstuffs. In addition, Warsaw was forced by Moscow to reject Western aid and to join the Council of Mutual Economic Assistance (Comecon) in 1949. The Polish economy became tied to the Soviet one and suffered substantial losses by selling commodities to the USSR below market prices. During the Six-Year Plan of 1950–1955, Poland adopted the Soviet model of industrialization, and introduced both the command economy and extensive bureaucratization. Private industry and trade were virtually liquidated. Most investments were allocated to heavy industry and armaments production. The consumer goods industry and services were neglected, and living conditions deteriorated. The Six-Year Plan, which resembled the Soviet Five-Year Plan of 1928–1932, increased several times under the pressure of the Cold War. The planning process, however, was never based on adequate statistics.

The growing burden imposed on the people led to the rebellion of 1956, which brought economic changes. Collectivization of agriculture was abandoned, and the peasants reverted to individual farming. Compulsory foodstuffs deliveries were reduced, and agricultural production begun to grow. The 1956–1960 Five-Year Plan transferred more investments to consumer goods, services, and construction. The state administration of industry was simplified and decentralized, workers' councils were established as a form of self-management, and planning and management reforms were initiated. After a couple of years, however, when the Gomułka regime had secured its control over society, the so-called Polish economic model was abandoned; management experiments were given up; workers' self-management was reduced to a minimum, and only some changes introduced after 1956 survived. Investments in heavy industry started growing again. Serious new problems were caused by a demographic explosion, a growing technological gap between the Western and the Communist camps, low labor productivity, insufficient reserves, supply shortages, mismanagement, insufficient investment and financial control, and a lack of a long-term economic strategy. Social frustration also grew, and the government's "retail price reform" triggered a rebellion in December 1970.

In response to the frustration, the new Gierek regime withdrew price increases and promised new reforms. The Five-Year Plan of 1971–1975 reallocated significant resources to the consumer goods industry and housing. Standards of living improved, and real wages increased. At the same time, several spectacular projects, such as the new coal-mining Lublin region, the Gdańsk Northern Port, the huge Huta Katowice steel plant, and the development of the car industry, were completed. Gierek's success, however, was based on large-scale borrowing from the West. New investments extended the previously planned investments by 31 percent. In 1971–1980 Poland bought 452 licenses. Even though most of them were imported from the West, some of them were of no economic importance or were even useless. The government planned to discharge the debt to the West by selling the licensed products, but Polish industries produced commodities that were worse than their Western equivalents and could not compete in the international marketplace. These problems were worsened by the recession in the West.

Gierek responded by borrowing more money. Investments and wages were growing much faster than industrial output. In 1976 the regime tried to restore market equilibrium by raising food prices, which triggered a new rebellion. The authorities curbed imports and the rate of investments. The economy began to decline, raw materials and food shortages appeared, and a black market thrived. Deteriorating living standards led to strikes and the establishment of Solidarity, the workers' trade union, in 1980. During the political crisis of 1980–1981, industrial stoppages, rising wages, and a shortened working week contributed to Poland's accelerating economic deterioration. Martial law and the economic modifications introduced by the Jaruzelski regime met with stiff social resistance. In 1988 both the authorities and the democratic opposition realized that Poland was sliding down toward a social catastrophe and that a political compromise was necessary.

CHANGES AFTER 1989

The economic problems faced by Poland after the fall of communism were unavoidable. In 1989 the first post-1945 sovereign Polish government inherited a very difficult situation characterized by hyperinflation (over 500 percent in 1990), an enormous foreign debt, hidden unemployment, inefficient industries, and a backward agricultural sector. To improve this situation, Poland moved from the command economy to the free market. In January 1990 the Bal-

Farmer and horse plowing cropland. (David Turnley/Corbis)

cerowicz Plan, also known as "shock therapy," was introduced. The government ended strict price controls, introduced tight monetary policies, started privatization, incorporated Poland into the global economy, and gained the support of the Western powers and the International Monetary Fund, which led to a debt restructuring advantageous to Poland.

The transition from the communist economy to a free market one was implemented harshly and rapidly without any educational or propaganda campaign. Initially, Western powers invested little in Poland. The strategy, designed by then finance minister Leszek Balcerowicz, included several new elements, such as the liberalization of domestic prices, rising imports, a tightening of enterprises' pay structures and of financial policy, the introduction of interest rates above the rate of inflation, the stabilization of the zloty against the dollar, and the introduction of zloty exchangeability. The banking and credit systems were reformed, and new capital and labor markets were created. In July 1990 the Sejm accepted privatization laws. In July 1991 the parliament introduced the income tax for private persons and, in 1992, the value added tax (VAT). Initially, the sudden introduction of free market principles generated a recession, but the recession was followed by an accelerating recovery. The shock therapy stimulated domestic competition. The private sector

became the principal agent of economic growth. The budget deficit was drastically reduced; perhaps more importantly, inflation dropped to 43 percent in 1992 and continued to fall. Foreign creditors reduced Poland's debt by 50 percent; the Warsaw Stock Exchange was opened in 1991, and the fully convertible zloty was denominated in 1995. The Polish economy stabilized, opened to the world, and in a relatively short time became one of the most dynamically developing economies of Europe. Between 1990 and 1998, average annual real growth in Polish gross domestic product amounted to 4.4 percent, which was the best result in Central Europe.

CONTEMPORARY CHALLENGES

Despite the heady days that followed the collapse of the Soviet empire and the return of true independence to Poland, over a decade later, even given the tremendous progress in many areas of society, Poland's transition from a Soviet bloc state to a European one continues to confront numerous challenges.

Poland's entry into the European Union (EU) in 2004 constitutes the most serious challenge to the entire Polish society. Poland has to adjust her laws and political and economic realities to Western European standards. In many fields, this adjustment will be a difficult operation. Some parts of Poland will be the poorest regions in the EU, and Poland's eastern border will be the eastern border of the united Europe.

Poland's agriculture is the most challenging issue, one that constituted a particularly difficult topic in the EU talks. About 27 percent of the Polish population works in or is maintained by agriculture (and contributes only 3.4 percent to the GDP), as compared with between 2 and 4 percent of the population in the most developed countries. Most Polish farms are small, lack modern equipment, and are barely able to produce for the market. They are destined to lose the competition against Western producers. Numerous Polish peasants will have to abandon their farms and join the army of unemployed. It appears that nobody in Poland has a solution to this problem. Populist and peasant politicians try to defend the traditional agriculture or manipulate this issue to win the votes of the threatened and immobile Polish peasants. Supporters of the free market economy and European integration are often accused of killing the Polish peasantry. A terrible choice has appeared: to modernize and quickly develop the country or to defend and maintain unproductive peasants.

Frequently, people do not realize that the situation in the agriculture is another burden inherited from years of communism. Immediately after World War II, in 1944 and 1945, the Communists, backed by the Red Army, introduced a radical land reform in Poland. The reform was motivated by political rather than economic reasons. The newly established communist authorities badly needed popular support. They did not have it in the Polish cities. Therefore, they were looking for this support in the countryside. The communists bribed the peasantry, dividing the estates of the landed gentry and the big farms of the so-called kulaks, the wealthy peasant farmers, and giving the land to the poor peasants. The communists did not worry about the economic consequences of this reform, because they intended to collectivize Polish agriculture anyway. In fact, however, they did not manage to collectivize agriculture, and Poland was left with antiquated, inefficient, nonmechanized small farms. In some parts of Poland, especially in former German territory in the west and in the north, where the Polish peasantry did not live before the war, the communist authorities established large state agricultural farms. Today, these regions constitute an area of economic and social disaster. The state agricultural farms went bankrupt, leaving their employees without work and on welfare. In some regions unemployment reaches thirty percent.

At the same time, the state will not be able to subsidize heavy industry and coal mining in the long run. Poland still remains one of the world's largest coal producers, but the coal sector provides only 3.7 percent of total industry sales. A similar situation exists in the steel industry, and in 1992 government consultants recommended the closure of half of the country's twenty-five steelworks by 2002. This has not happened, since, as in the agriculture, there are no new jobs for coal miners and steel mills workers. Therefore, the state is forced to subsidize these unproductive enterprises, which makes the state budget even tighter.

An extremely tight budget has painful consequences. The economy in Poland is divided into two parts: the private sector and the state sector. The private sector thrives: its employees earn good wages and live better every day. Simultaneously, however, the people who receive their salaries from the state budget are frequently grossly underpaid. Physicians, nurses, teachers, policemen, and clerks earn less in a month than a relatively modest businessman earns in one day. Sometimes, a university professor receives a paycheck several times smaller than his wife, who might work as a secretary in a private enterprise. As a consequence of all these problems, there is a great deal of frustration in Poland. Strikes, protest demonstrations, and blockades of railways and roads are almost an everyday occurrence.

The Polish health service is also going through a crisis, and the major healthcare reform initiated in 1999 has been unpopular. Hospitals, like schools, universities, theaters, public transportation, police, and other institutions maintained by the state budget, work poorly and are in bad shape.

Some Polish cities have changed so much that they are unrecognizable to someone who left them ten years ago. At the same time, however, little provincial towns and workers' districts in large cities have not changed at all; Polish standards of living are low, and life expectancy at birth in 2001 was 70.2 years for males and 78.4 years for females, compared with an EU average of 75.3 and 81.4 years, respectively. The birthrate fell sharply in the 1990s, and the fertility rate is continuing to decline.

Poland's economic situation is also affected by bad relations with Russia. In January 2002 the Polish government expelled nine Russian diplomats for spying. In February, young Polish anarchists, protesting against the war in Chechnya, broke into the Russian consulate in Poznań, tore up a Russian flag, and covered the walls of the building with swastikas. The Russians recalled their ambassador from Poland and commented on the incident in Poznań in a manner that recalled the Soviet phraseology of the Brezhnev era. Poles are also afraid that the union of Russia and Belarus might have negative consequences for them. However, the biggest Polish fear is that Russia will "unite" with Ukraine too. Poland considers this country a strategic partner, but Polish businessmen are afraid to invest there because, exactly as is the case with Russia, they think it is too risky. Both Russia and Ukraine are afraid that with Poland entering the European Union the eastern border of Poland will become the "Belgian curtain," leaving them out of Europe. Poland has already introduced a visa regime for travelers from its non-EU neighbors. The Kaliningrad region constitutes a problem, since after the EU enlargement (including the Baltic states), the area will be a Russian enclave within the EU. The Russian authorities have asked Poland and Lithuania for special transit rights to access Kaliningrad, but the request has been rejected.

In addition to the challenges facing the overall economy, Poland faces numerous other problems. Violent crime has risen sharply since the fall of communism, and organized crime has appeared. Unemployment is especially prevalent among young people who, because of lack of housing as well as unemployment, find it difficult to start families. Finally, the infrastructure (from railroads to the road network) continues to impede economic development; most of the nation's transportation needs a major upgrade, which would require both time and the allocation of scarce resources.

SELECTIVE BIBLIOGRAPHY

Barnett, Clifford R. *Poland: Its People, Its Society, Its Culture.* New York: Grove Press, 1958.

Bethell, Nicholas. *The War Hitler Won: The Fall of Poland, September 1939.* New York: Holt, Rinehart and Winston, 1972.

Biskupski, Mieczysław B. *The History of Poland.* Westport, CT: Greenwood Press, 2000.

Brückner, Aleksander. *Dzieje Kultury Polskiej* (A History of Polish Culture). 4 vols. Warsaw: Książka i Wiedza, 1958.

Burek, Ryszard, ed. *Poland: An Encyclopedic Guide.* Warsaw: Polish Scientific Publishers PWN, 2000.

Central Intelligence Agency. "Poland." In *The World Factbook,* http://www.cia.gov/cia/publications/geos/pl.html (accessed 15 July 2004).

Cieplak, Tadeusz N., ed. *Poland Since 1956.* New York: Twayne, 1972.

Coutouvidis, John, and Jaime Reynolds. *Poland, 1939–1947.* Leicester, UK: Leicester University Press, 1986.

Czerwiński, E. J., ed. *Dictionary of Polish Literature.* Westport, CT: Greenwood, 1994.

Davies, Norman. *God's Playground: A History of Poland.* 2 vols. New York: Columbia University Press, 1982.

———. *Heart of Europe: The Past in Poland's Present.* New York: Oxford University Press, 2001.

———. *Rising '44: "The Battle for Warsaw."* London: Macmillan, 2003.

Economist Intelligence Unit. "Country Profile 2002—Poland," http://www.eiu.com (accessed 15 July 2004).

European Commission. "Relations with Poland," http://europa.eu.int/comm/enlargement/poland/index.htm (accessed 27 July 2004).

Falk, Barbara J. *The Dilemmas of Dissidence in East-Central Europe.* Budapest: Central European University, 2003.

Garton Ash, Timothy. *The Polish Revolution: Solidarity, 1980–1982.* London: Granta Books, 1991.

Grodziski, Stanisław, Jerzy Wyrozumski and Marian Zgórniak. *Wielka Historia Polski* (A Great History of Poland), vols. 1–10. Cracow: Fogra, 1998–2001.

Gross, Jan T. *Revolution from Abroad: The Soviet Conquest of Poland's Western Ukraine and Western Belorussia.* Princeton: Princeton University Press, 2002.

Groth, Alexander J. *People's Poland: Government and Politics.* San Francisco: Chandler, 1972.

Jędruch, Jacek. *Constitutions, Elections and Legislatures of Poland, 1493–1993.* New York: Hippocrene Books, 1998.

Kancelaria Sejmu. "Deputies," *The Sejm,* http://www.sejm.gov.pl/english/poslowie/posel.html (accessed 27 July 2004).

Karpiński, Jakub. *Trzecia Niepodległość: Najnowsza historia Polski* (The Third Independence: The Contemporary History of Poland). Warsaw: Świat Książki, 2001.

Keegan, John. *The Battle for History: Re-Fighting World War Two.* Toronto: Vintage Books, 1995.

Kersten, Krystyna. *The Establishment of Communist Rule in Poland, 1943–1948.* Berkeley: University of California Press, 1991.

Korboński, Andrzej. *Politics of Socialist Agriculture in Poland, 1945–1960.* New York: Columbia University Press, 1965.

Korboński, Stefan. *The Polish Underground State: A Guide to the Underground, 1939–1945.* New York: Columbia University Press, 1978.

Landau, Zbigniew, and Jerzy Tomaszewski. *The Polish Economy in the Twentieth Century.* London: Croom Helm, 1985.

Lerski, George J. *Historical Dictionary of Poland, 966–1945.* Westport, CT: Greenwood Press, 1996.

Lubiński, Marek, ed. *Poland: International Economic Report 2001/2002.* Warsaw: Warsaw School of Economics, 2002.

Lukas, Richard C. *Forgotten Holocaust: The Poles under German Occupation, 1939–1944.* New York: Hippocrene Books, 1990.

Lukowski, Jerzy, and Hubert Zawadzki. *A Concise History of Poland.* Cambridge: Cambridge University Press, 2001.

Macmillan, Margaret. *Paris 1919.* New York: Random House, 2002.

Maik, Wieslaw. *Polska* (Poland). Poznań: Kurpisz, 2000.

Matynia, Andrzej. "Contemporary Polish Art." In *Poland Today—Culture.* Polish Information Agency, 1998, http://www.poland-cmbassy.si/eng/culture/todayart.htm (accessed 27 July 2004).

Michta, Andrew. *Red Eagle: The Army in Polish Politics, 1944–1988.* Stanford, CA: Hoover Institution Press, 1990.

Miłosz, Czesław. *The History of Polish Literature.* Berkeley: University of California Press, 1983.

Ministry of Foreign Affairs of the Republic of Poland. "Poland in Brief." http://www.msz.gov.pl/mszpromo/index_en.htm (accessed 15 July 2004).

Narkiewicz, Olga. *The Green Flag: Polish Populist Politics, 1867–1970.* London: Croom Helm, 1976.

Podgórecki, Adam. *Polish Society.* Westport, CT: Praeger, 1994.

Reynolds, Jaime. "'Lublin' versus 'London'—The Party and the Underground Movement in Poland, 1944–1945." *Journal of Contemporary History,* vol. 16, no. 4 (1981): 617–648.

Sanford, George. *Poland: The Conquest of History.* Amsterdam: Harwood Academic, 1999.

Sanford, George, and Adriana Gozdecka-Sanford. *Historical Dictionary of Poland.* Metuchen, NJ: Scarecrow Press, 1994.

Snyder, Timothy. *The Reconstruction of Nations: Poland, Ukraine, Lithuania, Belarus, 1569–1999.* New Haven: Yale University Press, 2003.

"Special Report: Poland and the EU." *The Economist,* 30 August 2003, pp. 16–18.

Toczyński, Tadeusz, ed. *Statistical Yearbook of the Republic of Poland, 2003.* Warsaw: Central Statistical Office, 2003.

Suchodolski, Bogdan. *A History of Polish Culture.* Warsaw: Interpress, 1986.

Szajkowski, Bogdan. *Next to God, Poland: Politics and Religion in Contemporary Poland*. London: Frances Pinter, 1983.

Taras, Raymond. *Consolidating Democracy in Poland*. Boulder: Westview Press, 1995.

Tworzecki, Hubert. *Parties and Politics in Post-1989 Poland*. Boulder: Westview Press, 1996.

U.S. Department of State. "Background Note: Poland," http://www.state.gov/r/pa/ei/bgn/2875.htm (accessed 27 July 2004).

Wandycz, Piotr S. *The Price of Freedom*. London: Routledge, 1992.

———. *The Lands of Partitioned Poland, 1795–1918*. Seattle: University of Washington Press, 1974.

Wieniewski, Ignacy. *Heritage: The Foundation of Polish Culture*. Toronto: Canadian Polish Congress, 1981.

Wikimedia Foundation. "Politics of Poland." *Wikipedia: The Free Encyclopedia,* http://en.wikipedia.org/wiki/Politics_of_Poland (accessed 27 July 2004).

Wróbel, Piotr. *Historical Dictionary of Poland, 1946–1996*. Westport, CT: Greenwood Press, 1998.

———. *The Devil's Playground: Poland in World War II*. Montreal: The Canadian Foundation for Polish Studies, 2000.

"Wyniki spisu powszechnego [2002]" (The [2002] General Census Data). *Gazeta Wyborcza*, 26 November 2002. http://www.gazeta.pl.

Zamoyski, Adam. *The Polish Way: A Thousand-Year History of the Poles and Their Culture*. London: John Murray, 1987.

CHRONOLOGY

180,000 B.C.E.	earliest traces of men on the territories of future Poland.
4000–1800 B.C.E.	Neolithic cultures.
2500 B.C.E.	Beginnings of agriculture.
1800–400 B.C.E.	Bronze Age.
600	First Iron Age cultures appear.
ca. 550 B.C.E.	Construction of the Biskupin stronghold.
ca. 500 B.C.E.	Invasion of Asian Scythians.
ca. 400 B.C.E.	Celtic tribes appear north of the Carpathians.
100–200 C.E.	Migration of Germanic tribes.
400–460	Rise and fall of the empire of the Huns in Central Europe.
550–750 C.E.	Asian Avars control Central Europe.
ca. 820 C.E.	Establishment of the Greater Moravian Reich (which included a part of Polish lands).
ca. 830–1370	Piast dynasty in Poland.
ca. 830	Piast dynasty takes power in the tribal state of Polanie in the region of Poznań.
966	Prince Mieszko I accepts baptism and introduces Christianity to his state.
990s	Silesia and the region of Cracow are incorporated into Poland.
1025	Bolesław the Brave (Chrobry) becomes the first king of Poland.
1138	Bolesław the Wrymouthed (Krzywousty) divides Poland among his sons.
1100–1400	The so-called German colonization in Poland.
1226	Teutonic Order is settled in Prussia.
1241	Mongols invade Poland.
1306–1333	Reign of Władysław the Elbow-Short (Łokietek) and reunification of Poland.
1340s	Polish conquest of Red Ruthenia (Halych Principality).
1370	Death of Casimir the Great (Kazimierz Wielki), the last Piast king of Poland.
1370–1385	Reign of Louis d'Anjou of Hungary and his daughter Jadwiga.
1385–1572	The Jagiellonian dynasty in Poland.
1385	Union of Krevo: personal union between Poland and Lithuania.
1410	King Władysław Jagiełło defeats the Teutonic Order at the Battle of Grünwald.
1454–1466	Thirteen Years' War and incorporation of Royal Prussia (the Gdańsk region), formerly controlled by the Teutonic Order, into Poland.
1493	Establishment of a bicameral parliament (Sejm and Senate).
1500s	Renaissance and Reformation in Poland.
1525	Secularization of the Teutonic Order state and its homage to Poland.
1529	Incorporation of Mazovia into the Polish kingdom.
1561	Incorporation of Livonia (today's Latvia) into Poland.
1564	Jesuits arrive in Poland; beginning of Counter-Reformation.
1569	Union of Lublin: closer union between Poland and Lithuania and transfer of Ukraine from the Grand Duchy of Lithuania to the Polish kingdom.
1572	Death of Sigismund II Augustus, the last Jagiellonian on the Polish throne.
1573–1795	The Polish-Lithuanian Commonwealth.
1573	First royal election; Henri de Valois elected.
1596	Union of Brest and the establishment of the Uniate Church.
1605	Polish intervention in Moscow.
1617	Beginning of Swedish wars.
1620	Beginning of Turkish wars.
1648–1657	Chmielnicki (Khmelnytskyi) uprising in Ukraine.
1652	*Liberum veto* used for the first time.
1655–1660	"The Deluge": Swedish invasion of Poland.
1665–1667	Civil war is triggered by the rebellion of Jerzy Lubomirski.
1683	Siege and Battle of Vienna.
1700–1721	Great Northern War.

1704–1710	Stanisław Leszczyński put on the Polish throne by the Swedes.
1717	Silent Parliament; beginning of the Russian protectorate over Poland.
1733–1735	War of Polish Succession.
1768–1772	Bar Confederation: the first anti-Russian uprising.
1772	First partition of Poland.
1788–1792	Four Years' Parliament (Sejm).
1791	Constitution of 3 May, the first European constitution.
1793	Second partition of Poland.
1794	Kościuszko's Uprising.
1795	Third partition of Poland.
1795–1918	The Period of Partitions.
1797	Establishment of the Polish Legion in French Service.
1807	Establishment of the Duchy of Warsaw.
1815	Congress of Vienna: Congress Kingdom of Poland, Grand Duchy of Poznań, and Republic of Cracow are formed.
1830–1831	November Uprising against Russia.
1846	Anti-Austrian uprising in Cracow and jacquerie in Austrian-occupied Galicia.
1848	Anti-Prussian uprising in the Poznań region, the end of the Grand Duchy of Poznań, and the emancipation of the peasants in Galicia.
1863–1864	Anti-Russian January Uprising.
1864	Emancipation of the peasants in Russian-occupied Poland.
1867	Broad political and cultural autonomy is established in Galicia.
1905	Outbreak of revolution in Russia and the former Congress Kingdom.
1914	Beginning of World War I and the establishment of the "Piłsudski Legions."
1915	German-Austrian occupation of the former Russian Poland.
1916	German-Austrian restoration of a puppet Polish kingdom.
1917	Revolutions in and collapse of Russia.
1918	Western powers recognize Poland as an independent state; the collapse of Germany and Austria and the end of World War I.
1918–1939	The Second Polish Republic.
1918–1921	Border wars against Ukraine, Germany, Soviet Russia, Lithuania, and Czechoslovakia.
1920	Battle of Warsaw and the expulsion of the Red Army from Poland.
1921	Peace treaty with Soviet Russia and the March Constitution.
1919, 1920, 1921	Anti-German Silesian uprisings.
1926	Coup d'état of Joseph Piłsudski and the beginning of his dictatorship.
1932	Non-aggression pact with the Soviet Union.
1934	Non-aggression pact with Nazi Germany.
1935	Acceptance of the authoritarian April Constitution and the death of Piłsudski.
1939	British Guarantee for Poland, the Molotov-Ribbentrop Pact, and the Nazi-Soviet invasion of Poland.
1939–1945	World War II.
1939	German and Soviet occupations of Poland.
1940	Closing of the ghetto of Warsaw and most other ghettos in Poland; the Soviets execute almost thirty thousand Polish officers at Katyn and other locations.
1941	Nazi invasion of the Soviet Union; the establishment of diplomatic relations between Moscow and the Polish government in exile in London.
1942	Systematic killing of the Jews starts in Auschwitz.
1943	Soviet Union breaks diplomatic relations with the Polish government in exile; the Warsaw Ghetto Uprising.
1944	Warsaw Uprising; the Soviets eject the Germans from eastern Poland and establish a communist puppet state.
1945–1989	Polish People's Republic.
1945	Western powers recognize the Provisional Government of National Unity in Soviet-occupied Poland.
1947	First postwar parliamentary elections and the establishment of a communist-dominated Sejm.
1948	Forced unification of the Polish political left by the communists; beginning of the collectivization and the Stalinist period.
1949	Poland becomes a member of the Council of Mutual Economic Assistance (Comecon); Stalinist purges in the Polish United Workers' Party (PZPR).
1952	Stalinist constitution accepted by the Sejm.
1953	Stefan Wyszyński, the primate of the Roman Catholic Church in Poland, is arrested.
1955	Warsaw Treaty is signed.
1956	Workers uprising in Poznań and the beginning of de-Stalinization in Poland; Władysław Gomułka becomes the first secretary of the PZPR.
1964	Intellectuals protest against the cultural policies of the regime.
1966	Celebrations of the millennium of Christianity in Poland.
1968	"March events": students' riots and anti-Semitic campaign.
1970	"December events": workers' uprising in Gdańsk and Gdynia; Gomułka is replaced

	by Edward Gierek as first secretary of the PZPR.
1976	"June events": workers' riots in Radom, Ursus, and elsewhere.
1978	Cardinal Karol Wojtyła is elected as Pope John Paul II.
1980	Establishment of Solidarity and the beginning of the Solidarity period.
1981	Martial law is implemented; the beginning of the Jaruzelski regime.
1984	Secret police murders Fr. Jerzy Popiełuszko.
1988	New wave of strikes forces the regime to talk to the opposition.
1989	Round Table Negotiations.
post–1989	Redemocratization and the Third Republic.
1989	Solidarity wins the first postwar partially free parliamentary elections and the first noncommunist government, headed by Tadeusz Mazowiecki, is formed.
1990	Lech Wałęsa wins the presidential elections.
1990	First fully free parliamentary elections; twenty-nine parties enter the Sejm. The Balcerowicz Plan, also known as shock therapy, is introduced in Polish economy.
1993	Postcommunist Left wins the parliamentary elections.
1995	Aleksander Kwaśniewski, a former communist minister, defeats Lech Wałęsa in the presidential elections.
1997	Solidarity Electoral Alliance (AWS) wins the parliamentary elections and establishes new government.
1999	Poland enters NATO.
2000	Solidarity-led governing coalition collapses, and the AWS cabinet becomes a minority government; Aleksander Kwaśniewski is reelected president of Poland.
2001	Postcommunist Left wins parliamentary elections and returns to power.
2004	Poland joins the European Union.

ESTONIA

MEL HUANG

LAND AND PEOPLE

Estonia is one of the most fascinating countries in Europe for many different reasons. Populated by a population not speaking an Indo-European language, advantageously located at the center of a busy trading Baltic Sea, disadvantageously located at a point coveted by regional powers, the small nation has been a significant—though underexamined—focal point of the continent's history.

Lying at an attractive location on the northeastern coast of the Baltic Sea, Estonia rests at a spot naturally fitting a role as a conduit of land-based and sea-based trade in the region. The country is surrounded by the Baltic Sea to its north and west, while the Russian Federation lies to the east across a population border remarkably stable over the centuries, and Latvia lies to the south.

Directly across the Gulf of Finland to the country's north is Finland, the Finno-Ugric kin of Estonia. The short distance between Estonia and Finland, in both geographical and kinship terms, proved to be a vital link throughout the centuries of the chaotic and often unpleasant history of the region. The capitals of the two countries—Tallinn, in Estonia, and Helsinki, in Finland—are in fact separated by only 85 kilometers, one of the closest pairs of capitals anywhere in the world. Numerous ferries and hydrofoils travel the short distance, as well as scheduled flights on airplanes and helicopters for the over 3 million individuals that travel between the two cities annually.

From Tallinn, Latvia's capital Riga is 307 kilometers away, while Russia's St. Petersburg is 395 kilometers away, all linked by major air, road, and rail networks. Sweden's capital Stockholm, 405 kilometers from the capital, is served by normal air and overnight ferry services. The close proximity to large metropolitan areas in neighboring states makes Tallinn a natural hub for transit and travel.

The modern Estonian state is 45,227 square kilometers, a little smaller than the size of a combined Vermont and New Hampshire in the United States or a bit larger than the Netherlands or Denmark. It shares lengthy land borders, totaling 676.8 kilometers, with the Russian Federation and Latvia, as well as maritime borders totaling 768.6 kilometers with Finland, Latvia, and the Russian Federation.

Estonia lies between 57°30'34" and 59°49'12" north latitude, placing it further north than Juneau, Alaska, at about the same latitude

A view of Tallinn's Old Town from Toompea. (Courtesy of Rein Linask)

as the southern tip of Greenland. This northern location brings significant differences in day lengths; for example in the summer, sunlight in the north lasts over eighteen hours a day and in the winter about six hours. However, despite its northern location, its coastal location keeps temperatures mild, and most of its ports do not fully freeze in the winter. The average temperature in 1999 was minus 1.9 degrees Celsius (28.5 degrees Fahrenheit) in January and plus 18.8 degrees Celsius (66 degrees Fahrenheit) in July, while the precipitation in 1999 was 640 millimeters.

The territory of Estonia is rather flat. In fact the highest point in the country is Suur Munamägi (The Great Egg Hill), which only rises 318 meters above sea level—the highest hill in the entire Baltic region. Over 60 percent of Estonia is at an elevation of 0–50 meters above sea level. Earth movements also mean that the northwestern part of the country is rising by about 2.5 millimeters annually.

Inland water accounts for about 6 percent of Estonia's inland territory, or about 2,830 square kilometers. Though many rivers flow through Estonia, most are small in size. The longest rivers are the Pärnu, at 144 kilometers, the Kasari, at 112 kilometers, and the Emajõgi (literally "Mother River") at 101 kilometers. Estonia also features many pockets of inland water, including about 1,500 natural, meteor-created, and man-made lakes. The largest are the

Võrtsjärv at 270 square kilometers, in the south of the country, and Lake Peipsi at 3,555 square kilometers (the fifth largest freshwater lake in Europe), on the border with the Russian Federation (only about half the lake is in Estonian territory). Lake Peipsi has formed a natural boundary between the Estonians and the Russians for centuries, which can be seen in the Russian name for the lake: Chudskoye ozero (Lake Chudski, the term *chud* being an ancient Russian term for Estonians).

One of Estonia's most fascinating features is its many islands, mostly on its western coast. Numbering over 1,500 and accounting for about 10 percent of the country's territory, the different-sized islands hold many different treasures. The two largest islands, Saaremaa at 2,673 square kilometers and Hiiumaa at 980 square kilometers are also popular holiday resorts and retreats, boasting the famous fourteenth-century Bishop's Castle in Kuressaare (the main city on Saaremaa) and the Kõpu Lighthouse (at the northern tip of Hiiumaa), the third oldest continuously functioning lighthouse in the world. Many of the islands also preserve strong local traditions, especially the two most distant and least inhabited islands, the 11.54 square kilometers Ruhnu (population 60) and the 16.4 square kilometers Kihnu (population 513), which even have their own Web sites. Some of the islands also boast strong ties to Sweden, as

A field of Lupine in southeastern Estonia, with a traditional Estonian farmhouse in the background. (Courtesy of Rein Linask)

Swedes have inhabited them for many centuries. Some of the smaller, uninhabited islands serve as nature reserves and have restricted public access for that purpose.

Estonians identify closely with the land; they show the closeness of their relationship with nature in the way they care for the land. Over 80 percent of Estonia's territory is rural or natural territory, ranging from grasslands to farmland and from forests to inland water.

Forests make up some 45 percent of Estonian territory, or just over 20,000 square kilometers. Ironically, due to Soviet agriculture policy, many people abandoned farming, and forests reclaimed the land, more than doubling the forested areas since 1940. There are records of 87 native and about 500 introduced species in the forests. The most common trees found in forests include Scots pine (41 percent), silver and downy birch (28 percent), and Norwegian spruce (23 percent). About a third of the large forested areas are under protection, giving naturalists some of the best examples of primeval forests anywhere in Europe. Forests play a major role in the economy as well, as wood and wood products accounted for 14.5 percent of exports in 1999.

Other natural areas in Estonia include meadowlands, marshes, and bogs. In the meadowlands there exist a wide variety of flora, while in some bog areas the peat thickness reaches seven meters. Peat is also used widely as an energy source, especially in rural areas. The Soomaa (literally Bogland) National Park in the western part of the country has some of the most fascinating examples of bog and peat in Europe. Some 20 percent of Estonian territory can be considered marshland and swamp forests.

Estonia has a rich variety of fauna, totaling over 12,000 different species. Over 11,500 species of invertebrates—including 10,000 documented insects—and 488 vertebrate creatures exist in Estonia today. For example, there are eleven species of amphibians, with some, such as the green toad and crested newt, under protection.

In different bodies of water around Estonia live different types of aquatic creatures, and these bodies of water are usually rich in fish stock. There are some 65 species of fresh and saltwater fish in Estonian waters. Lake Peipsi on the eastern border boasts large numbers of whitefish and a local specialty, the Peipsi smelt, a favorite delicacy when dried and salted. In the southern Võrtsjärv there are large numbers of pike perch and eels, both local delicacies. In the Baltic Sea there are large populations of herring, sprats, and flounder, as well as various shellfish and other aquatic treasures. Estonian waters actually account for 1 percent of the world's fish catch.

There are also a great variety of birds in Estonia, both indigenous and migratory. There are 333 different bird species recorded, and two-thirds of them breed in Estonia. Various resident species include the magpie, black grouse, seagulls, and, of course, the ever present pigeon. Some of the swamplands and isolated islands serve as home for many species, including the golden eagle and the osprey, as well as various ducks and owls. The national bird is the barn swallow, which is depicted on the back of the 500-kroon banknote.

There are 64 species of mammals recorded in Estonia, including the reintroduced red deer and European beaver. Some, however, such as the flying squirrel and European mink, are in danger of extinction. Many of the mammals live in the forests, such as elk (nearly 10,000), deer (30,000), wild boar (11,000), beaver (10,000), lynxes (1000), bears (600), and wolves (200). It is quite common to hear on the news of wildlife, such as a giant elk, wandering into town— sometimes into apartment buildings!

With the wide diversity of species, conservation has been a major part of Estonian thinking for decades. The first nature conservation zone was created on the island of Saaremaa in 1910, and in 1938 the Estonian parliament passed a landmark nature protection law (although it was never put fully into force due to the 1940 Soviet invasion). Today more than 10 percent of Estonia is under some form of protection.

Though not blessed with abundant resources, Estonia does boast large amounts of rocks and minerals, which have played a role in the architecture and economy of the people for centuries. The most common stone found in Estonia is limestone, the national stone. Much of the coastal cliffs are of limestone, with some of the most picturesque cliffs (especially at Ontika) dropping sharply down fifty meters to the Gulf of Finland. There is also a large supply of dolomite, with the best supplies found on the island of Saaremaa.

Estonia does boast a large quantity of oil shale in its northeast. Though burning at a relatively low caloric value (compared to coal or other fossil fuels), the large oil shale supply in Estonia keeps the country self-sufficient in generating electricity. There is also a significant supply of phosphorite and other minerals.

With the urbanization of society in the past century, the size of the agricultural sector has declined. For instance, in 2000 the share of agriculture in Estonia's gross domestic product (GDP) was only 3.3 percent, compared with about 15 percent a decade ago.

In Estonia there are about 12,000 square kilometers of arable land, alongside nearly 3,000 square kilometers of natural grassland, making agricultural land total about 14,300 square kilometers. There are also approximately 12,000 farms in production, with about 6 percent of the population employed in the agriculture sector.

Some of the most important crops are cereals and legumes (over 700,000 tons), potatoes (over 470,000 tons), and vegetables (about 53,000 tons). Other major agricultural products include milk (almost 630,000 tons), meat (about 52,000 tons), eggs (over 250 million), wool (71 tons), and honey (334 tons). There is also a healthy number of livestock: cattle (over 250,000), pigs (over 300,000), sheep and goats (over 32,000), and various poultry (almost 2.4 million).

Generally, Estonia's agricultural sector sustains the country, but trade in agricultural products also account for a part of consumed goods. Only about 7.4 percent of exports and 9.2 percent of imports (in January–August 2001) involved the agriculture sector. The main export items in that period include canned fish (22.7 percent), condensed milk (12.7 percent), fish fillet (11.4 percent), and frozen fish (11.4 percent), while the main imported agricultural goods include tobacco products (5 percent), poultry (4.5 percent), pork (4.1 percent), and sugar (4.1 percent).

Due to high competition in the agricultural sector, as well as the growing European integration process, there has been much encouragement for less traditional farming, such as organic farming, apiculture, and fish farming.

The population of the country, due to various figures such as emigration and a low birthrate, continues to fall. From data taken in the 2000 national census, the total population of Estonia is only 1,356,931. This is a considerable drop from the previous census, taken in 1989, which showed a population of 1,565,622. The 2000 census showed that the birthrate was 9.56 per 1000 inhabitants, compared to a mortality rate of 13.46 per 1000 inhabitants.

Estonia is increasingly becoming an urban society, as the population balance between urban and rural continues to swing further in favor of the former. In 2000 some 69.12 percent of inhabitants lived in urban areas. The capital city of Tallinn, on the northern coast, is the largest city, with 399,850 residents, or 29.25 percent of the national population. This is followed by the southeastern university city of Tartu at 101,240, the northeastern industrial city Narva at 68,538, another northeastern industrial town, Kohtla-Järve, at 47,484 and the southwestern resort town of Pärnu at 44,978 inhabitants. The population density as a whole is about 30 inhabitants per square kilometer. The country is divided into fifteen counties, as well as seven cities.

As for the ethnic breakdown, ethnic Estonians comprise 67.9 percent of the population, followed by Russians at 25.6 percent, Ukrainians at 2.1 percent, Belarusians at 1.2 percent, and Finns at 0.9 percent. The demographic balance between the indigenous and nonindigenous population was at one time a threat to the survival of the Estonian nation. The chart of population balance over the years indicates the massive change caused by Soviet policy of importing Russian-speaking workers following World War II.

Estonia is also a relatively young country, with just over a third of the population 25 or under. The life expectancy of children born in 1999 is 70.82 (65.35 for males, 76.09 for females). The gender balance favors females by about a 54–46 ratio.

One of the most unusual things about Estonians is their language, a member of the Finno-Ugric family. Estonian, like Finnish, sits on the Finnic side of the branch, and Hungarian lies on the Ugric side, the two branches being distantly related. The Finno-Ugric languages are not related to Indo-European languages, though centuries of coexistence have allowed for many loan words and structures to be interchanged between the two families.

Among the various Finno-Ugric speaking peoples, only Estonians, Finns, and Hungarians have reached statehood.

Table 1

Censuses	1922	1934	1959	1970	1979	1989	2000
Total	1,107 million	1,126 million	1,197 million	1,356 million	1,466 million	1,566 million	1,357 million
Ethnic Estonians	970 million	993 million	893 million	925 million	948 million	963 million	921 million
Percentage	87.7%	87.7%	74.6%	68.2%	64.7%	61.5%	67.9%

Other large Finno-Ugric peoples generally live in northern Scandinavia (such as the Sami), or in the Russian Federation (including the Komi, Udmurt, and Mari, among others). Many of them are dying out due to assimilation—very much the problem in Finno-Ugric areas in the Russian Federation due to linguistic Russification.

One of the smallest remaining Finno-Ugric groups is the Livonians, once a dominant group in present-day Latvia. Only a handful of people speak Livonian today, though Estonia has made efforts to help keep the kindred language alive.

The few thousand Setu people, living on both sides of the Estonian-Russian border around the Russian border town of Pechory (Petseri in Estonian, formerly a part of Estonia), are closely related to the Estonians. Most linguists consider the Setu language a distinct language, though it is related to the Võru dialect of Estonian. The Setu people are of Orthodox background, since for most of their history—unlike the Estonians—they have been under Russian rule.

As members of a small nation, Estonians have always excelled at languages. Most Estonians speak several foreign languages. Estonians can understand Finnish due to its closeness to Estonian, and Russian was a mandatory subject at school during the Soviet years. With most of today's television programs coming from Hollywood, most Estonians—especially the younger generation—speak English as well. One advantage for modern Estonians in learning languages is that most foreign-language programs are not voice-dubbed into Estonian; rather, Estonia follows the Nordic practice of subtitling the programs and keeping all the voices in the programs' original language. This is drastically different from other nearby countries such as Latvia, Russia, and Germany, which still overdub the voices into the local language.

Religion still plays a significant role in the life of Estonia, though as in the rest of Northern Europe, its role is diminishing. During the five-decade Soviet occupation, religion was severely discouraged by the occupying powers. Many of the most beautiful churches in Estonia, some over 600 years old, were turned into museums, storage units, or even "museums" celebrating atheism. However, since the restoration of independence in 1991, the faithful have once again been allowed to actively practice religion with no fear of government retribution.

The Roman Catholic Church gained its major footholds at the start of the thirteenth century in the Baltic lands, as both clerics and warriors forced the natives to convert by the sword. Since the Reformation in the sixteenth century, however, the Lutheran Church has played the most important role in the country's spiritual life. In 2000 there were about 180,000 official members of the Estonian Lutheran Church. Some other Protestant denominations have also grown, including Baptists and Methodists, and a small number of Catholic believers have remained. These denominations boast official membership of between 1,000 and 5,000.

There is also a community of so-called Old Believers, those who fled Russia in the seventeenth century following reforms to the Russian Orthodox Church; these Old Believers numbered about 5,000 in the year 2000. In fact, the Baltic lands served as a sanctuary for the Old Believers for centuries, with the strongest communities existing in Estonia and neighboring Latvia.

There are also many followers of Orthodoxy in Estonia not limited to particular ethnic groups. Like the Finns, many Estonians converted to Russian Orthodoxy in the nineteenth century after promises of preferential treatment by their Russian rulers. In 1920 the Estonian Apostolic Orthodox Church (EAÕK) was established and recognized by the Russian Orthodox Church. Three years later the Ecumenical Patriarchate in Constantinople issued a *tomos* (an ecclesiastical edict) bringing the EAÕK under Constantinople, but with extensive autonomy. About 20 percent of the population in 1941 identified themselves with the Orthodox faith, including Estonia's first president, Konstantin Päts (1938–1940).

When the Soviet Union invaded and took control of all aspects of daily life in 1944, the EAÕK leadership fled to Sweden and set up the church in exile. The following year officials from the Moscow-based church dismissed those EAÕK officials who had remained in Estonia and placed Estonia's Orthodox followers under Moscow's authority.

Following the 1991 restoration of independence, the EAÕK returned and reregistered itself in 1993 as the legal successor of the Interwar EAÕK; in 1996 the Ecumenical Patriarch Bartholomeos I restored the 1923 tomos, bringing the Estonian church back under the authority of officials in Constantinople. Patriarch Aleksius II of the Russian (Moscow) Orthodox Church, himself originally from Estonia, issued a tomos in 1993 placing the Estonian Orthodox Church under Moscow. This caused a split in the church, even though in 1996 Moscow and Constantinople agreed that each parish in Estonia could choose which church to follow. About 18,000 followers chose the EAÕK (under Constantinople), and the rest stayed with the Estonian Orthodox Church (under Moscow).

Islam has also grown in recent years to become one of the largest religions in Estonia. An estimated 10,000 in Estonia are believers in Islam at some level; most having come from

The Estonian Language

There are just over one million Estonian speakers around the world. Outside the country, Estonian speakers live in especially large numbers in Sweden, Canada, the United States, and Australia, most of them having fled the Soviet takeover in the 1940s.

Estonian is rich in vowels, with a limited number of consonant phonemes in use. The vowels are the standard *a, e, i, o, u,* as well as four others: *ä, ö, ü,* and *õ.* Most words are stressed on the first syllable, except a few rare cases of commonly used words (such as *aitäh,* "thanks," where the stress is on the second syllable) or borrowed words (such as *probleem,* "problem"). Lengthening of both vowels and consonants is a major aspect of the language; compare *kus* (where) to *kuus* (six), or even *maja* (house) to *majja* (into the house).

Like all Finno-Ugric languages, Estonian is a highly inflected language. Instead of the reliance on prepositions seen in most modern Indo-European languages, Estonian relies on case endings, fourteen of them to be precise (for example: "church" *(kirik),* "of the church" *(kiriku),* "in the church" *(kirikus),* "into the church" *(kirikusse),* and "from the church" *(kirikust).* Thus the fourteen case endings are not as intimidating as they might sound, since they simply replace prepositions. Verb forms are also much simpler than most other languages, and there is actually no proper future tense in the language.

A common book of prayers with explanatory texts in Estonian, Latvian, and Livonian, published in Lübeck in 1525, is believed to be the first printed matter in Estonian. The first true Estonian book was a compilation of Lutheran catechisms with parallel texts in the south Estonian dialect and Low German printed in 1535. Only fragments of this historic text, compiled by Pastor Simon Wanradt and translator Johann Koell, remain. The first print shops opened in Tartu in 1631 and in Tallinn in 1635, and the number of books published in Estonian reached about forty during the century.

Ironically, the southern dialect is closer to Finnish than the northern. However, the north Estonian dialect was established as the standardized version of the language. Many regional dialects are still spoken today, the most distinct being that of the people of the southeastern Võru region.

Estonian and Finnish are very closely related and are to some extent mutually intelligible. However, due to both sound and grammatical changes, it is much easier for Estonians to understand Finnish than vice versa. Look, for example, at the numbers one through ten in the following table. They are given in Estonian, Finnish, and Hungarian to show the family likeness in the Finno-Ugrian languages, in English and German to show the contrast with the Germanic Indo-European languages, in Lithuanian as an example of a Baltic Indo-European language, and in Polish as an example of a Slavic Indo-European language:

(continues)

Muslim parts of the former Soviet Union, such as Azerbaijan and Central Asia, during the period of Soviet occupation.

With total freedom of religion, other groups have since become active. There are growing numbers of other Christian denominations, such as the Mormons and Jehovah's Witnesses, and Buddhism is also attracting new believers. The Dalai Lama makes frequent visits to Estonia, citing Pühajärv (Holy Lake) in the southern resort town of Otepää as an inspirational site.

The Jewish community in Estonia was small (about 3,000) but very active during the 1920s and 1930s, and international Jewish leaders praised Estonia's policy toward its Jewish community during this period. Unfortunately, during the Nazi occupation of 1941–1944, the small Jewish community was essentially wiped out. Today, the Jewish community is back up to about 3,000, including some of the best-known individuals in the country, such as the highly respected semiotics professor Yuri Lotman, the world-famous conductor Eri Klas, and the media professor and former broadcasting chief Hagi Shein.

Under Soviet occupation, even the displaying of the Estonian flag or the singing of the Estonian national anthem resulted in arrest or even deportation to Siberia. Therefore Estonians feel very passionately about their national symbols. Many are depicted on Estonia's currency, the kroon (crown).

The national flag is a tricolor of even horizontal stripes of blue, black, and white. The flag originated actually as the symbol of a university student fraternity, the Estonian Students Union (EÜS), which was consecrated in Otepää on 4 July 1884. It was adopted as the national flag on 21 November 1918, nine months after the country's declaration of independence.

The country's coat of arms is a golden shield background with three blue lions, flanked by golden oak branches. The coat of arms, adopted on 25 June 1925, was actually derived from the old city coat of arms for the capital, Tallinn. The oldest imprint of this coat of arms dates back to 1294, when it was given to Tallinn by the Danish king, Valdemar II. The lion design resembles that on the coat of arms of the English national football squad.

The Estonian Language *(continued)*

English	Estonian	Finnish	German	Hungarian	Lithuanian	Polish
one	üks	yksi	eins	egy	vienas	jeden
two	kaks	kaksi	zwei	kettő	du	dwa
three	kolm	kolme	drei	három	trys	trzy
four	neli	neljä	vier	négy	keturi	cztery
five	viis	viisi	fünf	öt	penki	pięć
six	kuus	kuusi	sechs	hat	šeši	sześć
seven	seitse	seitsemän	sieben	hét	septyni	siedem
eight	kaheksa	kahdeksan	acht	nyolc	aštuoni	osiem
nine	üheksa	yhdeksän	neun	kilenc	devyni	dziewięć
ten	kümme	kymmenen	zehn	tíz	dešimt	dziesięć

The similarities between Estonian and Finnish are clearly visible, and the difference between them and the Indo-European languages is easily noticeable. But what happens commonly is that Estonian words tend to have one syllable less, since Finnish words generally need to end in vowels (or *n* or *s*). The following may serve as examples:

English	Estonian	Finnish
day	päev	päivä
island	saar	saari
land	maa	maa
man	mees	mies
port	sadam	satama
sauna	saun	sauna
sea	meri	meri
telephone	telefon	puhelin

The last example also shows how Estonian tends to borrow more words than the ultra-conservative Finnish. English words like "show" have penetrated the language despite breaking numerous Estonian spelling rules; some tried to make that word fit with the alternate spelling *šou,* but this looks quite odd even in Estonian.

One other peculiarity that Estonia and Finland share (aside from their unique languages and cultures) is the same melody for their national anthems. The melody was written by Finnish-German Fredrik Pacius in 1843, and became the Estonian anthem following the 1918 declaration of independence. The words to "Mu isamaa, mu õnn ja rõõm" (My Native Land, My Joy and Delight) were written by beloved Estonian poet Johann Voldemar Jannsen and put into the song for the first of the celebrated Estonian song festivals in 1869.

Other unofficial symbols of the country, aside from those mentioned above, include the national bird (the barn swallow), the national flower (the purple-blue cornflower), the national tree (the oak), the national rock (limestone), and others.

HISTORY

The history of Estonia is long and complicated, and the understanding of it is key to understanding the Estonian people. For centuries the Estonians languished under foreign domination, ranging from Germanic crusaders to expansionist Sweden, from Russia (trying to transform the country into Russia's "window to the West" to the Nazis (who saw it as *Lebensraum*), from resurgent Poland-Lithuania to the Soviet empire. During only about 4 percent of the past 800 years have Estonians enjoyed their independence.

The continuing saga of foreign domination shaped the Estonian nation through the centuries, both positively and negatively. The remarkable thing is that despite over 700 years of foreign domination (and, at times, active suppression), the Estonians kept their national identity alive and well. It is with this baggage, however, that Estonians today remain fiercely independent-minded and proud of their achievements.

This history of foreign domination is perhaps why Estonia's return to Europe is so remarkable. In 2004 Estonia rejoined the Western world fully by joining NATO and becoming a full member of the European Union. Locked into a secure Europe, Estonia can now place its full attention on exploring the future—something it has never had the luxury of doing in the last eight centuries.

The Cornflower—Estonia's national flower. (Courtesy of Rein Linask)

THE ANCIENT ERA (PRE-HISTORY TO 1200)

Most experts believe that the regional thaw in the ninth millennium B.C.E. created hospitable conditions for human settlements in the territory of modern-day Estonia. The warmer climate allowed forests to appear and wildlife to inhabit the region, which eventually led to human settlements. Archaeological discoveries place the earliest settlements at about 7500 B.C.E.

Several sites belonging to the so-called Kunda culture, named after the town near which a major discovery was made, have been discovered, including the earliest find in Pulli. There is no consensus regarding the exact origins of the Paleolithic (ca. 7500–4000) inhabitants of Estonia, though most believe they originated from somewhere in the south.

Closer in origin to modern-day Estonians were the inhabitants in the Neolithic period (ca. 4000–2500). The people of this era are classified in two separate groups, which most experts believe combined to form modern-day Estonians. The first group, believed to be from the east, is classified as the comb-pottery culture, named for the dis-

tinctive décor on earthenware discovered from excavations. These settlers are also thought to have brought with them among other things the Finno-Ugric language, the precursor of languages like Estonian and Finnish. The second group, arriving in the late Neolithic period, is called the boat-ax people, from the shape of the ax-heads discovered from archeological digs. Items related to the boat-ax people are found further south, and they are believed to be the primary ancestors of modern-day Balts, the Latvians and Lithuanians.

The absence of tin and copper (components of bronze) makes it difficult to distinguish the Bronze Age (ca. 2500–500 B.C.E.) when considering Estonia; rather, many ancient historians and archaeologists examine the period as one of transition from hunting and gathering and fishing to agriculture. The bronze items originating in this period that have been found were imported, though most items from this era remain stone-based. Despite that, this era remains important, as the transition to agriculture also saw the construction of fortified settlements. That also meant a sharper settlement pattern, which split the forefathers of the Estonians, north of the Daugava River (bisecting modern-day Latvia), and the ancestors of the Latvians and Lithuanians in the south. The so-called Pre-Roman Iron Age (ca. 500 B.C.E. to 1) saw some importing of crude iron tools, but there was no sharp change in society.

Though evidence hints at an earlier modest start to iron smelting, the Roman Iron Age (ca. 1 to 400 C.E.) saw the gradual replacement of stone with iron in Estonia. Though the supply was limited, iron ore was found in bogs, and smelting and forging activities increased. This activity also increased foreign contacts and trade, as indicated by Roman and other ancient coins found in archaeological digs. Even the Roman historian Tacitus spoke of the people living on the Baltic coast as "Aestii" (probably based on the Estonian name for Estonia, "Eesti," though experts remain uncertain).

The Middle Iron Age (ca. 400–800) represented a more chaotic era, with mass movements of peoples throughout the region, upsetting trade patterns established in the previous era. A large number of fortresses were built during this era to deal with land invasions from Slavs and maritime raids from Scandinavian Vikings. Viking chroniclers depicted major confrontations in Estonia, where even some Scandinavian kings fell in battle.

The Late Iron Age (ca. 800–1200) saw the continuation of armed conflicts, but also the revitalization of commerce. Slavic forces increased their raids into Estonia starting in the second millennium, and the area around Tartu fell several times to invading armies. These raids forced Estonians into building some larger fortifications, and some of their ruins remain standing today. Chroniclers also noted the activities of raids into Scandinavia by Estonian Vikings; one significant attack by Estonians (and likely other inhabitants of the eastern Baltic coast) sacked the key Swedish town of Sigtuna in 1187.

Prior to the medieval period, there was no centralized administration in Estonia. The main unit of administration was the *kihelkond* (parish), a loose grouping of villages led by an elder. Increasingly, loose groupings of parishes formed a *maakond* (region), though their consolidation was fragmented and haphazard. Though some of the regions cooperated with each other, the lack of a unified organization hindered joint resistance to attack, thus leading to the centuries of foreign occupation.

FOREIGN POWERS TAKE HOLD (1201–1238)

Increasing trade activities with German merchants during the Late Iron Age also brought pagan Estonians to the attention of Christian preachers. The first serious attempt to preach to the inhabitants of the eastern Baltic coast came around 1184, with the arrival of the Augustinian monk Meinhard, who was also ordained the Bishop of Livonia two years later. Meinhard was successful in baptizing Livonians (Finno-Ugric kin of the Estonians) and Lettgallians (a Baltic tribe that later formed the core of the Latvian people). However, attempts to baptize Estonians failed during that period. Meinhard's successor Berthold attempted a crusade in 1198 but was killed in the early campaign.

In many respects therefore, the real beginning of the period did not come until the arrival of the canon of Bremen, Albert, who was named as the third bishop of Livonia. Albert, along with a powerful army of crusaders, founded the city of Riga in 1201 on the site of a small Livonian fishing village. A crusading order, the Order of the Brethren of the Sword, was created the year after with the goal of forcibly converting the pagans. In 1204 Pope Innocent III confirmed the order in its crusading mission and the first serious invasion into Estonian lands happened in 1208. Much of what we know from this era comes from Henry of Livonia, whose chronicles are the best-known records from this era.

The order, along with their Livonian and Lettgallian allies, launched a series of attacks into southern Estonian regions. Slavic raids from the east exacerbated the situation in Estonian lands, especially when the Slavs cooperated with the order. The Estonians, for their part, counterattacked into both Slavic and order territory, which led to a three-year armistice with the order in 1211. However, as the armistice ended, the order (as well as their allies) resumed their attacks on the ground and by sea.

By 1215 some southern regions had fallen to the order, and people were forced to undergo baptism. Although Estonians continued to fight back, partly by working with their own Slavic allies, the Battle of St. Matthew's Day on 21 September 1217 saw the biggest setback for Estonian forces. The large army, led by a southern parish leader, Lembitu, the same inspirational leader who had succeeded in several victories against both the order and Slavs, failed in this crucial battle. Lembitu and thousands fell in the battle, and it marked a major turning point in the period.

Though victorious in the battle, Bishop Albert turned to the Danish kingdom for assistance in 1218, an appeal to which Pope Honorius III gave his blessing. The Danish king, Valdemar II, led the attack on northern Estonia, defeating the Estonian forces in June 1219 at the northern fort of Lindanise. Danish folklore tells of how the failing Danish forces were inspired by a red banner with a white cross falling from Heaven, which rallied them to victory; the symbol, the *Dannebrog*, later became Denmark's flag. The Danes built a fortress in Lindanise, which later became known in Estonian as Tallinn (*Taani* means "Danish" and *linn* means "fortress").

By 1220, mainland Estonia was effectively conquered, as the Danes held the northern part of Estonia and the Germans held the southern half. However, seeing the opportunity, Sweden, under youthful King Johan (Sverkersson), launched an attack on the western part of Estonia. His initial victory was, however, short-lived, as a military contingent from the island of Saaremaa decimated the Swedish invading force soon after.

The same Saaremaa force, encouraged by their victory in repelling Danish intentions on their island, led a major revolt across mainland Estonia. Beginning in 1222, the various Estonian regions pooled their military strength, and the counterrevolt began to reap results. By 1223, their combined forces, led by the islanders, had liberated most of Estonia. Only Tallinn remained fully under foreign control, and conquest of that key fortress remained elusive.

With the momentum of the revolt lost, foreign reinforcements began to take back lands liberated. By 1224, the last part of the mainland still under Estonian control, the fortress at Tartu, fell after the third siege undertaken by the order. And, in the winter of 1227, a huge army from the order invaded Saaremaa, successfully taking the island. All Estonian lands fell under foreign rule.

Freeing up its forces in the north, the order pursued further attacks in the south. However, the 1236 Battle of Saule (near modern-day Šiauliai in Lithuania) against the Lithuanians and their allies dealt the Order of the Brethren of the Sword a mortal blow. The weakened order was forced to seek help from the Teutonic Order based in Prussia, becoming in the end simply the Livonian branch of the entire Teutonic Order (and better known from this point onward as the Livonian Order).

Despite its weakened status, the order, now the Livonian Order, continued its aggressive activities. Even before this time, conflict between the order and the ecclesiastic power, which was divided into two bishoprics (with the order's territory bisecting them), had been common. Conflicts also erupted between the order and Danish holdings, a quarrel that even papal envoys failed to help mediate. In the end, the Treaty of Stensby, signed in 1238, ended the disputes, setting the border between the two foreign powers. The lands held by Denmark became known as Estland (Estonia) and the lands held by Germans—both religious and military—became known as Livland (Livonia). Though this one conflict was resolved, the coming era brought continual conflicts that plagued the Estonian territories for centuries.

OLD LIVONIA (1238–1561)

Conflicts were common in the Middle Ages. Uprisings by Estonians against their overlords happened often, and the Livonian Order and their religious counterparts also fought over control of territory. In the meantime, feudalism came to Estonia, as German landowners acquired lands that evolved into manor estates. Urban centers also developed with the immigration of German merchants and the granting of city rights to Tallinn (1248) and Tartu (1262), among others. Some of the architectural gems of both cities originate from this period.

One important development of this period was the growth of trade within the Hanseatic League, an innovative grouping promoting trade in the Baltic Sea region. Tallinn joined the Hanseatic League in the late thirteenth century, becoming one of the most important Hansa towns over the centuries; later Tallinn served as a major point in the trade route from London to Lübeck and Novgorod. Tartu played a major role in the trade route to Pskov, and Viljandi and Pärnu also joined the trading league. The league declined in influence in the sixteenth century, but the trade routes continued despite the league's slump. Many guilds also developed, especially in Tallinn, where some twenty maintained their trade beyond this period.

The Livonian Order, however, faced a continual decline in its power, with some spectacular defeats. The defeat in 1242 on the ice of Lake Peipsi by Alexander Nevsky did establish the lake and the Narva River as the effective border between the Western powers and the Slavs. The order also suffered badly at the 1260 Battle of Durbe. Despite these major defeats, the order also picked on their ecclesiastic partners in conquest, which led to several civil wars between the Germans that lasted into the fourteenth century.

The most significant event of the period came on 23 April 1343, St. George's Day, when a spontaneous revolt began near Tallinn and spread throughout the region. The Estonians manage to win control over most of the region around Tallinn, and then the revolt spread to other regions. Success was fleeting. The order retaliated and eventually won back all the lost territories, even in formerly Danish-held lands. The last of the lost territories—the island of Saaremaa—was retaken in 1345.

Though the St. George's Day Uprising failed, it did leave a lasting mark on Estonia. The Danish crown felt the cost of holding onto this territory to be too great; therefore, in 1346 Denmark sold its Estonian holdings to the Teutonic Order for a reported 19,000 silver Cologne marks. In the following year the master of the Livonian Order was put in control. The entire German-controlled territory was known as Old Livonia.

The Livonian Order suddenly became the ruler of most of Estonian lands, and it thus grew much more powerful than the two bishoprics. The order naturally took advantage of this situation and frequently attacked the bishoprics. Although a conference in Danzig (Gdańsk) in 1397 helped mediate the situation between the order and the ecclesiastic powers in the region, the balance established there held for only a short time, as the historic 1410 Battle of Grünwald saw the combined Lithuanian-Polish army decimate the Teutonic Order, neutralizing the Teutonic Knights as a regional power. The Livonian Order, as a branch of the Teutonic Order, suffered similarly, and the religious powers regained much of their power in the region.

Rapid expansionism all but ended for the order, not just from its weakened status but also from the final conversion of Lithuania and Samogitia (the Lithuanian highlands) in the early fifteenth century. Some normalcy developed in the region, as administrative units were organized. In the 1420s regional assemblies (*Landtage* in German) began meeting, as an early provincial government began to develop.

However, peace did not last, especially with occasional skirmishes with the Slavs from the east. The conflicts intensified with the rise of Muscovy, which began uniting the Slavic lands into what was to become the Russian Empire. The raids increased in frequency, but Moscow could not hold onto its territorial gains for any real length of time. The order, on the other hand, also claimed a few victories of its own, including the 1502 victory at the Battle of Lake Smolina. This battle resulted in a tense peace in the region for a short time, before Moscow's ambitions again led to full-scale war.

Shortly thereafter, another challenge to the power of the rulers of Estonia appeared, this time in the form of the Reformation, which reached the Estonian lands soon after it began in the West (arriving via Riga in 1523). While both the order and the ecclesiastical powers in the Baltic states remained steadfastly loyal to the Roman Church, urban centers increasingly shifted toward Protestantism. This split led to violence against Catholics and the Catholic Church. (Ironically, as religious violence spread, so too did culture, as this era also saw the first known printed text in Estonian, a book of Lutheran catechisms printed in 1535. There may have been earlier works in the early part of the sixteenth century, but no proof survives.)

At the same time, Moscow's territorial aspirations led to a new set of conflicts. Moscow's ruler, Ivan IV (Ivan the Terrible) looked at expansion toward the Baltic Sea, where his empire already bordered Estonia and other German territory in the Baltics; the Livonian Wars (1558–1583) began on 22 January 1558, as Russian forces invaded and crippled the already weak defenses of the order. The attack led to a full invasion campaign in the spring, with the key trading town and fortress of Narva falling in May. Tartu fell in July, marking the total collapse of the bishopric based in the southern Estonian city. A counter-campaign in 1559 by the order failed to push the Russians out of Tartu. Sensing the worst, the bishop based in Haapsalu chose to sell his bishopric to King Frederik II of Denmark for 30,000 thalers. Frederik II gave the territory to his young brother Duke Magnus, who landed with an army on Saaremaa in 1560.

The order's army attempted to attack the invading Russian forces, but was summarily defeated. The order's tenuous hold on power slipped further as Estonians revolted throughout the country. Despite reinforcements from Poland-Lithuania in 1560—effectively the overlords over the order since their collapse a century ago—the order's life span was limited. A devastating defeat near Härgmäe in 1560 marked the order's swan song.

Meanwhile, another power, the Swedish kingdom under King Erik XIV, entered the fray in 1561. Supported by many nobles in Tallinn, the Swedish army landed and took the city. By the summer, Sweden gained control over all of the northern part of the Estonian lands. The withered order now collapsed completely, as the master of the Livonian

Order and the archbishop of Riga both swore full allegiance to the Polish-Lithuanian crown, an action that marked the end of Old Livonia after more than three centuries of German control.

THE RISE OF SWEDEN (1561–1699)

Old Livonia was gone, but the wars continued. The Estonian lands were still divided between Denmark, Sweden, Russia, and Poland-Lithuania, and the four states continued to war over the ruins of Old Livonia. The Nordic War (1563–1570) erupted between Sweden and Denmark, and the conflict extended into their Baltic holdings. Poland-Lithuania had allied itself with Denmark, thus adding an extra dimension to the conflict. In 1568 a revolt in Sweden saw the installment of Johan III, the brother-in-law of the Polish king, Sigismund II Augustus, as king. Poland-Lithuania in 1569 also restructured and formed a commonwealth, replacing the dynastic union that had ruled both countries for almost two hundred years. With this change in regional dynamics, a peace was concluded in 1570 between Sweden and Denmark. However, this peace did not mark the end of the conflicts. Duke Magnus, who had a falling out with his brother, King Frederik II of Denmark, continued to assert his powers by attempting to form alliances with other powers, including Ivan the Terrible of Russia. Though Magnus failed in his earlier attempts to form an alliance, which angered his Russian overlord, by 1576 he (along with his Russian and Tatar allies) had taken control of a vast majority of Estonian lands. Poland-Lithuania was driven out of the region, while Swedish forces were confined to the area around Tallinn. Although some peasant attacks on Russian forces, especially one led by Estonian peasant Ivo Schenkenberg, succeeded in slowing the Russians, Russia had become the most significant power in the land.

Once Duke Magnus outlived his usefulness, Ivan the Terrible removed him from the picture. However, this change also coincided with the rise of Stephen Batory as the new king of Poland-Lithuania in the late 1570s, and the new king attacked the Russian forces, inaugurating a new phase of the war and adding a dimension to it. Sweden took advantage of Russia's second front by pushing out from Tallinn. By 1581, Sweden had recovered all of its lost northern Estonian lands, and carried the fighting into Russian territory. The two-front fighting cost Ivan the Terrible his conquests, and he concluded a truce with Poland in 1582, ceding the southern part of Old Livonia (including southern Estonian lands) to Poland-Lithuania. A year later the Livonian Wars formally ended with a peace treaty between Russia and Sweden, a treaty by which Sweden made substantial gains in Russian territory.

Although the Estonian lands were divided into three empires at the Livonian Wars' conclusion, stability was short-lived. Sweden controlled the north, Poland-Lithuania the south, and Denmark the island of Saaremaa. The inevitable conflict among the three broke out in 1600, as the Swedish king, Karl IX, advanced to take territory from Poland-Lithuania. War raged on and off well into the reign of the new Swedish King Gustav II Adolf (Gustavus Adolphus,

crowned in 1611), as the new king took Riga in 1621 and Tartu in 1625. Poland-Lithuania sued for peace, and the Treaty of Altmark handed all territories north of the Daugava River to Sweden.

Sweden and Denmark, the competing Nordic powers, also went to war in 1643. After two years of fighting, the Brömsebro Treaty was signed, in which Denmark ceded Saaremaa to Sweden. The year 1645 thus saw Estonian territories reunited under a single ruler, the crown of Sweden. Peace did not last long; Russia invaded in 1656 to try to reclaim lands lost during the Livonian Wars. Although the forces of Tsar Alexei I managed to take Tartu, they could not hold their initial gains, and the previous status quo was reaffirmed by a 1661 armistice. For the moment, Sweden controlled a land that had known little but struggle and war for decades.

Swedish rule came to be known as the "good old Swedish days" for many Estonians, as it represented some relaxation of the powers of the local nobility, even if the status of the peasants (as serfs) was not equal with that of their counterparts in Sweden proper (as freed peasants). Though later the Swedish crown moved to nationalize lands given earlier to Swedish nobles in order to refill the emptied royal coffers, they also began taking estates away from the German nobles. This policy led to one major factor in the Swedish Empire's later downfall in the Baltics, as the landed nobility resented the seizures and excessive taxation policy.

The Baltics became a major part of the Swedish Empire, as Riga became the largest city in the Empire. Narva was to become a "second capital" for the empire as well. Swedish rule also firmly established the Lutheran Church as the dominant religion. A gymnasium, or institution of secondary education, was founded in Tartu in 1630 by the Swedish governor-general, Johan Skytte; two years later it was transformed into Academia Gustaviana (Gustav Academy), a full-fledged university named for King Gustav II Adolf. This university, later known as Tartu University, became the second institution of higher education in the Swedish Empire. The same decade also saw an increase in number of books, as printing presses began working in Tallinn and Tartu.

RUSSIA'S WINDOW TO THE WEST (1699–1869)

In 1689 Peter the Great came to the throne of Russia. Unlike many of his predecessors, Peter looked to be an active part of Europe. However, Russia had little direct access to Western Europe, and Peter now sought to open a window to the West along the Baltic coast. The Great Northern War ensued.

The 1699 signing of an anti-Swedish pact by Peter the Great, Denmark's Frederik IV, and Poland's Augustus II led to the roots of a series of regional conflicts, better known as the Great Northern War. The war broke out on 12 February 1700, when troops from Saxony, the home of Poland's Augustus II, attacked Riga. The Saxon-Polish force pushed from the south, and the Russians attacked from the east, though Denmark sued for peace after Sweden placed Copenhagen under siege early in the conflict. The Swedish king, Karl (Charles) XII, brought his army to Estonia and met the Russian army at the Battle of Narva in November 1700. Despite being severely outnumbered, the Swedish army routed the Russians. However, the Russians were not completely defeated; a major victory at Erastvere in the same winter severely damaged Swedish defenses.

Swedish defeats mounted into 1702, as the Russians mercilessly plundered Estonian lands and boasted about it, as seen in letters from commanders at the front. A large Swedish fleet went down in May 1704, unable to control the waterway blocking Russia's renewed attempts to take Narva. By late summer, both Narva and Tartu were under Peter the Great's control. This line held for a few years, as the war quieted on Estonian territory. But by 1708 warfare flared up again, and the Swedes suffered another defeat at Vinni, the last large battle on Estonian soil. The rest of the Swedish army was decimated at the Battle of Poltava in June 1709, giving Peter domination of the region.

City after city continued to surrender to the Russian army, with Tallinn's capitulation on 29 September 1710 signaling the end of the campaign. The nobility in Estonia happily recognized Russian domination according to terms of the surrender, as they hoped to regain the powers they had lost under Swedish rule. The war however had proved to be costly. Plague had devastated Estonia, and there had also been a prewar famine; it is estimated that over 100,000 people died on Estonian soil during the period. The 1721 Treaty of Nystadt (Uusikaupunki) brought an end to the Great Northern War, giving Russia control of Sweden's Baltic lands. Warfare continued to flare up, including failed Swedish campaigns in 1741–1743 and in 1788–1790, but that did not change the Estonian situation. Russia now controlled Estonia as its window to the west.

The former domination of the German landlords returned with Russian control, as the wealthy German barons had openly supported Russia's Baltic aims in response to Sweden's attempt to curb their influence. The seizure of manorial property by the Swedish crown had come back to haunt them during the Baltic conflict, and Russia began returning lands to manor estates. The rights given to peasants were also curbed, much to the nobility's delight.

With Germans in control of the region, the manorial estates expanded their activities throughout the Russian period. Small industries even began to develop on some estates, including a large paper mill in Räpina, which started up in 1734. Though at times St. Petersburg challenged their powers, the German nobility increased their influence during this period.

At the same time, however, education for the masses did improve. Though the first printed text in Estonia had appeared two centuries earlier, the 1739 publication of the first full translation of the Bible into Estonian helped increase literacy. The first Estonian newspaper, *Tarto maa rahwa Näddali-Leht* (Tartu County People's Weekly Paper [in the southern dialect]), was published in 1806, though it was the appearance of *Eesti Postimees* (The Estonian Courier) in 1864 that really launched the Estonian media. In the early 1800s educational reform also took place, creating a basic framework for primary education. The first compulsory schooling system was launched in 1854, and became universal in Estonian lands within twenty-five years. Education was extended to girls in the 1850s.

Many Germans, imbued with the belief in nationalism of the German philosopher Johann Gottfried Herder and the ideals of German romanticism, also took up the cause of the Estonians, forming groups to study everything Estonian. The entrance of some Estonians into higher education also enlarged the body of material devoted to Estonia. In 1838 the Estonian Learned Society was founded at Tartu University by Friedrich Robert Faehlmann, who devoted himself to collecting folktales. This foundation also led to the formation of the Estonian Literary Society in 1842, to foster Estonian literature. A colleague of Faehlmann, Friedrich Reinhold Kreutzwald, helped turn the collected tales into what became Estonia's national epic, *Kalevipoeg* (Son of Kalev), which was published in full in 1863. Even in other fields Tartu University excelled, boasting world-renowned scientists such as the astronomer Wilhelm Struve (who pioneered the study of binary star systems) and biologist Ernst von Baer (the founder of embryology).

The condition of the peasants improved a little as time went on. St. Petersburg viewed the Baltic lands as an experimental territory, and actually abolished serfdom in 1816 in Estonia and 1819 in Livonia. Though officially freed from serfdom, the peasants were still restricted by the estate owners over arable land. Sometimes this led to peasant uprisings, including a major insurrection in Otepää in September 1841. Some peasants also converted to Orthodoxy, believing they would gain advantage from the tsar, but that was wishful thinking.

However, Tsar Alexander II, who freed all the serfs in Russia and is remembered as a liberal, also allowed for local administrative control to be enacted in Russia's Baltic holdings. In 1866 permission was granted to create a parish council system—much like the rural self-governing idea of centuries ago—giving power to the people and not just estate owners.

NATIONAL AWAKENING (1869–1917)

There are many symbols that can be used to mark the beginning of Estonia's national awakening, but none better than the first National Song Festival, held in Tartu in 1869. The hundreds that participated (with an audience of over 10,000) sang many foreign songs, but also began the trend of singing patriotic Estonian songs. One of the songs performed that day was "Mu isamaa, mu õnn ja rõõm" (My Fatherland, My Joy and Delight), written by Johann Voldemar Jannsen to music by German-Finnish composer Fredrik Pacius; this song later became Estonia's national anthem (and, it should be noted, the tune is ironically also the Finnish national anthem). Many speeches were made that day, turning the festival into an early national rally, introducing many faces that were to lead Estonia's national awakening in the direction of a movement for national independence in the decades to come. The song festival began a tradition in Estonia, and they have been held regularly ever since.

Johann Voldemar Jannsen became one of the first leaders of the national movement for his role in organizing the first

The Song Festivals

Throughout history Estonian culture has been under threat by foreign invaders and occupiers, but Estonians have managed to retain and even strengthen their culture despite pressures against it. One of the key institutions in the retention of Estonian culture since the national awakening in the latter part of the 1800s has been the national song festival. Throughout their history the song festivals have given Estonians a venue to celebrate their culture, especially their language and songs, even during the darkest periods of tsarist or Soviet repression.

The first National Song Festival was organized by the Vanemuine Cultural Society, the brainchild of the prominent Jannsen family (led by patriarch Johann Voldemar Jannsen and his daughter Lydia Koidula), and took several years of planning. The Jannsens also fought against opposition among other Estonian activists, who argued that the song festival tradition was too German in style. Nevertheless, the very first song festival was held 18–20 June 1869 in Tartu. An estimated 15,000–20,000 people attended this groundbreaking event to sing the few Estonian patriotic songs already composed and to hear passionate speeches on the state and future of Estonian culture. This event proved to be a major turning point in Estonia's history, as the celebration of Estonian culture evolved into a political struggle.

The song festivals were held on several more occasions in the nineteenth century: in 1879, 1880, 1891, 1894, and 1896. Tallinn hosted its first national song festival in 1880 and took over as the regular site by 1896, symbolizing the gradual shift of the country's focal point from education-centered Tartu to politically centered Tallinn. The 1910 song festival also featured an entire Estonian program, marking the maturity of the national movement in just a few decades.

Interrupted by war and the establishment of national independence, the song festival tradition was revived in independent Estonia in 1923 and scheduled to take place every five years. The popularity of the festivals continued to grow as the nation prospered under independence; an estimated 100,000 attended in 1938.

Soviet occupation in 1940 disrupted the tradition for a short period, but the tradition returned in 1947, albeit under the careful and watchful eyes of the Soviets. Soviet officials attempted to turn the events into propaganda sessions, but the collective emotions of the gatherings, often numbering more than 100,000 individuals, kept the passion of Estonian culture alive. Composer Gustav Ernesaks, for the 1947 festival, premiered his version of the Lydia Koidula poem "Mu isamaa on minu arm" (My Homeland is My Love), which has become an unofficial anthem since that day. The song festivals from 1950 to 1980 were held every five years, in addition to a special 1969 centennial festival.

The singing tradition of Estonians played a major part in the restoration of independence in the process so aptly called the Singing Revolution. Many of the mass gatherings and protests featured song, many of them sung for decades in the song festivals. The September 1988 "Eestimaa laul" (Song of Estonia) gathering was the focal point of the entire revolution, as hundreds of thousands of Estonians took part in the collective song for freedom. The national song festival in the summer of 1990 finally allowed its organizers and participants to express a half-century of pent-up emotions on the eve of the restoration of freedom.

Even after the restoration of Estonian independence the song festival tradition has continued, just as it did during the period of independence during the interwar years. Though the numbers in attendance have dropped somewhat since the heyday of the Singing Revolution, nevertheless a substantial percentage of the Estonian nation (about one out of every ten Estonians in the world) attends the festivals. Clearly, the national song festivals symbolize the continuity and the resilience of Estonian culture despite the centuries of foreign assault and occupation, and it continues to serve as the protector of this much cherished part of every Estonian's life.

song festival and his founding of newspapers, including *Eesti Postimees* in 1864. The entire Jannsen family played a major role in organizing cultural events, with the daughter of the patriarch, Lydia Koidula, becoming the most loved woman poet in Estonia.

The increase in interest in and output of Estonian literature also led to the founding of the Estonian Society of Literati in 1872. This group helped to craft a compromise spelling system that has remained much the same to this day, and continued to promote Estonian literature.

Meanwhile, the manorial estates continued to increase their role in industry, especially in the latter part of the nineteenth century. The largest company of the time (also the largest cotton works in Europe), the Krenholm textiles factory, was launched in Narva in 1858. Other large industries included the Dvigatel wagon carriage factory in

Tallinn and the Waldhof cellulose factory in Pärnu. This increase in trade and manufacturing accelerated the process of urbanization, as city dwellers tripled from the 1860s to the 1890s. The first railway, linking the port of Paldiski to St. Petersburg (via both Tallinn and Narva), was completed in 1870, and the network soon expanded to other cities.

However, the assassination of Tsar Alexander II and rise of his son, Alexander III, in 1881 marked a major change in policy toward the Baltics. A period of Russification ensued, with the imposition of Russian as the language of education in 1887. Despite this language regulation, many private academies, such as the Hugo Treffner Gymnasium, became preparatory schools for Tartu University. Eventually the Russification efforts eased (especially after the death of Alexander III in 1894), and the first Estonian daily, *Postimees* (The Courier) hit the streets in 1891.

Newspapers also provided voices for nationalism. Jaan Tõnisson made his earliest marks as *Postimees* editor. The nationalist paper, based in Tartu, pursued a more anti-German line than others. Tõnisson also founded the first local Estonian banking institution, the Estonian Loan and Savings Cooperative. His rival at this point, destined to remain a rival for the next half-century, was the Tallinn-based lawyer Konstantin Päts, who launched a rival paper, *Teataja* (The Herald) in 1901.

The turn of the century witnessed remarkable accomplishments politically, as Estonian and Latvian deputies in the Valga town council in 1901 took power for the first time; Valga became the first Baltic town to gain local control. This step was followed in 1904 by an Estonian-Russian coalition in Tallinn, making Jaan Poska the first Estonian mayor of Tallinn.

The social democracy movement also grew in Estonia in the very early years of the twentieth century, fueled by rapid urbanization. The 9 January 1905 massacre of peaceful demonstrators in St. Petersburg, which touched off the Revolution of 1905 throughout Russian territory, saw major strikes in Estonian cities. The protests continued, and bloodshed soon followed. On 16 October, the military killed 94 protestors and injured over 200 more. Similar events throughout the empire pushed Tsar Nicholas II to issue a decree (the October Manifesto) aimed at creating a constitutional monarchy and establishing a parliament, the Duma. Five deputies from Estonia (four Estonian, one Russian) were elected to the body in 1906. However, the parliament proved to have little power and subsequent Dumas were manipulated by the crown so that the national groups lost seats.

Nevertheless, Estonian political movements continued to develop. Jaan Tõnisson founded the Estonian National Progressive Party, while the social democrats founded the Estonian Social Democratic Workers Community (apart from the main Russian party). At the same time, various uprisings also occurred, though they were put down. The tsar's government reacted by declaring martial law and executing many protestors. Many political leaders also faced execution, and many fled, among them Konstantin Päts. Martial law remained in force until 1908.

The years before the outbreak of World War I therefore remained tense, as the Dumas had little power, and the situation in Europe deteriorated. It was the changing situation in Europe that finally brought the Estonians the chance to win their independence.

WINNING INDEPENDENCE (1917–1920)

World War I and the ensuing collapse of the tsarist regime proved pivotal in the history of Estonia. The unpopular war played a major role in the downfall of Tsar Nicholas II, and many of his radical rivals campaigned on a slogan of peace. The Baltic region became a major battleground during the Great War and the ensuing conflicts, which led to the (re)creation of five states on Russia's west—Estonia, Finland, Latvia, Lithuania, and Poland.

The February 1917 Revolution in Russia soon spread into the Baltics, and by early March, protests and strikes paralyzed Estonian cities, especially Tallinn. However, calm returned soon after, as the Russian provisional government on 6 March appointed Jaan Poska, the mayor of Tallinn, as the commissar of the Estonian province. With an Estonian appointed to govern Estonian lands, nationalists began to ask for more autonomy from Petrograd (formerly St. Petersburg). It worked to a point, as the provisional government on 30 March allowed for the merger of the northern part of the Livonian province into Estonia, uniting all of Estonian lands (except for some border areas, such as Narva) under one administration.

Poska's provincial government allowed many Estonians political power for the first time, and Estonian was established as the official language of the province. The commissar also called for elections to the Maapäev (Landtag, or diet). This first election to an Estonian body was held in May despite left wing agitation, which forced Poska to flee Tallinn at one point. The Maapäev, which convened in July, became Estonia's first national assembly.

As Russia's war against the Germans collapsed, Russian soldiers continued their retreat through Estonia. However, Estonia escaped much of the fighting early on due to its geographic position. It was not until September 1917 that German forces reached Estonian lands, taking the islands first. The Bolshevik October Revolution added to the chaos, as communist agents attempted to take power from the Maapäev. Though the Bolsheviks ordered the dissolution of the assembly and government, the Maapäev asserted itself as the official power in Estonia and declared sovereignty.

By February 1918, German forces decided to take Estonia once and for all, assuming control of most of the territory within weeks. During the German campaign, the leaders of the Maapäev-mandated provisional government on 19 February formed the Päästekomitee (Salvation Committee), composed of Konstantin Konik, Konstantin Päts, and Jüri Vilms, to officially express Estonia's independence. In the period between the Russian retreat and the German advance, many of the towns were taken over by voluntary military groups called Omakaitse (Self-Defense), and the Tallinn Omakaitse gained control from the Bolsheviks on 23 February. On 24 February 1918, the Päästekomitee officially proclaimed independence, forming a provisional government headed by Konstantin Päts. Though German forces

Konstantin Päts

Among the myriad of Estonian historical figures, the one individual who stands out is Konstantin Päts, considered to be the "grand old man" of Estonian independence. The controversial first president of Estonia played the most influential role in Estonian society in the first half of the twentieth century, ranging from his leadership in declaring independence in February 1918 to his acquiescence to Soviet military basing demands in 1939.

Päts was born in 1874 near Pärnu and later studied law at Tartu University. The young lawyer soon played an active role in the political scene of what was then the Estonian province of the Russian Empire. Advocating economic and political empowerment for Estonians, Päts founded the Tallinn newspaper *Teataja* (The Herald) in 1901 as a political vehicle. Postitions taken by the paper during the 1905 Russian Revolution turned Päts into a revolutionary in the eyes of the tsarist government, and Päts fled abroad for some time to escape a death sentence. When Päts returned in the latter days of the Russian Empire, he was jailed.

Päts was appointed as the chairman of the clandestine Päästekomitee (Salvation Committee), as the Bolsheviks attempted to curtail Estonia's hard-won autonomy. This committee on 24 February 1918 declared Estonian independence, and this act became the basis of the Estonian state. Subsequently, Päts was interned in a German prison camp until the opportunity opened to properly exercise the declaration of independence, following the collapse of the German Second Reich in November 1918.

Though Päts lost the early battles on forging the constitution and land reform laws, the creation of a landowning class by the latter in fact made his Farmers Assembly the most prominent during the era of parliamentary democracy. The Farmers Assembly played a major role in most of the era's ruling coalitions, and Päts served as Riigivanem ("State Elder," or de facto prime minister) seven times between 1918 and 1934.

On the other hand, Päts is also remembered for engineering a palace coup, on 12 March 1934, that ended liberal democracy in Estonia. For the remaining six years of Estonia's de facto independence Päts served as the country's authoritarian leader, albeit a mild one. There were no major repression campaigns, though Päts did for a period imprison or silence his opponents and critics. In 1938 Päts created the post of president, and he became the first officeholder. Though he is praised for uniting the country after several years of divisive politics and helping to restore Estonia's economic health, he is also blamed for giving in to Soviet demands for military bases and eventual occupation.

With the occupation of Estonia by the Soviet Union in June 1940, a rump parliament dismissed Päts. Although technically still president, he was arrested by the Soviets and deported at the end of July to Ufa in the Urals; he died in a psychiatric hospital in Tver in 1956.

The return and reburial of his remains in Tallinn in 1990 served as a symbolic moment on the eve of the restoration of Estonia's independence, though his role during the years before occupation, especially his giving in to Soviet demands, have remained sources of contention. Nevertheless, Konstantin Päts symbolizes the Estonian state during the interwar period, making him easily the most significant historical figure in the country.

moved into Tallinn that same day, independence had nevertheless officially been declared.

By 3 March 1918, German forces took all of Estonian territory; on the same day war-weary Russia signed the Brest-Litovsk Treaty with Germany ending its involvement in World War I. Now with the Germans in control, the provisional government was crushed. Most of Estonia's leaders were arrested and imprisoned, while the deputy head of the provisional government, Jüri Vilms, was shot near Helsinki.

The Allies naturally opposed the events in the Baltics, and on 3 May 1918 Estonia's lobbying efforts paid off with de facto recognition of its independence by France, Italy, and the United Kingdom. The Germans, however, went ahead with trying to create a Baltic Duchy of Estonian and

Latvian lands, and the German nobility elected a *Landesrat* (state council); Kaiser Wilhelm II recognized the duchy in September. This new entity was short-lived, as the kaiser was deposed in November; the provisional government reassembled in Tallinn on 11 November.

Unfortunately, trouble came from another direction, as the Bolsheviks chose to abrogate their treaty obligations with Germany and invade the Baltics. The Bolsheviks invaded from the northeast and southeast, beginning the Estonian War of Independence on 28 November 1918. The German forces were retreating, and the Kaitseliit (Defense League), created from the various regional groupings of Omakaitse, was ill equipped to defend Estonia; Narva fell quickly. The volunteers could not hold off the Russians, so the provisional government ordered full mobilization in December. However, by 21 December, the Bolsheviks took Tartu, holding half the country and threatening the rest. They also formed a Soviet authority based in Narva and caused widespread terror; the most infamous of their acts was the brutal murder of eighteen innocent prisoners, including the Orthodox Bishop Platon (who was later canonized).

However, the tide began to turn at the end of the year. Mobilization proceeded, and the Estonian army by January reached an estimated 13,000. Guerrilla warfare now shifted to a centralized command with the establishment of Johan Laidoner, a former tsarist officer, as commander-in-chief. The Estonian navy was established, and its leader, Johan Pitka, successfully attacked the Bolsheviks from the rear. Finnish volunteers also arrived at the end of the year, joined by other Scandinavians in the early part of 1919.

The Estonian counterattack began on 6 January 1919 with resounding success, taking Tartu on 14 January and Narva on 19 January. The Bolsheviks continued to retreat into Russia and Latvia, and the southern towns of Valga and Võru were liberated on 1 February. Though in the following few months Bolshevik forces broke through the line a few times, they were unable to occupy and hold Estonian territory. Estonian forces actually took the Russian city of Pskov in May and transferred it to their temporary allies in the White Russian monarchist forces.

With most of the country liberated and the battle lines stable, the provisional government called for the election to the Asutav Kogu (Constituent Assembly) on 5–7 April. The body met for the first time on 23 April 1919, with the democratic left wing taking a 65 percent majority of the 120 assembly seats. Socialist Party leader August Rei was elected the assembly's chairman, and his victory led to some key early legislation and to the constitution itself.

Unfortunately, warfare was far from over, and trouble came this time from the south, as German adventurers, called the Baltische Landeswehr ("Baltic Brigade") overthrew the Latvian provisional government of Kārlis Ulmanis in April. The plans of the Landeswehr leaders were to rebuild German control of the Baltic, and Estonian leaders decided to act preemptively. Clashes between the Landeswehr and Estonian forces began in early June (Latvian forces also played a role in the offensive, but it was Estonian-led). The decisive battle took place in Cēsis (Wenden in German, Võnnu in Estonian), and the Estonian military, led by Ernst Põdder, defeated the Germans on 23 June, the day still celebrated today as Estonia's Victory Day. The Estonians pursued the Germans all the way to the edge of Riga, helping to restore the Ulmanis government to power.

The White Russian forces meanwhile continued their war against the Bolsheviks, dragging the Estonians into the unwanted conflict. In October the White forces reached the outskirts of Petrograd, but failed to take the imperial capital and were eventually forced back to Estonia. The Allies finally gave up in December and withdrew their support for the Russian White forces, relieving Estonia of the major burden of aiding the anti-Bolshevik forces.

By this point, the Constituent Assembly had made significant strides in its work, including the passage of a radical land reform bill on 10 October. Over a thousand manor estates covering over 2 million hectares (over 96 percent of all estate lands), mostly owned by German nobles, were nationalized and redistributed to applicants. Over fifty thousand new homestead farms were created from this ambitious but controversial (especially when examining the minute level of compensation for the owners) program. A new currency, the mark, was also introduced in 1919, though it proved less than stable.

While the assembly was making progress in creating a new Estonian state, warfare continued to rage, as German and Russian adventurers once again occupied parts of Latvia, causing Estonian forces to help once again. Bolsheviks also pushed toward Narva again, and some of the bloodiest battles of the War of Independence were fought in defense of Narva. The Bolsheviks could not take Narva, and after a year of fighting the two sides signed an armistice at the end of 1919.

Negotiations for a permanent peace commenced fully in Tartu, headed by former provincial governor Jaan Poska. The lengthy talks resulted in a full annulment of Estonian debts to Russia and the awarding of 15 million gold rubles, as well as small strips of territory in the northeast and southeast. In the Tartu Peace Treaty, signed on 2 February 1920, Russia pledged to "give up forever" all sovereign rights Russia had in Estonia. The document has been called Estonia's birth certificate, as it was the first de jure recognition of the new state. The signing of the Tartu Peace Treaty marked the end of the War of Independence; the process of state building could thus commence fully.

ERA OF LIBERAL DEMOCRACY (1920–1934)

Finally in 1920 Estonia enjoyed the fruits of its struggle, as conflicts with all other combatants came to an end. Though the process of state building had begun earlier, Estonian officials could now move to create the structures of an independent state.

The Constituent Assembly adopted a new constitution on 15 June 1920, and it went into effect on 21 December 1920. The left-wing majority in the assembly helped to draft a very liberal constitution, one that kept most of the power in the hands of the 100-seat Riigikogu (State Assembly) and away from any one individual. In fact, there was no head of state per se; that role was held by the Riigivanem (State Elder), who also led the cabinet. While that might sound quite powerful, the Riigivanem in fact had very little power and acted at the whim of the parliament. The Left wanted to prevent the possibility of the rise of a strongman (but ironically it caused that exact outcome fourteen years later). Suffrage was granted to all men and women over the age of twenty.

Elections to the First Riigikogu were held in November 1920, and their results differed significantly from that of the Constituent Assembly. With many former left-leaning peasants now landowners and smallholders, radicalism had succeeded and so had lost its raison d'être. The right wing, embodied in the Farmers Assembly, gained 21 seats in the new assembly. The large Labor Party also shifted notably toward the center, leaving the left wing with just 29 out of 100 seats (a communist front organization won five seats). Konstantin Päts, the hero of the independence declaration and leader of the Farmers Assembly, thus became the first prime minister of a parliamentary Estonia on 25 January 1921.

On the foreign front, the Allied Supreme Council eventually offered de jure recognition of Estonia and Latvia on 21 January 1921, and Estonia joined the League of Nations on 22 September 1922. The United States was the last of the major powers to recognize Estonia, doing so in July 1922, marking the full international acceptance of an independent Estonia.

Relations with the other Baltic states were lukewarm, as each faced their own problems. Lithuania and Poland remained on the brink of war over the Polish seizure of Vilnius, and Finland sought to distance itself from its southern neighbors. The most important diplomatic accomplishment of this period was the conclusion of a major bilateral treaty with Latvia, including a defensive alliance, concluded on 1 November 1923. A mild trilateral cooperation agreement was also made with Latvia and Lithuania in 1934, but the agreement turned out to be weak.

Early on, the building of the national economy proved difficult, exacerbated by the Soviet Union closing its markets to Estonian goods at the end of 1922 (partly in response to crackdowns against communist agitators). Insolvency spread across the country by 1923, pushing the central bank to continue to print money, which in turn caused major inflation. By early 1924, most of the 15 million gold rubles paid by Russia was gone. In the spring, however, austerity measures and trade control helped stabilize the situation, and the economy finally began to grow.

There was little stability on the political front as well. The small National Christian Party was incensed at the parliament's plan to remove religious teaching from schools and managed to put the issue to a public referendum. The 1923 referendum dealt a defeat to the parliament, thus causing early elections. Elections to the Second Riigikogu were held in May 1923, marking a further shift to the right. The Farmers, alongside the Homesteaders, won 27 seats, while the socialist groups dropped to a total of 20 (though 10 seats were taken by communist front members).

Despite peace with the Soviets, there was always fear of subversive activities by Bolsheviks. These activities by agitators led to crackdowns, including the execution of the communist Viktor Kingissepp on 3 May 1922; the Soviets responded angrily, renaming a border town after the "martyr." However, Estonian fears came true on 1 December 1924, when an estimated three hundred communists attempted a coup d'état. About two dozen people were killed by the communists, including Transport Minister Karl Kark, but the revolt was quickly put down in hours by General Laidoner. The role of Moscow was apparent, with a massing of troops at the border and the approach of a naval fleet, but the failure of the coup prevented any escalation. However, the psyche of Estonia was shaken. Many communists were jailed or executed for their roles in the coup attempt, while the Kaitseliit (Defense League) was recreated as an armed civilian national guard force. A "rainbow coalition" of the Right, Center, and Left was formed under Jüri Jaakson of the National Center Party, a coalition that lasted for nearly a year.

The mid-1920s was an otherwise productive period. The ambitious cultural self-governing law for minorities gave minority groups extensive autonomy in education and organizational matters, a program that earned Estonia widespread praise and honor in the 1927 Jerusalem Golden Book for its progressiveness. And in 1925 the *Kultuurkapital* (the Cultural Endowment Fund) was introduced to offer state funding to expanding culture.

Elections to the Third Riigikogu were held in May 1926, which featured a mild continuation of the left-to-right trend. The socialist groups consolidated into a Socialist Workers Party, winning 24 seats, one less than in the former parliament. The center lost more ground to the two right-wing parties, which took 37 total seats.

One of the problems in the early years was the unstable currency, the mark. In 1927, as a result of the initiative of finance minister Leo Sepp, Estonia gained a substantial loan from Britain (mediated by the League of Nations) and restructured the monetary system. A new currency, the *kroon* (crown), was introduced on 1 January 1928, exchanged for 100 marks and pegged to the Swedish *krona* (crown).

The elections to the Fourth Riigikogu were held in May 1929, which saw very little change from the previous parliament. Both the left and the right gained only one extra seat from the center, but this meant that the body remained rather fractured and unable to deal with the increasing problems faced by the country.

The looming global economic depression also struck in 1929, and Estonia's economy teetered. The tremendous political disputes in the Riigikogu in dealing with the crisis did little to solve the problems, and the public came to see the parliament as hopelessly ineffective. Radicalism grew in many circles, especially among veterans of the War of Independence. The Central League of Veterans of the Estonian War of Independence (*Eesti vabadussõjalaste keskliit*) was formed in 1929 as an umbrella organization for veterans, and it expressed concern that Estonia's hard-won independence was being squandered by senseless bickering between political parties. Over time, the group radicalized, becoming known as the League of Veterans of the Estonian War of Independence (*Eesti vabadussõjalaste liit*), and became overtly political—though not necessarily within the system. The league did not run for offices; instead it pushed for a new constitution that would create a powerful chief executive and diminish the power of the parliament and the political parties.

At first, the effect of the league's campaign caused smaller political groupings to consolidate. In 1931 the two right-wing parties merged into the Agrarian Union, while various centrist forces merged into the National Center Party. However, the party mergers did little to improve the situation in the May 1932 elections to the Fifth Riigikogu, as the divisions among the three groupings increased. The government did, however, heed the warnings from the League of Veterans and drafted a new constitution that took into account some of the veterans' ideas. However, the veterans saw it as a watered-down version of what they wanted, and campaigned against it alongside the Socialists. The draft constitution was put to a referendum on 13–15 August 1932, and failed by a slim margin; only 49.2 percent of voters supported the draft.

The League of Veterans attempted to introduce their own draft constitution, but the parliamentarians beat them to it. The second draft constitution faced a referendum, and with loud campaigning by the League of Veterans against it, in the referendum of 10–12 June 1933 the second draft constitution was soundly defeated, with only 32.7 percent of voters in support. The league's protests increased, including one incident in Tartu that caused Riigivanem Jaan Tõnisson to declare martial law, curbing political activities. The popularity of Tõnisson also diminished, as his government in June devalued the kroon by 35 percent, a necessary but wildly unpopular move. The League of Veterans' draft constitution did face a referendum on 14–16 October 1933, and it won by a large margin (72.7 percent in support). Tõnisson lifted the state of emergency and resigned, and Konstantin Päts on 21 October 1933 became the caretaker leader until the new presidential elections mandated by the new constitution could be held.

The transition period saw the arrangement for elections under the new League of Veterans' constitution, with the focus on the race for the position of all-powerful president. The path to power for the League of Veterans seemed certain, as it scored major victories in local elections in most cities in January 1934. The titular leader of the veterans, retired general Andres Larka, was seen as the clear frontrunner of the race. Caretaker premier Päts and former commander in chief retired general Johan Laidoner were both put forward by the Right, while Socialist leader August Rei led the Left. There was little possibility, however, of the League of Veterans not winning the scheduled April 1934 elections, an outcome that was expected to lead to the end of parliamentary democracy in Estonia.

THE ERA OF SILENCE (1934–1939)

The last years of the independent Estonian republic became known as the era of silence, as parliamentary democracy was replaced by mild authoritarianism. Though many, especially the left wing, had feared that the League of Veterans would pursue just such a move, it turned out to be someone else who actually ended parliamentary democracy, someone who had been the living symbol of the independence declaration—Konstantin Päts.

The League of Veterans' constitution included a provision on transition, which essentially gave the caretaker premier the powers allotted to the powerful president. Using this provision, Päts acted, on 12 March 1934. Having already ascertained the support of the military, Päts named his close colleague General Johan Laidoner as commander in chief for a third time. Quickly members of the Kaitseliit national guards and cadets from the military academy took control of central Tallinn and apprehended members of the League of Veterans. Päts then suspended the elections and disbanded the league, arresting several hundred of its members. The civil service was purged of elements sympathetic to the League of Veterans as well. Karl Einbund, also of the Farmers Union, became the third member of the "triumvirate" after being named deputy premier.

The original six-month state of emergency was extended in September by a year, thus postponing all elections. The Riigikogu reconvened in the autumn and began criticizing the extended state of emergency. Einbund reacted by canceling the 2 October 1934 session of parliament, and it was never recalled again.

Though the Päts regime did not prove to be a harsh dictatorship, it did exhibit mild authoritarian characteristics. A tinge of nationalism also became evident, with the formation in 1935 of a national patriotic organization, Isamaaliit (Fatherland Union). A campaign was launched also to "Estonianize" German-sounding surnames, with deputy premier Karl Einbund taking the lead; he changed his name to Kaarel Eenpalu. By the summer of 1935, Päts gained control over all aspects of society, and felt safe enough to start releasing members of the League of Veterans from jail.

However, increasing agitation by the league and other opposition caused another crackdown in December, as alleged coup plotters were arrested at a meeting. A wave of arrests followed, which sent 133 people to jail, further consolidating the position of Päts. In that same year former Riigivanem Jaan Tõnisson, the main political rival of Päts since the turn of the century, had his beloved newspaper *Postimees* taken from him for statements against the regime.

Wanting to give some legitimacy to his regime, Päts announced that a new constitution was needed to bring the country back to a state of normalcy. A February 1936 referendum called on the people to give Päts the power to assemble a new constituent assembly aimed at drafting a new constitution. The referendum was successful (with 75.4 percent of voters in support), and Päts called for elections to the assembly in December 1936. The opposition boycotted the elections, as fair campaigning was not allowed; thus Isamaaliit candidates took complete control of the assembly. It began meeting in February 1937, drafting a constitution giving significant powers to a newly created president and limited power to a new bicameral legislature (an eighty-seat lower house elected by direct mandate and a forty-seat appointed upper house).

The 1938 Constitution went into force on 1 January 1938, and elections to the lower house were held in February 1938. The opposition won a significant number of votes even without campaigning, but took only sixteen seats. There was no election for the president, as Päts was the only candidate, making him the first president of Estonia in April 1938. Kaarel Eenpalu became prime minister.

Little changed following this period, as the state remained effectively an authoritarian one. However, Päts felt comfortable enough with the situation to grant wide-ranging amnesty to political prisoners from both the left and right. The opposition to Päts remained weak, as the country stood united, entering a period of deep anxiety and eventually facing the loss of its much cherished independence.

THE LOSS OF INDEPENDENCE (1939–1944)

The international situation in the late 1930s caused Estonians to fear the worst. Relations with both regional powers—the Soviet Union and Nazi Germany—deteriorated as the rhetoric of both sides intensified. Ominous signs affecting Lithuania signaled an international catastrophe: Poland forced Lithuania to restore diplomatic relations upon the threat of war on 17 March 1938, and Germany forced the transfer of the Klaipėda region (Memelland in German) on 20 March 1938 (just days after marching into Czechoslovakia).

Nevertheless, the signing of the Soviet-German nonaggression treaty on 23 August 1939 stunned Estonia as much as it did the rest of the world. The two ideological and geographic enemies sealed the agreement (known popularly as the Molotov-Ribbentrop Pact, after the two foreign ministers), creating fear in the other states of the region. Their fear was justified, as secret protocols in the pact divided the region between Germany and the Soviet Union, creating spheres of conquest; Estonia ended up in the Soviet sphere under the secret protocol. Though this fact was never confirmed at the time, Estonian and other Baltic officials feared the worst, especially as German forces rolled into Poland on 1 September 1939.

During the middle of September, a Polish submarine, the *Orzeł* (Eagle), drifted into Tallinn. Estonia, which had beforehand declared itself neutral, was obliged to quarantine the submarine. However, as the Soviet Union itself invaded Poland on 17 September, the sympathies of Estonians were clearly evident as the *Orzeł* "escaped" the following day. This incident gave Moscow a basis for charging Estonia with violating its neutrality.

Soviet Commissar for Foreign Affairs Vyacheslav Molotov proposed a mutual assistance pact with Estonia on 24 September. The pact involved the basing of Soviet naval forces in Estonia. Molotov hinted that if the deal were refused, force would be used. Using false propaganda about the attack of a Soviet ship in Estonian waters, Moscow further demanded the basing of 35,000 troops—more than twice the number in the Estonian military—to support the naval units. The deal was signed on 28 September after Estonian officials painfully agreed to the ultimatum (though the number of Soviet troops was limited to 25,000 under a supplementary protocol), attempting to avert a destructive war.

Though the Soviets guaranteed observation of the country's territorial integrity and respect for the sovereignty of Estonia, the influx of Red Army troops on 18 October 1939 painted a different picture, one that became even more clear as Hitler called all ethnic Germans back to the Reich on 7 October. Many then suspected the truth, that the Soviets and Nazis had colluded to divide the countries of the area between them.

Lithuania and Latvia also acquiesced to the Soviet demands for bases, but Finland did not. Therefore Moscow began its war against Finland, the so-called Winter War, in November 1940. Soviet forces violated the agreement with Estonia by launching attacks from its Estonian bases, which was most painful for Estonians, as they saw their ethnic kin bombed from their bases.

Soviet foreign commissar Vyacheslav Molotov signs the German-Soviet nonaggression pact in Moscow on 23 August 1939. (National Technical Information Service)

As the Nazis rolled through Europe, international attention focused away from the Baltics. Using this opportunity, Molotov and other Soviet officials intensified their anti-Baltic rhetoric and laid unfounded accusations of violations of the basing agreements. Lithuania was the first to get the final ultimatum from Moscow to form a sympathetic government on 14 June 1940; Estonia got theirs two days later. The government had no choice but to acquiesce without firing a shot, since the occupation was already a fait accompli, with 25,000 Soviet troops in the country. On 17 June, more Soviet forces crossed into Estonia, raising the number of occupying forces to about 80,000. The same day, General Laidoner signed a decree passing control of Estonia's communications to Moscow, and ordering the disarming of the people, including the national guards, the Kaitseliit.

Soviet officials and troops took part in public protests in Tallinn and other towns, attempting to suggest a homegrown revolution; however, there was little local support for the Soviets. Nevertheless, a "friendly" government headed by the left-wing academic Johannes Vares, known by his pseudonym "Barbarus," was installed on 21 June 1940 by the Soviet envoy, Andrei Zhdanov. Rigged one-candidate elections were called for early July, with the communist-front Estonian Working People's Union winning 92.9 percent of the votes. The rump parliament subsequently met on 21 July to ask to join the USSR, presenting the decision two days later; Moscow "accepted" the "application" on 6 August, finalizing the incorporation.

The governing system was changed to fit the Soviet model, and the people endured the painful collectivization and nationalization of private property. Moscow also imposed an unfair exchange rate in abolishing the kroon, and mass censorship began. Moscow also began deporting high-ranking civil and military officials, as well as the intelligentsia, most of whom were shot within a short time. The entire military leadership was essentially sent to their deaths, while President Päts was put into a mental institution in Russia.

In 1941, the level of repression by the NKVD, the predecessor of the KGB, increased sharply. With a looming conflict with Germany, the Soviets stepped up the "ethnic cleansing" of Estonia and the other Baltic countries. The focal point of the major deportations of innocents—many of them women, children, and the elderly—was 14 June 1941, when at least 10,000 Estonians were deported to the USSR. Within a year, the Soviets had been responsible for tens of thousands of deaths, executions, deportations, and incarcerations. Therefore when Germany attacked the USSR in 1941, many Estonians and other victim nations of Moscow (ranging from Ukrainians to Chechens) saw Germany as an agent of liberation that could drive out the murderous Red Army and NKVD.

On 7 July 1941, the German military reached the Estonian border from the south as Operation Barbarossa struck the Soviet Union. The Germans did not at first pursue full occupation, as they saw Leningrad as their target; however, that did not prevent Soviet agents from pursuing a scorched-earth policy throughout Estonia, leading to thousands more deaths. Many Estonians also took to the forest to fight the Soviets, calling themselves *metsavennad* (forest brothers).

The failure of the German Wehrmacht to take Leningrad caused the Germans to turn their attention to Estonia. By late August, Tallinn fell, and the Germans took the Estonian islands in September and October. The Nazi occupation period had begun, and for most Estonians, having seen the brutality of the Soviet occupation, the Germans were a welcome sight.

However, that feeling was short-lived, as the Germans gave little indication of supporting the restoration of Estonian independence. Estonia effectively became another province of Nazi Germany, a part of their *Lebensraum* (living space). Repression continued for Estonians and non-Estonians alike, including the opening of several concentration camps. An estimated 125,000 people died in the camps, including thousands of Estonians; however, most were Soviet prisoners of war and Jews from occupied lands. The only things the occupying Germans restored were military units they could use, such as the Omakaitse. However, many Estonians continued to fight as guerrillas against all occupation forces, and others chose to go to Finland to fight the Soviets.

At the same time, on the Soviet side, thousands of Estonians chose also to fight against the Germans. And with Germany forcibly mobilizing Estonian men, the horrific scenario of Estonians fighting Estonians occurred. By 1944, the German attack stalled, and the Soviets pushed back into Estonia. The Soviet Air Force bombed historic Narva in early March, followed by other cities throughout Estonia, including Tallinn and Tartu. The Germans were unable to stem the tide of the Soviets, though many Estonians continued to fight on against the Red Army. By the summer, the Soviets were certain to take control of Estonia.

During this period, some of the political leaders of the country who had evaded deportation and remained in the country formed a National Committee of the Republic of Estonia. The last prime minister of the country, Jüri Uluots, acted as president and appointed Otto Tief as acting prime minister; they declared the restoration of independence on 18 September 1944. That lasted only a few days, however, as the Soviets took Tallinn. Uluots escaped to Sweden, but most other leaders of the interim national government fell into Soviet hands and were executed. The Soviets soon took over the entire country, sealing the country's fate for a half century.

SOVIET OCCUPATION (1944–1985)

When the Soviet army returned in the late summer of 1944, Estonians had no illusions about what would happen, remembering the brutality during the first yearlong occupation. Estonia received very little help from overseas, as the occupation became de facto for most countries. Though most of the world, including great powers like the United States and Great Britain, did not recognize the Soviet annexation and continued to recognize the independence of Estonia and the other Baltic countries, it was clear that the occupation was not going to end by international pressure. Certainly the de jure recognition of Estonia's independence had limited meaning, as most of Estonia's diplomatic representatives were denied access to the Allied meetings. The perceived sellout of Central and Eastern Europe at Yalta ended most hopes for international support.

Many Estonians took to the forests and waged a guerrilla campaign against Soviet interests. Many well-known partisans became heroes, sabotaging Soviet equipment and robbing Soviet treasuries. The battles by the forest brothers, as they were known, continued into the 1950s, despite a crackdown by Soviet authorities and infiltration by agents. Foreign intelligence services, such as Britain's SIS, played a role in supporting the forest brothers, but they were infiltrated as well. Some estimate the number of fighters in the forests at over 10,000, usually working in small bands of 50 men.

The Soviets resumed the repression of 1940–1941, deporting tens of thousands more people to Russia. Forced collectivization of rural lands also proved to be most difficult for Estonian farmers, and their resistance led to the shocking deportation of over 20,000 people—mostly children and women—on the evening of 26 March 1949 to Siberia as retribution. The private sector disappeared in 1947 with the final nationalization programs, and the 26 March deportations broke the opposition to completing

Estonian Population Percentage

Ethnicity	1922	1934	1959	1970	1979	1989	2000
Estonians	87.7	88.7	74.6	68.2	64.7	61.5	67.9
Russians	8.2	8.2	20.1	24.6	27.9	30.3	25.6

collectivization of agricultural land. By late 1951, about 95 percent of farms were collectivized, and production fell to lows that were worse than those of wartime.

In the 1940s and 1950s policies of mass industrialization were pursued by Moscow. This had the added effect of diluting Estonia's population, thanks to the importation of workers from other parts of the USSR. As these newcomers spoke no Estonian and were not encouraged to learn the language, a major national divide began to occur.

Moreover, the governing system was formed much like those in other Soviet lands, with a Supreme Soviet as a pseudo legislature and the chairman of the Presidium of the Supreme Soviet as a pseudo head of republic. A committee of ministers acted as a republican government, with its chairman serving as the governmental leader. Most of the leaders were "Yestonians"—Estonians who had grown up in Russia (Russians tend to pronounce an initial letter e with a palatal y sound, leading to the nickname).

The repression continued until the death of Stalin in 1953; his passing helped to bring a thaw in the situation in Estonia, allowing, for example, the return of deportees to Estonia and an attempt to give an amnesty to the remaining forest brothers. Some 30,000 deportees returned to Estonia following the thaw, and most forest brothers gave up their struggle when they saw the lack of international reaction to the Budapest uprising of 1956. A few forest brothers, though, managed to hide out into the 1970s; the last of them, August Sabe, killed himself in 1978 after failing to evade his pursuers.

The thaw lasted into the 1970s, when Brezhnev launched further new programs of Russification and Sovietization. The use of Russian was promoted, while that of Estonian was discouraged; education, especially higher education, insisted on the use of the Russian language.

The Helsinki process, begun in 1975, was formulated to reduce tension between the West and the Soviet bloc by promoting dialogue aimed at reducing potential conflicts. The forum created, the Conference for Security and Cooperation in Europe (CSCE, later the OSCE), became a turning point in the history of the region. Spurred by the protest of various groups in the United States, Washington refused to yield to Soviet insistence on recognizing the incorporation of the Baltic states into the USSR. The Helsinki process also allowed for "Helsinki groups" to start up throughout the Soviet bloc, including Estonia. Later a group of forty-five dissidents from the three Baltic countries sent a letter to various governments such as the Soviet Union, the two Germanies, and the United Nations, calling for international recognition of the nature of the secret protocol of the Molotov-Ribbentrop Pact on the fate of the Baltic states and condemnation of its impact on the region. This action, known as the Baltic Appeal, led to a 1983 decision by the European Parliament to adopt a resolution calling for the restoration of Baltic independence. These kinds of appeals, as well as the hosting in Tallinn of yachting events in the 1980 Summer Olympics, alerted a number of foreigners as to Estonia's situation.

Estonians also could watch Finnish TV and listen to Finnish radio, thus making them more open to the world than many within the USSR itself, a critical factor as the Soviet empire imploded during the 1980s. Former president Lennart Meri used to joke that only in Estonia did people know that Lech Wałęsa (leader of Poland's Solidarity movement) had a moustache.

The first real protests in Estonia came from the generation born after the start of the thaw. Reacting to heavy-handed police actions after a September 1980 concert by the legendary punk group Propeller, the youth took to the streets on 1 October. Though this protest was put down quickly, it indicated the discontent among Estonia's youth. It also resulted in the so-called letter of forty—signed by forty well-known intellectuals—to the Soviet media highlighting social problems. Although the authorities cracked down on the forty, the letter was circulated widely underground.

THE SINGING REVOLUTION (1985–1991)

The entire process of restoring Estonia's independence has been dubbed the Singing Revolution, from the role singing played in demonstrating the will of the Estonian nation to become free again. The rise to power of Mikhail Gorbachev in Moscow began the restructuring of Soviet power throughout the USSR, allowing for the first time real dialogue. His glasnost (openness) and perestroika (restructuring) gave Estonians tools to begin the process of independence.

Before this period, many of the public protests or campaigns had been met by brutal suppression by the security services. However, the catalyst for what turned into national protests came in late 1986, when plans were unveiled to extensively mine phosphates in Kabala-Toolse. By the start of 1987, campaigners began organizing protests against what was seen as an environmental disaster. This first public expression of anger over Soviet policy evolved into a more political protest, as the number of public gatherings quickly expanded. In August 1987 a small group of activists formed the Estonian Group for Publicizing the Molotov-Ribbentrop Pact, which organized a political gathering at Tallinn's Hirvepark on 23 August 1987—the forty-eighth anniversary of the infamous deal.

The public gathers in the streets of Tallinn to commemorate Independence Day, 24 February 1990. (Bernard Bisson/Corbis Sygma)

By this time, talk of some form of economic sovereignty had begun. The breakthrough came in an article published in September 1987, calling for an independent economy for Estonia, written by Siim Kallas, Tiit Made, Mikk Titma, and Edgar Savisaar. The plan was called Isemajandav Eesti (Self-Management Estonia), or IME (which in Estonian means "miracle").

An increasing number of public expressions of anger over Estonia's hijacked history led to the formation of the Estonian Heritage Society in late 1987. Many of the 1988 public gatherings were scheduled to mark important dates: the Tartu Peace Treaty anniversary (2 February), Independence Day (24 February), the anniversary of the 1949 deportations (26 March), among others. It was at one of these gatherings that the banned blue-black-white national flag was used for the first time since the occupation began. The authorities attempted to confront the public at times, but they failed to deter public gatherings. A popular television program introduced the entire idea of forming an organization to support Soviet reforms, and in a short period the Estonian Popular Front for the Support of Perestroika became one of the largest public groups in the country.

By June, the Popular Front had organized large-scale rallies, putting significant pressure on the government. Moscow noticed the situation as well, and on 16 June sacked Karl Vaino as the first secretary of the Estonian Communist Party and replaced him with a moderate, Vaino Väljas. The Popular Front celebrated this success with a major rally attended by some 150,000 people in Tallinn, with the national flag waving unrestricted. By August, the Estonian National Independence Party was founded, with the goal of restoring Estonia's independence.

The singing aspect of the Singing Revolution took off with the rally Eestimaa Laul (Estonian Song) on 11 September, with over 300,000 in attendance. Many of the songs sung evoked national passions, some from the large repertoire of the various song festivals and others written by pop and rock stars using the poetry of Estonia's best-known historic poets.

Opposition to the Estonian movement gathered in the form of the International Movement of the Workers of the Estonian SSR and the Joint Soviet of Workers Collectives, both in mid-1988. These groups, mostly composed of Soviet-era immigrants and Russian speakers, protested to keep Estonia part of the Soviet empire.

As the Popular Front continued to grow, it absorbed many communists as well. This caused many other groups to push further, calling for the restoration of independence, though the Popular Front remained the largest public group. The Popular Front at first pushed only for autonomy, but eventually warmed to the idea of a restoration of independence after autonomy was rejected outright by an increasingly alarmed Moscow.

Moscow's attempts to calm the waters angered Estonians, and on 16 November 1988, the Supreme Soviet in Tallinn voted for a declaration of sovereignty (258 for, 1 against, 5 abstained), asserting that Estonian laws superseded Soviet all-union laws. Moscow responded with harsh warnings and verbal rebukes for Estonia's leaders. The Supreme Soviet followed up by passing on 18 January 1989 a language law making Estonian the official language, and marked Independence Day on 24 February by raising the national flag on the Pikk Hermann tower, something not seen since 1940. The most dramatic moment in the protests came on 23 August 1989, the fiftieth anniversary of the Molotov-Ribbentrop Pact, when about two million people joined hands from Tallinn to Riga to Vilnius, forming the Baltic human chain. Though at first Soviet officials denounced the protest chain, by the end of 1989 officials yielded to pressure and admitted to the secret pact for the first time.

Not willing to take things slowly, activists from various groups calling for restoration of independence formed the Committee of Citizens in 1989. The group began registering those people who were citizens of the Republic of Estonia (before the occupation began in 1940) and their descendants. Nearly 900,000 citizens were registered during a short period. Then a second parliamentary body in Estonia, the Congress of Estonia, was elected, this one by only registered citizens (with a turnout of about 590,000 citizens, or about 98 percent) of Estonia, in February 1990. The leadership of the Congress of Estonia, the Estonian Committee, was chaired by long-time dissident Tunne Kelam.

Even before that election took place, the Estonian Communist Party was splitting into two, with one side pro-Estonia, the other pro-Moscow. In the March 1990 elections to the Supreme Soviet, the pro-Estonia side won clearly in the first even partially free elections in decades. The Popular Front's Edgar Savisaar was elected head of the government, while Arnold Rüütel remained chairman of the legislative body. On 30 March, the government quickly proclaimed a period of transition to independence and restored all the symbols of the Republic of Estonia. Moscow reacted angrily to this, with Gorbachev "rescinding" the order from Moscow. Anti-independence protestors tried to storm the parliament in May, but Popular Front supporters defended the building and prevented a bloody confrontation. (Russian-speaking workers, however, embarked on a series of strikes that damaged the economy.)

Seeing the imminent collapse of the USSR, Moscow called for a referendum on the future of the USSR. However, the Baltic countries instead held a preemptive referendum on the question, "do you want the restoration of the independence of the Republic of Estonia?" Over 77 percent voted in favor. The Moscow-backed referendum was boycotted by most of the Estonian public, with turnout of less than a quarter of eligible voters.

The restoration of independence finally came as chaos descended upon Moscow itself. The coup by hard-liners on 19 August (which eventually led to the fall of Gorbachev) gave the Supreme Council the opportunity to declare immediate restoration of independence on 20 August. Estonia was once again free.

INDEPENDENCE

As the coup collapsed in Moscow, the issue of the independence of the Baltic states was firmly outside of Moscow's control. The Estonian government received its first de jure recognition of the restoration of independence on 22 August from Iceland, followed within days by a host of countries, including the European Community and most of Europe; surprisingly the United States was again late in recognizing the independence of Estonia, only doing so on 2 September. Sweden opened the first embassy in Tallinn on 29 August. The USSR itself recognized the Baltic countries on 6 September, and the three countries joined the UN on 17 September.

A constituent assembly composed of thirty elected members of the Supreme Council and thirty from the Congress of Estonia met for the first time on 13 September. A draft constitution was completed by the end of 1991, and after some polishing, the constitution passed a national referendum on 28 June 1992. The 1992 Constitution, which came into force on 3 July, stipulated that the country should be a parliamentary republic.

Elections to the Sixth Riigikogu were held on 20 September, at which the center-right won 51 of the 101 seats. On the same day, the first round of the presidential election was also held, with Supreme Council Chairman Arnold Rüütel taking the most votes, though he failed to gain a majority, receiving only 41.8 percent of the vote. Rüütel thus entered a parliamentary runoff with the ambassador to Finland, Lennart Meri, the previous foreign minister and well-respected documentary filmmaker. The parliament's center-right orientation facilitated the election of Meri over the left-wing Rüütel by a 59 to 31 vote. The young 32-year-old center-right historian Mart Laar became prime minister.

The governing system was solidified after the Riigikogu elections by the dissolution of both the Congress of Estonia and the government in exile. The third branch of government was complete with the first session of the Supreme Court in Tartu in May 1993, with Rait Maruste presiding as its chief justice.

The central bank, re-created on 1 January 1990, benefited from the return of Estonia's gold from safekeeping abroad. The central bank's governor, Siim Kallas (of IME fame) turned the gold into a large foreign currency reserve and reintroduced the kroon on 20 June 1992. The currency, introduced despite warnings from the International Monetary Fund (IMF), was more than fully backed by the foreign currency reserve and pegged strictly to the German mark, at a ratio of one mark to eight kroon. This monetary stability became the backbone of Estonia's economic development.

The main problem of the newly restored state was the presence of a large contingent of the Red Army. Tens of thousands of Russian troops remained after the restoration

Lennart Meri, former president (1992–2001). (Patrick Robert/Corbis Sygma)

The Sinking of the Ferry *Estonia*

Estonian history has been plagued by various tragic events, most notably the mass deportations of thousands of Estonians to Siberia in the 1940s. The most tragic of those events not linked to foreign occupation or war occurred on the stormy evening of 28 September 1994, when the ferry *Estonia* sank en route between Tallinn and Stockholm. The accident claimed the lives of 851 individuals.

In a country of approximately 1.5 million people, nearly everyone knew someone who died on the ferry. Some towns were hit especially hard. The country lost its most beloved rock singer. But everyone in Estonia has a personal tragic story connected to this accident. Every year the anniversary date of 28 September has become a tragic reminder of one of the worst maritime disasters in history.

The tragedy has been shrouded in controversy, as rumors and conspiracy theories continue to spread regarding the cause of the ferry's sinking. The many half-baked theories about explosions aboard the ferry fail to disappear, despite an international commission's findings that the bow door caused the sinking of the roll-on, roll-off ferry. Some adherents of the theories have gone so far as to make an illegal diving expedition to the wreck, an act considered a violation of sepulcher by nearly all regional countries, which have jointly declared the wreck a mass grave.

Though at the time the sinking affected the numerous shipping lanes in the Baltic Sea between the Nordic countries and Estonia, the route has since recovered and gained in strength. Tallinn has become one of the busiest ports in Europe, especially for tourism. After all, it was Ernest Hemingway who wrote that you could find at least one Estonian at every port in the world. The memories of the ferry's sinking remain and still evoke deep sadness among Estonians (and of course Swedes, who lost the most people in that tragedy); however, the love of the sea and maritime navigation continues to characterize Estonia and its people.

of independence, despite international organizations and various countries calling for their withdrawal as soon as possible. Continuous international pressure, especially by the U.S. Congress, eventually led to an agreement, signed by Lennart Meri and his Russian counterpart, Boris Yeltsin, in July 1994. The last Russian troops left Estonia on 31 August 1994.

A series of scandals over arms acquisitions from Israel and the sale of Soviet rubles led to the resignation of Prime Minister Laar, and a minority government, led by Andres Tarand, held power until the next scheduled elections in March 1995. The Seventh Riigikogu elections gave the center a significant victory, with a coalition comprised of centrist and rural forces winning 41 seats. Most of Estonia's foundational policies, however, were not changed, despite the change in political orientation of the government. Lennart Meri won reelection on 20 September 1996 in a special Electoral College, as no candidate received sufficient votes in the parliament. Arnold Rüütel again lost in the runoff to the now-popular Meri.

The government pushed hard for Estonia's membership in international organizations, especially NATO (the North Atlantic Treaty Organization) and the EU (European Union). Estonia first joined the Council of Europe, the continent-wide human rights body, taking the organization's chair in 1996 for a six-month period. Estonia also joined the World Trade Organization in late 1999. Estonia's reforms were finally rewarded in 1997 when Estonia was named among the leading contenders for EU membership.

In 2002 Estonia received invitations from both the European Union and NATO to become an official member.

NATO membership is seen as the culmination of a long search for real security, and the raising of Estonia's tricolor at NATO Headquarters in 2004 means the end of the security vacuum in the region. However, membership in NATO also means additional responsibilities placed on Estonia, and the country has made significant contributions to peacekeeping efforts in various hotspots, ranging from the Balkans to Iraq.

Estonia's joining of the European Union in mid-2004 is perhaps more important in many respects, as it impacts nearly everything from agriculture to travel. With a strong 66.83 percent majority in the referendum on joining the EU in September 2003, Estonians said a loud "jah!" to returning fully to the Western world and becoming part of Europe and its governing machinery.

Politically, the country has remained on the center-right in recent years. The country swung back to the right for the Eighth Riigikogu elections on 7 March 1999, when a three-party center-right coalition won just over a majority of seats. Mart Laar returned to the post of prime minister, holding it for nearly three years before resigning in January 2002 after the coalition collapsed. Siim Kallas, the "father of the kroon," became prime minister in late January, working in a coalition with his former IME partner Edgar Savisaar. Part of the pressure on the coalition came with the August-September 2001 presidential election, as the coalition failed to elect one of their candidates. In a runoff at the Electoral College, three-time candidate Arnold Rüütel, in a shocking surprise, won his job back as head of state after a decade. The Ninth Riigikogu elections in 2003 returned a slightly more centrist three-party coalition, with Juhan Parts becoming prime minister but continuing a similar liberal policy.

Though the history of Estonia is quite complicated and often difficult to follow, the basic aspects are clear—centuries of foreign domination and an independence that is highly cherished and treasured. The understanding of the difficult history faced by this small nation helps to explain many modern issues there, ranging from the search for "hard" security guarantees to the stringent application of the language law (designed to ensure that Estonian remains the only official language of the country, and to ensure that Soviet-era immigrants learn the language). Nevertheless, the important thing for Estonians is simple: the fate of the nation again rests in the hands of the Estonian people.

POLITICAL DEVELOPMENTS

The history of Estonia places a heavy burden on its political system today, the task of relegating the problems of the past, both homegrown and foreign-imposed, definitively to history. The modern Estonian political system evolved from the collective experience of its people through hundreds of years of occupation, as well as from lessons learned around the world. What has developed is a modern parliamentary democracy capable of addressing the problems of the legacies of history and the challenges of the future, especially those presented by the ongoing process of European integration.

The maturing of the political system in Estonia is much more impressive when one considers its history, especially the absence of self-determination through the last eight centuries. In fact, only about 5 percent of the time since the first foreign conquests in the thirteenth century has the indigenous population been in charge of its own development. The modern version of Estonian democracy began to develop only in 1990–1991, during the last part of the process of restoring independence.

For centuries following the arrival of the German invaders in the thirteenth century, Estonians lived under foreign systems of government in which most (if not all) Estonians were excluded from the process. Estonians lived under the brutal regime of the Livonian Order and the Roman Catholic Church, as well as the crowns of Sweden, Denmark, Poland-Lithuania, and Russia.

The early political evolution of Estonia is most dramatic during the Russian tsarist period. Though the German nobility retained control over the Baltic region, Russia used the territories as a laboratory for social reform. This came most notably in the abolition of serfdom in Estonia in 1816 (for Livonia, 1819), which freed Estonians legally from subjugation. The nineteenth century in Estonia showed a dramatic change among the indigenous population, as increased educational opportunities created not just an intelligentsia, but also visionaries and leaders. Estonians increasingly shifted their discussion from culture to politics and reform, alongside those Germans sympathetic to the changes taking place in Europe and in Estonia.

Though political control was still far removed from Estonians, the 1866 decision by St. Petersburg to create local parish councils paved the way for the development of a modern local governmental system. As a consequence of modernization and education, Estonians began to play a larger role in local politics. In 1901, for the first time, the indigenous population—a coalition of Estonians and Latvians—took over the town council of the town of Valga. The most spectacular triumph came in 1904, as Estonian deputies in Tallinn, having gained Russian support, took control of the city council, making Jaan Poska the first Estonian mayor of Tallinn.

The real catalyst for change came with the 1905 Revolution in Russia and the resulting bloodshed throughout the Russian Empire, including Estonia. The creation of a Russian parliament, the Duma, in the long run did little to promote the democratization of Russia or to improve the situation in Estonia; the election of several Estonian deputies, however, did bring political experience to a group of statesmen who went on to become the leaders of the Estonian political movement in the ensuing decades. It was also during this period that the first true Estonian political parties, such as the National Progressive Party, were founded to safeguard Estonian interests.

The 1917 February Revolution in Russia, which toppled the tsar, brought the best opportunity for Estonia to gain political power, as local activists convinced the Russian provisional government to merge Estonian lands (the Estonian province and the northern part of the Livonian province) into one administrative unit and for that unit to be led by a native. Tallinn mayor Jaan Poska was eventually named as commissar, and he soon called for elections to the first Estonian national assembly. The elections to the Maapäev (an Estonian translation of the German "Landtag") occurred, and the first sitting was held in the summer of 1917.

The development of the first indigenous legislative assembly came to a halt, however, with the Bolshevik October Revolution, which spilled into Estonia as Bolsheviks attempted to seize power. The Bolsheviks prevented the

Prime Minister Mart Laar (1992–1994, 1999–2002), one of the young leaders who forged the country's ambitious reforms. (Sean Gallup/Getty Images)

Maapäev from meeting, though the body managed to appoint a three-man National Salvation Committee, the Päästekomitee. The committee worked clandestinely during the Bolshevik terror and the German invasion of Estonia during the worst part of World War I. During an interregnum between the retreat of the Bolsheviks and the invasion of the Germans, the committee, on 24 February 1918, declared independence.

The political system could not develop for months due to German occupation; with the collapse of the German military in the autumn of 1918, however, the provisional Estonian government regained power. Successful in repelling foreign occupation during the War of Independence, the provisional government organized elections to the Constituent Assembly in April 1919. The body, dominated by the democratic left wing, structured the draft constitution and key pieces of early legislation in accordance with their ideology. The 1920 constitution sought protection against a concentration of power, thus the severely weakened executive. Most of the power rested in the parliament, the Ri-

igikogu, which could appoint and dismiss cabinet ministers at will. The head of the cabinet, the weak State Elder, served also as the ceremonial head of state but did not proclaim laws; that prerogative remained with the Riigikogu speaker.

The electoral system of the era also featured an idealistic vision of equality, based on a purely proportional system of representation. The lack of a minimum threshold meant that parliament was composed of many small parties who proved unable to make stable coalitions, thus paralyzing the government frequently, most notably during the crises around the global Depression of the late 1920s. This lack of ability to act angered the right wing and organizations representing veterans of the War of Independence, who lobbied for the creation of a strong presidency. Two attempts at a referendum for a new constitution (with a somewhat stronger executive power) failed due to lack of support from the veterans; the third referendum on a draft constitution by the veterans succeeded. This 1934 constitution focused power on an elected president and away from the fractious parliament.

The political freedom of Estonia fell for once to a domestic force, when caretaker prime minister Konstantin Päts, the hero of the declaration of independence, undertook a palace coup. The country moved into a mild form of authoritarianism, as the parliament was not recalled; corporatism and nationalism were both employed to jumpstart the economy and society. Though an attempt at re-democratization happened later in the 1930s, with the creation of a new bicameral parliament, it was nothing more than window-dressing, as the opposition was not allowed to function openly. Though the Päts regime did not prove to be unpopular, it did stymie the country's political development.

In 1939 the Molotov-Ribbentrop Pact was concluded between Nazi Germany and the Soviet Union; shortly thereafter Estonia fell under Soviet occupation. Sham elections were held, and the rump parliament voted to join the USSR. Though local conspirators held many leadership positions, Moscow and its local representative, Andrei Zhdanov, directed their actions. Attempts to Sovietize the political system occurred, but were halted by the Nazi invasion of the USSR in June 1941. The three-year Nazi occupation saw Estonia run as a territory for future colonization in Germany's Lebensraum (living space). When the Soviets retook Estonia in 1944, the Sovietization of the political system continued. The legislature was renamed the Supreme Soviet, while the republic's government became the council of ministers. The de facto head of republic became the chairman of the presidium of the Supreme Soviet, or simply the legislature's speaker. Many of the leaders were so-called Yestonians, ethnic Estonians who had grown up in Russia and did not speak Estonian.

The Soviet system did not allow for any true political development, as the system and its management remained foreign-imposed and foreign-controlled. The "elections" to the local and all-Union supreme soviets were single-candidate ballots, and always featured nearly 100 percent turnout and nearly 100 percent support for the Communist Party candidate. Many Estonians eventually joined the Communist Party following the end of the brutal Stalinist period, using membership as a method of career advancement.

By the mid–1980s, leadership positions in Estonia were primarily in the hands of Estonian-born Estonians (not Yestonians), and they took advantage of the Soviet programs of glasnost and perestroika (openness and restructuring). Public protests occurred with greater frequency, evolving from environmental concerns to more national issues. Nongovernmental organizations (NGOs) were formed to address historical issues and to commemorate historical events, such as the mass deportations of the 1940s and Estonia's Independence Day. Eventually political organizations began to form, first to support perestroika, later to advocate full independence. Thus, the political development of Estonians happened via NGOs campaigning both within and outside the system, and the political leadership began to shift toward the nation's point-of-view.

By the end of the 1980s, Estonians of all beliefs were fully engaged in political activities. Independence activists continued to campaign, registering the citizens of Estonia for a parallel political body, the Congress of Estonia. The Popular Front, which chose to work within the system in the Supreme Soviet, asserted the republic's superiority in legislation, superseding all-Union laws. The election to the Supreme Soviet in 1990 was nearly free and fair, and pro-Estonia delegates held the majority, making the Popular Front the leader of the republic's government. A republic-wide referendum in early 1991 showed overwhelming support for Estonian independence.

Though this chain of events resulted in two parallel bodies of power, the (renamed) Popular Front in the Supreme Council and the Estonian Council in the Congress of Estonia, both worked to achieve independence. With the eventual restoration of independence in August 1991, the two bodies came together and formed equal parts of the new Constituent Assembly. This Constituent Assembly drafted the basic document that created the foundations for the modern Estonian political system.

The modern Estonian political system reflects many qualities of its counterpart between the world wars, but heavily tempered by the collective experience of the people of the perils of both ultraliberal parliamentary democracy and authoritarianism. The product created and enshrined in the 1992 constitution by the Constituent Assembly is a modern parliamentary democracy, built with integral safeguards and expressly stipulated checks and balances. The key was to create a *Rechtstaat,* a state based on the rule of law.

Unlike its 1920 counterpart, the 1992 Constitution places a significant amount of power in the executive, personified by the head of government, the prime minister. The cabinet, made up of the prime minister and the ministers who head the various ministries, is entrusted with the day-to-day governing and administration of the state. Various departments, bureaus, inspectorates, and offices are under the government or one of the ministries; for example, the European Integration Office is part of the cabinet office, while the Border Guards are under the Interior Ministry. Government decisions are made democratically by the cabinet, needing majority support for their enactment. For the most part the civil service remains depoliticized, with only the ministers being purely political posts; the permanent

undersecretaries remain civil servants, as do department and inspectorate directors (despite temptations to politicize the posts). The government and ministries also introduce a significant amount of legislation, including the annual budget.

Also, unlike the 1920 constitution, the position of head of state, the president, was created by the 1992 constitution. The president serves as the ceremonial head of state, as well as the supreme commander of the country's national defense. The president also promulgates laws and has the ability to challenge legislation by veto; if the parliament returns a vetoed law unchanged, the matter goes to the Supreme Court for a decision. The president also officially nominates ministers and other key positions, though all nominations require parliamentary confirmation.

Though the executive holds significant power, the parliament, or Riigikogu, remains the support base for the executive. All major government posts, ranging from ministers down, hold their posts at the confirmation and with the confidence of the parliament. The legislature is responsible for introducing, amending, and passing legislation. The political parties establish factions within the 101-member parliament. The parliament is also divided into ten permanent committees, such as the Foreign Affairs Committee, the National Defense Committee, and the Legal Committee. The management of the parliament's affairs comes from the elected chairman and two deputy chairs; one of the deputy chairs usually goes to an opposition MP.

The judiciary plays an independent and major role in maintaining the court system, and also serves as an independent arbiter between the legislative and executive branches. The Supreme Court is responsible for ruling on the constitutionality of legislation during a presidential-parliamentary disagreement over legislation passed but not promulgated by the president. The chief justice of the Supreme Court, who is first nominated by the president and later confirmed by parliament, nominates the other justices, who require parliamentary confirmation. Justices at all levels are appointed by the president, on the recommendation of the chief justice of the Supreme Court, and serve for life terms.

The State Audit Office remains an independent state body responsible for overseeing the use of state funds, while the Legal Chancellor's Office serves as an independent analyst considering the constitutionality and legality of pending legislation.

Parliamentary elections are held every fourth year under a modified proportional representation system. The country is divided into eleven electoral districts based on geographical boundaries, with the total mandate divided by population numbers. Suffrage is universal for all Estonian citizens over the age of 18, and candidates must be citizens over the age of 21. The voters technically vote for an individual, but the vote counts also in the party count. Certain candidates who reach a specific vote level are automatically elected within their party lists, though the slots within each electoral district are divided by proportional representation within the district. Those slots not filled by the automatically elected candidates are filled in numerical order in the district party list. Parties, however, need to gain at least 5 percent of all votes throughout the country to be considered for the seat distribution, a much needed safeguard to prevent extremely small or localized movements from fracturing the parliament's composition.

Estonia is not a very centralized country, as many responsibilities, ranging from municipal utilities to public transportation, lie at the local level. The country is divided into 15 counties, which in turn are split in many local authorities with their own local councils and governments; despite the ongoing process of merging small local administrative units, there remain nearly 250 in 2001. Local elections are held every three years, also under a proportional representation system.

Presidential elections are held once every five years, with the responsibility first resting in the parliament. Candidates are nominated by at least one-fifth of MPs (members of parliament) from among its 101 members, and winning candidates require a supermajority of at least 68 MPs in support. The parliament is given three chances—with the final round being a runoff of the top two vote getters—to achieve that supermajority. In case the parliament fails, a special Electoral College is convened. The Electoral College is composed of the 101 parliament members as well as representatives from all the local councils (for the 2001 presidential elections there were 266 local council representatives). A minimum of 21 Electoral College members can nominate a candidate, and a simple majority elects a new president. If the Electoral College fails to elect a president in two rounds, the second being a runoff of the top two vote-getters, the process returns to the parliament and repeats. Candidates for the presidency must be native-born Estonian citizens at least forty years of age; there is also a two-term limit.

The 1992 Constitution achieved a good balance of power among the three branches of government, creating safeguards against the overextending of power by the government, the president, or the parliament. Though European integration, as well as the surprise opposition victory in the 2001 presidential election, has provoked debate about amending the Constitution, for the most part the political system created in the early 1990s has functioned well as the foundation for the country's continual development.

Despite its lack of a continuous democratic tradition, Estonia has managed to build a relatively stable party system since the restoration of independence. Unlike many other countries in Central and Eastern Europe, Estonia has not suffered from a large amount of party fracturing; instead, the party system has actually seen consolidation over the years, creating more stable parties, parties based on philosophy rather than on personality.

Ironically, one of the cleavages created before the restoration of independence remains, the split between the Estonian Popular Front, those who worked within the Soviet system toward freedom, and the Estonian Citizens Committee, those who created a parallel structure outside of the Soviet system as a continuation of the state occupied in 1940. For the most part, the Citizens Committee established itself on the center-right, while the Popular Front held the center and the center-left. Many of the figures who played major roles in the two organizations remain in the political fray, split along similar lines, though on much more contemporary problems than the method of achieving freedom for the country.

Since the first post-Soviet general elections in 1992, the center-right has held the most influence, whether in the government or in opposition, in large measure due to the foundations the center-right governments of 1992–1995 built for Estonia's future development. A strong left-wing force never developed during this period (as happened in other states in the region), leaving the political battleground in the right and center.

The main right-wing conservative force in Estonia grew from the Estonian Citizens Committee, which has manifested itself today as the Pro Patria Union. This party was formed by a merger of its conservative predecessor Pro Patria with the nationalist Estonian National Independence Party. In the 1992 general elections these groups won twenty-nine and ten seats respectively; the leader of the merged parties, the then–thirty-two-year-old Mart Laar, served as prime minister until scandals forced him out of power in late 1994. The two groups ran as a coalition in the 1995 general coalitions but faced public backlash for the difficult economic reforms that affected many in Estonian society, earning only eight seats. By the 1999 elections, however, the parties had merged and stormed back to victory with eighteen seats, returning Laar to the prime minister's office. Though it has evolved, the party aligns itself with the Christian Democratic and conservative movements in Europe, boasting a pro-family and national-minded platform. The party also continues to support the liberal economic policies it created in the early 1990s, which have received some support from the liberal wing.

Several other right-wing movements also played minor roles during this period, but they have not lasted over time. A small right-wing breakaway of Pro Patria, the Right-Wingers, won five seats in 1995, but the group merged into other parties by the 1999 elections. The right-wing nationalist Estonian Citizens, led by a retired U.S. military officer, campaigned on an exclusionary policy toward Estonia's Russian speakers; the party fared well in 1992 with eight seats, but failed to win any seats by 1995 and has since disappeared. Even a semiserious pro-monarchy group gained eight seats in the 1992 elections but has since disappeared.

With the probusiness environment created in the early years of Estonian independence, it was not surprising to see a liberal movement become one of the strongest political orientations by the mid-1990s. The Reform Party, led by the father of the kroon and former central bank president, Siim Kallas, pursued ultraliberal laissez-faire policies and gained the support of the growing number of entrepreneurs. The party campaigned on further reduction of the tax burden of both the public and businesses, the preservation of liberal trade policies, and strict fiscal and monetary policies. This probusiness and tax-cutting platform earned the Reform Party nineteen seats in the 1995 elections, as the party worked in coalition with centrists for a part of the election cycle. The party remained successful in the 1999 elections, winning eighteen seats. Kallas became prime minister in early 2002 in a caretaker coalition with centrists.

Since 2001 the political movement Res Publica has turned its attention to elected office. One of the oldest political movements in Estonia, Res Publica for years resisted transforming itself into a party; instead its members usually ran with the like-minded Reform Party, and sometimes the Pro Patria Union. However, the group has since risen to challenge the established center-right with substantial membership and funding. This "new" party managed to craft a three-party coalition after the 2003 general elections, making its leader, Juhan Parts, prime minister.

The evolution of the party known as the Moderates is among the most complex and convoluted of all of the Estonian political movements. The party has its roots in the Moderates coalition from the 1992 and 1995 elections, which linked the Estonian Social Democratic Party and the Rural Center Party with a centrist platform; the Moderates won twelve seats. Despite its Social Democratic background, the party remained centrist and worked closely with the center-right; its leader, Andres Tarand, served as a caretaker prime minister in 1994–1995 up to the general elections. The 1995 elections also saw the Moderates lose out due to the unpopularity of difficult reforms; they won only six seats. In the run-up to the 1999 general elections, the Moderates joined a coalition with the right-wing People's Party, a relationship that was formalized soon after the coalition won seventeen seats. The merger looked odd from an ideological point of view, as the People's Party was actually a merger of right-wing nationalist and agrarian parties, whereas the Moderates had Social Democratic backgrounds; the merged party remained technically loyal to the Social Democratic banner, but worked closely with the center right.

The Pro Patria Union, Reform Party, and Moderates signed a cooperation agreement before the 1999 general elections, proposing to work together in a postelection government. The three lists won 53 of 101 seats, and they gave the prime ministerial job to the Pro Patria Union leader Mart Laar. This government, which lasted from March 1999 until January 2002, broke apart due to personality differences; however, the curious aspect was that it represented the three major political affiliations of Europe: conservatism, liberalism, and social democracy.

The political center in Estonia has become the major battleground, as there are no truly left-wing parties with any amount of substantial support. The populist Center Party, a descendant of the Popular Front, leads the centrist movements. Though often employing populist left-leaning ideas, such as the abolition of the flat tax system, the party is far from being truly left wing; however, the lack of a true left wing gives the Center Party much of the natural left-wing voter support.

Having led the independence process from within, the Popular Front began collapsing at the restoration of independence; it won only fifteen seats in 1992. Reconfigured into the Center Party, the group won sixteen seats in 1995 and worked in a centrist coalition, until a scandal involving party leader and then–interior minister Edgar Savisaar tapping private conversations of his political opponents forced them out. The party remains the main beneficiary of a lack of left-wing parties, winning twenty-eight seats in 1999, the largest share, but it was kept out of the government for another three years until the previously mentioned center-right coalition collapsed in early 2002.

Rural centrist groups, especially the Estonian People's Union, represent another strong centrist movement. Originally called the Rural People's Union, the group continued to gain strength with the uneven economic development throughout the country. Despite the small share of agriculture in the overall economy, there remains a significant voter base for the rural-based party. As urban development outpaced rural development, the party scored well in 1995 by running with the centrist Coalition Party and other groups (see below), winning in total forty-one seats. The Rural People's Union, before the 1999 elections, decided to move beyond simply rural interests by inviting the smaller Rural League and the Families and Pensioners Party to merge into the new movement, to be named the People's Union. The party fared less well in 1999, winning just seven seats, but managed to score an upset victory in 2001 with the election of its founder and honorary chairman Arnold Rüütel as president. Despite modest numbers in the 2003 elections, the People's Union managed a place in the center-right ruling coalition.

One of the most interesting cases in the center can be seen in the rise and collapse of the Coalition Party. Originally designed as a probusiness centrist party, this "party of power" brought together many rich businessmen to create a stable business environment. Running in the 1992 elections as the "Safe Home" coalition, the group gained seventeen seats. Rising before the 1995 elections, it teamed together with several small parties, as well as the Rural People's Union, to take a dramatic victory with forty-one votes. The party's Tiit Vähi and Mart Siimann held the prime minister's job through the entire parliamentary cycle, but its uninspiring platform and lack of solid ideology left the party decimated by the 1999 elections, in which it and coalition partners won only seven seats; with further defections of both party members and coalition partners, the party maintained only one seat by 2001 and formally dissolved.

Several parties have also risen as self-designated representatives of the large Russian-speaking communities in Estonia, the largest being the United People's Party. Often several parties run in a coalition to maximize their chances to break the 5 percent minimum barrier, a challenging task, as many Russian-speakers choose to vote for mainstream parties. These parties failed to gain representation in the 1992 elections, but managed to win six seats in 1995. The same result was achieved in 1999, but with the help of the solidly left-wing Estonian Democratic Labor Party, the renamed Communist Party. None of the parties, including the Democratic Labor Party and the United People's Party, can achieve the 5 percent minimum themselves, and their strength remains weak. Most of these parties campaign for the easing of citizenship and language laws, as well as increased social spending. These parties, not surprisingly, do much better in local elections, in which non-citizens are allowed to vote. However, as a sign of the maturation of politics away from ethnocentric voting, even in such local elections the Russocentric parties have recently been sharply down in number of seats won.

Among new Central and Eastern European democracies, Estonia has demonstrated a relatively stable party system, with many of the same political forces active throughout the post-Soviet period. Considering the political evolution of Estonia over the centuries, and especially its history in the twentieth century, the achievements of recent years are even more impressive. This stability of political parties has helped to preserve a stable political system, allowing for reforms to be pursued and maintained. This stability demonstrates the maturity of the political system despite its youth, a very Estonian characteristic in general.

CULTURAL DEVELOPMENT

Among the small nations of the world, Estonia has one of the most developed and diverse cultural environments. Though "high culture," such as literature and art, only developed in the nineteenth century, when both education and opportunities finally opened up to Estonians, the strength and breadth of cultural achievements for a nation just over one million strong is enormous. Estonian cultural figures rank among the best known, even if their Estonian links are less frequently known.

Nothing brings out more strongly the importance of culture in Estonia than the fact that the national awakening of the late nineteenth century was first a cultural awakening. That awakening was, however, only the beginning; the period of independence between the world wars was the catalyst for a newly found creativity throughout the entire population. The 1925 establishment of the Kultuurkapital (Cultural Endowment Fund) helped to fund a new generation in all areas of culture, ranging from the already strong field of literature to the developing genre of cinematography. Various professional associations, such as the Estonian Writers Association and the Estonian Academic Society of Composers, also formed to increase activity in the individual genres.

The invasion of the Soviet Red Army in 1940 decimated Estonian culture; many figures were imprisoned or killed. Many of the most prominent figures were denied permission to work. Others also fled overseas, a large number congregating in the capital of Estonian culture in exile, Stockholm. Although these émigrés continued the tradition of Estonian culture, the predominant theme of many of these works had to do with the ordeal of exile, the longing to return home, and opposition to the Soviet occupation and its installed regime.

Though the Soviets attempted to halt cultural development for a significant period of time through censorship and repression of creativity among Estonians, the cultural achievements of the nation continued. Many ingenious, creative minds worked around the censors in imaginative ways, and audiences became used to reading between the lines, focusing on the imagery. It is of little surprise that the restoration of independence process was led by cultural figures who attempted to create a second national awakening. The role of culture in the fight for freedom cannot be underestimated.

Today Estonian culture is enjoying a renaissance, and at the same time it is facing a crossroads. The country's restored freedom, which has also meant the reinstatement of the Kultuurkapital, has led to a new generation of cultural figures finding ways to express themselves. The continuing internationalization of pop culture, however, especially in the form of the influence of Hollywood and other forms of American culture, has presented a major challenge to this new generation. They face a hard choice: they can remain true to their roots, they can enter this international culture, or, the biggest challenge, they can attempt to bring the two together. In any case, the success of Estonian culture in the first decade of restored independence has given this new generation the energy and determination to bring Estonia fully back into the mainstream of the Western world.

LITERATURE

Of the various forms of culture in Estonia, literature has perhaps the most fascinating development, and the development that can be described in most detail. The growth of literature has paralleled the country's development in many ways, ranging from the national awakening movement to the various ups and downs the country faced over the years.

Though the first printed text in the Estonian language—translated catechisms—appeared in the early 1500s, it took several more centuries for Estonian literature to develop fully. One of the best early pieces of literature came as a 1708 poem by a poet named Käsu Hans, lamenting the sacking of Tartu in the Great Northern War, but it was only in the 1800s that the expansion of education opportunities for the indigenous population fostered the rapid growth of Estonian literature. The earliest of the pioneers was Kristjan Jaak Peterson (1801–1822), who wrote some of the earliest Estonian poems before his untimely death; however, his work was only revealed decades after his passing.

The Estonian Learned Society was founded in 1838 to promote knowledge of Estonia in various areas, including language and literature. The society helped to coordinate activities by Estonian scholars of both native and foreign origin, including the increasing study of Estonian folk culture. Though most of the learned societies of the time were German, and the Estonian Learned Society membership was composed chiefly of German so-called Estophiles, there were several Estonians among the group. Among them were two Estonian doctors who changed the course of Estonian literature: Friedrich Robert Faehlmann (1798–1850) and Friedrich Reinhold Kreutzwald (1803–1882).

Through the society, the two doctors began collecting folklore from around Estonia and the Estonian parts of Livonia. Oral literature had been an important part of folk culture, and this compilation was the first effort aimed at its recording. When Faehlmann died, Kreutzwald took over the task and began compiling the material into the national epic, *Kalevipoeg* (Son of Kalev). With creative additions and influence from the Finnish national epic, *Kalevala,* Kreutzwald completed the epic—the first major piece of literature in Estonian. Due to censorship issues, the compilation was published only in 1862 in Finland.

Kalevipoeg is a tale of the complex character from whom the epic takes its name, a character who symbolizes Estonia in all its aspects—its triumphs, struggles, laments, and joys. The lengthy epic, written in a poetic form using an old Estonian folk poetry meter, focuses on both the national struggle, chiefly against enemies symbolizing the German crusaders, and also the personal struggle within the complex title character. Reflecting the situation of the age, the story ends with Kalevipoeg stuck, guarding the world from the gates of hell, ready to return to the world some day to liberate Estonia. The political symbolism used in the epic has made it a rallying point for the various freedom movements over the years.

The next major figure in the world of Estonian literature is beloved poet and drama pioneer Lydia Koidula (1843–1886). At this point all areas of Estonian literature began developing, leading to the creation of the Estonian Society of Literati in 1872. The number of works in Estonian increased dramatically, as the society promoted the use of Estonian in all aspects of life. The society also played a significant role in standardizing the spelling system for the language, something to which both Kreutzwald and Koidula left lasting contributions.

Much of the early literature was romantic in nature, especially in its dramatization of Estonian folk culture and traditions. The collection of folklore continued, spearheaded by cultural leaders like Jakob Hurt (1839–1906), whose portrait is on the ten-kroon note. However, as the political situation of the country changed, so too did its literature. Increasingly in subsequent years literature focused on realism—often critical—and played a major role, alongside the song festivals, in the national awakening movement.

In the latter part of the nineteenth century, a fresh crop of Estonian literary talent had entered the scene, taking full advantage of the opportunities created by trailblazers like Koidula and Kreutzwald. Many poets emerged, such as Juhan Liiv (1864–1913), who could create beautiful passages about nature and with equal ease craft the most intense symbolism in his patriotic poems, despite the massive oppression of the Russification years in the 1880s. Another genre in which major progress was made was historical novels, such as the 1880 book *Tasuja* (The Avenger) by Eduard Bornhöhe (1862–1932), depicting the (much romanticized) 1343 St. George's Day uprising. The 1902 story based on

Lydia Koidula

One of the most fascinating cultural figures in Estonia is the beloved poet Lydia Koidula, whose beautiful poetry remains as popular and relevant as ever nearly 150 years after its writing.

Rarely can a nation claim a nineteenth century female poet as its most beloved national poet. Born in 1843 in the town of Vändra, Koidula received an enlightened upbringing from her well-known father, the pioneering newspaper founder and author of the national anthem, Johann Voldemar Jannsen. Koidula took advantage of the pioneering secondary girls' school founded in Pärnu in the 1850s and trained to be a teacher.

Though busy with work at her father's newspaper, Koidula began serious creative writing in the 1860s, ranging from short stories to poems. One collection of her early poems, *Emajõe ööbik* (The Nightingale of the Emajõgi), showed both the lyrical quality of her prose and the passionate patriotism she could invoke through words. Koidula became known as the premiere national poet, overcoming most gender barriers that hindered her work.

Many of her poems were set to music during the national song festivals, which she and her family helped to organize. "Mu isamaa on minu arm" (My Homeland is My Love), accompanied by various tunes over the decades, remains an unofficial anthem for the Estonian nation, and even became the emotional focal point of the Singing Revolution more than a century later, as Estonia moved to regain independence.

Koidula also established Estonian drama, writing the first original staged play in Estonian: *Saaremaa onupoeg* (The Saaremaa Cousin). The play was first performed in 1870 at the pioneering Vanemuine Cultural Society (later Theater), which Koidula and her family also founded.

Koidula left Estonia after marrying a military physician in the mid-1870s, moving to Kronstadt, near St. Petersburg. She continued her writing until her premature death in 1886. Later her remains were returned to Estonia to be buried among the nation's most prominent figures in the Forest Cemetery in Tallinn.

Reverence for Koidula among the Estonian nation is clearly noticeable, nor is it limited to their love for "Mu isamaa on minu arm." Her poetry remains popular, and her role in the history of Estonian literature—establishing the long tradition of Estonian drama and national poetry—makes her among the most important figures in the evolution of Estonian culture. This public reverence is also clearly evident on the 100-kroon banknote, which is graced by Koidula's portrait.

the 1858 Mahtra uprising, *Mahtra sõda* (The Mahtra War) was among the most important works of writer Eduard Vilde (1865–1933), the first truly successful Estonian novelist.

At the start of the twentieth century, with the harshest Russification campaigns ending and social turmoil appearing, a new generation of literary figures emerged to continue the national movement. In 1905 the Noor-Eesti (Young Estonia) movement was formed, bringing together the efforts of some of the most gifted writers of the new century. The main principle Noor-Eesti followed was "Let us be Estonians, but also become Europeans," emphasizing that Estonian culture had to take its rightful place among other high European cultures. One of the leading figures of Noor-Eesti was the poet Gustav Suits (1883–1956), best known for his 1905 volume *Elu tuli* (Life's Fire), which played a major role in modernizing Estonian poetry. Another of the movement's leaders was master storyteller Friedebert Tuglas (1886–1971), who produced popular short stories one after another, as well as becoming one of the leading literary critics of the land. The contributions of the Noor-Eesti to the literary world were major, including the works of linguist Johannes Aavik (1880–1973), who modernized the Estonian language. The 1905 Russian Revolution drove many members of the socially conscious Noor-Eesti out of the country, and their travels around the world expanded their horizons even further. The Estonian Literary Society was created in 1907, and the publication of the first Estonian literary journal, *Eesti kirjandus* (Estonian literature) had begun a year earlier.

The quality of Estonian literature continued to improve in the early years of the twentieth century. Oskar Luts (1887–1953) created one of the lasting classics of Estonian literature in 1912, with his tale of school life, *Kevade* (Spring), and poet Ernst Enno (1875–1934) expanded the scope of Estonian poetry into more exotic themes. Drama also became even more popular, with the growth of theater companies around the country, and August Kitzberg (1855–1927) became one of the leading playwrights, especially with his 1912 tragedy, *Libahunt* (The Werewolf).

The establishment of independent Estonia gave Estonian literature the further ability to develop without the threat of censorship, and the plethora of authors created a rich array of works in all disciplines and topics during the two decades of independence between the world wars. One of the earliest movements of this period was Siuru (Wonderbird), formed already in 1917, which included the poet and Nobel Literature Prize nominee Marie Under (1883–1980), who experimented controversially with eroticism, as well as Henrik Visnapuu (1890–1951), who possessed a gift for constructing lyrical verse as well as potent imagery. The establishment of the Estonian Writers Union in 1922, as well as the Kultuurkapital (Cultural Endowment Fund), helped to develop literature even further.

The indisputably most excellent literary work of the independence period is the five-part epic *Tõde ja õigus* (Truth and Justice) by Anton-Hansen Tammsaare (1878–1940), depicting the conflict between truth and justice experienced by a family over the years of the national awakening. Tammsaare contributed several other major novels in this era, such

as the fantastic but fun *Põrgupõhja uus Vanapagan* (The New Devil of Põrgupõhja) and the relationship-focused *Elu ja armastus* (Life and Love), making him the best-known novelist in Estonian literature and winning him the honor of appearing on the twenty-five-kroon note. Another giant among the large number of gifted novelists was August Gailit (1891–1960), with his grotesque fantasy *Purpurne surm* (The Purple Death) and his international hit *Toomas Nipernaadi*. Many others left major works during this period, including the so-called Tallinn trilogy by Karl Ristikivi (1912–1977), the opposing rural trilogy by Albert Kivikas (1898–1978), the psychological work *Armukadedus* (Jealousy) by Johannes Semper (1892–1970), and the coastal folktale *Öitsev meri* (The Blossoming Sea) by August Mälk (1900–1987).

All aspects of literature flourished in this period, especially poetry. Alongside the old masters from the Noor-Eesti period and the younger generation of Siuru, other poets like the left-wing thinker Johannes Vares (1890–1946; known as Barbarus) and Betty Alver (1906–1989) also emerged. Unfortunately, Vares was used as a puppet for the Soviet occupation authorities and committed suicide in 1946, after seeing the true nature of Soviet communism. Drama also continued to grow in popularity, with the satirical plays of Hugo Raudsepp (1883–1952) playing a major role.

The Soviet occupation and World War II wreaked havoc on the Estonian literary world. Several of the authors mentioned above, Raudsepp, for example, among them, died after being deported to Siberia, and others were prohibited from publishing or placed in some form of internal exile (Tuglas and Alver among others). A great number, however, fled overseas (Suits, Under, Gailit, Mälk, Ristikivi, Visnapuu, and more), many finding a base in Stockholm. They continued to publish overseas, though the focus had now shifted to issues relating to their exile, and their works were not available back in Estonia. The few works that emerged in Estonia in the following years were tainted heavily by dogma and imposed communist sympathies.

Only the death of Stalin and the coming of the thaw period made it possible for Estonian literature to be revived. A new generation of writers and poets took advantage of this opportunity. Poetry saw a major revival with the coming of this new group, including Nobel Literature Prize nominee Jaan Kaplinski (b. 1941), who experimented with exotic oriental concepts, Paul-Eerik Rummo (b. 1942), Hando Runnel (b. 1936), a master at patriotic works in an era of harsh censorship, and Juhan Viiding (1948–1995; also known as Jüri Üdi), the most playful and darkly symbolic of the group. The latter two have become even more popular over the years, as many of their poems have been turned into pop and rock songs. Drama also regained its popularity, with one of the best known being *Nimetu saar* (The Nameless Island) by playwright and poet Artur Alliksaar (1923–1966). Many of the poets faced repression and censorship throughout the Soviet occupation, especially in the stagnant 1970s, when Russification intensified.

However, the most celebrated writer of that time and up to the present day is Jaan Kross (b. 1920), a perennial nominee for the Nobel Prize in Literature. A victim of both Soviet and Nazi captivity, Kross has been a prolific poet, novelist, and short story writer for a half century. He is best known for his historical novels, especially the internationally acclaimed 1978 *Keisri hull* (The Tsar's Madman), about a German baron and his "madness" in pushing the Russian tsar toward reform. Kross is the only Estonian author with several novels and short stories in English translation, and his work has earned him critical praise in many of the world's most prominent literary reviews.

With independence regained, Estonian literature is again experiencing a renaissance. The old masters, such as Kross, continue to produce masterpieces, and the work of the exile community has been discovered and merged into the overall literature pool. At the same time, a new generation of writers is again emerging, including the brilliant young writer Andrus Kivirähk (b. 1970), giving literature an infusion of fresh blood. If the quality of the literature of the previous independence period is any indication, then the future of Estonian literature is indeed bright.

ART

Many forms of culture flourished in Estonia during periods when native Estonians were given no opportunity to take part, art being a prime example. Some of the masters of the European art world left exquisite examples of their work in Estonia, especially the most famous Tallinn churches. For example, the paintings by Bernd Notke (1436–1509) and Hermen Rode (1430–1504) at the Niguliste (St. Nicholas) Church are among the most memorable pieces in the country today. Tallinn-born Michel Sittow (1468–1525) became a well-known Renaissance painter and served in the Danish royal court, with his pieces exhibited in major museums around the world.

Only in the nineteenth century, when Estonians were encouraged to dabble in the arts, did Estonian artists begin to make their mark. One of the most prominent Estonian artists of the century was Johann Köler (1826–1899), best known for his portraits and landscape paintings. Köler worked in the Russian imperial court in St. Petersburg, and also played a significant role in the national awakening movement.

With the growing national movement, Estonian art gained in prominence, and art schools sprung up in Tallinn and Tartu. One of the most revered artists of the period was Kristjan Raud (1865–1943), a master of romantic imagery. Raud is best known for his powerful illustrations in the 1935 printing of the national epic *Kalevipoeg,*; he is honored on the one-kroon note. His twin brother Paul Raud (1865–1930) was also a prominent portrait painter of the period. Eduard Wiiralt (1898–1954) became the best-known Estonian graphic artist, winning acclaim throughout Europe with his illustrations.

Estonian sculpting was founded by August Weizenberg (1837–1921), who created some of the most stunning figures of history and legend. Amandus Adamson (1855–1954), famous for the Russalka memorial in Tallinn, is best known for his patriotic monuments; unfortunately most were destroyed by the Soviet authorities after the occupation.

The painting Joonas *(Jonah) by Jüri Arrak, which depicts the biblical story, has become a symbol of Estonia's escape from Russia. (Juri Arrak/Artists Rights Society, New York/EAU, Tallinn)*

The occupation crippled the art world for a period until a new generation appeared. Among the rich and diverse group of artists in Estonia today, one of the best known and most memorable is Jüri Arrak (b. 1936), who boasts one of the most instantaneously recognizable styles in the world today. Blending myth and fantasy, Arrak has created scores of powerful images, ranging from the thought-provoking to the fear-evoking; he conjures up powerful emotions in his works. His works have been exhibited all around the world to major acclaim. Another of the most well-known and talented artists is Mark Kalev Kostabi (b. 1960), born to Estonian exiles in California and now one of the leading figures of the New York contemporary art scene. His works are exhibited in world-famous galleries such as the Metropolitan Museum of Art and the Guggenheim Museum, and is forever linked to the hard rock world with the cover of the popular "Use Your Illusion" album by rockers Guns n' Roses.

MUSIC

Of all the arts, Estonians have experienced the most international success in music, especially in recent times. The importance of music, especially the song festivals, in the lives of Estonians cannot be overestimated, and the pride the nation takes in its musical achievements is major, ranging from the work of Estonia's many world-famous figures in classical music to the victory of Tanel Padar (b. 1980) and Dave Benton (b. 1951) in the 2001 Eurovision Song Contest—the first person of African descent to have won the

European pop contest in its forty-six-year history. (Given that Estonia has no significant black population, for the Caribbean-born Benton to have won the contest is testimony to the openness of Estonian society.)

At the first national song festival in 1869, there was not much Estonian-originated music. A few of the pieces, however, including settings of the poems of Lydia Koidula, were composed by the festival's conductor, the Estonian Aleksander Saebelmann-Kunileid (1845–1875). But by the turn of the century, many of the foundations of Estonia's musical development, such as the first symphony orchestra in 1900, had been laid.

Many of the early pioneers of Estonian composition were educated in Russia by some of the biggest Russian names in classical music. Rudolf Tobias (1873–1918) was a pivotal figure in Estonian music, composing some of the earliest major Estonian pieces, including the mammoth 1909 oratorio *Des Jonah Sendung* (Jonah's mission), based on the Biblical story of Jonah and the whale. Tobias is honored on the fifty-kroon banknote. His contemporary, another pioneer in developing the oratorio tradition, was Artur Kapp (1878–1952), especially with his 1931 *Hiiob*, based on the Biblical story of Job. Also from the St. Petersburg school was the grand old lady of Estonian music, Miina Härma (1864–1941), best known for organ works and choral pieces, as well as her conducting.

The early twentieth century saw Estonian composers achieving firsts for their nation. Artur Lemba (1885–1963) created some of the earliest and most lasting operatic and symphonic works, while Cyrillus Kreek (1889–1962) focused on folk motifs, an approach that also brought success to future generations of Estonian composers. Eugen Kapp (1908–1996), son of pioneering composer and music professor Artur Kapp, also created some of the best-known ballets and operas of the era, and Gustav Ernesaks (1908–1993) created some of the most memorable patriotic choral pieces, which played a major role in the Singing Revolution decades later. Heino Eller (1887–1970) was a prominent composer and teacher, responsible for producing the next generation of composers that put Estonia on the world's musical map.

The best known of Eller's students is Arvo Pärt (b. 1935), one of the most famous figures in today's classical music scene. His passion for religious choral music, seen in such works as the 1994 *Litany* and the 1982 *St. John's Passion,* has made his pieces some of the most sought-after in the world today.

Another of Eller's students is Eduard Tubin (1905–1982), the best-known traditional symphonist from Estonia. His ten (plus one unfinished) symphonies have been frequently performed in Northern Europe, and his pieces have continued to gain popularity years after his death. Tubin fled Es-

Dancers take part in a traditional folk dance festival. (Courtesy of Rein Linask)

tonia at the onset of the Soviet occupation, producing many of his finest works in exile in Stockholm.

Two of Eller's other students who played major roles in perpetuating the teaching tradition are Lepo Sumera (1950–2000), an excellent symphonist who also pioneered the use of electronics in classical music, and Jaan Rääts (b. 1932), whose flexibility and ingenuity has made his material, including his works for piano, popular among musicians. These two figures played a major role in the development of the next generation of Estonian composers.

Another of Estonia's best-known contemporary composers is Veljo Tormis (b. 1930), a pioneer in Estonian choral music, especially in his inclusion of ancient themes and motifs, as well as the folk traditions of various Finno-Ugric peoples. His 1972 *Curse upon Iron* conjures up feelings of the supernatural, while his six-part cycle *Forgotten Peoples,* written over two decades starting in the early 1970s, is based on the motifs of folk melodies from the smallest Finno-Ugric nations, such as the Livonians and Vepsians.

The new generation of composers, such as the rhythmic Raimo Kangro (b. 1949) and the exotic Peeter Vähi (b. 1955), have also made significant breakthroughs in bringing Estonian music to the rest of the world. The most prominent of the new generation, however, is Erkki-Sven Tüür (b. 1959), who is today one of the most sought-after composers all over the world. His flexibility in style and ingenuity in approach made his pieces, especially the experimental *Architectonics* chamber cycle, among the most popular throughout the classical music world. He has also composed various symphonies and in 2001 premiered an opera based on the life of Raoul Wallenberg, the heroic Swedish diplomat who saved the lives of Jews during the Holocaust. Tüür's origin as a symphonic rock musician in the band In Spe gives his music a further experimental, and thus exciting, aspect.

Alongside the many famous Estonian composers in today's musical world, Estonia has also produced many of the most active and recorded conductors. The most famous among this group is Neeme Järvi (b. 1937), who is among the most prolific conductors in major classical recordings today, taking the baton for hundreds of recordings in the past two decades. He has led some of the most famous orchestras in the world, such as the Royal Scottish Orchestra, the Gothenburg Symphony Orchestra, and, since 1990, the Detroit Symphony Orchestra. His children have also followed in his footsteps and become international stars in the music world: Paavo (b. 1962) is the music director at the Cincinnati Symphony Orchestra and one of the most in-demand guest conductors in the world; daughter Maarika (b. 1964) is one of the top flautists in Europe today; and Kristjan (b. 1972) is another in-demand conductor and music director of the adventurous Absolute Ensemble.

Another of Estonia's best-known conductors is Eri Klas (b. 1939), principal conductor and music director of a series of top European orchestras and operas, popular for his energetic and animated style. And continuing the tradition of choral music, Estonia's Tõnu Kaljuste (b. 1953) is among the worldwide leaders in this field, responsible for many of the top choral recordings over the past two decades.

Estonia has also produced successful musicians in other genres, ranging from folk to rock, from pop to jazz. The rock music scene in Estonia was seen as the strongest within the Soviet empire, experimenting with a combination of Western influences and homegrown ideas. The rock band Ruja, formed in 1971, helped to create a truly Estonian rock scene. Rock singers Ivo Linna, with his band Rock Hotel, and Tõnis Mägi, both with unique and powerful voices, have been on the forefront of Estonian popular music for several decades, while blues rock group Ultima Thule have been the best-known live act for many years. Even the experimental and provocative punk band Propeller had an effect on the beginnings of the Singing Revolution during its brief existence. Estonia also pioneered progressive rock in the former Soviet world with the aforementioned Ruja, as well as the groundbreaking symphonic rock of Mess and In Spe, the latter mentioned above as the brainchild of today's classical music genius, Erkki-Sven Tüür.

Estonian pop music has increasingly taken on foreign influences, especially in recent years. Europop and techno, as well as rap and grunge, are all popular styles. Alongside many of the crooners of the older generation, the symbol of modern Estonian pop music is Maarja Liis Ilus (b. 1980), boasting a voice of power and emotion and bringing her two entries to the Eurovision Song Contest to among the top. Many of Estonia's pop and rock acts are crossing borders to play in nearby countries.

Overall, Estonian music can be considered the nation's best export. For such a small nation, Estonia has produced scores of world-famous musicians, composers, and conductors, and international interest in Estonia has grown exponentially because of its proud musical tradition.

FILM

Cinematography in Estonia has a surprisingly long history and has compiled a rich and diverse collection of works over the past century. Since the first folk documentary made at the end of the nineteenth century by Johannes Pääsuke (1892–1918) and the first short feature film, *Karujaht Pärnumaal* (A Bear Hunt in Pärnu County) in 1916, the genre has developed into a small but strong means of expression for Estonia's cinematographers.

The costs involved in filmmaking, however, kept the genre rather limited during the interwar independence period, with only a limited number surviving from that period. Even back then, foreign films made the most impact on the public; nevertheless, Estonia did contribute actress Miliza Korjus (1909–1980) to the booming Hollywood film industry. Many budding film studios disappeared due to financial problems, and the creation of a national film institution came only in the 1930s authoritarian period. The first major figure of Estonian cinematography was Theodor Luts (1896–1980), though the nature of the Estonian market took Luts to a successful career across the Gulf in Helsinki. Still, he was responsible for major Estonian works such as the 1927 patriotic feature film *Noored kotkad* (Young Eagles).

Ironically, the cinema industry in Estonia took off only during the Soviet period. With the state film studio becoming

Ruja: Estonia's Rock Band

Though rather underexamined, the rock music scene has played a significant role in the social evolution of Estonia, especially during the latter half of the Soviet occupation. With the slow permeation of rock music from the West (such as the Beatles), a small rock scene began to develop in the 1960s. However, the first true Estonian rock band came into being in 1971, in the form of Ruja. For nearly two decades after their founding, Ruja reigned as the most influential rock band in the country, in both musical and social terms.

Started in 1971 with the goal of creating a specifically Estonian rock band, Ruja focused on strong music and strong lyrics in Estonian. Poems written by some of the country's top poets of the past and present were skillfully woven into increasingly complex musical compositions by bandleader and keyboardist Rein Rannap. The band rapidly gained popularity over the 1970s, even as Margus Kappel replaced Rannap, while the band's music evolved and joined the complex world of progressive rock. Some of the material of this era rivaled the work of famous contemporaries in the genre like Yes and Emerson, Lake and Palmer. The unique guitar work of Jaanus Nõgisto and the emotional but powerful vocals of Urmas Alender created the trademark Ruja sound.

The band faced various forms of official repression, ranging from banning their activities to arrest. Periodically, their pieces were banned, and, though recorded, were not released. It was not until 1980 that officials allowed the release of a four-track EP (a short album), now a major collector's item. The Ruja of the 1970s most prominently used the lyrics of controversial poet Juhan Viiding (who also used the pseudonym Jüri Üdi) to express some of the pent-up anger among the nation's youth.

That anger spilled over at the beginning of the 1980s as Russification campaigns, aimed at fostering Russian culture at the expense of Estonian, increased. Ruja transformed its sound, with Rannap back in the band, for a more simplistic style that quickly propelled them back to the top. Taking advantage of the growing public discontent, Ruja used various styles of music, including pop, rock, folk, and reggae, among others, to bring the words of beat poet Ott Arder to the yearning public. Tens of thousands of Estonians went to Ruja concerts as they performed their anthem, "Eile nägin ma Eestimaad!" ("Yesterday I saw Estonia!"), a sharply written song with heavy critical overtones directed against the Soviet system. Many of the seeds of the Singing Revolution of the latter half of the 1980s were planted during this short period, with Ruja becoming the focal point of youth discontent and collective emotional expression.

The frequent member changes led to further problems within the band in the mid-1980s. Though new keyboardist Igor Garšnek brought a new and complex flavor to the music, to the delight of its legion of fans, the band began to fall apart from within. Tension was exacerbated by a KGB-trained provocateur who served as the band's manager, and the band loss much of its Estonian appeal by trying to crack the Russian market, even singing in Russian. Ironically the founding principle of the band, its opposition to the Soviet system, led to its collapse in 1988. Though Ruja played a major role in sowing the seeds of the Singing Revolution, it had self-destructed by the time of the protests. Some of the band's members fled overseas to escape increased repression during the last years of Soviet rule.

A decade after the band's collapse, Ruja again made history by releasing the first boxed set in Estonian music history, a five-CD compendium of their entire career. This is the lasting legacy of the band, as reunion would be impossible. Urmas Alender, the voice and soul of the band for its entire history, was among the 851 killed in the tragic sinking of the ferry *Estonia* in September 1994. However, Ruja lives on in the hearts of hundreds of thousands of Estonians, young and old, who remember the impact this ambitious rock band had on their lives and their country.

known as Tallinnfilm, the studio produced many memorable local classics, as well as developing the overall quality and professionalism of the industry. Some of the features in the 1960s and 1970s adapted well-known pieces of literature, though many are original and even quietly challenging to the ideas of Soviet domination. Some of the best known from this period are the 1969 *Viimane reliikvia* (The Last Relic) and 1983 cult favorite *Hukkunud alpinisti hotell* (Hotel of the Perished Alpinist), directed by Grigori Kro-

manov (1926–1984), as well as adaptations of literary pieces by Kaljo Kiisk (b. 1925).

However, the field of documentary filmmaking was the area in which Estonian artists found the most success during the Soviet period. Mark Soosaar (b. 1946) became the most celebrated among the documentary filmmakers, with an intense and fascinating focus on individuals. His 1973 *Kihnu naine* (The Woman from Kihnu) won the top award in Italy, while his 1997 *Isa, poeg ja püha toorum* (Father, Son, and Holy Torum) took honors in Paris and San Francisco. Another well-loved documentary maker is Lennart Meri (b. 1929), the first president of Estonia after the restoration of independence (1992–2001), who made fascinating films about the cultures of small ethnic groups. His *Linnutee tuuled* (Winds of the Milky Way) was critically acclaimed around the world, even winning an award in New York.

Perhaps the best-known area of Estonian cinematography is animation, in which Estonians have won various international awards and critical acclaim. The person who personifies this success is Priit Pärn (b. 1946), responsible for many of the country's top animation films since the 1970s. His first film, the 1977 *Kas maakera on ümmargune?* (Is the Earth Round?) brought him into the genre; he also worked as a graphic artist and caricaturist. His subsequent films earned international praise, including the 1984 *Aeg maha* (Time Out), which earned top awards at film and animation festivals in Bulgaria, Portugal, and Spain. His 1987 *Eine murul* (Luncheon on the Grass) drew even greater acclaim, winning top recognition in various film festivals in Australia, Portugal, and elsewhere. His 1995 film *1895* won still more acclaim in far-flung festivals in Korea and Canada. But his masterpiece must be the 1998 *Porgandite öö* (Night of the Carrots), which won animation awards in Canada and the United States and is recognized as one of the top animation films of the decade.

The Estonian film industry faced difficult financial times with the restoration of independence, but the innovations, such as the interesting 1993 black-and-white-turned-color *Tallinn pimeduses* (Darkness in Tallinn), have continued. The Black Nights film festival, held since 1997, has also helped budding filmmakers expose their material to the international film world. Hollywood films dominate the market today, and those in the local cinematography industry are learning to find a niche for their material.

SPORTS

The achievements of Estonian athletes through the years have been tremendous for such a small country. Though its climate would obviously favor winter sports, success has been achieved in all areas, ranging from cross-country skiing to track and field, from cycling to wrestling.

One excellent indication of Estonian sporting success can be seen by its number of medals in the Olympic games through the years: twenty-eight (including nine gold medals). This count is only indicative of Estonia's success as an independent competitor; it does not include the numerous medals won during both the late tsarist era and the half-century of Soviet occupation.

Early Estonian success came in strength-related events, such as wrestling and weightlifting. The first ever medal by an Estonian came at the 1912 Stockholm summer games, as Greco-Roman wrestler Martin Klein (1886–1947) won a silver medal after a nearly twelve-hour match against his Finnish semifinal competitor left him too exhausted for the final. It was in the 1920 Antwerp summer games that Estonians competed under their own flag for the first time, with resounding success, bringing home three medals. Alfred Neuland (1895–1966) brought back Estonia's first gold medal, in weightlifting, while silvers were won in the marathon and in weightlifting.

Olympic success continued at the 1924 Paris summer games, bringing back six medals. Eduard Pütsep (1898–1960) brought home a gold for Greco-Roman wrestling, while Neuland this time brought home a silver for weightlifting. Four bronze medals—two for weightlifting, one for wrestling, and one for decathlon—were also won. The Estonian soccer team also took part, losing to the United States 0–1. The 1928 Amsterdam summer games also brought success with five medals. Freestyle wrestler and later two-time U.S. champion Osvald Käpp (1905–1995) and Greco-Roman wrestler Voldemar Väli (1903–1997) brought home golds, alongside one silver for weightlifting, and bronzes won for Greco-Roman wrestling and sailing. The worldwide economic depression made Estonian participation in the 1932 Los Angeles games limited, and no medals were won there.

However, it was at the controversial 1936 Munich summer games that Estonia found its most successful games, winning five medals, including two golds by master wrestler Kristjan Palusalu (1908–1987). Palusalu thus became the first and only wrestler in Olympic history to win the heavyweight wrestling events in both Greco-Roman and freestyle, going down in the record books. (He also managed to escape Soviet captivity twice, escaping from Russia back to Estonia.) Silvers were won in freestyle wrestling and boxing, while bronzes were won in wrestling and weightlifting.

During the half-century Soviet occupation, Estonian athletes competed with the Soviet team and won various medals. The sailing events of the controversial 1980 Moscow summer games, boycotted by the West, were held at the Pirita suburb of Tallinn. It was only in the 1992 Barcelona summer games that Estonian athletes were allowed to compete under their own flag, bringing home one gold in cycling and a bronze in sailing. The gold medal winner, cyclist Erika Salumäe (b. 1962), had been the dominant track cyclist in the world in the 1980s, winning several world championships and the gold (as part of the Soviet team) in the 1988 Seoul summer games. Estonia had its worst showing ever at the 1996 Atlanta summer games, with no medals at all. The 2000 Sydney summer games brought home three medals, including two bronze medals in the unlikely event of judo. Decathlete Erki Nool (b. 1970) won a gold medal and took his place among the best athletes of the world.

Ironically Estonia found much less success in the winter games, winning no medals during the interwar period. There were some wins during the Soviet occupation, and then Estonia won its first three winter medals at the 2002 Salt Lake City winter games. One of the top cross-country skiers in the world, Andrus Veerpalu (b. 1971), brought home a gold and a silver, while his countryman Jaak Mae (b. 1972) brought home a bronze, also in cross-country skiing.

Outside of the Olympics, some Estonian athletes are world-famous in their sports. Cross-country skier Kristina Šmigun (b. 1977) is among the top competitors, winning various events in the international circuit. Jane Salumäe (b.

Estonia's Erki Nool carries his nation's flag after winning the gold medal in the men's decathlon at the Sydney Olympic Games, 28 September 2000. (Reuters/Corbis)

1968) has won various marathons around the world, including the 2000 Los Angeles Marathon. Budding tennis star Kaia Kanepi (b. 1985) is one of the highest-ranking junior players, winning the junior French Open in 2001. Basketball player Martin Müürsepp (b. 1974) was surprisingly picked in the first round of the 1996 NBA draft by Utah, while World Rally driver Markko Märtin (b. 1975) is one of the sport's rising stars. Cyclist Jaan Kirsipuu (b. 1969) has won several stages of the Tour de France in recent years. Estonia's soccer players have also found success in some of the top leagues around the world; of these, the most prominent is goalkeeper Mart Poom (b. 1972), who played with Derby County of the English Premiere League and is often called the best technical goalkeeper in England.

One of the most celebrated of all sporting figures in Estonia is chess master Paul Keres (1916–1975). Keres became one of the top players in the world for a remarkably long time, from the 1930s up to his death in 1975. Though he never achieved the title of world champion, partially because of the disruption caused by World War II, Keres remained one of the most feared challengers for the title for nearly four decades. He was recognized through his play

and the books he wrote as one of the top chess strategists in the world, and he is honored by a tournament named for him in Vancouver and by his portrait on the Estonian five-kroon note—probably the only chess master on any banknote in the world.

Sports remain one of the most important aspects of the lives of Estonians, as its athletes join the most competitive circuits around the world. With regained freedom, the ability for Estonian athletes to compete with the best around the world, under their own flag, keeps the flame of athletic excellence alive in the country.

SCIENCE AND TECHNOLOGY

The world of science and technology has played an important role in developments in Estonia, as the small northern European nation has sought to carve itself a niche. Ever since the creation of Tartu University in 1632, Estonia has contributed to the understanding of our natural world in various areas.

Due to the social situation in Estonia over the centuries, many of the most renowned figures to emerge from Tartu University were of Baltic German extraction, mostly from the nobility. Higher education opportunities were for the most part unavailable to Estonians until the nineteenth century. Nevertheless, Estonians today still take pride in the many German scientists who called Estonia home over the years. Tartu University and its research institutions have been outstanding centers of research for centuries. For example, the founding of the Tõravere Observatory in 1824 saw the installation of the largest telescope in the world, and the Tartu University Clinics, founded in 1802, became a regional center for medical innovations.

One of the most famous scientific figures in Estonian history is Karl Ernst von Baer (1792–1876), who pioneered the science of modern embryology. Born into a noble family in Järva region, Baer became one of the most renowned researchers in the biological sciences in the German academic world. Many of his greatest accomplishments came at the University of Königsberg, during his appointment as professor of both zoology (1821) and of anatomy (1826). Baer also founded the zoological museum in the Prussian imperial city. However, Baer is best known for his 1826 discovery of the mammal ovum (which of course includes the human ovum), a discovery that, along with his subsequent research and publications, created the foundations of modern embryology. Baer is remembered fondly in Estonian scientific history, and his portrait graces the two-kroon note.

Another of Estonia's most renowned scientific figures is the surgeon Werner Zoege von Manteuffel (1857–1926), who brought hygiene into surgery by pioneering the use of rubber gloves. Earlier surgeons generally used bare hands to perform operations. This change in practice by the Estonian-born German noble, working at the prestigious Tartu University Clinics, helped to modernize surgical medicine. Another famous medical name from Estonia was Alexander Schmidt (1831–1894), who formulated theories on blood coagulation and transfusion, becoming one of the pioneers of hematology.

Tartu University was a center of excellence in chemistry during the nineteenth century. One of its most prominent students was the Riga-born Wilhelm Ostwald (1853–1932), winner of the 1909 Nobel Prize in Chemistry. Ostwald played a major part in the development of both physical chemistry and electrochemistry, and formulated a well-known law on diffusion. Physicist Moritz Hermann Jacobi (1801–1874) discovered electroforming and the subfield of galvanoplastics with his experiments, and Ivan Kondakov (1857–1931) made one of the first major advancements in 1901 in polymerization, a step toward the invention of synthetic rubber.

The strength of the astronomy program at Tartu, with the installment of the largest telescope in the world at the time, brought many high-quality researchers. The director of the Tõravere Observatory, Friedrich Georg Wilhelm Struve (1793–1864), made a pioneering study of the stars by measuring the distance to the star Vega. Struve also made significant advances in the study of double stars and contributed greatly to their cataloguing. The binary pair Struve 2398 was named after the pioneering astronomer.

With the gradual availability of higher education opportunities for Estonians starting in the nineteenth century, Estonians themselves soon became world renowned in various scientific disciplines. Independence finally turned Tartu University into an Estonian institution, but its high quality and rigorous standards of scientific research continued.

One of the best-known Estonian scientists is the astronomer Ernst Julius Öpik (1893–1985), who pioneered many different areas within his discipline. Researching at Tartu's famous Tõravere Observatory, Öpik furthered the research of his predecessor Struve by discovering a methodology to accurately estimate nebulae distance, a method that was proven accurate later by Edwin Hubble. Both Struve and Öpik helped the astronomy world rethink the size of the universe by their breakthroughs. Öpik, during his long career, also discovered White Dwarves in 1915, as well as making a series of surprisingly accurate measurements of distances and densities of heavenly bodies. Tragically, like many other top Estonian scientists, when the Soviet occupation came, Öpik fled Estonia for the West. Nevertheless, Öpik continued his research at the Armagh Observatory in Northern Ireland for the remainder of his life. A minor planet is named after him. Members of his family also contributed both to the sciences and to their adopted country, with his nephew Lembit becoming a member of the British Parliament in the 1990s. Another pioneer in astrophysics from Tartu University was Jaan Einasto (b. 1929), who continued the work of his predecessors in studying the evolution of the universe. His research on gravitational pull in turn developed one of the first sets of evidence for the existence of dark matter, which remains one of the most intriguing areas of research today. Einasto remains at the forefront of astrophysics research in areas such as red shifts and galaxy clusters.

Continuing with the strong traditions of chemistry advances, the independence era also featured many breakthroughs in the field. One prominent chemist was Paul Kogerman (1891–1951), who pioneered the chemical study

The German chemist Wilhelm Ostwald (1853–1932). He was awarded a Nobel Prize in 1909 for his work on chemical equilibrium. (Hulton-Deutsch Collection/Corbis)

of oil shale, a vital resource in Estonia, and served as the last education minister of the country before occupation (for which he was deported to a prison camp).

Again following tradition, Tartu became a center of innovation in the medical field from its famous clinics. One of the most prominent figures was Ludvig Puusepp (1875–1942), who made some early major breakthroughs in the delicate field of neurosurgery. Tartu-trained surgeons have gone on and made significant advances in the treatment of various diseases, including Parkinson's Disease.

The field of linguistics also saw many specialists working in Tartu. Many of the aforementioned literary and linguistic figures worked at Tartu to further standardize the language. One of the most important steps in the development of Estonian was the compilation of the massive 1200-page Estonian-English dictionary by Paul Saagpakk (1910–1996), exiled from Estonia during World War II and working in a series of American universities. That dictionary is an invaluable resource for translators today. And Russian-born Yuri Lotman (1922–1993) was among many Jewish academics who fled the anti-Semitism throughout the Soviet Union to Tartu, where many gathered during the Soviet period as refugees. Lotman founded the study of cultural structural semiotics, playing a major part in the advancement of Russian language studies.

The most exciting development of recent years is the founding of the Estonian Genome Foundation, which in 2001 began the process of cataloguing the genome of the Estonian population. This massive database would be the most thorough and largest database for one single population, which would be of invaluable help to genetic researchers in further developing advances in genetic engineering.

The University of Tartu has been a continually active center of research excellence over the centuries, and is continuing its high quality work in the twenty-first century.

ECONOMIC DEVELOPMENT

The economic development of Estonia, especially in the past century, has been nothing less than a roller-coaster ride, a direct consequence of the chaotic and harsh history the country has faced. Some of the worst aspects of Soviet-imposed centrally planned socialism devastated the economy that had developed during the more prosperous interwar years, leaving the economy in ruins after decades of occupation.

During the period in which Estonia regained its independence, the country moved to abandon the failed planned economic system and crafted an alternative system more closely akin to that of its Nordic neighbors. Sticking by an ambitiously liberal economic plan, this small northern European country turned things around, becoming one of the most dynamic economies in Europe in less than a decade after being freed from its Soviet shackles. The memories of the past, of a dreadful and dull economic development, continues to fuel the dynamism of the modern liberal economy created by Estonian policymakers, an economic model that has even attracted the praise and attention of the most laissez-faire figures around the world.

Few would have imagined in 1991 that in just a decade, the country would boast one of the freest economies in the world, according to the U.S.-based think tank the Heritage Foundation. Estonia is recognized as being among the most successful reformers of the former communist bloc, and it has earned the nickname of the "Baltic tiger" for its rapid economic growth.

ESTONIA AS A TRADING POST

The Hanseatic League was among the most important medieval organizations, controlling the prosperous trading routes in the Baltic Sea. The league linked dozens of cities on the Baltic coast and beyond, ranging from its primary cities of Hamburg and Lübeck to famous trading towns like Gdańsk (Danzig), Riga, Bruges, Bergen, Stockholm, and even London. Estonian towns also played a major role in this early pan-European trading bloc, becoming a vital part of the league in the latter part of the thirteenth century.

Four of Estonia's biggest towns—Tallinn, Tartu, Pärnu, and Viljandi—became part of the Hanseatic League. Tallinn was a bridgehead for trade linking Novgorod to other towns like Lübeck and London, while Tartu played a significant role in trade with Pskov. The Estonian Hanseatic towns became prosperous from trade during the medieval period, as did Narva, which remained formally outside of the league due to trade disputes with other Hanseatic towns. Estonian grain, as well as fish, furs, and stone, found a large market in Flanders and Russia. Estonian towns acted as a conduit for trade between the Russian principalities and towns and Western Hanseatic cities, with salt imports to Russia serving as a major part of Tallinn's trade activities.

Many guilds developed during this period, gathering merchants, tradesmen, craftsmen, and others into organized institutions to promote and perpetuate their specialty. By the late medieval period, nearly two dozen guilds operated in Tallinn, though only a very few allowed native Estonians to take part.

But as the Hanseatic League lost its influence starting in the sixteenth century, Estonian cities also faced major economic problems. The opening of other trading routes in and out of Russia devastated some of the cities, especially inland towns such as Tartu and Viljandi. Under Swedish rule, however, the cities of Tallinn and Narva continued to prosper; salt destined for Russia continued to be stored in Tallinn, while Estonia's grain export trade to Sweden thrived. Luxury items such as spices, metals, tobacco, alcohol, and fruits also played a larger role in trade.

During the Swedish period, larger enterprises also came into being, such as brickyards and lime kilns, as well as sawmills; the Hüti glass factory opened in the seventeenth century as a new type of enterprise. However, the Great Northern War of the early eighteenth century devastated the economy, as people were killed, fields burned, and factories destroyed. By the time Estonia formally passed into the hands of the Russian Empire, there was little left of the old economy.

Under the Russian Empire, trade routes were reestablished. Grain remained the main export item, though the felling of the vast forests increased with the growing importance of timber and paper. The Räpina paper mill was founded in 1734, the oldest continually operating industry in Estonia. Other manufacturing also increased throughout the eighteenth and nineteenth centuries, though frequently disturbed by war and other strife.

Though the peasants were "freed" early in the nineteenth century, peasants remained tied to the land; however, the focus slowly moved from grain to more productive crops, such as potatoes, and cash crops, such as flax. Another important trend was the gradual entry of native Estonians into the economic picture, especially with the growth of smallholder farmers.

Textiles also grew in importance in the latter half of the nineteenth century, most strikingly with the opening of the Krenholm plant in Narva in 1858. Since then, Narva has been the industrial center of Estonia. Railways also developed in this period, with the Paldiski–Tallinn–Narva–St. Petersburg line opening in 1870. Machine and metal plants were also founded, as well as factories producing armaments, ships, cement, and other goods. Distilleries opened as a side operation of manors. Estonia's paper mills produced some 70 percent of all paper in the Russian Empire by the

The Port of Tallinn has become one of the busiest commercial and tourism ports in Europe. (David Rubinger/Corbis)

start of the twentieth century. Estonia became a major industrial center within the Russian Empire, with over 50,000 employed in industry at the time of World War I.

During this late tsarist period, cooperatives sprung up, especially among native Estonians, to help prop up the economic state of the native population. The movement began with sales of dairy goods, developing later to joint procurement of farm machinery. The Estonian Loan and Savings Cooperative was also opened in 1902, the first national bank. However, all economic development came to a halt with the outbreak of World War I.

AN INDEPENDENT ESTONIAN ECONOMY

The end of World War I and the Estonian War of Independence gave Estonians for the first time in centuries control over their economic development. With an economy in tatters after the war, as Russia removed many industrial enterprises to Russia proper during the war, Estonia continued to rely on Russia for trade (partially aided by the trade benefit aspects of the 1920 Tartu Peace Treaty). A new monetary system had to be crafted, as several foreign currencies circulated during the transitional period. The Estonian mark was introduced in 1919, but it never gained the stability needed for the economy really to develop. The economic situation was exacerbated by war debts (to the United

States, Britain, France, and Finland) equaling some 5 billion marks, which overwhelmed the 15 million gold rubles given as reparations by Soviet Russia.

The early period of independence saw economic problems increase. A land reform law ended the manor economy, as estates were divided to form smallholder farms; over 50,000 new smallholding farms were created from this ambitious but controversial program; however, many proved to be unsustainable. The Bank of Estonia, a new national central bank, was created to help develop the economy through loans; unfortunately, many of the loans went into default, and most of the Russian reparation had disappeared by the start of 1924. The economic strains were exacerbated by Russia's closing of its market to Estonia at the end of 1922.

The government began an austerity program in 1924 to bring the country back to economic health, by cutting state spending, restricting imports, and creating more stringent requirements for loans. A land bank *(Maapank)* was founded to help develop the agriculture sector, which remained the most important aspect of the economy. Within a few years, agricultural output began to recover, returning to the prewar situation. Industrial reform also occurred, with the growth of the chemical, timber, and cellulose industries. Even the much-maligned mark was replaced in 1928 by a stable new currency, the kroon, which was pegged to its Swedish namesake.

The global economic depression however hit Estonia hard, as trade levels crashed in 1929. Both agriculture and industry suffered with the loss of export possibilities, and unemployment increased. Belatedly, the kroon was devalued by 35 percent in 1933; although the move was highly unpopular at the time, it did pave the way for gradual economic recovery. During the authoritarian period under Konstantin Päts, economic recovery continued, thanks in large part to the active participation of the state. Various councils and institutes were created, as the state increased its stake in the economy. As trade resumed to a healthy level, Germany and Britain remained the country's main trade partners; however, the increasingly tense politics of Europe at the time played havoc with trade patterns, as Berlin often used trade as a carrot to influence Estonia's policy. By the late 1930s, nevertheless, Estonia's economy was healthy and growing, with living standards high compared to other Central and Eastern European countries. Then World War II and the loss of independence devastated the economy.

THE IMPOSED COMMUNIST SYSTEM

The wartime occupations of Estonia destroyed much of the economy developed over the two decades of independence. The occupation of Estonia by Soviet forces in the summer of 1940 decimated the local economy, as Moscow began nationalizing private industries and collectivizing smallholding farms. Most of the larger businesses, as well as half of the country's housing, were nationalized. An artificially low exchange rate for the kroon to the ruble devastated savings. The major deportation of 14 June 1941 of over ten thousand Estonians added to the economic collapse. The three-year German occupation did not relieve the situation, as Estonia remained in the battle zone. The Nazis tried to coopt surviving industries for their war use, and transferred many of the nationalized companies to new German ownership.

The Soviet Red Army retook Estonia in 1944, occupying the country for nearly another half century. The nationalization policy was reimposed, as well as the collectivization of farms. Over 900,000 hectares were expropriated in the few years following reoccupation, and many of the expropriated lands were given to new settlers from Russia and elsewhere in the Soviet Union. Rapid collectivization began in 1946, along with a crackdown against the kulaks (as farmers seen as better off than the rest were called) in 1947. The repression of the kulaks started as oppressive taxation, eventually leading to mass deportations. Those who resisted collectivization were given one-way tickets to mass graves or Siberia, with the result that more than 95 percent of all farms were collectivized by 1951.

By 1947, the private sector had totally vanished. Rapid industrialization also occurred soon after reoccupation, especially the development of the oil shale industry. Though the beginnings of this development had taken place during the independence period, Soviet planners expanded oil shale mining and processing in the late 1940s, taking over the industry in the northeast of the country. The village of Sillamäe was converted into a closed industrial city for the Soviet military-industrial complex, with all of its workers imported from the USSR. Estonia was progressively being integrated into the planned Soviet economy.

As time went on, the situation began to stabilize, especially with the death of Stalin and the thaw period, as surviving deportees began to return to Estonia. Agriculture recovered, alongside a rapidly growing industrial sector, including the construction of large oil shale–burning power plants to power Estonia and parts of northwest Russia. In the 1970s, however, the economy of the USSR experienced stagnation, exacerbated by the growth of a shadow economy.

With the arrival of social activism in the 1980s, calls for growing economic independence from Moscow also arrived on the agenda. In 1987, with Gorbachev calling for economic innovations and reform, a plan was developed in Estonia for a major rethinking of the local economy. The "miracle" plan published by Siim Kallas, Edgar Savisaar, Mikk Titma, and Tiit Made on 26 September 1987 called for an economic separation from the rest of the USSR by asserting local administration and control, creating a market trade system with the USSR, and introducing a local currency. As public demands for sovereignty grew, more ambitious plans for economic reform were adopted. Moscow relented partially, and Estonia gained approval for building a domestic economy independent from Moscow.

During the brief period (1990–1991) leading to the restoration of independence, much economic reform occurred. The Bank of Estonia was revived as the country's central bank, as Tallinn asserted control over monetary policy. The Estonian government put forward a budget separate from the all-Union budget. Finally, prices were gradually liberalized, and a private sector started to develop. Within this short period of time, alongside the rapidly changing political situation, Estonia broke down the centralized planned economic system and reasserted control over its own economy.

RESTORING ESTONIA'S FATE
INTO ITS OWN HANDS

With the restoration of independence in August 1991, Estonia finally completely reclaimed its own economy. The world of 1991 was very different from the world of 1918, with European integration and globalization making economic development more dynamic, but at the same time more difficult. With the election of a young, center-right government in 1992, the country embarked on the liberal and far-reaching reforms, which have helped create the economic success enjoyed today.

The foundation of the economic revival was laid in the summer of 1992 when the Bank of Estonia, led by miracle plan drafter Siim Kallas, reintroduced the kroon as the sole legal tender in Estonia. At the time, international financial organizations such as the IMF (International Monetary Fund) warned Estonia not to take such a drastic step. The return of Estonia's gold supply, which had been kept in safety overseas by adherents of the internationally supported policy of nonrecognition of Estonia's annexation by the USSR, gave the country the tools it needed to take such a step. The gold helped the central bank acquire a significant sum in foreign currency reserves, ensuring that the kroon would be more than fully backed. The currency at its introduction was pegged to the German mark at a ratio of 1 mark to 8 kroon, a pegging that has never changed. (When the euro replaced the mark, the peg was kept identical at 1 euro to 15.65 kroon.) This stable currency became the foundation of the ambitious economic policy of the government of then 32-year-old prime minister Mart Laar, who came into power a few months following the successful launch of the kroon.

Alongside a strict monetary policy, the second foundation of Estonia's successful economic restructuring was a strict fiscal policy. A law was passed requiring Estonia's annual national budget to be balanced. This legal stipulation gave the government much less room to maneuver with spending, especially with borrowing. Estonia has taken very few foreign loans over the years; governments have maintained fiscal discipline, largely because they recognize the problems a dept burden would place on maintaining the legally-mandated balanced budget. This restraint has kept Estonia from falling into the vicious debt circle faced by many other emerging markets, keeping the country's international ratings among the strongest in Central and Eastern Europe.

The government of Mart Laar pursued a set of reforms so drastic they have been described as shock therapy; along with their strict fiscal and monetary policies, they established probusiness and proinvestment policies. A flat 26 percent income tax was established, a model that has actually earned the praise of tax reform campaigners in the United States. In the late 1990s a specific corporate income tax was also abolished, to promote reinvestment by companies. A regime allowing for full repatriation of profits encouraged foreign investors to pump money into the Estonian economy. This step was essential, given the negative trade balance that developed, as Estonia continually imported modern equipment and machinery to modernize its economy. The large tourism sector, with over 3 million foreign tourists (mostly from Finland) annually, also helps with the balance of payments.

Despite the trade imbalance on the side of imports, the government, acting on the principle of free trade, did not impose import duties. Instead, free trade agreements were pursued with a wide array of countries; by the end of the 1990s Estonia boasted free trade deals with most of Europe. Though the trade imbalance remained through the decade, the trade volume increased by a significant amount. Over a short time Estonia also managed to redirect its foreign trade away from Russia and the Commonwealth of Independent States (CIS) to the EU, especially after Sweden and Finland joined the latter in the mid-1990s. Already in 1995 nearly 57 percent of exports went to the EU, compared to just over 22 percent to the CIS; by 2000 more than three-quarters of Estonia's exports went to the EU, compared to less than 4 percent to the CIS. These new trade patterns would seem to suggest that Estonia has returned to its position as an important trading post, the position it enjoyed during the days of the Hanseatic League.

Bank notes from two eras of independence: 10 kroon notes from the Interwar period and from today. (Mel Huang)

The most telling sign of Estonia's economic development is its growth. Since the mid-1990s, when Estonia managed to stop the post-Soviet economic slide, the country has boasted some of the most impressive growth numbers in the region (such as a 10.4 percent GDP growth in 1997). Though inflation was a major problem in the early 1990s and at times since, due to an overheated economy, the consumer price index rise in the end of the 1990s stayed under 5 percent annually.

Another major aspect of Estonia's economic policy since the restoration of independence is the ambitious privatization program. With the help of the German privatization agency Treuhand, the Estonians established a similar office. The privatization of larger entities included the setting of operational conditions for the private purchasers, ranging from investment guarantees to employment level requirements. This approach prevented the development of local robber barons of the kind that emerged during privatization in Russia. At the same time, it encouraged the engagement of foreign (mostly Nordic) companies, which not only made much-needed investments but imported wholesale their proven management and accounting systems. By 2001, a decade after the restoration of independence, most of Estonia's industries were in private hands; Estonia was one of the largest recipients of foreign direct investment. For example, Estonia received a massive $570 million in foreign direct investment in 1998, and has pulled in a total of $2.3 billion since the restoration of independence according to the Estonian Institute. On the other side of the account,

Estonia's growing investment in other countries, namely Latvia, provide another sign of economic development and maturity.

Over the years following the restoration of independence, many new industries have risen to make their contributions to the new economy. Estonia has become a major transit point for Russian oil, making the rail transshipment and port sectors among the most lucrative. Estonia has also developed a strong homegrown banking sector, with Hansapank (the idea of a group of friends during the late Soviet days) becoming one of the most successful banks in the region. Since the late 1990s, Nordic banking giants have purchased all of Estonia's major banks, integrating Estonia into the Nordic banking sector. Even the Tallinn Stock Exchange in 2002 became a part of the Helsinki Stock Exchange, the first among Central and Eastern European bourses to merge into a larger international partner. Informational technology (IT) also grew as an industry, with computer manufacturer Microlink becoming one of the best-known brands in the region. Telecommunications also merged into the Nordic market, as many new innovations, such as payment for public parking by mobile phone, were first tested in Estonia. With the large influx of tourists, especially many one-day tourists from Finland, the service sector has become one of the major employers and revenue generators for the country (alongside its role in helping the balance of payments).

Over the same period, heavy industry, most of which is based outside of Tallinn and in the northeast of the country, has continued to decline. The decrepit heavy factories could not compete in the globalized economy at market prices, and have either transformed themselves to more targeted items (such as car safety belts) or have been mothballed. Even the mining of indigenous oil shale, the fuel for the country's power plants, has declined with the dwindling chemical industry. The agriculture sector also has taken a major downturn, even with the prospects of EU support funding on the horizon.

Estonia's industrial policy is clearly linked to marketing itself as part of the new economy, with its focus on IT, high-tech, telecommunications, banking, tourism, services, and entertainment, and distancing itself from the old economy of heavy industry, mining, manufacturing, and farming. Though the continual globalization process leaves the small Estonia in precarious shape if the world economy falls into recession, its advantageous position for trade ties with Russia—as in the Hanseatic days—allows Estonia some flexibility.

Estonia also actively pursued EU membership from the mid-1990s, and was named as a front-runner in 1997. Most of Estonia's trade involves EU members, and a large part of Estonia's investments come from the EU's Nordic members. With the kroon pegged to the euro, Estonia was already a de facto member of the European Monetary Union. The gradual task of adhering to the EU's body of regulations and rules, the *acquis communautaire,* will continue even after the accession to the EU, but membership will give Estonia a voice in the transformation of European economic structures. This goal was achieved in May 2004, when Estonia and nine other countries officially joined the EU.

Overall, the economic development of Estonia since 1991 has been remarkable. Estonia managed to shake off the remnants of foreign-imposed central planning and engage itself as a vigorous member of a globalizing capitalist market. The impressive aspect is that Estonia is joining the global economy on its own merits, on its own terms. The policy of the first Laar government, which carried through other successive cabinets, became the mantra for Estonia: "trade, not aid." It is little wonder that Estonia has been nicknamed "the little country that could."

CONTEMPORARY CHALLENGES

As Estonia celebrated the tenth anniversary of its restoration of independence in the year 2001, the challenges of the new millennium have replaced many of the initial problems that the country faced with the regaining of freedom. With the reform period essentially over, the new challenges facing Estonia mirror those facing many European and other modern societies; nevertheless, the legacy of the Soviet occupation remains and continues to force Estonians to tackle the lingering problems inherited from history.

For many years after the restoration of independence, the main priorities for the Estonian state had to do with joining the European Union (EU) and the North Atlantic Treaty Organization (NATO). The rapid changes necessary to conform to both organizations forced Estonia to quickly adopt drastic changes in many aspects of society, ranging from military restructuring to trade liberalization. The all-encompassing nature of EU integration required all areas of Estonian society to work toward that goal; diverse issues ranging from motor vehicle regulations to customs requirements all come under the influence of EU harmonization.

Despite joining both the EU and NATO, some of Estonia's foreign policy challenges remain. Relations with Russia, the former colonial ruler, remain lukewarm at best. Though economic links are strong—primarily due to Estonia's role in the transshipment of Russian goods, especially hydrocarbons, to European markets—Russia continues to impose a double tariff on Estonian goods. Russia has also failed to continue fruitful negotiations on concluding a border agreement, despite the fact that the de facto border with Russia is now the EU-Russian border.

Most of Estonia's significant challenges in the new millennium, however, are domestic in nature.

INTEGRATING A POSTCOLONIAL POPULATION

The issue that plagued Estonia even before the restoration of independence was the integration of its minority populations. Due to World War II and Soviet policy, the population balance of the country shifted drastically following the loss of independence in 1940; in 1934 Estonians represented over 88 percent of the population, whereas in 1979 they constituted only about 64 percent. During the Soviet occupation, workers from various parts of the former USSR were brought into Estonia to work in the new heavy industries based in the northeastern part of the country. Given policies aimed at preventing displaced Estonians from returning to cities in the northeast like Narva, the ethnic makeup in the northeast became nearly 100 percent non-Estonian. The Soviets converted Sillamäe into a closed city for nuclear research and prevented ethnic Estonians from returning there after World War II.

During the Soviet period, a majority of these migrants did not integrate with the indigenous population. There was little need, as official Soviet policy promoted Russification (the promotion of Russian culture and language), and even an attempt to integrate by a non-Estonian would have been perceived negatively by Soviet officials. Thus, most of the non-Estonian migrants spoke no Estonian. During the period leading up to the restoration of independence, the issue of citizenship was of major concern to most of the occupation-era migrants; the restoration of Estonian citizenship fell only to those (or their descendants) who were citizens before the initial Soviet occupation in 1940. Most migrants faced naturalization, which at first was difficult due to linguistic problems.

Following the restoration of independence, many ethnic Estonians chided the Russian-speaking communities for not learning Estonian during the decades they lived in Estonia. (Although many call members of this minority population Russians, they are, in fact, multiethnic, drawn from all over the former USSR, though they are Russian speaking.) Yet during that time for the Russian-speaking population there was neither the will—as Russian was the functional language of the republic—nor the way—learning Estonian was discouraged. Nevertheless, naturalization for most of the Russian-speaking population required a rudimentary knowledge of Estonian.

At one point in the early days of restored independence, ethnic tension brought on by the citizenship and language issues (Estonian having been restored as the sole official language) caused some activists in the predominately Russian-speaking northeast to seek autonomy; this attempt was quickly outlawed. For the most part, those favoring breaking away tended to change their minds quickly, especially given the political and economic chaos in Russia. Despite any problems in development in Estonia, the industrial city of Narva is clearly in better economic shape than its sister city across the Narva River in Russia, Ivangorod (formerly the Estonian city of Jaanilinn). Some inhabitants of the formerly closed city of Sillamäe also favored autonomy at first, but even this city eventually reaped the rewards of freedom.

Nevertheless, the issue of integrating the population remains. Though naturalization was made easier following heavy-handed international advice (largely from OSCE, the Organization for Security and Cooperation in Europe, which acts as a human rights watch in Europe, but also from the EU), and the passage rate of the language and civics exams stands far above 90 percent, there remain a significant number of permanent Estonian residents who are either citizens of a foreign country or are stateless persons. By the turn of the millennium, over 100,000 individuals had been naturalized as Estonian citizens. At the same time, an estimated 250,000 remained stateless; that is, they held so-called noncitizen passports, or had taken other citizenship (most, over 80,000, took Russian citizenship, while fewer individuals took citizenship in other countries, such as Ukraine). Though many anticipate another major naturalization jump as Estonia joins the EU, as members of the Russian-speaking population seek to enjoy the benefits of being European citizens, the issue of integration remains a major concern.

Though the naturalization numbers far exceed those of neighboring Latvia, where the issue is even more contentious and the percentage of the population that speaks the national language is even smaller, the issue remains a major concern. The lack of a strong domestic Russian-language media pushes the large number of Russian-speakers, even those who are integrated in the sense that they are able to speak Estonian or are naturalized citizens, to use the media from Russia. The difference in approach, especially in news programs, could be clearly seen during the NATO campaign in Yugoslavia, with the Estonian-based press being pro-NATO and the Russia-based press firmly siding with Belgrade. The state has done little to pursue projects such as ETV-2, a proposed public television channel with substantial programming in Russian (which was to be like Finland's YLE-2 public channel, with its high proportion of Swedish-language programs).

Though most in the public sphere no longer accuse the population yet to be naturalized of being a fifth column for Russia, there remains unease over the large number of noncitizens in the country (approximately 20 percent of the total population). The deadline for integrating the school system (i.e., combining the Estonian-language schools, the Russian-language schools, and the mixed schools) has continued to be pushed back due to political bickering, though the right for minorities to be educated in their native language is guaranteed by law. Those non-citizen students who pass their Estonian language courses automatically comply with the language requirements for citizenship, an easing that has been brought about by international pressure.

Despite the large number yet to be integrated, the program has been seen as somewhat successful. Many younger non-Estonians view integration and citizenship as necessities to reap the rewards of the economic success of the country, especially given that it will be a common European citizenship. Though non-citizens are allowed to vote in local elections, citizenship is required for taking office and voting in national elections. The various political movements focusing on the Russian-speaking population are failing to increase their electoral base in national elections despite the growth in naturalized citizens, which indicates that the political system is becoming denationalized, in the sense that people do not vote along ethnic lines. This trend is also noticeable in these parties' sharp decline in local elections, in which even non-citizens are allowed to vote, a trend that demonstrates the remarkable integration of the polity.

Estonia's approach to integration, which is tougher than that of other European countries in its insistence on some degree of mastery of the national language, has in the new millennium been praised by Danish officials, who have even suggested that Europe, in dealing with its own integration crises, should learn from the Estonian example. Nevertheless, the challenge to integrate the minority populations will remain for the long term, and will be inextricably tied to Russia's own development, especially its acceptance of its postcolonial reality, as well as to the nature of its bilateral relations with Estonia.

BALANCING REGIONAL DEVELOPMENT

Impressive as Estonia's economic growth has been, it has not been without problems. One major problem is drastically unequal development in different parts of the country. Basically, Tallinn, the capital, has received most of the investments and reaped most of the rewards, while rural communities and the former industrial heartland of the country's northeast have suffered, experiencing little of the rewards of economic progress. Tourists, for the most part, have rarely ventured out of Tallinn, especially the million of Finnish day tourists, interested mostly in shopping and alcohol. With its large concentration of expatriates, Tallinn has also grown increasingly cosmopolitan, as evidenced by the large selection of ethnic restaurants and the many languages heard on its streets. The same cannot be said of rural towns like Viljandi, the cultural heart of central Estonia, nor of Narva, the industrial hulk on the northeast.

Though the Estonian government has embarked upon limited decentralization by moving the Ministry of Education to Tartu, the university town (joining the Supreme Court in Estonia's second city), the focus of every aspect of the new Estonia, including politics, economics, society, entertainment, tourism, and activism, is indeed in Tallinn. Less political clout from rural sectors meant a generally recognized urban-focused political elite for the first post-restoration decade; the election of Arnold Rüütel as president in 2001 was a direct reflection of growing rural discontent with the Tallinn-centered political world.

Though Tallinn accounts for just under one-third of the country's population, it represents the bulk of the country's economy. Unemployment (especially white collar) is significantly lower there than in the rural south or the industrial northeast. The contrast between modern glass skyscrapers in Tallinn and mothballed crumbling smokestacks in Kohtla-Järve is indicative of the uneven development. The dramatic difference in standards of living in Tallinn and in other areas is increasing as Tallinn's role in regional commerce continues to increase, and despite the creation of a ministerial post for dealing with regional affairs, there has been little in the way of major initiatives to offset this lack of harmony in development.

An additional difficulty can be seen in the industrial northeast, where many of the industries, such as mining, chemicals, textiles, and food processing, are labor intensive but low paying. The inability for some of the Soviet-era industrial giants to adapt to new economic realities exacerbates the out of balance development by contributing to unemployment. Moreover, a large percentage of the region's population is Russian-speaking, making the issue more important to solve to prevent any growth in discontent among the country's minority population.

Bringing a better balance of development throughout the country is necessary for Estonian society as a whole to enjoy the rewards of its post-Soviet success. Tallinn has symbolized the success of the first post-restoration decade, Narva its failures. The challenge for Estonian policymakers is to redress the balance and to correct those failures, and bring the economic miracle of the first decade to all corners of the country.

SAVING A FRAGILE ECOLOGY

One of the many negative legacies left by the Soviet occupation is the precarious state of Estonia's ecology. Many Soviet-era industries, including secretive factories working for the Soviet military-industrial complex, created widespread pollution of the environment, ranging from chemical to radioactive. The lax environmental regulations of the Soviet period, exacerbated by a general lack of concern for the environment by Soviet planners, gave Estonian protestors the fuel to begin mass national protests in the late 1980s. Though some major projects, such as the mining of phosphates that would have severely damaged the local ecology, were stopped, the overall state of the environment inherited by the Estonian government following the restoration of independence was incredibly bleak.

The industrial complexes, many in the country's northeast, spew out pollution at an alarming rate. Even the indigenous fuel for the country's power plants and chemical industry, namely oil shale, causes major pollution in postfiring sediments in landfills and airborne particles from the smokestacks. Major investments were necessary to cut down the level of pollution in those enterprises that survived the transition to a market economy. The desire to be self-sufficient in electricity (and not be dependent on Russian exports) forces Estonia to continue to use the dirty oil shale, but significant investments have been made to bring oil shale firing to a level compatible with EU regulations, as well as the Kyoto agreements.

In addition, the Soviet military and its industrial complex left a myriad of environmental disasters. As Russian troops pulled out of Estonia in 1994, they left behind hundreds of installations in decrepit condition. Often sabotage also afflicted the environment, as ships were stripped and scuttled in various bodies of water. Jet fuel was dumped into wells or the ground, poisoning both the water system and the soil. Various chemicals and pollutants seeped noticeably from the abandoned bases, as everything valuable was stripped by the outgoing Soviet military. Worse, at the former closed city of Sillamäe, a radioactive lake remained from the former Soviet atomic research facility that threatened to seep into the Baltic Sea.

Significant investments have already been made to control the environmental damage from the Soviet occupation, though the problems are long term in nature. The country has an extra impetus to move quickly in order to proceed with European integration, since here again it is crucial to adhere to the EU's strict environmental regulations. The most dangerous pollution sites, such as the radioactive lake in Sillamäe, have been contained to prevent

Finding Estonia's Nokia

In a 1999 speech, former president Lennart Meri challenged Estonia to find the so-called Estonian Nokia, a reference to the company that put Finland on the world map. Many felt that Estonia's northern cousin's success with marketing Nokia around the world created Finland's reputation as a center for high tech manufacturing, and has in turn perpetuated Finland's economic growth. Meri thus challenged Estonia to find its own Nokia in order to put Estonia on the global map.

Both entrepreneurs and the media took up the challenge, and Meri's words became a common catchphrase in the newspapers. Many felt that few outside of Estonia knew much about the country and its economic success (a fact corroborated by poll results among European businessmen) and that the nation needed a magnet to draw more foreign investments. This call for a one-product remedy for Estonia's lack of image caused various pundits to speculate on the possibilities, ranging from the high-quality cross-country skis by Viisnurk to the wave of Estonian fashion models, led by supermodel Carmen Kass (a candidate for a seat in the European Parliament in June 2004), who grace the catwalks of the world's fashion capitals. Others joked that a better mission would be to find Estonia's McDonald's, to ensure a penetration into global pop culture. The hosting of the 2002 Eurovision Song Contest, which brought hundreds of millions of viewers to focus on Tallinn, the capital, helped to promote the country's image, but the nation still lacked a product with which the name Estonia could be linked.

The question was not to find an Estonian success story—there were many, ranging from a continent-wide Internet-recruitment service (CV-Online) to the many world-famous contemporary classical music composers (such as Arvo Pärt and Erkki-Sven Tüür) and conductors (Neeme Järvi and Tõnu Kaljuste). The goal was to find a single product that could help define Estonia to the world. This has become more important over time as the predominance of Nordic investment capital in the Estonian economy, and their command over Estonian businesses, continues to increase.

Perhaps the best-known Estonian name in global culture comes from a very unlikely place, percussion instruments, or, to be precise, cymbals. The world's number two cymbal maker, Paiste, originated in Estonia in the early part of the twentieth century. The family business played a major role in the development of contemporary music, especially with the advent of the drum kit, which helped to launch rock and modern jazz. The company relocated during the Soviet occupation, and became a truly global venture, with a major presence in the United States and Switzerland. Its "homecoming" to Estonia in the early 1990s was a symbolic gesture acknowledging its tie to its roots. Despite this name recognition, however, Estonians continued to search for a modern, homegrown Nokia equivalent.

The most recent candidate for this position has been the Estonian Genome Project, one of the most ambitious genetics projects in the world. The goal of cataloguing the genome of the Estonian nation, creating perhaps the largest database for a single population in the world, has brought Estonia's small but advanced genetics industry to international prominence.

Still, the search for Estonia's Nokia continues, driving both entrepreneur and politician to work towards this goal. Though it could prove to be a fruitless chase for the end of the rainbow, it nevertheless brings out the best and most creative aspects of the country and its people.

---

an imminent leak into the water system. However, the damage, estimated to be in the billions of dollars, will take decades to repair.

The only environmental advantage of the Soviet occupation came with the reforestation of the land. With the brutal forced collectivization of farms, many fields were simply abandoned and eventually reclaimed by the forest. At the turn of the millennium, some 45 percent of Estonia is covered by forests, giving the timber and wood-processing industry sufficient resources without threatening the country's natural environment. Estonians have a cultural affinity with forests; thus the reforestation has been one refreshing result of Soviet policies.

The many nature reserves in Estonia have also seen an increase in ecotourism. Many small islands off the coast are closed as nature reserves, and cooperation between tourism and environmental officials have successfully marketed this aspect of Estonia. Though few and far between, the success stories of Estonia's ecological situation remain encouraging signs for the healing of the country's precious land.

A MODERN PLAGUE ARRIVES

As every age seemingly has its own plague, the modern age's scourge has been AIDS. This incurable disease has severely crippled many countries around the world, and increasingly the problem has spread into the former Soviet bloc. Formerly insulated from intravenous drugs, the quickest method of spreading HIV, the virus that leads to AIDS, former Soviet bloc countries have experienced a sharp increase in the proliferation of drugs, which has also meant the rapid growth of HIV infection. Estonia has not escaped from this modern plague.

For many years after the restoration of independence, the number of registered HIV infected patients in Estonia remained remarkably low, despite the spread of IV drugs in various parts of the country. Then a quick upsurge in positive diagnoses in 2000 caused alarm, as the problem was isolated in the northeastern city of Narva, a city economically depressed and predominantly Russian-speaking. Within a few months, the number of registered HIV patients grew from nearly zero to over three hundred, and cases sprung up in other industrialized towns in the region, such as Kohtla-Järve.

Politicians worry that the slow spread westward of HIV cases will reach Tallinn at some point, which would cause a major social catastrophe. At the same time, the localization of the cases in Russian-speaking Narva has exacerbated both the problems of integration and of regional development. Major antidrug and safe-sex campaigns have been conducted throughout Estonia, including the Russian-speaking communities, and the trend has slowed for the time being.

Politicians also fear that treatment for the large number of HIV cases will seriously impact the Health Fund, as the number of positive diagnoses, near 2500 in mid-2002, represented almost 0.2 percent of the population, according to statistics compiled by the Social Ministry. The huge cost for the state will come in the future, as the HIV patients fall ill and require extensive medication and hospitalization. This is clearly a major challenge for the long term, not just for Estonia, but also for Europe and the world, another good example of the worldwide nature of many of Estonia's most pressing challenges.

By no means are these three challenges the only ones that Estonia faces in this new millennium. Various other concerns also challenge the country's policymakers and society. The gap between the better-off and the poor is increasing as the country becomes more prosperous, leaving some who have missed out on the positive results of market reforms in dire straits. EU integration and globalization bring Estonia closer to the world, but some fear that they will also dilute or even threaten the survival of the Estonian language and culture. The predominance of Nordic capital in Estonia has brought strength to the local economy and helped create the economic miracle of Estonia, but some feel a concern that Estonia might become nothing but a backyard for Nordic companies.

These challenges and issues will continue to test a new generation of Estonian policymakers, as well as society in general. The country has shed its Cold War legacy by joining the EU and NATO and by fully reintegrating into the Western community of nations, but these concerns, which also afflict many other European and North American countries, will certainly remain as challenges for years to come. In many ways, the normalization of Estonia's domestic challenges, now so like those of other developed European countries, is a reflection of the success of its post-Soviet reforms. The new challenges will be more difficult to solve.

SELECTIVE BIBLIOGRAPHY

Clemens, Walter. *The Baltic Transformed: Complexity Theory and European Security.* Lanham, MD: Rowman and Littlefield, 2001.

Crowe, David. *The Baltic States and the Great Powers: Foreign Relations, 1938–1940.* Boulder: Westview Press, 1993.

Estonian Foreign Ministry. http://www.vm.ee/eng (accessed 16 July 2004).

Estonian Government Portal. http://www.riik.ee (accessed 16 July 2004).

Estonian Institute. *Estonica: Encyclopedia about Estonia.* http://www.estonica.org (accessed 16 July 2004).

Estonian Ministry of Social Affairs. http://www.sm.ee (accessed 16 July 2004).

Estonian National Electoral Committee. http://www.vvk.ee/engindex.html (accessed 16 July 2004).

Hiden, John, and Patrick Salmon. *The Baltic Nations and Europe: Estonia, Latvia and Lithuania in the Twentieth Century.* 1991. Reprint, London: Longman, 1994.

Kasekamp, Andres. *The Radical Right in Interwar Estonia.* Basingstoke, UK: Macmillan, 2000.

Laar, Mart. *Little Country That Could.* London: Centre for Research into Post-Communist Economies, 2002.

———. *War in the Woods: Estonia's Struggle for Survival, 1944–1956.* Washington, DC: Compass Press, 1992.

Laur, Mati, Tõnis Lukas, Ain Mäesalu, Ago Pajur, and Tõnu Tannberg. *History of Estonia.* Tallinn, Estonia: Avita, 2000.

Lauristin, Marju, and Mati Heidmets, eds. *The Challenge of the Russian Minority: Emerging Multicultural Democracy in Estonia.* Tartu, Estonia: Tartu University Press, 2002.

Lauristin, Marju, and Peeter Vihalemm. *Return to the Western World: Cultural and Political Perspectives on the Estonian Post-Communist Transition.* Tartu, Estonia: Tartu University Press, 1997.

Lieven, Anatol. *The Baltic Revolution: Estonia, Latvia, Lithuania and the Path to Independence.* New Haven: Yale University Press, 1993.

Marandi, Rein. *Must-valge lipu all: Vabadussõjalaste liikumine Eestis 1929–1937.* Vol. 1, *Legaalne periood, 1929–1934;* vol. 2, *Illegaalne periood, 1934–1937* (Under the Black-White Flag: The Veteran's Movement in Estonia, 1929–1937. Vol. 1, The Legal Period, 1929–1934; vol. 2, The Illegal Period, 1934–1937). Stockholm: Centre for Baltic Studies, University of Stockholm, 1991.

Medijainen, Eero. *Saadiku saatus: Välisministeerium ja saatkonnad, 1918–1940* (The Fate of the Diplomat: The Foreign Ministry and the Embassies, 1918–1940). Tallinn, Estonia: Eesti Entsüklopeediakirjastus, 1997.

Misiunas, Romuald, and Rein Taagepera. *The Baltic States: Years of Dependence, 1940–1990.* 1983. Reprint, Berkeley: University of California Press, 1993.

Raun, Toivo. *Estonia and the Estonians.* Stanford, CA: Hoover Institution Press, 1991.

Sprudzs, Adolf. *The Baltic Path to Independence: An International Reader of Selected Articles.* Buffalo: William S. Hein, 1994.

Taagepera, Rein. *Estonia: Return to Independence.* Boulder: Westview Press, 1993.

Tarulis, Albert. *Soviet Policy toward the Baltic States, 1918–1940.* South Bend, IN: University of Notre Dame Press, 1959.

Trapans, Jan Arveds, ed. *Towards Independence: The Baltic Popular Movements.* Boulder: Westview Press, 1991.

Vihalemm, Peeter, ed. *Baltic Media in Transition.* Tartu, Estonia: Tartu University Press, 2002.

Von Rauch, Georg. *The Baltic States: Years of Independence, 1917–1940.* 1974. Reprint, New York: St. Martin's Press, 1995.

CHRONOLOGY

7500 B.C.E.	The oldest known settlement in Estonia established.
600 C.E.	Large-scale attacks by Sweden on Estonian lands commence.
1186	First Bishop of Livonia, Meinhard, ordained to intensify efforts to convert the Baltic peoples.
1187	Estonians sack key Swedish town of Sigtuna.
1198	First notable attempt by Catholic Church to convert Estonians by military force.
1201	Riga (Latvia) is founded by Germanic crusaders as base for crusades and seat of a bishopric.
1202	Order of the Brotherhood of the Sword founded to subjugate local population in the Baltic lands; Pope Innocent III confirms Order two years later.
1208	Germanic crusaders begin major raids into Estonian lands.
1210	Russian princes attack Estonia, opening eastern front for defenders.
1212	Armistice reached between Estonian forces and crusaders.
1219	Danish forces land in Estonia; Tallinn (originally Reval) founded.
1224	Foreign forces complete domination of mainland Estonia by capturing Tartu.
1227	Estonia comes under total foreign rule as the islands are captured.
1238	Stensby agreement establishes the partition of Estonian lands by the Danes, the Livonian Order, and two bishoprics.
1242	The "battle on the ice" on Lake Peipsi, in which Russian prince Alexander Nevsky defeated Germanic crusaders; Lake Peipsi becomes de facto border with Russian principalities.
1248	Tallinn granted city rights; becomes key member of the Hanseatic League later in the century.
1343	Saint George's Day uprising.
1346	Danish crown sells its Estonian possessions (including Tallinn) to the Teutonic Order.
1410	Lithuanian-Polish joint army defeats Teutonic Order at Grünwald, marking the decline of the crusading orders along the Baltic.
1523	Reformation reaches Estonia.
1525	First text in Estonia, a book of common prayers, is published.
1558	Russian invasion of Estonian lands marks beginning of the Livonian Wars.
1559	Denmark purchases western bishopric and reenters Estonia.
1560	Polish-Lithuanian forces take control of most forts owned by the Livonian Order.
1561	Swedish forces reenter Estonia, taking control of the north (including Tallinn) from remnants of the Livonian Order, which ceases to exist.
1563	Conflict between Denmark and Sweden begins, extending to Estonia; conflict ends in 1570, with Denmark's possessions reduced to the island of Saaremaa.
1577	Sweden and Poland-Lithuania jointly push Russian forces back.
1582–1583	Peace treaties among warring parties signed, ending the conflicts; northern Estonia remains Swedish, southern Estonia remains Polish-Lithuanian, and Saaremaa remains Danish.
1600	Conflict commences between Sweden and Poland-Lithuania for control of Baltic lands, lasting nearly thirty years.
1629	Peace of Altmark signed between warring parties, giving Sweden control of the Estonian mainland.
1632	Academia Gustaviana, later to be renamed Tartu University, is founded as the second institution for higher learning in the Swedish Empire.
1637	First Estonian grammar book written by Heinrich Stahl.
1645	Denmark loses Saaremaa in peace agreement after three-year war with Sweden; all of Estonia now under Swedish rule.
1656	Russia attacks Swedish-controlled Estonia, but Swedish forces evict Russian forces in the short war.
1695–1697	Mass famine kills estimated 20 percent of population.
1700	Polish-Lithuanian and Saxon forces attack Swedish-controlled Riga, setting

	off the Great Northern War; Russian forces attack Narva to enter war.
1709	Swedish forces comprehensively defeated by Russians at Poltava; Russian forces take control of most of Estonia despite another decade of warfare.
1721	Peace of Nystadt signed, giving Estonia and other Baltic lands to the Russian Empire.
1739	So-called Rosen Declaration establishes full serfdom in Estonia.
1806	First Estonian-language newspaper published.
1816	Tsar Alexander I abolishes serfdom in Estonia; Livonia follows two years later.
1838	The Estonian Learned Society is founded, sparking the cultural awakening that continues throughout the 1800s.
1858	The Krenholm textiles factory established in Narva, marking the start of industrialization in Estonia.
1862	The national epic, *Kalevipoeg,* is published.
1869	The first Estonian National Song Festival is held in Tartu, becoming a major force in the national awakening.
1870	The Baltic railway, linking the ports of Paldiski and Narva to Tallinn and St. Petersburg, is completed.
1872	Estonian Society of Literati founded to promote literature in Estonian.
1884	The Estonian Students Society consecrates its blue-white-black flag, which later becomes the national flag of Estonia.
1887	Russian established as only language of education, marking the peak of the Russification campaign.
1904	Coalition of Estonians and Russians take control of Tallinn Town Council from Germans.
1905	The 1905 Revolution breaks out in Estonia.
1909	Tartu-educated Wilhelm Ostwald wins the Nobel Prize in Physics.
1914–1918	World War I.
March 1917	February Revolution reaches Estonia with massive public chaos; Jaan Poska becomes first Estonian appointed as governor (now commissar), and Estonian is declared official language; northern Livonia is also merged with Estonia in the province.
May 1917	The *Maapäev,* the first Estonian legislative body, is elected; body convenes in July and confirms its first government.
October 1917	Bolshevik Revolution spreads to Estonia.
19 February 1918	The Committee of National Salvation formed by the *Maapäev* leadership to assume control of Estonia.
20 February 1918	German forces invade the Estonian mainland.
23 February 1918	Bolsheviks evacuate Tallinn.
24 February 1918	The Committee of National Salvation declares Estonian independence.
3 March 1918	German forces assume control of all of Estonia; Estonian leaders arrested, and committee member Jüri Vilms executed in Finland.
3 May 1918	Britain, France, and Italy give de facto recognition to Estonian independence.
28 November 1918	Bolsheviks attack Narva, starting the Estonian War of Independence.
December 1918	Russians take control of much of Estonia with brutal repression.
1 February 1919	Estonian forces manage to expel all Bolshevik forces from Estonia.
5–7 April 1919	Constituent Assembly is elected by the people and convenes on 23 April; the democratic left takes majority.
23 June 1919	Estonian forces, assisted by Latvian forces, crush the German *Landeswehr* force in the Latvian city of Cēsis, ending a potential German threat.
10 October 1919	Radical land law redistributes land to the peasantry.
2 February 1920	The Tartu Peace Treaty (Estonia's "birth certificate") is signed by Estonia and Soviet Russia.
15 June 1920	Constituent Assembly adopts the Estonian constitution.
November 1920	First parliamentary elections held; center-right wins majority.
21 January 1921	The Supreme Allied Council offers de jure recognition of Estonia; the United States waits until the summer of 1922.
22 September 1922	Estonia joins the League of Nations.
May 1923	Elections held to second parliament after referendum loss on religious education; center-right gains seats.
December 1923	Estonia and Latvia sign treaty for a defensive alliance.
1 December 1924	Bolsheviks fail in coup attempt; Communist Party banned.
May 1926	Elections to third parliament held, center-right again wins.
1 January 1928	The kroon is introduced as the national currency, replacing the unstable mark (introduced in 1919).
1929	The Estonian League of Veterans of the War of Independence founded as major pressure group on constitutional reform; later shows semifascist tendencies.
May 1929	Elections to fourth parliament held; center-right remains in control.

13–15 August 1932	First referendum on constitutional changes, aimed above all at creating a powerful executive, fails by small margin.
10–12 June 1933	Second, watered-down referendum fails by large margin.
Summer 1933	The government devalues the kroon by 35 percent, helping the economic recovery following the worldwide Depression.
14–16 October 1933	Third referendum to create a strong executive (submitted by the League of Veterans) wins by big margin, and presidential elections scheduled for March 1934; Konstantin Päts is appointed as caretaker head of government.
12 March 1934	Palace coup by Päts, citing fascist tendencies of the League of Veterans, ends parliamentary democracy; mild totalitarian rule creates Era of Silence.
February 1936	Elections held for new constituent assembly; silenced opposition candidates boycott vote; new constitution creates bicameral parliament, but power remains with the executive; approved the following year.
24 April 1938	Päts is elected as Estonia's first president after constitutional change.
23 August 1939	Nazi Germany and the Soviet Union sign Molotov-Ribbentrop Pact, including secret protocols to carve up the Baltic countries.
18 September 1939	Polish submarine *Orzeł* escapes from internment in Tallinn Harbor, leading to Soviet complaints; Estonia cannot defend neutrality.
28 September 1939	After Soviet threats, agreement is signed, establishing Soviet bases in Estonia.
16 June 1940	Moscow issues ultimatum to Estonia to replace government with one sympathetic to the USSR.
17 June 1940	The Red Army occupies Estonia.
17 July 1940	Results of rump one-candidate elections announced by Soviet authorities, with 92.9 percent "turnout."
6 August 1940	Assembly votes to request membership in the USSR.
1 June 1941	Mass deportations of population to Russia, estimated at 10,000.
7 July 1941	German forces enter Estonia weeks after declaring war against Moscow; by October the entire country is taken over.
18 September 1944	Acting President Juri Uluots appoints new Estonian government, and independence is declared re-established.
24 November 1944	Red Army takes control of all of Estonia; "forest brother" partisans fight guerrilla campaign against Soviet power until the 1950s.
May 1947	Forced collectivization of farms begins.
25–26 March 1949	Mass deportations of the population, estimated at over 20,000.
1965	Regular ferry links with Finland begin.
1978	The last forest brother, August Sabe, kills himself when ambushed by KGB.
December 1978	New stringent policy of Russification embarked upon, including the introduction of the Russian language to kindergarten-age children and discouragement of the use of Estonian.
September 1980	Mass protests by students ensue after concert by punk band Propeller, and soccer match cancelled, becoming first major set of protests for democratization.
November 1980	Stemming from protests, the so-called "Group of Forty" intellectuals draft an open letter to Soviet authorities to address problems such as Russian immigration, Russification, and youth policy.
Spring 1987	Protests began to stop massive phosphorite mining, starting the revolution process.
23 August 1987	Protest in Tallinn's Hirvepark becomes first mass political protest.
April 1988	The Estonian Popular Front for the Support of Perestroika is founded.
August 1988	The Estonian National Independence Party is formed, with the ultimate goal of restoring Estonia's independence.
11 September 1988	Eestimaa Laul song festival becomes the symbol of the Singing Revolution, with over 300,000 in attendance.
16 November 1988	The Estonian Supreme Soviet adopts declaration of sovereignty.
24 February 1989	Flag of independent Estonia is raised on Independence Day on Tallinn's Pikk Hermann tower for the first time in nearly fifty years; the Committee of Citizens is formed and begins collecting database of citizens of Estonia before the 1940 occupation and their descendants.
23 August 1989	Over a million people create human chain from Tallinn to Riga to Vilnius to protest the Molotov-Ribbentrop Pact.
24 February 1990	Elections to the Estonian Congress, a parallel legislative body created for registered citizens of Estonia; body meets in March.
18 March 1990	First multicandidate election under Soviet rule; reformers win most seats, leading to split in the Estonian Communist Party.
30 March 1990	The Supreme Council adopts decision on transition toward independence.

3 March 1991	Referendum on independence in Estonia, with 77.8 percent in support.
20 August 1991	The Supreme Council declares the restoration of Estonia's independence during turmoil in Moscow after coup.
22 August 1991	Iceland becomes the first country to recognize Estonian independence.
6 September 1991	The USSR recognizes Estonian independence.
17 September 1991	Estonia joins the United Nations.
20 June 1992	The kroon is reintroduced as the national currency.
28 June 1992	Referendum approves a new constitution.
20 September 1992	Parliamentary elections and first round of presidential election; center-right parties take majority of seats.
5 October 1992	Lennart Meri is elected president by the parliament; then confirms 32-year old Mart Laar to head a center-right government.
13 September 1993	Baltic Free Trade Agreement is signed.
9 May 1994	Estonia becomes an associate member of the European Union.
31 August 1994	The Red Army completes its withdrawal from Estonia and Latvia.
28 September 1994	The ferry *Estonia* sinks en route from Tallinn to Stockholm; 851 die.
March 1995	Parliamentary elections give the center a working majority.
20 September 1996	Lennart Meri reelected president by electoral college.
March 1999	Parliamentary elections bring the center-right back to power.
September 2001	Arnold Rüütel, former titular head of republic during the late Soviet days, is elected president.
November 2002	Estonia receives official invitation to join NATO.
December 2002	Estonia receives official invitation to join the European Union.
March 2003	Parliamentary elections keep the center-right in power.
September 2003	Two-thirds of Estonians vote to join the European Union.
29 March 2004	Estonia officially joins NATO.
1 May 2004	Estonia officially joins the European Union.

LATVIA

ALDIS PURS

LAND AND PEOPLE

The Republic of Latvia is situated on the eastern rim of the Baltic Sea in Europe around the geographic coordinates of fifty-seven degrees north latitude and twenty-five degrees east longitude. The state's regional placement has often determined its politics and history. Traditionally Latvia, along with the other Baltic States, Estonia and Lithuania, has been seen either as an Eastern European country, one of the western borderlands of Russia, or a republic (and since 1991, a former republic) of the Soviet Union. The Baltic states themselves prefer a regional association with Scandinavia and see themselves as part of Northern Europe. These ambiguities in geography are associated with a difficult and traumatic history and a region in transition.

Perhaps only the political geography of the country is simple. At 64,589 square kilometers, Latvia is slightly larger than West Virginia, and it has 1,150 kilometers of borders with other countries. Latvia, although a small European state, is larger than Denmark, Estonia, Switzerland, Netherlands, Belgium, and Albania. Nevertheless, the farthest distance across Latvia (from Liepāja in the west to Zilupe in the east) is nearly 450 kilometers, or roughly the equivalent of the distance between Riga and Stockholm, in Sweden, or between Berlin, in Germany, and Copenhagen, in Denmark. Estonia borders Latvia to the north and shares a 339-kilometer border with Latvia. Russia lies due east with a 217-kilometer border. Belarus lies to the southeast, sharing a 141-kilometer border, and Lithuania is due south with a 453-kilometer border. The Baltic Sea provides 531 kilometers of coastline to the west and north of Latvia. As of 2002, the treaty with Russia delimiting the border had not been signed, nor had Latvia's parliament ratified the maritime boundary agreement with Lithuania.

The internal political geography of Latvia has also fluctuated considerably over many centuries, and is in fact currently undergoing considerable substantive change. The capital is Riga, situated on the Daugava River not far from the Gulf of Riga. Traditionally Latvia is divided into four provinces (singular *apgabals*): Kurzeme to the west, Zemgale in the center, Vidzeme in the east-northeast, and Latgale to the southeast. These provinces are closely linked to regional identity and still determine national electoral territories (with the addition of Riga as an electoral territory), but have a limited administrative presence. Local government revolves around counties (singular *rajons*) and municipalities (singular *pilsēta*) with a continuing, but diminishing, role played by several hundred parishes

©2001 maps.com

Riga and the Daugava River. (Tibor Botgnar/Corbis)

(singular *pagasts*). Latvia currently has twenty-six counties: Aizkraukle, Alūksne, Balvi, Bauksa, Cēsis, Daugavpils, Dobele, Gulbene, Jēkabpils, Jelgava, Krāslava, Kuldīga, Liepāja, Limbāži, Ludza, Madona, Ogre, Preiļi, Rēzekne, Riga, Saldus, Talsi, Tukums, Valka, Valmiera, and Ventspils. Each of these counties has an urban center by the same name acting as its administrative seat, and most include several other smaller urban centers. Unique among Latvia's towns and cities, however, are the seven largest cities (Daugavpils, Jelgava, Jūrmala, Liepāja, Rēzekne, Riga, and Ventspils), which are autonomous administrative divisions. The general administrative division of Latvia, however, is in the midst of a controversial process of rationalization, amalgamation, and consolidation of local governments, a process that anticipates the drastic reduction of their number.

Latvia's physical geography is not immediately awe-inspiring, but it has a subdued, serene, unique pastoral beauty. As a whole, the country is composed primarily of low-lying plains, which begin at the coastline and sweep eastward, interrupted by forests and occasional hills and minor highlands. On a continental scale, Latvia is part of the great east European plain that stretches from the Baltic Sea in the north to the Black Sea in the south and is loosely bordered by the Ural, Carpathian, and Caucasian mountain chains. Through this entire region, including Latvia, there

are few hills that rise above 300–400 meters. Within this relatively small variation in elevation, however, Latvia showcases a surprising array of hills, valleys, swamps, and forests. Hundreds of lakes (officially, 2,256, ranging in size from small to large), as well as several major rivers and many more streams, create many river-valley systems. Various ice ages, having covered Latvia in more than a hundred meters of ice, have contributed to Latvia's geography by carving swathes through the countryside and by depositing giant granite boulders in seemingly incongruous places.

Latvia's coastal plain impinges between five and forty kilometers into the interior. The sandstone foundations of most of the coastline facilitate a gradual, evolving geography that lacks the stark fjords of Scandinavia. Similarly Latvia does not have many natural harbors and instead relies on major river deltas for harbor towns and cities. The constant ebb and flow of the tides of the Baltic Sea has also resulted in the frequent march of dunes and beaches into the interior and the presence of many shallows and sand bars along the coast (particularly in the Gulf of Riga). For the most part, dune formation is gradual, and there are few places, such as Jurkalne, with cliff-like dunes approaching twenty meters in height. Until the past few centuries (with the intervention of man), the ambiguous coastline and moving dunes threatened to overtake the lowlands that reached from Riga to Bauska and Jelgava in central Latvia. The inland city of Jelgava, for example, is only eight to fifteen meters above sea level, and Riga is less than twenty-five meters above sea level. The entire central plain is a mix of peat bogs, sandy soil, relatively fertile agricultural land, and forest composed of pine, fir, birch, and aspen.

A highland region cut through by the Venta and Abava river valleys dominates the western province of Kurzeme. These highlands are a continuation of the Lithuanian highlands, and seldom rise more than 150 meters above sea level; the two tallest hills are 200 and 190 meters above sea level. Although geographically the elevation is relatively insignificant, the appearance is often deceiving. Along the Venta River, for example, the elevation drops more than 100 meters in less than 5 kilometers, giving the impression of significant change. The nearby Abava River Valley is particularly noted for several caves on its shores and for the Abava Falls *(Abavas rumba),* which drop a paltry half meter. Many of the region's hills, combined with its valleys, provide wide landscapes of subtle beauty. Microclimates within this region, as well as its proximity to the coast, have allowed the most northerly vineyards in the world in Sabile. A similar highland region is found in Latvia's eastern province of Vidzeme. The Gauja River valley divides these highlands, and frequent lakes and streams periodically break the highland effect. This river vally is also home to one of Latvia's most important national parks. The smaller, but occasionally more dramatic, Amata River Valley in the same region includes some of Latvia's most notable cliffs. Further south, but still in the Vidzeme highlands, is Latvia's highest point, Gaiziņš Hill *(Gaiziņ kalns),* at 312 meters.

A lake plain dominates much of the province of Latgale immediately south of the Vidzeme highlands. This plain is roughly 60 meters above sea level and covers more than 7,000 square kilometers of land. Lake Lubane, Latvia's largest lake, covers 82 square kilometers of the lake-studded plain. Throughout the province of Latgale, there are some 650 lakes, including almost all of the benchmarks in terms of largest (Lubāne and, second largest, Rāznas Lake), deepest (Drīdzis Lake at 65.1 meters), and with the most islands (Ežezers, or Ješa, Lake, with at least one hundred islands). Before considerable human effort had been put into it, this lake plain with its many lakes flooded on a frequent basis, and the region was frequently impassable to land traffic due to extensive swamplike conditions. Along the edges of this plain are two more highlands that ring the edges of Latgale. In the south and southeast, the highlands are also dotted with exceptionally many lakes, while along the western edge of Latgale a highland plateau surrounds the Daugava River valley.

The river systems and their various watersheds are quite extensive. Altogether there are several hundred rivers, streams, and creeks in Latvia, almost all of them eventually flowing into the Baltic Sea or the Gulf of Riga. There are, however, four major rivers, the Daugava, Lielupe, Gauja, and Venta, and another half-dozen notable rivers. The Daugava River (also known as the Dvina, or Duna) is Latvia's largest river system and the eleventh longest in Europe. The Daugava's source is in Russia, and its entire length is over 1,000

Silver birches in a Latvian forest. (Niall Benvie/Corbis)

kilometers, 367 of which are in Latvia. Its width varies considerably, as does its depth (from more than a kilometer wide to more than 10 meters deep). The Daugava was an important transit river (carrying everything from Vikings to floating lumber) for centuries, but its navigability was sporadic, due to periodic rapids and heavy currents. The freezing of the river in winter and the consequent breaking of ice in the spring further limited its usefulness to humans; rapid thaws often led to devastating floods. Despite these troubles, the Daugava River holds a central place in folk traditions, customs, and lore. In the twentieth century, hydroelectric dams tamed the river's excesses and tapped into its energy potential. Similarly a series of bridges have reduced the Daugava's ability to stymie land transportation. These technological advances, however, are seen as bitter-sweet; the building of a hydro-electric dam by the Soviet government, for example, submerged an important national symbol, a cliff near Koknese called Staburags (the cliff was almost 19 meters high and was considered the setting of the climactic battle in Latvia's national epic, *Lāčplēsis* [The Bear Slayer]).

After the Daugava River, the Lielupe (literally "large river") is Latvia's second largest. The primarily Lithuanian rivers Mūsa and Mēmele flow together near the Latvian town of Bauska and form the Lielupe River. The Lielupe is a wide, relatively shallow river that flows slowly across the heart of Zemgale, ultimately entering the Daugava River near its entrance to the Gulf of Riga (at one time the Lielupe flowed directly into the Gulf). The river is easily navigable and allowed for the rise of the interior port city of Jelgava. Its many small tributaries provide a considerable amount of natural irrigation for the fertile agricultural lands of Zemgale.

Latvia's two other largest rivers are the Venta River in the western province of Kurzeme, and the Gauja River in the eastern province of Vidzeme. The Venta originates in Lithuania and flows down the Kurzeme highlands, finally emptying into the Baltic Sea (the port of Ventspils is built around the river delta). The constant and occasionally dramatic drop in elevation means that the Venta has many rapids and is mostly not navigable. Near the town of Kuldīga, the falls are at their severest with close to a 3-meter drop (and the widest falls in Latvia at 110 meters). Between Kuldīga and Ventspils, however, the river slows, the riverbed deepens, and navigation is possible. The Gauja River snakes 452 kilometers through Vidzeme and is Latvia's only large river entirely within the state's borders, although 20 of those kilometers form part of the border with Estonia. As with the Venta, the Gauja begins in highlands and drops relatively quickly to sea level (flowing into the Bay of Riga). The change in elevation leads to rapids, cliffs, caves, and an impressive river valley. Both of these river valleys help the surrounding areas (most improbably) refer to themselves as the Switzerlands of Kurzeme and Vidzeme respectively.

Complementing the extensive river systems are thousands of lakes. Every part of Latvia has a considerable number of lakes, with the exception of the plains in Zemgale. Latgale, as mentioned, has particularly many lakes, and they cover nearly 1.5 percent of the total area of the province. Most of these lakes, however, are small and relatively shallow. There are only fourteen lakes that cover more than 10 square kilometers of territory; some of the more important are Rāznas Lake, Lubānes Lake, Burtnieku Lake, Engūres Lake, Usmas Lake, and Papes Lake (the latter two have unique ecological value). Other lakes, such as Liepājas Lake, Alūksnes Lake, Babīša Lake, Ķīšu Lake, and Juglas Lake, are on the outskirts of cities and have become fixtures of the urban geography.

Latvia's natural resources are relatively limited. There are few mineral resources, primarily confined to amber, peat, limestone, and dolomite. The discovery of offshore oil reserves in neighbouring Lithuania, however, has recently stimulated interest in the potential oil wealth of Latvia's shoreline. Still, the most abundant natural resources are forests, arable land, and hydroelectric power. There have also been attempts to harvest wind power along the coasts. The extent of these resources has fluctuated considerably with human activity. The forests of Latvia, for example, were gradually reduced through the nineteenth and first half of the twentieth century. Most of this felling was driven by a demand for more arable land. The money to be made from the sale of lumber also earned the resource the nickname "green gold." After World War II, however, that demand receded considerably, and much previously tilled land went fallow. As a result, Latvia was one of the few countries in the world with more forests at the end of the twentieth century than at its beginning. More recently, however, that trend has again reversed, and felling of timber has considerably expanded. Still, nearly forty-six percent of Latvia's territory is covered with forests and woodlands. The ebb and flow of forest versus arable land conversely affects arable land and permanent pastures, which currently comprise roughly 40 percent of the state's territory.

A long geologic history has shaped Latvia's flora as much as its geography. The Ice Ages covered Latvia in more than one hundred meters of ice and effectively ended all botanical growth. As the ice receded, Latvia's environment took on a tundralike character, which remains in today's peat swamps. Over the next several millennia, swamplike vegetation encroached from the east, and in periods of dry, warm weather, forest vegetation arrived from the southwest. As a result, Latvia's territory is a mixture of deciduous and coniferous forests with intermittent prairies and swamplands. The Gulf Stream effect and close proximity to the Baltic Sea sustain a more temperate climate than Latvia's northern geographical location would seem to permit. In eastern Latvia, however, these factors weaken, and the climate and corresponding flora approach continental, northern norms. Zones of varying humidity and temperature further diversify the environment and leave Latvia with several distinct ecological zones over a relatively small territorial space. Near the coast, in the warmest regions, for example, ivy and yew trees have been found. As late as the Middle Ages, much of Latvia was covered with forests of a great variety of trees, including pine, fir, birch, aspen, oak, linden, elm, ash, maple, hazel, blackberry, and others. These forests were, and continue to be, rich with many forest berries and mushroom varieties.

Human activity, however, has substantially altered the terrain. As the human population grew, forests were cleared for more arable land. Generally, forests on the most fertile land were cleared first, thereby substantially changing the nature of Latvia's forests. Over time, forests decreased and became confined to sandy soil or semi-swamplands. As a result, the biological diversity lessened, and today's dominant coniferous tree is the pine, and the dominant deciduous trees are ash and birch. Likewise, many of Latvia's swamps and marshes have been drained, reducing the indigenous flora native to these environments. Nevertheless, swamps still account for 10 percent of Latvia's territory, and some of the largest and ecologically most significant are within national parks in Vidzeme (Gauja National Park), and Kurzeme (Slītere National Park). Just as the forests have mushrooms and berries, the swamps produce cloudberries in the spring and cranberries in the fall.

In the same way, Latvia's fauna changed with the shifts in the environment and, more recently, due to human activity. Prehistoric mammoths and rhinoceroses were victims of the Ice Age, but most extinction is tied to man. Several hundred years ago, European bison, brown bears, and lynx were common throughout the region. By the late 1800s, however, bison had been hunted to extinction, and bear and lynx were found only in isolated pockets in some of Latvia's most untouched forests. Similarly, moose once roamed through many of Latvia's forests and swamps and are now primarily found in the northeast. Some large mammal populations, such as wild boar and wolves, have varied considerably over the past two centuries, moving in and out of Latvia according to human activity (or inactivity). The racoon dog arrived in the eastern portions of Latvia, for example, only in the twentieth century. There are also a great many small mammals, including deer, rabbits, foxes, squirrels, martens, bats, rats, mice, and hedgehogs. Maritime mammals are limited to seals, although dolphins on occasion have reached the western shores of Latvia.

More than mammals, Latvia's wealth in fauna is in the more than three hundred species of birds that make Latvia their home at least for part of the year. The western shores of Latvia are particularly important as a part of the migratory route of arctic birds. The most impressive of Latvia's birds is the stork, which arrives in the western half of Latvia from northern Africa in the late spring and summer. Latvia's swamps also have considerable numbers of predatory birds, including small eagles, owls, and endangered cranes. Fish are fairly abundant in the Baltic Sea and Bay of Riga. Pilchard, flounder, cod, and salmon have all been important staples of Latvia's fishing communities, while freshwater eel, trout, pike, and catfish are caught in Latvia's rivers and lakes. Crawfish and lamprey are exceptional delicacies. Of the many amphibians, reptiles, and snakes, there is only one indigenous poisonous snake.

Changes in the use of some agricultural land during the Soviet era reversed some ecological trends in isolated places. On the one hand, the mechanization and intensification of agriculture with the heavy use of chemical fertilizers adversely affected Latvia's flora and fauna. Runoff from industrial concerns and the lack of waste conversion equipment severely compromised the health of many of Latvia's rivers and lakes, and even the Baltic Sea. Soviet military bases were some of the worst offenders in contaminating soil and groundwater with toxic chemicals and petroleum products. Many collective farms, on the other hand, abandoned arable land, which led to some forest recovery (and accompanying recovery of wildlife). More beneficial to Latvia's wildlife was the Soviet Union's prohibition of most human activity along the Baltic Sea as a security measure (in order to monitor the border). Outside of the few coastal cities and towns, the shorelines were mostly free of human activity. These regions are now the healthiest ecosystems of Latvia and have received international recognition for their potential in recreating European coastal marshland habitats. The migratory birds are a particularly important component, as is a recent World Wildlife Fund program that is reintroducing wild horses to the region.

Migrations of peoples is similarly central to the history of the region. The Livs, a Finno-Ugric people, have lived along the eastern shore of the Baltic Sea for the longest uninterrupted time. The ancestors of modern Latvians and Lettgalians have similarly lived in the region for millennia. The ancestors of modern Lithuanians and Estonians have lived

along the undefined borders equally as long. Germans, Russians, Jews, Poles, and other Slavic peoples began to arrive in the region from the twelfth century. Some of these populations arrived in the territory of modern Latvia in sizable numbers only in the last few hundred years. Others have been forcibly removed or killed in the past century and are no longer present in contemporary Latvia in considerable numbers. The nature of all of these communities, their relations with each other, and their claims of "belonging" to the region are extremely controversial. These details belong to the history of Latvia.

HISTORY
EARLY DEVELOPMENTS
Humans first travelled along the eastern shores of the Baltic Sea around 9000 B.C.E. This early habitation was short-lived and a part of more general wanderings. Prolonged human habitation probably began some six thousand years ago (roughly 4000 B.C.E.). These first settlers were from two distinct migrating peoples, the Finno-Ugric people and the Indo-European-speaking people. Most of the Finno-Ugric people migrated further north, populating present-day Estonia and Finland, but some remained along the Daugava River and the Bay of Riga. These were the ancestors of the Livs. Proto-Baltic people settled in the region soon after, and displaced some of these Finno-Ugric people to the north. Over the next several thousand years, all of these primitive societies moved through Mesolithic and Neolithic developments into the Bronze and Iron Ages. By the first century of the Common Era, these societies were becoming more and more differentiated linguistically and culturally. The migration of Germanic and Slavic peoples into Eastern and Central Europe pushed onto the Baltic periphery through the first several hundred years of the Common Era and further impacted the developing differentiation. Gradually, the Livs emerged as a distinct people within the Finno-Ugric peoples, and the Selians, Lettgallians, Semigallians, and Couronians did likewise within the Baltic peoples (as did the Lithuanians, the closest ancestral relatives of the modern-day Latvians).

From the fifth to tenth century, these peoples developed loose alliances between clans. Their societies became more complex. There were limited agricultural innovations, more clearing of forests, agricultural surpluses (resulting in the storage of grain), and limited participation in long-distance trade. The societies developed a division of labor and the production of metals. With these changes came differentiation in wealth and early state construction. Rule was likely tied to chiefs of clans and the control of hilltop fortresses. Roughly 470 hills (some estimates are far higher) constructed for fortification have been identified in Latvia, but relatively few have been thoroughly examined archeologically. Society was likely divided between the more powerful and wealthy and the poor (potentially slaves as well). The nature of these people's religious beliefs is clouded by the lack of sources, but they probably held beliefs similar to those of Germanic and Nordic paganism, with a heavy emphasis on the animist properties of natural forces.

Lake Pape

Lake Pape and the fishing village that surrounds it (also called Pape) are in the far southwestern tip of Latvia, bordering the Baltic Sea and near the Lithuanian border. Since independence, two different approaches to the future of this region have emerged. Wildlife conservationists see the region as an ideal nature preserve. Soviet prohibitions on construction near the seashore (a state border) translated into the area remaining a relatively pristine environment. Furthermore, the area is generally depopulated and is on an important migratory route of many birds. To international organizations such as the World Wide Fund for Nature (WWF) and its Latvian chapter, the region's natural environment is key. The WWF-Latvia has begun an ambitious (and initially successful) campaign to recreate a coastal wetland environment. Key to the campaign was the reintroduction of wild horses, horses that had not existed in the Pape area for at least two hundred years. The chosen horses, imported from the Netherlands, are technically not wild, but de-domesticated Przewalski horses originally native to Poland. Since the first introduction of the herd in 1998, it has taken to its new environment and has successfully wintered and foaled young. The horses are meant as an important component in the fragile ecosystem, since they will break up ground and graze vegetation. Ultimately the WWF hopes to introduce European bison, which, with large predators such as wolves or bear, would complete the ecosystem.

There is however, an alternate vision of preserving the natural habitat of the Pape region. Some local residents and ethnographic enthusiasts understand the natural environment in a radically different way. To these enthusiasts, Latvians in their traditional setting are a component of the natural environment. They believe that isolation and neglect, as well as the Soviet restrictions, have indeed helped preserve the region, but to them the most important items maintained were old fishermen's homes and lifestyles. Their ideal for preservation is closer to a living version of the open-air ethnographic museum (the open-air museum outside of Riga is probably Latvia's most popular museum). Instead of the resurrection of wetlands, this project draws from the mainstream vision of ethnic Latvian identity as tied to a lost, rural, static experience. The desire to reclaim this identity, to these believers, becomes stronger as Latvia joins multinational organizations and merges with more general Western or global patterns. Thus in the wetlands and villages of Pape an old struggle is currently under negotiation; concerns drawn from transnational issues (in this case the preservation of nature) versus the preservation of traditional culture and identity.

The Latvian Language

The Latvian language is one of the two surviving Baltic languages in the family of Indo-European languages. Lithuanian is the closest linguistic relative to Latvian, and both these languages have some root similarities to Sanskrit. These linguistic ties hint at the very distant nomadic migratory past of the Baltic peoples. For several thousand years, however, these Baltic peoples have resided along the eastern shores of the Baltic Sea. Over this long time period a process of differentiation set in, to be reversed by a more systematic process of standardization over the past several hundred years.

The Baltic languages were spoken languages with no written component until well after the arrival of Germans and Russians in the twelfth century. Initially German clergy and merchants were uninterested in recording the languages of the indigenous people and left their own account of conquest and Christianization in Latin and German. Indigenous languages were viewed as peasant tongues spoken by *undeutsch* (non-Germans) and aroused little interest, other than the occasional description of the local peasants that included a few terms in local languages. There was no attempt to record the language as is. The initial impetus for a recorded, written language came from Martin Luther's call for sacred texts and sermons in vernacular languages. Initially, this invigorated the development of the vernacular language of the elites, German. Some German pastors, however, took Luther's demand to its logical conclusion and began to write religious texts in the local peasant languages. These early hymns, catechisms, and sermons represented the first attempts to codify the indigenous peasant languages. The supreme accomplishment of the era was Ernst Glück's translations of the New and Old Testaments in 1687 and 1694 respectively.

Those who wrote the Latvian language were almost exclusively educated Germans up through the eighteenth century. Their unfamiliarity with the language often produced awkward and overly formal composition. Particularly

(continues)

The Latvian Language *(continued)*

difficult was the attempt to force a fluid peasant language, with considerable regional differentiation, into the grammatical rules of High German. The created language was comprehensible, and it improved rapidly, but still it was not the spoken language of indigenous peasants.

During the nineteenth century, the stilted and formal nature of written Latvian began to change. Herder's elevation of peasant peoples, or nations, brought new attention and a desire to record folk songs, legends, proverbs, and customs. More and more written Latvian texts addressed secular issues, although most were still written by Germans, including the first Latvian language newspaper. By the 1840s, however, more and more educated Latvians were writing in their mother tongue and expanding the language considerably.

The Latvian language was central to the national awakening of the mid-nineteenth century. Early nationalists fought to defend the intrinsic merits of what had been considered a peasant tongue by celebrating the folk heritage. These same nationalists attempted to prove the modern capacity of the language by creating for it all of the accoutrements of any "respected language," from novels, epic poems, and translations of the classics to scientific language. When the existing Latvian was found lacking, Latvian nationalists invented new words drawing on Latvian roots, prefixes, and concepts. They worried (and continue to worry to this day) about the many "foreign words" in use in spoken and written Latvian. Their task, however, was (and still is) a difficult, if not impossible, one. German and Russian power and influence were inevitably reflected in the language. A great many words are borrowed from German and Russian. There is within this choice of vocabulary a rich social history. Words of luxury, leisure, business, government, and science were initially exclusively German or Russian (and now are apt to be English). Only in the second half of the nineteenth century (and on) were "Latvian" versions suggested. Further complicating the matter was that there was no uniformity. Some families used German-sounding words while other used Russian ones. This choice often, although not always, betrayed an accompanying Germanophilia or Russophilia.

The following example will illustrate the situation. Traditionally there is no peasant Latvian word for suitcase. Common usage has adapted *koferis* from the German *Koffer* and *cemodans* from the Russian *cemodan*. Some Latvians will use *soma,* a traditional Latvian word that means bag, but its non-specificity has limited its general adoption as "suitcase." Most recently, English words have flooded into the Latvian language through the popular media, pop culture, and the social sciences.

The greater use of written Latvian, particularly with the spread of print media, introduced a standardization of the language, which was taken further by the demands of nationalists. A universally accepted grammar and a series of orthographic reforms defined the Latvian language in the first half of the twentieth century. The first two phases removed Germanic letters and influence. The more controversial third reform further simplified rules of spelling (the word for archive, for example, went from *archivs* to *arhivs*) during the early period of Soviet rule. Some nationalists consider this reform a step towards Sovietization and Russification and continue to resist its use.

The process of codification and standardization largely succeeded in creating one Latvian language. Regional dialects have for the most part disappeared, although idiosyncrasies in speech have remained, particularly in the northwest and along the Daugava River. The exception to this rule is the Latgalian dialect spoken in southeastern Latvia. This region, Latgale, experienced its own distinctive historical and economic development. Because it was more closely linked to Poland and Catholicism, for example, the impulse to express the sacred in the vernacular was muted. By the nineteenth century, the dialect was distinct. The national awakening in Latgale at the beginning of the twentieth century suggested unsurely that Latgalians were a distinct subset of Latvians, even potentially a separate nation. Since that time two conflicting processes have gone on, one of standardizing Latgalian to Latvian, the other of celebrating Latgalian identity. Latgalian is the most widely spoken and written dialect-language in Latvia.

From the late 1980s on, the official language of state has become a defining political issue in independent Latvia. The demand to give Russian official language status is widely shared by the roughly 40 percent of the population that is not ethnically Latvian (primarily Russian). Latvians more generally, and nationalists particularly, see the continuation of Latvian as the sole official language of state as vital to the long-term survival of a small nation's language in the face of Russian influences from the east and the globalizing impact of the English language. As it has been from its beginnings, language in Latvia is an intensely symbolic and political sphere.

The language itself is close to its peasant roots. The number of words is not overwhelming, but idiom usage and an almost infinite possibility of word play with recognized prefixes and suffixes gives the language considerable richness and flexibility. Reflecting its peasant heritage, the Latvian language is at its most articulate with nature. If the Inuit, for example, have a great many words for snow, Latvians have a great many for potato. Similarly the Latvian closeness to nature may have influenced the language's penchant for widespread diminutive usage.

The Baltic peoples' relations with neighbouring peoples are difficult to determine. The difference between trade and tribute was not always clear, but it is reasonable to assume that Vikings and the early Russian princes were superior in status to the local chiefs, and that as their power increased in the tenth and eleventh centuries they impinged on the region more frequently.

RUSSIAN AND GERMAN INFLUENCES

By the beginning of the twelfth century, Russian princes aligned with the grand prince in Kiev received periodic tribute from the Baltic "tribes" and exported Orthodox Christianity to them. Nearly simultaneously, in the middle of the twelfth century, Germanic priests and merchants arrived in the western half of Latvia and traveled through it by the river systems. In the 1160s a German priest, Meinhard, built a church in Ikšķile and attempted to convert the Livs. By the time of his death in 1196, Meinhard's efforts had yielded few converts, but they did bring recognition from Rome. Meinhard's replacement, Berthold, attempted to use force to win converts and lost his life in battle with the Livs in 1198. This sudden reversal led his successor, Albert, to more carefully plan and coordinate military action and conversion. He arrived with some five hundred knights in 1200 and established a more defensible German city, Riga, in 1201. The pattern for the conversion and conquest of the eastern Baltic was set. The Bishop of Riga used a knightly order, the Swordbrothers, threats, and promises to extend Christian (and thus German) control.

Throughout the century, the bishop and the Swordbrothers fought against the various chiefs of the Baltic peoples, forcing conversion upon defeat. Although the Swordbrothers were wiped out in a decisive defeat at Saule in 1236, they reformed as the Livonian Order in 1237 and continued the conquest. The Couronians and Semigallians resisted the longest, but by 1290 the German crusade was complete. As the Germans intruded from the west, the age-old pressure from the Russian princes to the east subsided with the Mongol Invasion of 1237–1242.

The arrival of German, and to a lesser extent Russian, religion, trade, and statecraft is a fundamental watershed in the history of Latvia. Conquest led to subjugation and a radically different kind of social organization, but also the introduction of many new technologies and innovations. The most important innovation was written language. The earliest direct, written accounts of people in the territory of Latvia begin with the arrival of literate German and Russian priests and lords. The almost complete lack of written sources for all of the preceding time forces us to rely on a very incomplete archeological record. Further distorting the understanding of early Baltic societies is the fact that the first records of Baltic "tribes" were written by their conquerors. These conquerors, particularly the Germans, saw themselves as bringing Christianity to heathens and saw little reason to document their earlier ways.

The Livonian Order, representing the German knights, merchants, and priests, ruled the region as a feudal state for the next several hundred years. Medieval Livonia was not a

The steeple of St. Jacob's Lutheran Church in the Old Town section of Riga. (Steve Raymer/Corbis)

unified modern state. The territory was a patchwork of feudal grants and jurisdictions. Some lands were church lands, usually under the control of the Archbishop of Riga. Other lands were the fiefs granted to the individual knights. Collectively these lands (including modern-day Estonia) were considered the territory of the Livonian Order, and were known as Livonia. Further complicating the structure of the decentralized state was the semiautonomous position of the cities. Wealthy German burghers dominated these cities, chief among them Riga. Several of the cities were members of the Hanseatic League (Riga from 1282) and became important regional mercantile centers. In the early fifteenth century, the four notable social orders (the clergy, the Livonian Order's masters, the vassals, and representatives of the cities) tried to solve the jurisdictional confusion by creating the Livonian Diet. The Diet, however, was unable to effectively mediate the many internecine struggles, and medieval Livonia remained a decentralized state into the sixteenth century.

The centuries of Livonian rule were also the formative era of social and protonational differentiation. The triumphant German knights of the Livonian Order settled into landed estates and ruled over the remnants of the Livs, Selians, Semigallians, Lettgallians, and Couronians. Although fully developed serfdom did not come into legal existence until the sixteenth century, the pattern of German lords and Baltic peasants slowly set in. The Baltic peasants owed rents, services, and labor to the German lords, who also controlled the administration of justice. These German lords maintained their general German identity, but also took on a Baltic veneer that with time became Baltic German identity. The loss of political authority for the chiefs of the various Baltic peoples tended to blur the distinctions between them and their former subjects. By the sixteenth century, peasants were increasingly referred to as non-Germans, or *Letten* (Latvians). Although the Letten shared a common ethnicity, this term referred to a social class of peasants more than to a modern nation. Some successful peasants tried to assimilate into the Baltic German milieu of the towns or into the Catholic clergy and thereby lose their status as Letten.

Two dominant movements of the sixteenth century, the Reformation and the rise of national monarchies, shredded the foundations of the Livonian State. In the German lands, Martin Luther challenged the status quo of the Roman Catholic Church in 1517, and in less than ten years his reformist views were embraced across Livonia. The Reformation in Livonia, as throughout Europe, was a complex mixture of genuine changes in religious belief and the use of the call for religious reform as a political and social tool for change. In Livonia, as throughout much of Northern Europe, the towns, particularly Riga, embraced the Reformation for political as well as religious change. Likewise, most Baltic German lords adopted Lutheranism for themselves and their serf peasants. The Counter-Reformation was particularly strong south of Livonia, in Lithuania, but for the most part by the middle of the sixteenth century Livonia had become Lutheran.

The success of the Reformation meant a change in the language of the church. Luther believed that the "Word of God" should be in the language of the people and spearheaded the translation of holy texts and the preaching of sermons in the vernacular. In Livonia this initially meant services in German, but religious figures quickly extended this idea to the peasant languages. As a result of this need, German pastors began to slowly forge a written language from the spoken language of the Latvian peasants. At the same time, the Lutheran Church was more receptive to peasants becoming pastors than the Roman Catholic Church had been. Although the development of a written Latvian language and its use by preachers and pastors took decades (even centuries), the slow codification of language, a building block of national identity, began in the decades following the Reformation.

THE SIXTEENTH TO THE EIGHTEENTH CENTURIES

The regional, national monarchies began to consolidate power and expand their territories during the sixteenth century. Aggressive and ambitious kings in Sweden and Poland looked at the decentralized Livonian State as a potential area for expansion. It was Tsar Ivan IV (Ivan the Terrible) of Muscovy, however, who began the actual wars that led to the end of Livonia. Ivan began the Livonian Wars in 1558 with the seizure of the cities of Narva and Dorpat (Narva and Tartu in modern Estonia). He then marched his armies into central Livonia toward Riga. The old medieval Livonian Order proved no match for the Muscovite armies, and the Baltic German lords and towns looked desperately for potential allies. (At the same time, many Latvian and Estonian peasants used the ensuing chaos and disorder to stage peasant rebellions.) The most likely allies against the advance of Ivan IV were the kings of Poland-Lithuania and Sweden. The Baltic Germans of northeastern Livonia allied themselves with Sweden, while the western and central part of Livonia (as well as Riga) appealed to Sigismund II Augustus of Poland-Lithuania. This realignment transformed Ivan's attack on Livonia into a major regional war. Increasingly, Sweden and Poland allied with each other and beat back the Muscovite incursion. These wars lasted several decades and devastated the countryside, leading to several outbreaks of plague and famine. By the first half of the 1580s, Muscovite Russia was pushed out of the territory, and Livonia ceased to exist. The former allies, Sweden and Poland-Lithuania, followed their respective peace treaties with Muscovy by attacking each other for the spoils. Warfare continued on and off until the Treaty of Altmark in 1629. This treaty set a new political geography for the region for the next century.

After the dust of nearly six decades of intermittent warfare settled, there were three separate political entities on the lands of modern Latvia. The Swedish king ruled the northeast (and modern Estonia) and Riga. The southeast became a part of Poland-Lithuania, and the center and west became the semi-independent Duchy of Courland. The first duke of this new duchy was the last master of the Livonian Order, Gotthard Kettler (1517–1587). Kettler's duchy was a vassal state to Poland-Lithuania, but the degree of its autonomy varied throughout its existence.

Kettler began his rule by rebuilding after the Livonian war. The cost of such reconstruction outstripped the resources of the duke's treasury, and he was forced to draw from his vassals or create new vassals. This set a precedent for the remainder of the duchy's existence; the duke may have ruled, but he could not rule without his landholding nobles, and they demanded a share of power. In 1570 the nobility received a guarantee of almost absolute power over their lands (and all peasants on them) in return for financial aid in reconstruction. Almost twenty years later, after Gotthard's death, the nobility used the struggle of succession between the duke's two sons to receive more concessions. Even during the reign of Gotthard's grandson, Jacob, the most successful of the Courland dukes, the power of the nobility was not challenged.

Jacob carefully built the wealth of his duchy on a vibrant merchant economy. He built a merchant navy, conducted long-distance trade, and briefly established two overseas colonies in Gambia and Tobago. His short-term success, however, led to negative long-term consequences. The Polish crown became more interested in a wealthy vassal and played a growing part in ducal intrigues. The Swedes, also attracted by wealth, raided the duchy with increasing frequency. The cost of the overseas ventures and of an increasingly lavish court life for the duke and much of the nobility weakened the fiscal strength of the autonomous duchy and likely led to greater impoverishmnet for the majority of the duchy's inhabitants, the peasants. After Jacob's death, the duchy lacked an equally vigorous ruler, and the power of the dukes declined, first submitting to the Polish court and later to the Romanov court of imperial Russia during the eighteenth century.

Swedish rule in what had been northeastern Livonia was markedly different from ducal rule, but also had some similarities. The territory became attached more closely to the Swedish crown (unlike the distant Polish role with its ducal vassal) and was part of Sweden's attempt to build an empire around the rim of the Baltic Sea in the seventeenth century. As a result, a Swedish governor ruled the territory for the Swedish king. The allegiance of the Baltic German nobles, however, was based on their continued control of their peasants. The Swedish crown wanted to centralize administration, but relied on a decentralized system revolving around local Baltic German control. This paradox was never completely solved. The Swedish crown alternately reaffirmed or undermined Baltic German aristocratic power. The greatest assaults against the local lords, moreover, were not motivated by sympathy for the Baltic peasants, but by displeasure with collected tax revenue. In 1681, for example, the Swedish government reviewed manorial rights and substantially lowered the number of recognized manors (assigning the remainder as crown land). This was a strike against the Baltic German lords, but often even those lords who lost their rights were allowed to retain their lands and privileges. Other corners of the territory were simply overlooked in the review. For Baltic peasants throughout the territory, on crown land or noble land, tax burdens increased, because Baltic German lords passed their tax increases on to their peasants; the ambitions of the Swedish crown were ultimately costly to the peasants.

Riga became a part of the Swedish Empire during the seventeenth century (surrendering to the Swedes in 1621), but also retained many of its autonomous rights and privileges. The city, the largest in the region, grew to several thousand inhabitants and became an important mercantile center. The wealthiest merchant families controlled the urban economy and politics. A standard, and mostly Baltic German, guild system established the foundations of the town. Riga's primary goods of trade were masts, sails, grains, timber, fur, and honey. Much of this trade was long distance, international trade that ended in the ports of the Netherlands and northern Germany and drew in raw materials from the Russian interior. The goods from the interior of Russia, particularly timber, were floated down the Daugava River in huge quantities. As with the Duchy of Courland and the Swedish territories, Riga fit a common pattern: a Baltic German elite controlled local affairs and managed a difficult, yet loyal, relationship with an outside power.

By the end of the seventeenth century, social divisions dating from the time of the Teutonic conquest remained. New sovereigns and foreign influences did not change local political patterns. The ruling elite, feudal lords, town burghers, and religious hierarchy were German; the peasants were not. If anything, the lot of the peasants became considerably worse throughout Polish, ducal, and Swedish territories, as legally sanctioned serfdom became absolute. In the continuing spirit of the Protestant Reformation, however, the Lutheran Church in the Baltic region continued to produce religious material in the language of the people. In the 1680s and 1690s, for example, a Baltic German pastor, Ernst Glück, finally produced the first Latvian translations of the New and Old Testaments. Glück planted oak trees to commemorate the accomplishment, and they still stand in the northeastern town of Alūksne. Other Baltic Germans, most notably Christoph Fürecker, began translating religious hymns into Latvian, but later reversed course by translating Latvian idioms and proverbs into German. This process began the long road to a uniform, printed peasant language. Similarly, the gradual and slow intensification of serfdom throughout the seventeenth century bound peasants together by a somewhat common social and economic experience. By the eighteenth century, the eastern Baltic littoral was home to a Baltic German landed elite ruling over peasants who could be called Latvians, all under more distant Swedish or Polish sovereigns.

The greatest exception to this rule was the southeastern territory of the old Livonian state that became a part of Poland-Lithuania outright after the Treaty of Altmark. This eastern region, known as Polish Inflanty, moved more closely into the Polish orbit in the seventeenth century. Daugavpils (also known as Dvina and Dunaburg) became the largest and most important urban area, but was still relatively small and overwhelmingly focused on river trade and traffic. The Counter-Reformation removed many Lutheran congregations and entrenched Catholicism throughout the region. Moreover, Polish lords replaced Baltic German ones, as the Polish-Lithuanian crown used this newly conquered territory to reward vassals with tracts of land in this newly acquired region. As a result, the region developed differently from the areas under Swedish or autonomous rule in terms of economic, political, cultural, and linguistic trends for several centuries. In Polish Inflanty, the local serfs served Polish rulers and remained outside of the early nationalizing influence of the spread of the printed word. These people, known as Latgalians, ultimately developed a different dialect of Latvian, with unique cultural components as well. Economic and political development was equally distinct from that in the west and northeast of modern Latvia. Latgalians remain unique: they are seen as either a subset of the Latvian nation with a distinct language and identity or, by some, as a unique nation.

The geopolitical impetus that hurried the demise of Livonia and the arrival of Polish and Swedish power was the western expansion of Muscovy. Ivan IV lost the Livonian wars and soon afterward died without an heir. This dynastic crisis led to the "Time of Troubles" (1584–1613) in Muscovite Russia. The Time of Troubles saw Swedish and Polish incursions into Muscovite territory and a constant spate of pretenders to the Russian throne. Ultimately, Muscovite society rallied around a new dynasty, the Romanovs, and repelled foreign influences. The chaos and devastation (made worse by the excesses of Ivan IV's reign) hampered renewed Muscovite expansion throughout the seventeenth century. A massive religious schism (religious refugees, the "Old Believers," became the first Russian communities in the territory of modern Latvia) further concentrated Muscovite politics on internal matters. By the end of the seventeenth century, however, a newly aggressive and confident Muscovy looked westward toward the Baltic Sea.

The young tsar, Peter I, embodied this new confidence and ambition. Peter the Great was first and foremost a great conqueror. His comprehensive reforms of Muscovite society were designed to address military weaknesses. His military conquests in the west came ultimately at the expense of the Polish and Swedish crowns.

Peter the Great's military campaigns in the Baltic region began in 1700. As the Polish king raided Swedish possessions, Peter attacked and captured Narva in present-day Estonia. Charles XII, the king of Sweden, defended his Baltic possessions (beating Peter at Narva), but ultimately was defeated at the Battle of Poltava in what is now Ukraine in 1709. Soon afterward, a Russian army captured Riga in 1710, and Swedish power in the eastern Baltic came to an end. The subsequent peace treaty, the Treaty of Nystadt, was not signed until 1721, but the collection of campaigns and battles referred to as the Great Northern War established Russian power on the shores of the Baltic. Peter transformed Muscovy into the Russian Empire and became its first emperor. Swedish territory, such as the province of Livland, became a Russian possession, and the military balance in the region shifted so fundamentally that the Duchy of Courland became increasingly tied to Russia (and its new capital St. Petersburg) rather than Poland. Years of constant warfare and the ensuing outbreaks of plague and famine, however, devastated Livland; its population plummeted by as much as 40 percent.

Eighteenth-century history in the lands of contemporary Latvia is the story of the gradual, yet relentless, rise of Russian hegemony, but with a veneer of Baltic German influence impinging into Russia. As early as the campaigns of the Great Northern War, a Baltic peasant girl under the wardship of Pastor Ernst Glück caught the eye of the Russian emperor. Ultimately she became his second wife and one of his short-lived successors (as Catherine I). Her own national identity is variously described as Lithuanian or Latvian, but under the guidance of Ernst Glück she was partially educated in a Baltic German milieu.

The Duchy of Courland was the institutional center of Baltic German influence and played an even more influential role in the palace politics of the Russian Empire following Peter the Great's death. During the Great Northern War, the last of the Kettler dynasty, Ferdinand, became duke. Ferdinand tied the duchy more closely to Russia by marrying Anna, the daughter of Tsar Ivan V, who briefly reigned as "co-tsar" with his younger half-brother Peter II, but Ferdinand personally seldom lived in or ruled over his

ducal realm. Many other Baltic German aristocrats of the duchy followed a pro-Russian policy and supported the candidacy of Ernst Johann Biron as duke after Ferdinand died childless in 1737. Biron's candidacy linked the duchy permanently to the Russian court; Anna had become tsarina in 1730, and Biron was her lover. The duchy remained a separate entity until the reign of Catherine the Great and the partitions of Poland, but practically was henceforth under Russian control.

Repeating the experience of the end of Livonia's existence, the Baltic German nobility in the eighteenth century somewhat effortlessly shifted their political allegiances, yet maintained and increased local control. The widespread depopulation caused by the wars and plagues led to labor shortages on the nobles' estates. Their response was to press for further legal rights over the remaining peasants. In practice this meant that the peasants were required to provide more labor to their lords. As the lifestyles of the nobility became more extravagant (particularly those who were involved in the palace intrigues of St. Petersburg), even more was squeezed from the peasants. The Baltic German nobility succeeded in limiting peasant mobility in order to maintain their labor supplies, and they preserved their monopoly over local justice. Some nobles even claimed that their rights over serfs amounted to full property rights. All of these changes made the legal definitions of serfdom more severe, and by the end of the century most peasants had become a social order of hereditary serfs.

Although the legal and material conditions of serfs throughout Livland and Courland deteriorated throughout the eighteenth century, there were at the same time religious and literary developments that countered this general trend. Pietism became the first Christian movement to make fundamental inroads into peasant communities.

Until the Lutheran Reformation, there were few attempts to make Christianity accessible to the Baltic peasants. Even after the arrival of Lutheranism and some translations of religious texts into Latvian, the close link between the Baltic German pastor and the Baltic German lord alienated peasants from Christianity. The ideas of the Moravian Brethren (also known as the Herrnhut Movement), however, were substantially different. These pietistic missionaries preached the equality of all Christians (despite social distinctions), trained Latvians for positions in the clergy, and encouraged literacy so that each Christian could have a personal relationship with the Scriptures. The movement spread quickly in Livland, before it was forbidden in 1742 as a potential threat to social order. Although the movement's tangible effects were few, the encouragement of literacy and a kind of egalitarianism continued to develop into the nineteenth century. The spread of literacy and the expanding demand for religious texts led to more and more publications in Latvian. The Baltic German clergy still wrote almost all of these books, and they forced the "peasant language" into German grammatical laws. Nevertheless, written Latvian slowly became standardized and codified. By the end of the eighteenth century, some books on nonreligious topics were also published, and other Baltic Germans began to write about Latvians in German.

Near the end of the eighteenth century, social, economic, cultural, and linguistic patterns strengthened across the political divide of Russian Livland and the nominally independent Duchy of Courland. In both of these territories, a Baltic German nobility ruled over Latvian serfs. Although these serfs had almost no rights, their similar conditions, combined with the spread of a standardized language, and a growing awareness of and literacy in that language, created a more general Latvian identity, that replaced the remnants of the more localized identities of a previous age. The gradual absorption of all Latvian lands into the Russian Empire as a result of the partitions of Poland accelerated this development. Nevertheless, "Latvianness" did not yet exist as a conscious national identity. Instead, Latvianness was synonomous with social position, or essentially peasantdom. To be a Latvian was to be a peasant and vice versa; those few Latvians that acquired the accoutrements of education, literacy, clergy status, and perhaps merchant wealth assimilated into the Baltic German world.

The first partition of Poland occurred in 1772 when Catherine the Great, the tsarina of Russia, exploited civil conflict in Poland to deftly create an international coalition of Prussia, Austria, and Russia against Polish interests. Poland lost nearly one-third of its territory to these three powers, including the loss of Polish Inflanty to Russia. The local Polish nobility maintained some of their local control (although not as successfully as the Baltic Germans historically had), but the territory increasingly became administered as a part of Russia. This sovereign change continued the pattern begun by the Treaty of Altmark, which placed the peasants living in this territory under different conditions and with different socioeconomic development from those in Livland and Courland. As a result, Lettgallian districts, the Lettgallian language, and Lettgallian peasants continued to develop a distinct identity, though one that was related to that of Latvians.

After the first partition, Poland-Lithuania was severely compromised, and over the course of the next twenty-five years Russia, Austria, and Prussia dismantled the remainders. The third and final partition, in 1795, also included the still nominally autonomous Duchy of Courland. By 1763, Biron's son, Peter, was duke. Peter's rule brought the duchy ever closer to Russia, and by the 1790s most of the duchy's nobility were eager to accept Russian rule if they could maintain their local control. When Poland-Lithuania ceased to exist in 1795, the duchy lost its theoretical liege lord. Catherine the Great eased Peter's loss of the duchy by purchasing his lands and providing him a substantial pension. The Courland nobility in turn swore allegiance to the Romanov dynasty, and Courland as an autonomous entity disappeared along with independent Poland-Lithuania.

UNDER RUSSIAN RULE

Russian rule over the eastern Baltic, although realized in military terms by Peter the Great's victories in the Great Northern War, became a reality through Catherine the Great's diplomacy. At the turn of the nineteenth century, all of present-day Latvia was a part of the Russian Empire. Livland and Courland, with their Swedish and autonomous pasts, became the core of the Baltic Provinces (which also included Estland, a part of modern Estonia). The Baltic German nobility remained in local control and easily accepted Russian imperial authority (often moving into imperial service in St. Petersburg as well). Lettgallia, with its distinct past and closer connection to Poland, became more closely attached to greater Russia itself.

Serfdom was the dominant social, political, and economic system of the Baltic Provinces as they became a part of tsarist Russia (not coincidentally serfdom was also the dominant social, political, and economic system of imperial Russia). By the end of the eighteenth century, however, serfdom was coming under increasing pressure from economic change, peasant unrest, and philosophical criticism. The philosophers of the European Enlightenment attacked the institution, even receiving some vague, theoretical support from Catherine the Great in her correspondence with many of these philosophers. The French Revolution in 1789 (and the execution of the French king Louis XVI in 1792, as well as the Pugachev Rebellion in Russia in the mid-1770s) tempered Catherine's desire for reform, but Enlightenment thinking influenced others, including the Baltic German Garlieb Merkel.

Merkel despised serfdom for humanitarian reasons, but at the same time he wrote about serfs as a potentially explosive social force. Merkel prophesied widespread Latvian peasant unrest if serfdom was not abolished.

The fulfilment of Merkel's prophecies seemed close at hand at the beginning of the reign of Tsar Alexander I, the grandson of Catherine the Great, when Latvian peasants rose in rebellion near the town of Valmiera (in an episode known as the Kauguri unrest). The army had to intervene to restore order, which was not accomplished until after an artillery barrage. The uprising convinced Alexander of the need to reform serfdom. The resulting Livland Peasant Law of 1804 did not question the validity of serfdom, but did redefine its nature. Labor services were defined on paper and payable with money. The law also created local courts that could review whether obligations exceeded legal norms. The law was a theoretical step toward the emancipation that ultimately came after the Napoleonic invasion of 1812 (the invasion crossed through the southern portion of Courland). Its consequences, however, also produced the opposite short-term results, as lords increased labor services when they were put into writing and the local courts were entirely dominated by representatives of the Baltic German lords. Nevertheless, the spirit of reform and the questioning of the foundations of serfdom had begun.

When Alexander I returned from Paris after the final defeat of Napoleon, he assented to a full emancipation of serfs in the Baltic Provinces (first in Estland in 1815, followed by Courland in 1817, and finally in Livland in 1819). Emancipation affected more than a half million serfs, but it left much to be desired among these newly freed peasants. The actual emancipation acts envisaged a slow transition to full liberty with no land for the peasantry. Throughout Livland and Courland, former serfs remained tied to the land with restrictions on their mobility well into the 1830s and 1840s.

Moreover, they continued to owe some labor dues to their former lords, and most entered into contracts that stipulated the giving of labor for rent. The Baltic German lords continued to control the administration of justice in the countryside. On the surface, therefore, little changed with emancipation. In Lettgallia even less changed, as emancipation did not come to Lettgallian peasants until the general Russian emancipation of 1861.

The limitations on emancipation further strengthened the hand of the Baltic German land-owning nobility. Freed from contractual responsibilities to serfs, many lords raised rent prices on their former serfs. With the restrictions on mobility, the ex-serfs were forced to accept the Baltic German demands. Still, the increasing importance of legal, written documents further stimulated the desire to acquire rudimentary literacy and led to the widespread formalization or introduction of surnames (often given by Baltic German lords, with occasional comical or malicious intent).

The shortcomings in the emancipation legislation led to more tension, not less. Small disturbances and peasant unrest became more commonplace. By the 1840s, Latvian peasants in Livland became convinced that conversion to the tsar's religion (Orthodoxy) would lead to a better life (usually with a gift of free land in the south of Russia from the pleased monarch). The ensuing mass conversions and migrations to Ukrainian lands and the east were difficult to manage for a conservative, status quo regime. On the one hand, the tsar considered himself the defender of Orthodoxy, but he also relied on the Baltic German nobility and did not want to provoke social unrest. Ultimately, the rumors were discouraged (as were converts), and a government committee looked into the underlying roots of social unrest, the land problem. Some initial steps were taken in the 1840s to allow for the purchase of land, but the sale of land to Latvian peasants did not become common practice until the 1860s.

New reforms also loosened the restrictions on peasant mobility. As a result, the second half of the nineteenth century witnessed great transformations in the Baltic countryside: land ownership, migration, and dramatic population growth. By the last quarter of the nineteenth century, from 30 to 40 percent of arable land was owned by Latvian smallholders. Still, most Latvians were landless, and increasing numbers relocated to Baltic towns and cities. This trickle became a flood when industrialization began to create opportunities for employment in the cities and population growth exacerbated land hunger in the countryside.

The backdrop to the change in the social fabric of the countryside was increasing tension between Baltic Germans, Latvians, and Russians. Throughout the nineteenth century, local conditions changed considerably, as Latvian peasants developed a sense of national consciousness. Simultaneously, St. Petersburg moved to stamp out regional differences in an effort to rationalize peculiarities and create a more uniform empire. Baltic Germans reacted to both of these challenges by mobilizing their energies to maintain local hegemony and imperial prerogatives.

The modernizing Russian Empire struggled with the unique nature of the Baltic Provinces. On the one hand, the provinces were economically more sophisticated than the bulk of Russia and seemed to offer an example for the rest of the empire. Baltic German nobles, often with superior skills and training, moved effortlessly into leading positions within the tsarist bureaucracy and military. On the other hand, the Baltic Provinces were quite different from the rest of the empire, and these differences flew in the face of the contemporary logic that demanded a standardized state. As the Romanov empire modernized, it grew less tolerant of regional differences. Modernization and standardization required greater Russian involvement, and this pattern intensified particularly in the second half of the nineteenth century (spurred on by the industrialization of the late nineteenth century). Moreover, the same regional differences grew more defined as a Latvian national movement struggled against Baltic German hegemony in local affairs.

LATVIAN NATIONAL AWAKENING

The Latvian national awakening began in the middle of the nineteenth century, with the Baltic German ruling elite as its initial target. Ironically, educated Baltic Germans laid the foundations of the national awakening. By the end of the eighteenth century, German thinkers had turned away from the Enlightenment and toward romantic nationalism. Johann Gottfried Herder, who taught in Riga for four years, exemplified this change. Herder believed that nations, or peoples, each a distinctive *Volk*, created history and that the nations of Eastern and Central Europe were worthy of study. He believed the best way to study these peasant nations was through their folk culture. Herder's writing included some discussion of Latvian folk songs with a few translations.

After Herder moved west, he became far more influential, and his influence in the more general German cultural world convinced Baltic German intellectuals to study their peasants. This academic pursuit led to the creation of societies (such as the Society of Friends of Latvians) for the study of Latvian folk customs, and the publication of the first Latvian language newspapers. For these Baltic Germans, this exercise was little more than an intellectual affair, but it did further standardize a written Latvian language and provided that language with many more secular titles. Theoretically, thinkers like Herder suggested that the Latvian nation was equal to any other in value and provided an opportunity for Latvian advancement. Practically, these thinkers helped found an institute for the training of primary school teachers. The majority of the institute's students were Latvian, and they formed the nucleus of the first generation of Latvian nationalists (their nationalism often learned through German texts).

By the 1850s, the gradual extension of schools led to more literacy among Latvians in town and country. A handful of Latvian students (such as Krišjānis Valdemārs, Krišjānis Barons, and Atis Kronvalds), buoyed by the nationalist ideas of Herder and his disciples, began to identify themselves as Latvians. They studied at the University of Dorpat, where they digested the latest developments in Europe and Russia. They followed the lead of European nationalist students,

Portrait of Johann Gottfried von Herder. (Bettmann/Corbis)

such as the Young Italians and the Young Germans, and called themselves the Young Latvians. From the mid-1850s to the mid-1880s, this first generation of Latvian nationalists advocated a cultural program that defended the merits of the Latvian language and people. Very often their efforts included the buttressing of the peasant Latvian language with the creation of new words, epic poems, and patriotic hymns. Their banner publication was the *Petersburg Newspaper (Pēteburgas avīze),* ultimately closed due to Baltic German pressure.

Andrejs Pumpurs, a Latvian officer in the tsarist army, exemplified these early efforts and the still nascent and ambiguous sense of this new identity. Pumpurs drew liberally from Latvian stories and wrote a national epic, *The Bearslayer.* He also, however, volunteered to fight for Serbia, motivated in part by pan-Slavic sentiments (a general movement that emphasized a common cultural bond among all Slavic peoples). Others of his generation, such as Atis Kronvalds, wrote often about "the Latvian question," but seldom in the Latvian language. Many of these students had begun the path toward assimilation into the Baltic German world and consciously arrested this development in adulthood. The results, at times, were Latvian nationalists more comfortable speaking and writing in German than in Latvian

and married to German women. Not surprisingly, their program was seldom revolutionary. The linguistic and cultural program of these early nationalists was thus not particularly threatening to the established Baltic German elite, which saw value in the recording of folk customs and lore. When the program began to press for an indigenization (that is, a Latvianization) of administration, however, the two ethnic groups became competitors.

The Young Latvians began to identify Baltic German hegemony in the Baltic Provinces as the obstacle to further Latvian advancement. These early Latvian nationalists encouraged Latvian economic development and appealed to the imperial Russian government to limit Baltic German control over the countryside. Baltic Germans were generally slow to respond to the challenge and largely continued to cling to an idea, rapidly becoming archaic, of social order and not ethnic determination, or in other words they believed the sucessful and the educated by definition of their accomplishment became a part of the Baltic German world. The Young Latvians' appeal, however, coincided with the Russian government's desire to modernize the state after the disastrous Crimean War (1853–1856). The imperial court identified diversity and regional uniqueness as a hindrance to the rational standardization of the empire around "Autocracy, Orthodoxy, and Nationality" (Russian), the official credo of the monarchy in the nineteenth century. A vibrant slavophilism around the court also questioned the desirability of Baltic Germans in high places, particularly with the rapid growth of Prussian might. In the Baltic Provinces, St. Petersburg first targeted the dominant position of the German language by decreeing the use of Russian in administrative and educational institutions. The Young Latvians supported this Russification as a strike against Baltic Germans.

Soon, however, the ultimate results of Russification disappointed all parties. The Baltic German nobility had seen themselves as stalwart defenders of the Russian empire since the time of Peter the Great. Suddenly their position was under attack from the tsar's administration itself. The nobility steadfastly clung to a series of "capitulations" that Peter the Great had granted the Baltic German nobility during the Great Northern War. Baltic Germans believed that their local control was sacrosanct, and they mobilized their resources to defend their privileges. Although their influence steadily eroded, they were able to maintain regional hegemony until World War I. Throughout this time period, however, they were increasingly hostile to Latvian demands and almost equally suspicious of Russia's plans.

Latvians, although they initially supported Russification, began to see the increase of Russian authority not as a tool to limit Baltic German power, but as a new threat to Latvian identity.

The Russian state was similarly disappointed. The hopes for standardization and rationalization of the empire were frustrated by successful Baltic German lobbying at the court and intransigence in the Baltic Provinces. When, for example, schools were to be run in Russian, the Baltic Germans withdrew funding for local education, thereby seriously undermining the success of the reforms. Russification, and the reactions to it, helped create polarized, activist societies organized increasingly on national principles.

Throughout the second half of the nineteenth century, the countryside slowly became more complex and differentiated. The Baltic German nobility still dominated, but with the midcentury reforms that allowed Latvians to buy land, some became prosperous smallholders. Most Latvian peasants, however, remained agricultural laborers and sharecroppers. Increasingly, Latvians left the land and moved to the towns and cities of the Baltic Provinces or to the southern regions of imperial Russia. Traditionally towns had been Baltic German oases in a Latvian peasant sea, capable of assimilating limited numbers of aspiring Latvians into a German cultural milieu. Most Baltic Germans believed that station defined Germanness; an educated Latvian peasant or wealthy Latvian merchant *became* German. Industrialization and urbanization, which took on revolutionary demographic proportions in the last quarter of the nineteenth century, overwhelmed the old established order and reinforced the ideas of national identity of the Young Latvians. Literate Latvian workers and smallholders provided a market for the literary and journalistic production of the Young Latvians, and their reading public similarly gave them a popular base of support. The Young Latvians' moderate program, however, could not satisfy all of the demands of the late nineteenth century.

A potential counterweight to national identity began to develop and emerge in the last decade of the nineteenth century. Socialism and the workers' movement emerged from industrialization and urbanization throughout Europe. As Russia industrialized rapidly after 1880, Riga became an important industrial center. Large factories sprang up all over Riga, as well as in other towns across the Baltic Provinces. Rural landless Latvians flocked to these factories for jobs, as did Russians, Poles, Jews, Ukrainians, Lithuanians, and Belarusians. Multiethnic factories and towns developed amid the ethnic tensions of Russification and the material poverty of early and rapid industrialization. A workers' movement was inevitable, and in a repressive, authoritarian state like Russia it was destined to develop along illegal and conspiratorial lines.

The workers' movement developed along Marxist lines, supposedly due to the semimythic voyage of a young intellectual, Jānis Pliekšāns, to Germany. Pliekšāns is supposed to have returned to the Baltic Provinces with a suitcase full of contraband Marxist literature and introduced other likeminded young intellectuals to Marxist thought. These intellectuals shared an animosity toward the previous generation, the Young Latvians. They believed that the previous generation's moderate program did little to better the condition of the majority of Latvians. They saw efforts within the system as ultimately futile and began to suspect the Young Latvians were most interested in defending the interests of the few propertied and educated Latvians. Furthermore, they saw their stress on rural solutions as inadequate to the changing, increasingly industrial character of the cities and towns of the Baltic Provinces. In Marxism, these idealistic young intellectuals saw a rejection of the previous generation, the appeal of revolutionary change, and the supposed inevitability of "scientific laws of history."

This early Marx-inspired movement became known as the New Current (*Jaunā Strāva*) and worked closely with the newspaper *The Daily Page (Dienas lapa)*. Pliekšāns edited the daily and ultimately adopted the pseudonym Rainis, by which he is best remembered. The newspaper introduced Marxist ideas to its readers through reviews of recent literature and theater performances. In these quasi-literary activities, several of the New Current's activists, including Rainis and his equally significant and active wife Elza Rozenberga, known by her pseudonym Aspāzija, proved to be more accomplished literary masters than subversive politicians. Nevertheless, after a series of strikes broke out in Riga in 1897, *The Daily Page* was closed and many of the leading members of the New Current, including Rainis, were deported to Siberia. Ultimately, Rainis and Aspāzija went into exile in Switzerland, but the Marxist movement had sunk deep and permanent roots.

The radical movement soon moved from literary criticism to involvement with actual workers, as evidenced by the strikes of 1897, which led to the establishment of an underground illegal Marxist workers' party, the Latvian Social Democratic Workers Party, in 1904. Although the party was aware of the similar Russian Social Democratic Party, it initially kept its independent status. Nevertheless, the world of conspiratorial politics brought many of Latvia's socialists into contact with the ranks of empire-wide radical parties.

The turn of the twentieth century was a time of enormous change in Riga and in the Baltic Provinces generally. Urbanization and industrialization spilled over from Riga to include Liepāja (Libau), Jelgava (Mitau), Ventspils (Vendau), and Daugavpils (Dvinsk). Even small towns like Sloka and Limbaži grew considerably, thanks to industrial enterprises. Industrialization also brought modernization; Riga led the empire in introducing technological innovations such as electric lights, telegraphs, telephones, and streetcars. Socioeconomic diversification became more pronounced, with great variations between skilled and unskilled workers, rich and poor merchants, and prosperous farmers and destitute peasants. The various political programs of Latvian nationalists, Latvian socialists (as well as Russian, Jewish, and Polish socialists), Baltic Geman elites, and Russian administrators vied with each other in a limited political system. Elections were neither universal nor democratic, and political and economic power remained in the hands of imperial administrators and Baltic German elites.

Ultimately the competing, yet potentially complementary, forces of national and class identity erupted in the Revolution of 1905. The Russian Empire fared disastrously in the Russo-Japanese War of 1904, and a resulting peace procession in January 1905 in St. Petersburg turned into a massacre when tsarist troops opened fire on the demonstrators ("Bloody Sunday"). Within days a similar demonstration in Riga also met the gunfire of tsarist troops, leaving dozens dead. Throughout the empire, people responded with near unanimity against this perceived injustice. In the Baltic Provinces the initial target of anger was the Baltic German elite. Workers (Latvian and Russian) went on strike in the cities, while the predominantly Latvian countryside rose in agricultural strikes and later rebellion. Dozens of manor houses were burned, and peasants organized their own autonomous governments. Strike committees wielded considerable power throughout the towns.

At the end of 1905, however, the tsar regained the upper hand throughout his realm with the October Manifesto, which successfully divided popular opinion. The October Manifesto allowed for a pseudo-parliamentary body (a duma) and seemed to guarantee some civil rights. With its promulgation, liberals and the bourgeoisie were ready to resume working for reform within the new system. Radicals, however, saw the manifesto as a sign of weakness and pushed for a more radical revolution. But with the nation now divided over how to react to the October Manifesto, the tsar soon regained control over the situation. Imperial troops restored order and repressed Latvians and Russians alike. Troop detachments aided by Baltic German aristocrats undertook punitive expeditions in the countryside, summarily executing or punishing suspected radicals.

After the incomplete revolution, local and imperial politics included more popular (although not democratic) participation. The October Manifesto created the Duma, a consultative body elected by *curias*, proportionate electoral bodies that ensured that the workers and peasants did not receive seats in proportion to their numbers. In 1906 the first elected Duma pushed the limits of the new system and tried to transform itself into a legislative body. Nicholas II responded by dismissing the Duma and calling for new elections. The rebellious majority, including the elected Latvian deputies (among them Jānis Čakste, a lawyer from Jelgava) retired to Vyborg in Finland and called for renewed revolution (the Vyborg Declaration). The tide, however, had turned, and the tsar, buoyed by a loyal army and aristocracy, carried the day. Nicholas II further dismissed the second Duma, and after his prime minister, Peter Stolypin, altered the electoral qualifications, the Duma became a largely subservient, consultative body. For the Baltic Provinces the new electoral laws meant fewer Latvian deputies in the Duma, and those that were elected were considered pragmatic conservatives.

Municipal politics in the Baltic Provinces revolved around similar curias and ethnic electoral lists. In the larger cities, including Riga, the Baltic German elite was able to play Latvian and Russian voters against each other and maintain power. In a few smaller towns, however, elected Latvian majorities took over local councils. Few, however, thought the political transformation complete. Radicals saw a betrayed revolution and planned for the next; in the Latvian case this included the Latvian Social Democratic Workers' Party becoming a member of the Russian Social Democratic Party and at times supporting the radical Bolshevik faction led by Lenin. Most felt, however, that though the new system was far from perfect, it could perhaps be reformed from within. Across all quarters, however, the Revolution of 1905 and its aftermath divided groups by class and ethnicity.

The ethnic makeup of the Baltic Provinces at the end of the imperial era is difficult to deduce. The first (and only) Imperial Census of 1897 did not ask for national identity, but for "mother's tongue," and was incomplete for the areas that later became Latgale. Drawing from this material and other city and regional censuses, Latvians made up more than 68 percent of the total population of modern Latvia. Russians accounted for nearly 8 percent (12 percent with Belarusians), and Baltic Germans were an additional 6 percent of the population. A sizable Jewish population numbered more than 7 percent of the total population. Cities and towns, particularly Riga, were much more multiethnic. Riga was home to Russian administrators and soldiers, Russian, Latvian, and Jewish merchants and workers, and Baltic Germans. By 1913, the city had more than 500,000 inhabitants, 42 percent of whom were Latvian, 19 percent Russian, 13 percent Baltic German, and 6 percent Jewish. Most other urban centers in the Baltic Provinces were similarly multiethnic. Throughout most of Courland and southern Livland, the countryside was overwhelmingly Latvian. Further east, however, in the region of Latgale, sizable Russian, Jewish, Polish, and Belorussian communities created an ethnic mosaic. If 58 percent of the region was ethnically Latvian, there were eleven parishes where the Latvian percentage fell well below 50 percent.

WORLD WAR I

No European power was prepared for the scope of destruction in World War I, but least of all Russia. World War I was disastrous for the Romanov empire. Whether the war caused or contributed to the Revolutions of 1917, Russia, like the other multiethnic autocracies of Europe, did not survive the war. Many of the "captive nations" attempted to break free from Russian rule (particularly after the inception of Bolshevik rule), and Latvia, along with Finland, Estonia, Lithuania, and Poland, succeeded. World War I enabled independence, but it also exacted a terrible price in physical destruction and massive demographic change.

The war began in August 1914 with Russia aligned with France and the United Kingdom against the Central Powers of Germany and Austria-Hungary. The Allied Powers' war plan imagined a rapid Russian mobilization and invasion from the east to squeeze the Central Powers into quick defeat. The Central Powers, on the other hand, through the German High Command's Schlieffen Plan, looked toward a quick rout of France through a great circling motion through Belgium before Russian armies could make much headway into Germany's eastern regions. As with so much else in World War I, neither plan worked as expected. The hoped-for quick rout of France stalled in the trenches of the Western Front that became so emblematic of much of the war in the west. In the east Russia mobilized more quickly and successfully than anticipated and moved into the territory of modern Poland. The Latvian deputies in the Duma (like almost all of the deputies) greeted the war with official speeches of loyalty and determination. However, in the late summer of 1914 early defeats turned to routs at the Battles of the Masurian Lakes and Tannenberg (more Latvians died at these two battles than at any others during the war). The German army pressed into the Baltic Provinces on the heels of a fleeing Russian army in disarray and confused civilians. The impending occupation unleashed a flood of at least

700,000 refugees eastward. The Russians evacuated the industrial equipment (and workers) from Riga and several other urban centers in the Baltic Provinces and encouraged the migration of local populations (often with implicit or direct force). By the fall of 1915, the front stabilized halfway through the Baltic Provinces along the Daugava River (Dvina), with a severely depopulated Riga perilously close to the front.

Over the next three years, the common experience of Latvians was deprivation. Some remained in the province of Courland, now occupied by the German Army and administered as *Ostland* (Eastland). Here Baltic Germans began to rethink their generations-old allegiance to the tsarist crown, particularly in light of Latvian violence during the Revolution of 1905 and frequent Russian assaults on Baltic German privileges. Some of these Baltic German elites saw their continued local dominance as most likely within a victorious German empire, and they began to organize for such an outcome. The Latvian peasants in the region, however, were subjected to military justice, requisitions of labor and supplies, and even the arrival of some German settlers.

East of the Daugava River, the situation was very unsettled with an active military front, troop concentrations, local populations, and war refugees. More unsettling was the experience of the displaced, probably the majority of Latvians. Some took refuge in Livland, while others moved further into the interior of Russia. Tsarist authorities did not want to add to the supply problems of St. Petersburg and Moscow and encouraged war refugees to the Caucasus and to the far east. War refugees were spread across the entire empire, with inadequate provisions made for their most basic needs. Other displaced Latvians included those conscripted into the army and those workers evacuated with their factories.

Increasingly the Russians could not deal with the refugee crisis and military failures and begrudgingly allowed society to organize as well. Latvian Refugee Associations began to care for Latvian refugees across the empire, and the Latvian Duma deputies and army oficers successfully lobbied for the creation of ethnic Latvian regiments, more popularly known as the Latvian Rifles, that came to be used in military action on Latvian territory. The regiments distinguished themselves in the Christmas Offensive of 1916 outside of Riga, but the rest of the army was unable to press the momentary advantage, and initial confidence turned to despair. Ultimately, across the entire empire this despair led to the February Revolution of 1917, touched off by bread riots in St. Petersburg.

Revolution deepened across the empire, and "dual power" emerged. Dual power was essentially a situation in which after the tsar's abdication two conflicting institutions claimed power, the provisional government and the Soviet of Workers, Peasants, and Soldiers. There was some cooperation between the two, but after Lenin's return to Russia in April, the Bolshevik Party, a small minority within the Russian socialist movement, agitated for the Soviet to claim complete power. Initially these demands were unpopular, but since neither the provisional government nor the Soviet could effectively meet the many problems of Russia, more

people turned to the Bolshevik vision. By May 1917, the Latvian Rifles sided with the Bolsheviks and provided them with needed military muscle for the next several years. In Latvia, and particularly in Riga, dual power was short-lived, and the Soviet wielded most of the real power.

In August 1917 a new German offensive captured Riga and initiated the long process that culminated in the Bolshevik seizure of power in October 1917 (by the old calendar; November 1917 by the Julian Calendar). After the Bolshevik Revolution, the German army occupied the remainder of the Baltic Provinces in the spring of 1918 to force a conclusion to the peace negotiations between the Bolsheviks and the Central Powers at Brest-Litovsk. The Bolsheviks acquiesced, and the German military and many Baltic Germans began preparations for annexation of the region.

Through the first three quarters of 1918, Germany seemed likely to acquire the Baltic Provinces, and many refugees began to slowly return. The collapse of the German army on the Western Front, however, mooted the Brest-Litovsk Treaty. The victorious Allies were determined not to allow German gains in the east after defeat in the west. They were, however, equally worried about the spread of the Communist Revolution from the east into the political vacuum of Central and Eastern Europe. This concern set the stage for alternative visions of a postwar Baltic and led to a resumption of fighting for two more years.

INTERWAR LATVIA

There were two visions of postwar society that battled in the war's immediate aftermath (along with a desperate, rearguard attempt by Germany and Baltic Germans to maintain dominance over the region). Latvian Bolsheviks, such as Pēteris Stučka, the brother-in-law of Jānis Rainis, building on socialism's popularity from the time of the Revolution of 1905 and the support of the Latvian Rifles, attempted to tie the region to nascent Soviet Russia. In December 1918, on the heals of the defeat of Germany, Soviet armies moved into the region hoping to extend the revolution and began to create a Latvian Soviet Republic. Initial military success took these Soviet armies through almost the entire region by the end of January 1919, leaving only a few opponents along a sliver of land around Liepāja in resistance. The Latvian Bolsheviks, however, quickly lost popular support due to their heavy-handed method of ruling Riga and their ideological stand against private property. Their persecution of class enemies encouraged ardent supporters, but lost most general support. Similarly, a perception existed that their first concern was the survival of the Soviet state with its capital now in Moscow, rather than with a Latvian Soviet state.

Just prior to the Latvian Bolsheviks' attempt to create a Soviet state, a group of nationalists and non-Bolshevik socialists gathered in Riga to declare a national independent Latvia. Their political opinions varied considerably, and they compromised with Baltic Germans and the still present representatives of the German occupation in order to unite against a perceived common enemy—Bolshevik rule. On

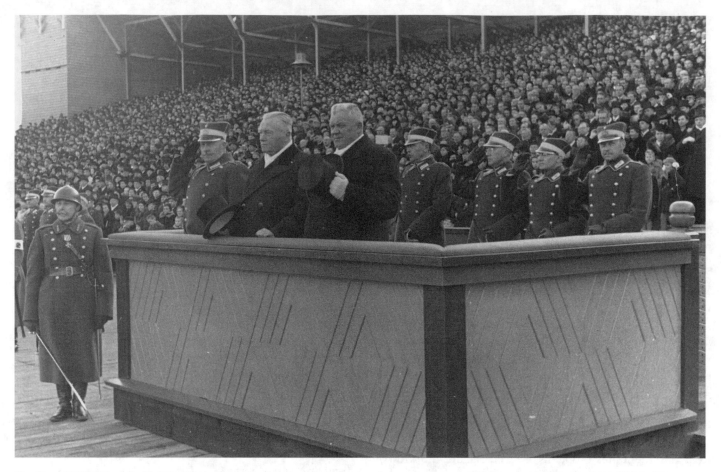

President Kārlis Ulmanis, his War Minister, and leading generals reviewing the troops during an Independence Day parade in 1935. (Getty Images)

17 November 1918, a group calling itself the National Council, consisting of representatives of political parties and other organizations, met and on 18 November declared the independence of Latvia.

Jānis Čakste was chosen as the provisional head of the council, and Kārlis Ulmanis, an agronomist who had studied at the University of Nebraska, became the first head of government as minister president (a position similar in function to that of a prime minister). Ulmanis led the largest agrarian party, the Farmers Union (*zemnieku savienība*), and faced almost immediate insurmountable obstacles. The national government had no army and could not effectively resist the Bolshevik Latvians' occupation of Riga in January 1919. Ulmanis and his cabinet of ministers fled westward toward Liepāja with a tiny, newly created army of a few volunteer officers and idealistic student soldiers led by the former tsarist officer Colonel Oskars Kalpaks. The national government contained seemingly irreconcilable interests. The socialists still hoped for a socialistic state (although not a Bolshevik one) and saw the Baltic German elite as class enemies. Hard-line Latvian nationalists also saw the Baltic Germans as the age-old enemies of the Latvians. The Baltic Germans and German volunteer army *(Freikorps),* on the other hand, hoped to maintain Germanic hegemony over the Baltic region.

At first the Germans, led by General Rüdiger von der Goltz, controlled more of the weapons and troops; they grew tired of Latvian national and socialist demands and staged a coup against the Ulmanis government in April 1919, installing a conservatve Latvian pastor, Andrievs Niedra, as the new minister president. The Latvian army was in disarray, due to the recent death of their founder in action, and Ulmanis took refuge on a British ship in Liepāja harbor. The new commander of Latvian forces, General Jānis Balodis, attempted to maintain allegiance to Ulmanis while cooperating with the Germans militarily against the Bolsheviks.

The national government seemed a spent force. As the Latvian Bolsheviks stumbled, however, and the Allied Powers reacted negatively to German machinations in the east, the Latvian nationalists gained in strength. The Ulmanis cabinet promised radical agrarian reform that would take land away from the Baltic German nobility and give it as property to Latvian peasants. More importantly, those who volunteered for the Latvian Army would be entitled to the land. Ulmanis also promised that a democratically elected Constituent Assembly would decide the ultimate law of the new state. Through 1919 this program drew popular support, and the combined German-Latvian army pushed the Bolsheviks out of Riga in May. In June a combined force of Estonian and Latvian troops turned on their difficult Ger-

Kārlis Ulmanis

Kārlis Ulmanis, independent Latvia's first minister president and authoritarian ruler from 1934 to 1940, dominated much of interwar political history. His legacy and memory remain intensely controversial and contested. Ulmanis, the son of a peasant landowner, studied agronomy and participated, in a tentative way, in the Revolution of 1905. Although by no means a significant leader or radical in 1905, he did fear tsarist retribution and emigrated to the United States through Germany. In the United States, Ulmanis studied agriculture at the University of Nebraska. By the start of World War I, Ulmanis returned to Latvia and began organizational work in Latvia's second largest political party, the Latvian Farmers' Union (Latviešu zemnieku savienība). Through 1918, Ulmanis was instrumental (although not central) to building a coalition of Latvian political parties to support the establishment of an independent Latvian state. The Latvian National Council that convened on 17 November 1918 and declared independence the following day voted to make Ulmanis the state's first minister president.

With independence established, Ulmanis became a fixture in Latvia's parliaments and cabinets. He came to embody the conservative establishment of the Latvian Farmers' Union, and he was often accused of corruption and quasi-dictatorial aspirations. On 15 May 1934, Ulmanis as minister president seized full political power by dismissing the Saeima, banning political parties, and ruling through an emergency cabinet. Important figures in the new regime such as General Jānis Balodis and Marģers Skujenieks were gradually marginalized, and Ulmanis emerged as the unquestioned leader. In 1936 Ulmanis assumed the state president title by his own decree; this act still polarizes Latvians, with supporters claiming Ulmanis as Latvia's fourth state president and detractors refuting the claim as illegal. Ulmanis' regime became steadily more centralized, adhering more and more to the *führerprinzip* (i.e., the principle of blind devotion to the leader, as seen in Nazi Germany) with Ulmanis as *vadonis* (leader). Surrounded by sycophants, he succumbed to the trappings of power. The regime adopted the fascist aesthetic current in much of Europe, but Latvia's limitations often prevented its full implications from being carried out.

In 1939 Ulmanis acceded to Moscow's ultimatum and allowed Soviet bases on Latvian territory. In June 1940 he decided not to resist full Soviet occupation and dismissed his cabinet. He remained state president until 21 July 1940, when he was deported to the Soviet interior. As with so much about Ulmanis, the wisdom of these decisions is still hotly contested. Some believe that he should have fought or at least offered token resistance to the loss of Latvian independence. Others see these moves as calculated to preserve as much human life and material wealth as possible in a time of crisis. His continuation as state president one month into occupation is seen by some as an attempt to mitigate Soviet rule, by others as a selfish attempt to cling to some position. Following Ulmanis' deportation, his ultimate fate was largely a mystery until the early 1990s. With access to considerable KGB files, the historian Indulis Ronis ascertained that Ulmanis was kept under house arrest until the Nazi invasion of the USSR approached the Caucasus. He was then transferred to prison; his health deteriorated, particularly during a transport across the Caspian Sea, and he died from kidney failure in 1942.

Ulmanis remains a controversial figure. His supporters see him as Latvia's greatest political figure of the interwar era and responsible for its relative prosperity. They also see him as a potent symbol of martyrdom to Soviet occupation. His detractors, however, see Ulmanis as an egotistical dictator with fascist pretensions whose rule weakened Latvia's ability to withstand Soviet occupation. The controversy is deeply embedded in the emotions of the debaters and not likely to pass.

man allies at the Battle of Cēsis, and Ulmanis returned to Riga triumphantly as the head of the government. A Russian adventurer, Pavel Bermondt-Avalov, rallied a German army for an assault on Riga in November, but a Latvian counterattack, supported by British naval fire, finally defeated the Germans. By January, aided by Polish troops, the Latvian army drove the Bolshevik Red Army out of Latgale and began to negotiate a ceasefire that led to armistice in August of 1920. Improbably, from the point of view of 1917 or 1918, the nationalists won their state.

Even before the conclusion of hostilities, the new state managed to hold elections to the Constituent Assembly. Jānis Čakste presided over the assembly and became Latvia's first state president (he served into his second term, until his death in 1927). The brilliant minister of foreign affairs, Zigfrīds Anna Meierovics, became the minister president, as a consensus builder replacing the more partisan Ulmanis. Meierovics served in the cabinet until his untimely death in an automobile accident in 1925. The Constituent Assembly and the *Saeima* (parliament) that soon followed reflected the massive demographic changes that Latvia had suffered during six years of war and revolution. The industrial evacuation of Riga more than halved its population, from 517,522 in 1914 to 181,443 in 1920. Latvia's population had fallen from 2,552,000 in 1914 to 1,596,131 in 1920. With the return of refugees, the population increased to 1,844,805 by 1925 and 1,905,900 by 1935, but Latvia was a far more rural and more ethnically Latvian state between the wars than before or after. The ethnic Latvian population increased from 68.4 percent to 74.9 percent over the years of war. Similarly, the urban population fell from 40.3 percent of the total to 23.8 percent. The results of this massive demographic and ethnic change colored the politics of the interwar period.

Latvian nationalists succeeded in founding a state, but its formation diverged from their nation-state ideal. Latvia's ethnic minorities (more than a quarter of the population), primarily Russians (11 percent), Jews (5 percent), and Baltic Germans (4 percent) fought for their rights. Coalition governments at all levels were forged from many parties, and Latvia's minority politicians enshrined and defended minority rights in return for general political support. Minority schools, media, and cultural institutions flourished. Some Latvian nationalists, however, saw this as a dream betrayed. They hoped for a state for the ethnic Latvian nation. Geography and democratic rights and procedures, however, built a nation-state with strong, vibrant minority communities. Latvian nationalists increasingly believed that the power of the state must be used to create a more Latvian Latvia (extremists called for a "Latvia for Latvians").

The most pressing need facing the new state was reconstruction. Almost half of Latvia's parishes witnessed actual battle during the many years of war. One-tenth of all of Latvia's buildings were destroyed during the war. The heavy casualty toll on men widened the sexual imbalance from 37,515 more women than men in 1897 to 152,277 more in 1920. The hallmark of the early Latvian state was radical agrarian reform. Most of the land of the Baltic German aristocracy was expropriated and distributed to the landless. This reform involved substantial economic change (from wheat production on large estates to small scale pork and dairy farming) and created new socioeconomic divisions, between farmers who owned farms before the reforms and those who received land as a result of the reforms; but ultimately the reform brought social peace to the countryside and gave the bulk of the population an investment in the new state.

In the 1920s Latvia witnessed a renaissance. The fine arts and literature blossomed, scholarship mushroomed (the University of Latvia was founded in 1919), the economy began to recover, and the state started to create a viable social safety network of health, education, and welfare legislation. Gustavs Zemgals, a lawyer and long-time liberal, became the second state president after the death of Jānis Čakste, and parliamentary elections, as well as local government elections, occurred on a regular basis.

The Great Depression, however, curtailed many of these advances and strengthened the appeal of the extremist Right and Left. Latvia's native fascist party, the Thunder Cross (Perkoņkrusts) called for a fascist solution, while the underground Communist Party suggested a Bolshevik answer for the country's economic ills. Under these political strains and the continuing pressure of the Depression, Latvia's delicate political system started to unravel, laying bare the weaknesses in the constitution. By 1934, many believed the existing parliamentary democracy could not solve the problems of the day.

On 15 May 1934, Kārlis Ulmanis and General Jānis Balodis led a coup that resulted in the installation of an authoritarian regime. The Ulmanis regime outlawed all political parties, (arresting most Social Democrat activists), but relied on the support of the Farmers' Union, the bureaucracy, and the right-wing paramilitary organization the Home Guard (aizsargi). The coup was bloodless, in part due to general apathy, rather than to mass enthusiasm. Authoritarianism influenced by fascism seemed to be the political solution of much of Europe.

The coup tried to create the ethnic domination that democracy could not by adopting the idea of a Latvian Latvia as state policy. The treasury maneuvered to replace Baltic German businesses with state-run cartels. Business licenses were routinely denied to Jews, and the once progressive minority education system was gradually weakened. The press became an indirect arm of the state. The regime, however, was also the only Eastern European government to ban anti-Semitic literature, and Ulmanis tried to maintain good relations with conservative leaders of minority communities. Nevertheless, the trend, clearly stated in the regime's propaganda, was for the state to create a "renewed, united Latvia" (atjaunotā, vienotā Latvija) devoted to its infallible leader (vadonis), Kārlis Ulmanis. Although direct opposition was muted, the regime to a great extent isolated the country and had little ability to meet the impossible demands of a changed geopolitical Europe in 1939.

WORLD WAR II

On 23 August 1939, the Soviet-German Non-Aggression Pact (the Molotov-Ribbentrop Pact), whose secret protocols envisioned the division of Eastern Europe between Hitler and Stalin, was signed. This pact threw Latvia, Finland, Estonia, Lithuania, Poland, and Romania into a state of crisis. On 5 October 1939 the Soviet Union forced Latvia to sign a Mutual Assistance Pact. In late 1939 and early 1940 Adolf Hitler called for the "repatriation" of Baltic Germans to the Third Reich. This repatriation was a harbinger of Latvia's inability to protect its own citizens in the face of a suddenly ominous international environment. In June 1940 the Soviet Union presented Latvia (and Estonia and Lithuania) an ultimatum to accept occupation. Fearing the destructive consequences that would result from refusal, all three states complied. By the beginning of August, all three were "accepted" into the USSR.

Andrei Vishinsky, the notorious prosecutor of the Moscow Show Trials of the late 1930s, arrived at the Soviet embassy in Latvia, and directed the political transformation of Latvia from an independent state to an occupied component of the USSR. A handpicked cabinet took control,

The Holocaust in Latvia

The murder of almost the entire Jewish community of Latvia was one of the gravest tragedies of World War II. The nature of local participation in the Holocaust and the Latvian community's response to it continues to be controversial. In 1935 Jews made up nearly 5 percent of the population of independent Latvia, roughly ninety thousand people. Jewish communities were well established in all of Latvia's larger cities (particularly Riga, Daugavpils, Liepāja, Jelgava, and Rēzekne) and there were many Jewish shtetls throughout Latgale and southeastern Zemgale. The interwar years, although not without problems, brought considerable advantages to the Jewish community. Tsarist-era restrictions on where Jews were allowed to live disappeared, and Jews enjoyed the full rights of all citizens of Latvia. Latvia's minority education laws made provisions for Jewish schools, and a general cultural renaissance took place in the Jewish community. Newspapers, societies, and political parties demonstrated the vitality of Latvia's Jewish communities.

At the same time, the economic conditions of many Jews, particularly in Latgale, remained impoverished, and a general systemic and societal anti-Semitism existed, outside of the strict parameters of the law. The Ulmanis regime continued a mixed policy toward Latvia's Jews. On the one hand, Ulmanis purged Jews from the state administration because of their religious background and used the economic power of the state to "Latvianize" the economy, often at Jews' expense. Ulmanis, however, also outlawed anti-Semitic literature, provided state subsidies to Jewish religious bodies, and maintained close personal ties with important conservative Jewish leaders. Compared to the violent and official anti-Semitism of other Eastern European countries, Latvia was a relative sanctuary. This degree of protection made the events of the Holocaust in Latvia so much the more shocking.

As Nazi armies invaded the Soviet Union (and the Soviet-occupied Baltic states), execution squads (Einsatzgruppen) began to organize the murder of Latvia's Jews. Nazi propaganda skillfully but deceptively depicted the terrors of the preceding year of Soviet occupation as the work of Jews. Some Latvians organized and worked with the Nazis, most infamously the Arājs commando unit organized by Viktors Arājs. Almost immediately "killing actions" executed thousands of Jews in Liepāja, Jelgava, Daugavpils, and Riga. Perhaps one-third of Latvia's Jews were murdered in this fashion in the first three months of Nazi occupation. The remainder were detained in the Riga, Daugavpils, and Liepāja ghettos. Most of these Jews were killed in November and December of 1941. Later in the war, the Nazi regime transported European Jews to concentration camps in Latvia (particularly to Salaspils), but most of Latvia's Jews, at least 90 percent of them, were killed by the end of 1941. After the war, Soviet authorities executed several Latvian collaborators, but many others fled westward with the more general flow of refugees. Arājs was eventually captured and tried in 1979 in West Germany, and others were killed later, such as Herberts Cukurs, killed in Uruguay in 1965. Other alleged Latvian war criminals, however, are still suspected to be at large.

The legacy of the Holocaust still haunts Latvia in two fundamental ways. The first is in the form of the question of the degree of Latvia's complicity in the murder of their compatriots. At the time, Latvia was an occupied country and had no ability to make or influence Nazi policy. Historians still debate whether during a brief period of chaos (an interregnum) Latvians initiated the murder of Jews. Clearly the design of the "final solution" rested with German Nazis. Individual Latvians (perhaps as many as 2,500) volunteered to participate in tasks ranging from the transport of Jews to execution sites to actually murdering Jews. Latvia also had several brave individuals who harbored Jews, protecting them from harm (many of these have been recognized as righteous gentiles). Neither group was representative; it seems that most Latvians knew about the Holocaust, but did little to prevent or assist it. This same lukewarmness, this same lack of concern, characterizes the second fundamental way in which the Holocaust still casts a shadow over Latvia. The government has taken considerable steps to recognize the murderous events, but many assert that the government devotes more attention to alleged Soviet war criminals or Soviet crimes than the Holocaust. More generally, the population is simply unconcerned. They see the Holocaust as a part of history and little more. Little attention has been placed on the near complete disappearance of a historic community of Latvia. A general amnesia, a general forgetting of that community's vitality and vibrancy, and its essential part in the life of the region, has become a second kind of Holocaust.

headed by the biologist Augusts Kirhensteins, with a famous novelist, Vilis Lācis, as minister of the interior. From June 1940 until June 1941, tens of thousands of Latvia's political, social, cultural, and economic elite were deported to Siberia (more than 14,000 on the night of 14 June 1941). Kārlis Ulmanis was deported to the south of Russia at the end of July and ultimately died in a Soviet prison in 1942. The Soviet regime systematically dismantled the independent state and "sovietized" the economy and society. The seeming ethnic Russian content of Soviet power, coupled with its initial warm reception by some of Latvia's ethnic minorities (and Social Democrats), suggested to Latvian nationalists a national catastrophe. It was clear, however, that the minorities, particularly religious communities such as Russian Old Believers and Jewish conservatives, and the Latvian Social Democrats suffered equally from Soviet deportations.

As a result of the first year of Soviet occupation, many Latvians greeted the Nazi invasion of the USSR in June 1941 as a liberation. Nazi occupation, however, proved no less malevolent to the institutions of the Latvian state or to its inhabitants than had the Soviet. Within the first year of Nazi rule, more than 90 percent (about 80,000) of Latvia's Jews were murdered in the Holocaust, often with the active, voluntary participation of Latvians. The Nazi regime's intent, beyond this "final solution" of the racial question, was to exploit the region for its war effort and to colonize the region after the war. The Nazi regime created a "Self-Administration" of Latvian politicians to manage local affairs, but with constant German supervision. After the Nazis' disastrous defeat at Stalingrad in early 1943, the Nazi regime began to conscript Latvians into the 15th and 19th Waffen-SS Divisions of the German army. Ultimately, 146,000 Latvians were conscripted into the German military, in direct violation of the Geneva Conventions' prohibition on conscription in occupied territories. The Soviet Union similarly conscripted at least 43,000 Latvians. Latvians also volunteered for both.

Representatives of pre-coup Latvia's largest political parties tried to resist both Nazi and Soviet designs on Latvia. On 13 August 1943 they formed the Latvian Central Council, headed by Konstantīns Čakste, the son of the first president. The council's attempts to create a nucleus of an independent armed force was ruthlessly suppressed by the Nazis, and its leadership was arrested. Čakste died in the Stutthof concentration camp in 1945. Other members of the council were arrested and executed by the Soviet secret police after World War II, as they continued to work for an independent Latvia.

SOVIET RULE

As Soviet armies threatened to reoccupy Latvia, more than 100,000 Latvians with memories of the first year of Soviet occupation fled westward as refugees. They became the nucleus of the Latvian émigré communities in Western Europe, North America, and Australia. Those that remained suffered the full hardship of a vengeful Soviet army and wartime scarcity. Latvia lost roughly 30 percent of its prewar population to death, murder, and flight. Latvia, Estonia, and Lithuania were the only European states to lose their independence during World War II and not have it restored at the conclusion of the war. Although Western Europe and the United States did not recognize the Baltic states' forced incorporation into the USSR (and Baltic diplomatic representatives remained in Washington, D.C.), the end of the war meant the loss of independence and complete Soviet occupation until 1991.

The Sovietization of Latvia's society returned as soon as Soviet troops entered Latvian territory. Within the first two postwar years, thousands were deported or executed as collaborators with the Nazi regime. Many in Latvia continued to resist occupation, forcing Moscow to fight a protracted partisan war that lasted until the early 1950s. In 1949 forced collectivization led to the deportation of more than 43,000 kulaks (including 10,000 children) in order to break the rural support of the partisans, and to bring Latvia in line with Soviet agricultural norms. Most crippling to Latvia, however, were the Soviet Union's five-year plans, intended to bring about the massive, rapid heavy industrialization of Latvia.

Industrial manpower had to "relocate" to postwar Latvia to satisfy the industrial demands of the five-year plans. Accordingly, 41,000 Russian, Belarusian, and Ukrainian workers moved into Latvia in 1946 alone. Most newly arrived immigrants settled near the new industrial factories in and around Riga. More than half a million workers moved to Latvia between 1945 and 1955. Joining the workers, between 1945 and 1951, were roughly 9,000 Communist Party functionaries. The first postwar Soviet census demonstrated the magnitude of the demographic change caused by war and Soviet policy. There were 170,000 fewer Latvians in 1959 than in 1935, but 388,000 more Russians, 35,000 more Belarussians, and 28,000 more Ukrainians. In superficial ways, Soviet Latvia returned to pre–World War I demographic patterns, with increasing urbanization, industrialization, and fewer ethnic Latvians. The speed of this change, however, the nature of it, and the replacement of many ethnic communities with a single Russian-speaking minority were all radically different.

There was little or no change in the terror of Soviet occupation until after Stalin's death in 1953. Nikita Khrushchev, who emerged from the power struggle after Stalin, limited mass terror, which led to at least a momentary thaw, political, economic, and cultural. General amnesties released many who had survived the Gulag (the Soviet prison system), including at least 30,000 Latvians.

Latvian communists initially pushed for reforming the nature of government and its goals. Using Khrushchev's policy of alliance with non-Russians, the so-called "national communists" strenghtened the ethnic Latvian position through the creation and subsidization of cultural and educational systems. They were, however, far less effective in limiting the rapid pace of industrialization and the influx of immigrants into Latvian territory, which threatened the ethnic Latvian population with eventually becoming a minority population in their own titular republic. Eduards Berklavs was the most influential of the national communists, but after their 1959 purge by hard-liners who took a

During World War II, Riga was occupied by the forces of Nazi Germany following the German invasion of the USSR. (Hulton-Deutsch Collection/Corbis)

stance closer to the wishes of the USSR (together with an official rebuke from Moscow), reforms stalled. When Arvids Pelše became the first secretary of the Latvian Communist Party in 1963, he took a hard line toward all expressions of nationalism or "narrow localism."

After the dismissal of more than 2,000 Latvian communists who were sympathetic to national communism, the Russian and Russian-speaking communities acted like occupiers in the eyes of ethnic Latvians. The party and gov-

ernment reflected this "foreignness"; Russian was adopted as the language of the ruling party, the government, and economics. Only one-third of the Latvian Communist Party was ethnically Latvian (the lowest percentage in the USSR) and only 5 percent of Latvians belonged to the Communist Party. From 1960 to 1989, the continued influx of immigrants hurried the Russification of Latvia, in fact if not in policy. Another 330,000 Slavic workers settled in Latvia during these thirty years. By 1979, fewer than 20 percent of the Russians living in Latvia could speak Latvian. By the middle of the 1980s, Soviet policy had created a Latvian Soviet Socialist Republic with a titular nation that felt threatened with extinction and a Russian-speaking population that felt as if they were an integral part of a Russian USSR.

Augusts Voss led the Latvian Communist Party from 1966 to 1984, almost co-terminously with Leonid Brezhnev's rule of the USSR, an era that is remembered for stagnation and an absence of political reform. After decades of upheaval, this period brought a degree of relative prosperity. Years of industrialization and modernization had minimized the rural and agricultural sections of the economy. Collective farms lacked state investment, and many people left the countryside for the town and city. Towns such as Valmiera, Olaine, and Ogre developed new industries, fiberglass, textile, and pharmeceutical respectively. Along with this limited progress, however, came many of the social problems associated with industrialization and modernization, such as marked increases in crime, suicide, abortion, and divorce. Alcohol abuse became an endemic problem throughout Latvian society. Ultimately, these social problems, together with poor productivity, threw the Soviet planned economy into crisis, a crisis that was not seriously addressed until Mikhail Gorbachev took office in 1985.

Gorbachev inherited an economic depression in an economy completely controlled by the state. These dificulties cast doubt over the USSR's ability to maintain a military establishment that could compete with the United States, particularly in developing ever more sophisticated equipment. Gorbachev introduced economic reform, perestroika (restructuring), to revive the economy. As hard-line oppposition resisted these reforms, Gorbachev introduced glasnost, or openness, in the hope of encouraging public participation and mobilization. In Latvia and in the other Baltic Republics, however, debate rapidly turned to the issue of the environment and then of history. In 1986, for example, a public campaign in Latvia, as in Estonia, successfully stopped the construction of a hydroelectric dam on environmental grounds (though equally troubling to the protestors was the project's need for more workers from outside of the Baltic Republics). Soon afterwards, Latvian dissidents, such as the human rights group Helsinki–86, pushed for a reappraisal of the "voluntary" incorporation of Latvia into the USSR.

"Calendar demonstrations" began in 1987, marking anniversaries such as the signing of the Nazi-Soviet Non-Aggression Pact or Latvia's Independence Day. In 1988 this protest movement expanded considerably, when reform-minded members of the Latvian Communist Party and leading intellectuals from the "creative unions" formed the Popular Front of Latvia (Latvijas Tautas Fronta; LTF). At the founding conference, which took place 1–2 June 1988, an old member of the Communist Party and journalist, Mavriks Vulfsons, stated openly that Latvia was violently occupied by Soviet military forces in June of 1940. The Latvian National Independence Movement (Latvijas Nacionālā Neatkarības Kustība; LNNK) formed soon afterward, on 17 June 1988, as a national mass movement demanding the restoration of full independence.

Ethnic Latvians overwhelmingly desired autonomy or independence, but after the demographic changes brought on by four decades of Soviet occupation they accounted for just 52 percent of the Republic's population. Movements such as LNNK and the more extremist For Fatherland and Freedom (Tēvzemei un Brīvībai; TB) demanded the exclusion of the bulk of the non-Latvian population from political decision making. To these organizations, all Soviet-era migrants were not legal citizens of the state.

The Popular Front shied away from this confrontational tactic and sought to prove its legitimacy to Moscow and the world through a series of electoral victories. Opposing these ethnic Latvian movements was an opposite popular front, the Interfront, which appealed to non-Latvians and hoped to keep the USSR whole. Despite the activities of Interfront, the Popular Front broadened its appeal to many non-Latvians and made common cause with similar movements in Estonia and Lithuania (most famously culminating in the Baltic Chain of 23 August 1989, in which the people of the three Baltic nations linked hands in a show of solidarity).

Elections to the Supreme Council in March and April 1990 returned a Popular Front majority. Anatolijs Gorbunovs, the highest ranking reform-minded Latvian communist, was elected chair of the Supreme Council, and Ivars Godmanis, a leader from the Popular Front, became the prime minister. The Popular Front decided not to follow Lithuania's directly confrontational method of unilaterally declaring independence and looked for a transition toward independence. On 4 May 1990, the Supreme Council of Latvia passed the "Declaration about the Renewal of the Independence of the Republic of Latvia," which called for a transition of indeterminate time to full independence. How to negotiate with a recalcitrant Moscow remained a serious problem. For more than a year a kind of dual government existed in Latvia, with, for example, an attorney general who was loyal to Moscow and another one who was loyal to Riga.

After many months of indecisive moves and countermoves, the Soviets attempted a response at the beginning of 1991. On 13 January 1991, Soviet paramilitary units attacked key installations in Vilnius, Lithuania (most infamously, the television tower attack left fourteen dead) and followed that with attacks on Latvian government buildings on January 20. Tens of thousands of Russians and Latvians flocked to Riga to construct human barricades across the city to defend the Popular Front government. After several tense days, the military backed down. Soon after, on 3 March 1991, 73.68 percent of Latvians voted in favor of independence. Many Russians decided Latvian nationalism was less onerous than the Soviet reaction. Following the failed coup attempt in Moscow in August of 1991 that sought to overthrow Mikhail Gorbachev and restore the "glory" of the Soviet empire, Latvia formally declared independence on 21 August 1991, and almost immediately received international recognition.

Demonstration during movement for independence in Latvia, 26 January 1991. Anatolijs Gorbunovs is in the foreground (left). (Svartsevich Vladimire/Corbis Sygma)

POLITICAL DEVELOPMENTS

Independence led to the emergence of politics and the political pursuit of interests in a multiparty forum, something without precedent in the Soviet Union and absent from Latvia for fifty-seven years. From 1991 on, and even more after 1993, the long historical themes of Latvia are harder to discern, and more contemporary observations about political and economic change come to the fore. Ethnic tension has emerged as the dominant division within post-Soviet Latvia, but not the only division. Latvian nationalists and Russian-speaking communities both felt a degree of betrayal (imagined and real) with the shape of the new state. After August 1991, the Supreme Council became the de facto parliament of the newly independent state, and its Council of Ministers became the acting government. The confusion and ambiguities of the dual government of the preceding years evaporated, but administation remained chaotic. Logic dictated that a new election should return a full parliament, but when to hold the election and who should vote became hotly contested. The Godmanis Cabinet stayed in office until the summer of 1993, struggling with these fundamental questions, as well as with the massive tasks of state construction and economic transformation with the authority of a lame duck government.

The government accepted the idea, first suggested by the extreme nationalists, that citizenship would be defined according to the idea that the state was a renewal of the interwar Republic and that therefore only the citizens of the original republic and their descendants could vote in the first parliamentary elections of newly independent Latvia. This in itself did not lead to absolute ethnic discrimination. Nearly a quarter of the interwar Republic's population was composed of ethnic minorities, and those citizens and their descendants were legally recognized as citizens. The letter of the law did not specifically deny citizenship to Russians and other Slavs living in Latvia. Technically, citizenship had no ethnic component whatsoever. Most of the Russian-speaking population, however, had moved to Latvia after Soviet occupation and was therefore disenfranchised by this definition of citizenship. Many Russians believed that the citizenship law was a symbolic connection to the past that would soon be revised. Some demanded the "zero option," which would grant citizenship to everyone living in Latvia on 21 August 1991. Others expected "zero plus one," an option by which the link to the interwar state would be established, but a quick move to grant citizenship with few requirements to those that did not immediately qualify would soon follow. Many members of the Popular Front had promised exactly this path toward citizenship in the campaigns of early 1991, hoping to build support beyond the ethnic Latvian community for the mobilization for confrontations with Moscow. Strategies for immediate electoral gain, together with the collapse of the USSR, however, led to the discarding of a rational, comprehensive approach and to disregard for the fulfillment of promises.

Once the citizenry was defined, ethnic Latvians became the absolute majority of the electorate. Politicians new to campaigning, and most likely with some degree of involvement in the Communist Party's rule over Latvia, found themselves appealing to an electorate that doubted their commitment to perceived ethnic Latvian interests. Increasingly, these politicians played the ethnic card, realizing that the great majority of the electoral community was ethnically Latvian.

Once the elections for the *Saeima* (parliament) were set for the spring of 1993, party formation began in earnest. Learning from the political crises of the interwar years and the weakness of many party coalition governments, the Godmanis Cabinet drafted and passed a modified electoral law that included a 4 percent threshold for representation in parliament. Ultimately twenty-three political parties or movements contested the elections to the fifth Saiema. Many of the parties resurrected names, symbols, images, and personalities from the interwar years. The Farmers' Union, for example, was re-formed, and its list of candidates was topped by Guntis Ulmanis, whose granduncle was Kārlis Ulmanis. The Christian Democratic Union and the Democratic Center Party also claimed links to interwar parties of similar names.

The largest political party of the interwar years, the Social Democratic Workers' Party, also re-formed itself, but fell victim to divisions within its left wing over the roles various members had played in the Soviet era and split into other left-wing parties, such as Latvia's Democratic Labor Party, headed by a former KGB major, Juris Bojārs, banned from running for office, and the awkwardly named Harmony for Latvia–Revival for the Economy led by Jānis Jurkāns, a minister of foreign affairs in the Godmanis Cabinet, who had been sacked for opposition to the restrictive citizenship law. The parties of the Left were rounded out by the Green Party (whose nonenvironmental policies were far from leftist) and the unrepentant Communist Party members, who called their new party the Equal Rights Movement, led by Alfreds Rubiks, in jail for treason for his role in the tumultuous events of 1991.

The Popular Front, headed by the acting minister president Godmanis, also contested the elections, but increasingly seemed a spent political force. Its raison d'être had been achieving independence, and with this goal accomplished, many of its most popular politicians left for other parties (or formed their own). Other figures, such as Godmanis himself, lost popularity and support rapidly from 1991 to 1993. No longer leading a mass opposition movement, but rather a government, these figures became the lightning rods for growing anger at economic collapse, corruption, and social confusion. The Popular Front that had succeeded in uniting so many people against Soviet rule be-

came the first casualty of independent politics and did not surpass the 4 percent mark required for representation. Instead, the dominant political party of the fifth Saeima was the newly created Latvia's Way Movement (Latvijas ceļš).

Latvia's Way was an electoral list of the most popular politicians in Latvia and notable émigré Latvians as well. Their unifying concern seemed to be a centrist, democratic, yet nationalist party focused on the West. The list included the telegenic and consistently most popular politician Anatolijs Gorbunovs. Latvia's Way's well-run campaign and professionalism garnered them thirty-six seats, by far the most of any of the eight parties that overcame the 4 percent threshhold.

In July 1993, after nearly sixty years, Latvia's parliament, the Saeima, reconvened. Latvia's Way formed a minority coalition government with Latvia's Farmers' Union. Compromise on the part of Latvia's Way concerning the Farmers' Union's candidate for state president, Guntis Ulmanis, sealed the coalition, with the candidate of Latvia's Way becoming minister president.

Latvia's political system, like that of much of Europe, includes a unicameral parliament from which a government is formed with the consent of a simple majority. The leader of government, the minister president, fills the functions of a prime minister, while a state president (elected by the Saeima) fills ceremonial roles. The state president can return legislation to the Saeima for a second reading, but cannot refuse to ratify a law that has passed this hurdle. In addition to the prominent ceremonial diplomatic role, the state president can dismiss the Saeima. The minister president and the council of ministers form the government.

The tasks before the fifth Saiema were daunting, and, in a larger sense, are still being addressed. The Republic of Latvia had to transform itself from a component of a one-party, socialist command economy to a multiparty democracy based on a market economy. Almost everything had to be done from scratch, from law codes to economic regulations to matters of justice to international issues. Two of the most immediate policy issues were Latvia's place in an international context, particularly the still open question of Russian military bases on Latvian soil, and the issue of Latvia's non-citizens. (Economic transformations will be discussed under "Economic Development.")

Arguably the most immediate concern of the new state was the continuing presence of Russian troops on Latvian soil. During the nearly five decades of Soviet occupation, Latvia's territory was incorporated into the larger Soviet military body. The long sea border made Latvia strategically important and the home to tens of thousands of troops and hundreds of military bases of every kind. Independence came quickly in 1991, without much regard for how and when to evacuate Soviet troops (from December of 1991, Russian troops). With considerable confusion in post-Soviet Russia, the return of hundreds of thousands of troops from all across Eastern Europe and the former Soviet Union was difficult to organize. Financial constraints and housing shortages played a part in Russian hesitancy, but increasingly the Russian government saw the presence of Russian troops on Latvian soil as a political tool. Boris Yeltsin's government attempted to link troop withdrawal with greater political rights for the disenfranchised, predominantly Russian population of Latvia. Latvia's governments (from the time of the Godmanis government), on the other hand, refused to recognize any such linkage and saw Russian troops as a clear attack on Latvia's sovereignty. Russian tactical interest in leasing for several years an intelligence-gathering installation near Ventspils, a naval harbour in Liepāja, and a phased radar array at Skrunda further complicated matters.

Ultimately the Birkavs government presided over troop withdrawal in 1994, achieved after the United Nations General Assembly and the Congress of the United States rejected any linkage between minority rights and Russian troop withdrawal. The Skrunda tower was demonstratively blown up on live national television in 1995, and the final small detachment of Russian troops left Latvia in 1999.

Although Latvia's governments successfully kept the Russian government from linking troop withdrawal with minority rights, the legal status of the disenfranchised was a pressing issue for the fifth parliament. More than 700,000 people were in legal limbo, and Latvia's government had two fundamental tasks to confront: to define the process for naturalization, and to define the legal rights of non-citizens. Simply put, although non-citizens do have many rights, they also face legal differentiation and discrimination. Naturalization could allay some of these concerns, but Latvia was slow to define the legal standards for naturalization. Ultimately, after the fall of the Birkavs government, a similar coalition government, headed by Māris Gailis, also from Latvia's Way, defined the requirements for naturalization in 1994. Citizenship would be granted with a residency requirement, a language examination, and an examination on the basics of Latvia's history and constitution. More troubling to the international community were the so-called windows to citizenship. The windows were floating ethnic quotas intended to slow the number of non-Latvians receiving citizenship in any specific year. Legally, the citizenship law created a naturalization process that applied a collective principle to individual applicants. The OSCE (Organization for Security and Cooperation in Europe) and the European Union (as well as many other international bodies and countries) reacted unfavorably to the new citizenship law, but with the voting population still limited by these very same laws, domestic concerns ran opposite to international pressure.

The Russian-speaking community responded by devoting all their political efforts to changing the citizenship law. The next parliamentary elections in the fall of 1995 heightened tension even further. Latvian politicians campaigned on questions about naturalization and the rights of non-citizens. Ethnic politics also masked the generally weak party structures and served to distance one candidate from another, particularly since most parties had similar economic messages. Parties differentiated themselves with personalities, ethnic issues, and scandal mongering. The alternative was the still divided Left. One faction on the Left tried to merge a nationalist image with a leftist economic agenda. The nonrepentant socialist Left, led by the jailed Alfreds Rubiks, pushed for open citizenship and a multi-

ethnic Latvia. Their program of citizenship appealed to the disenfranchised 700,000 Russian-speaking non-citizens of Latvia and deepened the ethnic cleavage in Latvian politics. Ethnic Latvians saw the Left (and its leadership) as questionable in loyalty to the state and beholden to ethnic Russian (and perhaps Moscow) interests. Similarly, many ethnic Russians who could vote had to choose between a party that represented their citizenship concerns and one that promised to fulfill their other socioeconomic desires. The short-term results for the Left were that its considerable popularity did not translate to equal votes, due to the existing citizenship laws.

The elections to the sixth Saeima in the fall of 1995 showcased popular frustration with the existing political order. There was a general sense that the ruling parties benefited too much from power, with frequent charges of corruption and abuse of power. The most disaffected of the electorate suprisingly supported a dubious populist politician, Werner Joachim Siegerist, and his For Latvia Movement. Siegerist, a newspaper publisher in Germany with alleged ties to far-right political groups, ran for, and was elected to, the fifth Saeima as a deputy of the LNNK. His electoral campaign included free bus trips to polling booths with complimentary refreshments and bananas. The mainstream dismissed such stunts, but Siegerist and his political movement tapped into popular anger. Dismissing parliament, Siegerist spent his time campaigning widely in pensioners homes, hospitals, and schools, donating money and supplies and promising more if elected. His movement stunned the political scene with its significant electoral gains, matched only by a left of center coalition. Almost from its beginning, the sixth Saeima seemed destined to political paralysis, as no coalition of parties was able to create a government. Ultimately, an extraordinary solution was taken by most parties acting together, united by their concern with keeping Siegerist from political power. Andris Šķele, a wildly successful businessman who had not run for parliament and was not tied to any party, became minister president of a grand coalition government.

The Šķele government, and the entire sixth Saeima, seemed to have a caretaker nature, until Šķele proved to be a strong and driven leader. He used a political crisis to win more power from his reluctant supporters in parliament and guided the Latvian government on a conservative fiscal policy of cutting government spending and aggressively pushing privatization and market reform. Šķele grew too popular for the established political parties and lost parliament's confidence in the year before elections to the seventh Saeima. He was replaced by Guntars Krasts of the right-wing, nationalist coalition party TB/LNNK as minister president. Thanks to the political confusion of the sixth Saeima, Guntis Ulmanis easily won reelection in parliament as state president when his term ended in the summer of 1996.

Despite the near constant state of political crisis, the sixth Saeima continued to pass brick-and-mortar kinds of legislation that laid the groundwork for the state. Significant legal, structural reforms included extending the term of the Saeima to four years from a rather short three years (and also extending the term of the state president to four years) and raising the electoral threshhold to 5 percent. The unratified second section of the Constitution (similar to the U.S. Bill of Rights) was also finally accepted. A controversial reform of local governments also began amalgamating Latvia's many levels of local government into large blocks. Under considerable international pressure, the government amended the citizenship law in the summer of 1998 to grant citizenship to children born in Latvia since 1991 and to end the controversial quotalike windows. The nationalist Right, however, launched a signature drive to force a referendum on the matter that was scheduled to coincide with the elections to the seventh Saeima in the autumn of 1998. The two simultaneous elections caused considerable excitement and political suspense. The former minister president, Andris Šķele, formed a new political party, the People's Party (Tautas partija), and seemed likely to be the primary victor in the elections. Simultaneously, the electorate had to decide whether it favored a restrictive citizenship or the more accommodating (although to many, still inadequate) version preferred publicly by the European Union.

The results of the referendum favored the more lenient citizenship laws, and Šķele's party did win the most seats of any party, but several other parties immediately formed a coalition to keep the People's Party out of power. Vilis Krištopāns, a member of Latvia's Way who had served as minister of transportation, became the minister president in a controversial new cabinet. Šķele's supporters saw conspiracy and underhanded dealings about specific economic decisions behind the coalition, while Šķele detractors questioned the mercurial leader's authoritarian tendencies and source of wealth. The government, however, was short-lived and fell by June of 1999. A new government, still led by a member of Latvia's Way, Andris Berziņš, but with People's Party participation (minus Šķele) took office and governed throughout the duration of the seventh Saeima. In June 1999 Guntis Ulmanis's second term as state president expired, and tradition held that state presidents can only serve two terms. As in the original election of Andris Šķele to office, a compromise candidate was suggested when no party would back another party's candidates. Vaira Viķe-Freiberga, an émigré academic, became the first female head of state of a former Soviet Republic. Her command of several European languages and academic standing quickly raised her public standing, and she has remained one of the politicians with the highest popularity ratings in Latvia; she won support from eighty-eight deputies for her reelection in June of 2003.

The Berziņš government oversaw the continued reorientation of Latvia toward Western European economic and military institutions, and piloted Latvia through generally poor international economic waters in relatively good shape. The Russian economic crisis, for example, was severely felt in some economic quarters, but generally economic performance has been impressive. Likewise, the more liberal citizenship law ushered in a period in which tens of thousands of non-citizens passed the examinations and received their citizenship.

Vaira Vike-Freiberga, Latvia's president. (Maher Attar/Corbis Sygma)

Minority issues, however, did not disappear. The citizenship law set out how Latvia's non-citizens could achieve citizenship, but it did little to manage the relationship between ethnic Latvians and the large Slavic (primarily Russian) communities within Latvia. Ethnic tension moved to the arena of official language laws and the language of instruction in minority schools. This continues to be the flashpoint between nationalists, who set government policy that decrees Latvian as the only official language and raises the amount of instruction in Latvian in schools, and Russian activists, who struggle against what they see as assimilationist governmental policy. As the electorate more accurately reflects the current ethnic makeup of Latvia, more compromise is probable, but the issue is still divisive.

Elections to the eighth Saeima in 2002 repeated several recurring themes in the political landscape of independent Latvia. Many of the parties of the center and right aligned themselves again against Šķele and his People's Party to keep it from power, but Šķele himself no longer played the role of the political outsider who could be the savior of Latvia's political scene. This role was now occuppied by Einārs Repše, the successful head of the Bank of Latvia throughout independence, who now headed the newly created New Era Party (Jaunais laiks). Like Šķele before him, Repše had considerable momentum moving into the elections, and his new party won the greatest number of seats. Unlike Šķele, however, Repše was able to patch together a coalition of four of parliament's six parties, with himself as minister president. The elections also saw the considerable weakening of the traditional right-wing nationalist party and the disappearance in parliament of Latvia's Way. In early 2004, however, the Repše government fell and was replaced by a coalition that included the People's Party, led by the Green Farmer Union deputy Indulis Emsis.

Latvia's Way had placed itself as the floating center of Latvian politics from its inception and had played a kingmaker role in almost every government (providing every minister president with the exception of Šķele and Krasts). Many of its leading politicians became synonomous with the ministries that they headed through successive governments; in many respects, Latvia's Way was the face of power in Latvia. Frequent scandals, charges of corruption, and a degree of arrogance in power, however, took their toll on the party. Equally damaging was the inability of Latvia's Way to present itself as the "least terrible option" among many untested or potentially radical parties. Šķele's and Repše's parties both ate considerably into Latvia's Way's support. At this writing, the future of the party, now outside of power, remains unclear.

Through three elections to parliament with seemingly extreme swings of fortune for many parties, some general trends are clear. The extreme Latvian nationalist party to some degree has been co-opted into the existing political status quo. Although this may calm the more extreme slogans within parliament itself, it has not meant the complete collapse of an extreme nationalist constituency. These groups find themselves largely outside of traditional politics and turn to symbolic acts or work on rallying popular opposition to the European Union as a loss of national sovereignty. The Left has similarly lost its believed close connection to the communist past and to Moscow. Some members of the Left have not abandoned this orientation, but they seem increasingly in the minority, and the Left has emerged victorious in municipal elections. The political center has moved somewhat to the right (particularly on minority issues), but has become the battleground between different political parties and individual egos.

The new strong leader with an outsider image and a promise of clean government has become commonplace in the last three elections. That leader, having gained office, becomes a disappointment, and that disappointment sets the stage for the next incarnation of the same phenomenon. This trend is a symptom of two interrelated developments. All political parties are weak in institutional structure and strength. They are usually defined by their most popular politician(s) and have small memberships. Members do not influence and create party policy from the grassroots, elites decide things, and on many issues there is very rudimentary consensus across many different parties. As a result, the common people see themselves as alienated from political decision making. Adding to this perception, and building on the weakness of mass parties, is the dominant impact of economic interests. Parties and politicians are perceived as tied to specific economic interests, and this perception adds gravity to instances of corruption and abuse of power. As is probably true for all modern states, the development of the economy and politics are inseparable in modern Latvia.

CULTURAL DEVELOPMENT

Two dominant themes are central to the history of Latvia's cultural development. The first is ethnic Latvian identity, as seen in artistic and cultural representation. Modern Latvian nationalism originated during the middle of the nineteenth century among the educated sons of Latvian peasants. Latvian national identity has always been tied to peasant identity and to the dominant themes of nature and human beings in relation to nature. Along with the acceptance of national identity, however, came the industrialization and modernization of the Baltic provinces at the end of the nineteenth century. Throughout the twentieth century and into the twenty-first, more and more "foreign" ideas and concepts have altered that supposed original peasant identity. Much of ethnic Latvian cultural development has revolved around this issue of incorporating the new into Latvianness. At the end of the nineteenth century, for example, the first artists and writers began to construct a cultural representation of urban life that was both urban and Latvian. These innovators met considerable resistance from traditionalists. At the end of the twentieth century and moving into the twenty-first, artists and writers struggle with "American consumerism" and new strains of internationalism and "cosmopolitanism," with equally vigorous resistance from traditionalists defending what they see as the core rural values of ethnic Latvian identity.

The second dominant, and related, theme concerns the place of nonethnic Latvian cultural developments in Latvia. The question is how to accept (or not accept) the cultural developments of "others" within the territorial constraints of Latvia (and beyond). The questions are simple, but the answers are contested. Is the art and literature of Baltic Germans, Latvia's Jews, and Russians a part of Latvian cultural development? How do they relate and interact with ethnic Latvian culture? Can a Russian paint "Latvian" art, and so on? Do the political refugees of the twentieth century who settled in the United States, Canada, Australia, and Western Europe play a part in Latvian cultural development? How "Latvian" are cultural developments whose origins are "borrowed" from abroad? Although no art or culture is produced in a vacuum and must draw on local circumstances, small nations are particularly sensitive to questions of cultural preservation as a component of ethnic survival. These two themes (and several more that grow from them) provide a conceptual framework for outlining the cultural developments of Latvia.

The earliest examples of a cultural development on the eastern shores of the Baltic Sea are provided by some archeological artifacts and linguistic and anthropological reconstructions of early Baltic life. A Baltic animisitic religion in all likelihood welded all cultural and philosophical ideas into a holistic worldview. A primary deity, Dievs (God), seems to have been a heavenly father figure, with a potential constellation of lesser deities such as Pērkons (Thunder) and the earth goddesses Laima and Māra. There seems to have been little organized religious hierarchy devoted to these deities; rather some individuals led rituals (often associated with places in nature such as oak trees) and probably sacrifices as well. Song, dance, jewelery, custom, and ritual were probably intertwined and mutually reinforcing. Possessions are believed to have signified social status, differentiating between elders, warriors, and common people, as did the nature of burial (one of the best archeological sources for this era). There is no written record of this time period (and almost no outsiders' descriptions as well), but there is a surviving folklore, particularly the *dainas,* a kind of folk song. The dainas mention some of these pre-Christian deities, and although their authenticity is not questioned, the nature and age of their contents are. Most dainas were only transcribed in the second half of the nineteenth century, and even given the remarkable durability and accuracy of oral traditions in nonliterate societies, one cannot generalize about a supposedly constant, unchanging pagan society and culture of one thousand years ago from a few fragments.

The earliest culture in the Baltic with a solid historical record, therefore, that of the Baltic German Christian crusaders, underlines the importance of the theme of foreignness and its place in Latvian culture. Initial German production had few details specific to the region, but nevertheless included important innovations. The first stone buildings, for example, in the eastern Baltic were built by Germans in the new German towns of Ikšķile and Riga. These earliest stone buildings were churches and fortifications, which with time became cathedrals and castles. In this manner, Riga's three oldest cathedrals had their origins by 1225: St. Peter's in 1209, the Doms Cathedral in 1211, and St. Jacob's in 1225. Eventually, German-built stone churches and castles were constructed across the territory as an extension and symbol of German control. The building of a German castle in Jelgava in 1265, for example, testified to the defeat of the Semigallians by the Teutonic Order.

Through the thirteenth and into the fourteenth century, this first wave of stone construction built castles: in Sigulda by 1207, in Cēsis by 1210, in Kuldīga by 1245, in Aizpute by 1248, in Kandava by 1253, in Daugavpils by 1275, in Rēzekne by 1285, and in Ludza as late as 1399. Most of these buildings, however, were primarily functional. Town architecture around them remained predominantly wooden, and the towns themselves rather small. The overwhelming cultural influence was northern German, reflecting strongly a sense of Christendom as a whole. Only in the sixteenth and seventeenth centuries did the lands of mod-

Dundagas Castle. (Courtesy of Aldis Purs)

ern Latvia begin to build something culturally unique on this initial foundation.

The sixteenth century witnessed the Protestant Reformation, a radical schism throughout Western Christendom. An important tenet in Lutheranism and many other Protestant sects was the importance of the individual's own communion with God. This necessitated sermons and religious writing in vernacular languages. The Roman Catholic Church responded in kind, with its own attempt to involve the congregation in a manner heretofore not seen. These currents began the long path toward a written Latvian language. Small as the popularity of the Roman Catholic Church in Latvia was, a Catholic catechism by Peter Canisius, published in 1585, must be accepted as the first full-length book in Latvian. A Lutheran counterpart was published in 1586 and 1587, and for several decades into the seventeenth century almost the entirety of literature in Latvian served religious purposes.

Latvian as a written language therefore began somewhat artificially and through a curious prism: the Baltic German priest or preacher. This early literary production was written in what Baltic German clergy imagined to be the peasant language around them. The grammar borrowed heavily from German (as did the orthography and vocabulary), and the finished product must have been quite different from the spoken language. Still the growing usage of a Latvian written language required some standardization, which was accomplished by Georg Mancelius in 1638 with his German-Latvian dictionary. Mancelius also published a collection of sermons in Latvian, among other religious texts. The Lutheran pastor Ernst Glück finally translated the Old and New Testaments into Latvian between 1684 and 1694. Perhaps more groundbreaking than these works, however, were Christoph Fürecker's translations of German Lutheran hymns into Latvian. Fürecker, unlike the others, was not a preacher, and although a German, he was married to a Latvian woman. These characteristics may have helped him add a vibrancy to his translations that seemed closer to actual spoken Latvian. His hymns (a complete set of 180 hymns was published in 1685) became standards in most Latvian congregations and suggested that the written language was capable of expressing emotion and mood, unlike the other rather stiff, formalistic translations of the seventeenth century.

During the first two centuries of a written Latvian religious language, however, the lands of modern Latvia were torn apart by wars. The Livonian Order collapsed in the 1560s, and Polish and Swedish rule replaced it. Ultimately during the reign of Peter the Great, Russia staked its claim of hegemony over the region, a hegemony that was ultimately achieved by Catherine the Great. During the many long years of war and in their immediate aftermath, cultural production almost ceased. The wars and the new politics, however, introduced new ideas and experiences, as well as trends and fashions from Warsaw and Stockholm (and ultimately St. Petersburg). These trends manifested themselves in the lands of modern Latvia, as the Baltic German aristocracy curried favor with their new sovereigns.

Architecture provides an example of the influx of new tastes in the seventeenth and eighteenth centuries. After Peter the Great's effective use of artillery, the old stone fortifications and castles became anachronisms. Functional castles and relatively modest churches became ornate palaces (equally symbols of the Baltic German aristocracy's power) and cathedrals decorated in the latest styles and with the newest accoutrements. An early organ for the Dom Cathedral, for example, was created by a Polish master in 1601. Similarly, the House of the Blackheads (a German order of bachelor merchants) in Riga was substantially renovated between 1619 and 1625. Through many of these years, no architectural style was uniformly adopted. The same House of the Blackheads, for example, always kept a Gothic style, while churches built near the end of the seventeenth century and into the beginning of the eighteenth century, such as the Church of Peter and Paul built in Riga in the 1720s, followed classical style. By the third decade of the eighteenth century, baroque architecture became the standard.

The dominance of baroque architecture in the manors and palaces of the Baltic German aristocracy (as well as the cathedrals of the Baltic German clergy) further highlights the theme of outside influences in the cultural development of the lands of modern Latvia. Peter the Great brought several Italian baroque architects to Russia to help design St. Petersburg, and those architects (and others like them) quickly became fashionable in the Baltic Provinces as well. The duke of Courland, Ernst Johann Biron, a favorite of Tsarina Anna, commissioned the Italian architect Bartolmeo Francisco Rastrelli to design a general palace in Jelgava and a summer residence in Rundāle (near Bauska). Work on these two greatest examples of baroque palace architecture in Latvia began in 1737 and 1736 respectively. Both residences approached the splendor of the Winter Palace outside of St. Petersburg. A palace coup in St. Petersburg in 1740 deposed Biron, but he was granted amnesty in 1763 and returned to Courland to complete both palaces. The interiors were lavishly decorated with Italian art and German furnishings. These two palaces (although only intermittently in use throughout their existence) set the architectural style for aristocratic manors for the next century. The Dominican Cathedral at Aglona, begun in 1768, mirrored the adoption of the baroque for church architecture as well.

Baroque remained the dominant architectural theme of manors and churches until the eclectism of the second half of the nineteenth century. Eclecticism borrowed easily from many time periods and is difficult to pin down to any specific design. The palace at Cesvaine, begun in 1896, for example, is eclecticism's vision of a romantic hunting lodge. The palace near Stameriene or the small and large guild halls in Riga are other examples of eclecticism. By the end of the nineteenth century, *Jugendstil* architecture began to be fashionable, but by this date so many different styles were popular that never again could any one style gain the predominance of, say, the baroque in the late eighteenth century.

At the end of the eighteenth century, new strains of European intellectual thought, specifically the Enlightenment and romanticism, began to enter the lands of what is now Latvia along the conduit of Baltic Germans who were in touch with a wider German world. Although both of these

Jugendstil

Jugendstil is an international architectural style, also known as art nouveau. Riga has perhaps the best and largest collection of this architectural style of any city in the world. Whereas a single building or two may be of note in other European cities, Riga is home to complete city blocks of this turn-of-the-century style.

Architecturally, Jugendstil is defined by ornamentation adorning the balconies, doors, and roof lines. The ornamentation is primarily drawn from myth and is of a stylized, elongated character. Lions, mythic faces, and natural elements are often prominent in Jugendstil architecture. Riga's relative wealth of this style is due to a confluence of socioeconomic factors in the city at the end of the nineteenth century and the beginning of the twentieth. At that time, Riga was one of the epicenters of industrialization in tsarist Russia. Factories, port facilities, and commercial interests drew tens of thousands of peasants to the city and brought considerable wealth to industrialists and successful merchants alike. Politics revolved around the growing power of Latvian nationalism, emergent socialism, and the existing Baltic German elite's attempt to maintain hegemony. Although political participation was very limited (and municipal government's ability to set policy equally limited), there was an electorate, and that electorate was defined in part by property qualifications. Moreover, apartment houses were needed for workers, as well as buildings for offices. All of these factors fed into a building boom.

The Baltic German elite still set the more general aesthetic trends, and from around 1900 they built considerably in the Jugendstil fashionable in northern Europe. Wealthy Latvians who were building to meet the property requirements of franchise matched Baltic German constructions as a symbol of prestige and equality. Architects such as Mihail Eisenstein (1867–1921), the father of the filmmaker Sergei, designed building after building in the period 1900–1910. Eisenstein's legacy can particularly be seen on Alberts Street, Elizabetes Street, and Strēlnieku Street. Some Latvian architects such as Eižens Laube (1880–1967), Aleksandrs Vanags (1873–1919), and Konstantīns Pēkšēns (1859–1928) incorporated traditional Latvian elements into their stylized building ornaments. By 1910, both the economic boom and the mania for Jugendstil subsided. War and independence weakened the financial basis of renewed private construction from 1914 to 1940. State construction in the 1930s and in Soviet times moved away from the ornamentation of Jugendstil. Many of the masterpieces became communal apartments and fell into general disrepair by the 1980s. With independence restored, Riga's wealth of Jugendstil architecture was recognized as part of the cultural heritage of Europe. The buildings have been painstakingly and lovingly restored and are some of the prime architectural jewels of Latvia.

currents touched only a few people, their impact became quite pronounced. Johann Gottfried Herder and Garlieb Merkel began to fundamentally alter the way in which Baltic German society imagined and interacted with Latvian peasants. As discussed above, in the discussion of the Latvian national awakening, Herder spent a brief period of time in Riga (from 1764 to 1769), and his exposure to Latvian folk traditions played a part in his development of the concept of das Volk, "the people," or "the nation," as the creative building block of culture and history.

When earlier Baltic Germans introduced a written Latvian language, the reason was to convey the specifics of Christianity to passive, receptive, and barbaric Latvian peasants. Herder began to believe that the simple Latvian peasants constituted a people, and, in that sense, a nation, and like other peoples had something to contribute to humanity. Herder's discussion of the value of all peoples was primarily cultural, but others drawing upon his writings developed nationalism as a political force in the nineteenth century throughout Europe. Merkel, a Baltic German, anticipated some of these developments and moved beyond the cultural concerns of Herder by suggesting that Latvian peasants could become a revolutionary political force, rising against oppressive Baltic German control. Both of these ideas played an important part in the general and political history of the lands of Latvia in the nineteenth century, as discussed above, and they also shaped cultural developments.

At first, the new cultural developments, particularly in a literary Latvian language, continued to be produced by educated, fashionable Baltic Germans. Many of these young students were ardent followers of Herder, and if he collected Latvian folk songs, so would they. They also began to describe Latvian folk customs, traditions, and superstitions in an organized manner, first in 1817 in the Courland Society for Literature and Art, but by 1824 in the Society of Friends of Latvians. Furthermore, they published their work in collections and began two weekly newspapers in the Latvian language: The Latvian Newspaper (Latviešu avīze) and Friend of the Latvian People (Latviešu ļaužu draugs). Although this was primarily an academic pursuit motivated by authentic interest in Latvian folklore, it led to the first considerable body of secular literature in Latvian.

With the continuing growth of literacy among Latvian peasants, the number of secular titles published in Latvian increased, and old patterns of assimilating educated Latvians faltered. In more general terms, these developments funneled into the rise of the Young Latvians in the middle of the century. In political history, the Young Latvians and succeeding activists struggled over the role and destiny of the Latvian nation. Their cultural pursuits were similarly motivated.

Outside of the political controversies between the Young Latvians and the established Baltic German elite (seen in the history of the Young Latvians' newspaper, *The Petersburg Newspaper*), the cultural pursuits of this first generation of Latvian nationalists attempted to prove Herder's assumption of the equality of peoples. Latvian poets and writers expanded the abilities of written Latvian to prove the language was more than a peasant tongue. Early innovative works such as Andrejs Pumpurs's *Lāčplēsis* (Bearslayer; published in 1888) were conscious constructions of the missing elements in the Latvian cultural pantheon. Nineteenth-century nationalists looked to premodern epics as bellwethers of national identity and character. The neighboring Finns and Estonians had recently published national epics of their own, and Pumpurs felt compelled to follow. Whether Pumpurs's epic was more a product of his own fantasy than grounded in Latvian folklore, whether it was of questionable artistic merit—these questions were irrelevant; Latvians had an epic poem.

Far more successful in artistic terms was the first full-length Latvian novel, *Mērnieku laiki* (The Time of the Surveyors), written by the Kaudzītis brothers in 1879. Although the first of its kind, the novel succeeded in becoming an instant masterpiece and towered over the genre for years to come. In political terms, the novel follows two parishes, showing all the reactions and machinations associated with the surveying of peasant land. The character of Švauksts, a caricature of a Latvian attempting to be German, is often discussed as a signpost of how far Latvian identity and self-awareness had developed in a few decades. The novel, however, represents far more than just this. All sorts of Latvians are brilliantly depicted as flawed, but ultimately sympathetic, characters involved in events of local yet momentous importance. They are at times powerless, but they also manipulate and maneuver as much as possible. Along with the depiction of the many minor characters, there is a tale of love and tragedy, which employs many of the more melodramatic plot twists of nineteenth-century novels. The real artistry in the novel, however, remains the descriptions of individuals and their interactions. The novel's descriptions are so timeless that its many characters are almost timeless tropes for Latvian society.

Mērnieku laiki's setting, in the countryside, is equally important for the development of Latvian culture. At the moment that Latvian ethnic identity crystallized and the first generation of cultural nationalists strove to prove the worth of the Latvian people, the overwhelming majority of the people were peasant. Those of the Baltic German elite who resisted the fundamental conviction of Latvian nationalists that they were representatives of a true people, a nation and not a social standing, pejoratively equated "peasantness" and "Latvianness." In reaction, the first generation of cultural

nationalists reclaimed peasantness and made it the cornerstone of Latvian identity. Authors wrote Latvian stories in their "natural" setting, the countryside and the peasant farm.

Painters followed a similar path. Already in the eighteenth century and into the nineteenth century, painters who were ethnically Latvian became accomplished in the Baltic Provinces and in the Russian Empire. Painters such as the nineteenth-century artists Johann Egink and Robert Konstantin Schwede excelled at the classical style; their subjects were primarily classical themes, court portraits, and altars. By the middle of the nineteenth century, Latvian painters influenced by the European turn toward romanticism and by the Young Latvians painted Latvian peasants as subject matter. Karl Huhn serves as a good example of the change in subject matter and style in one career. Huhn was classically trained in St. Petersburg and lived in Paris. Much of his career and artistic production fits into the accepted themes of the Russian and French art establishments. While in Paris, for example, Huhn planned to paint a great historical canvas, *On The Eve of St. Bartholomew's Night*. Ultimately, he was appointed professor of Historical Painting at the academy in St. Petersburg. Among his works in a romantic-realist style, however, were also paintings and sketches of Latvian peasants, Midsummer Eve celebrations, and landscapes of Latvia, all of which anticipated the development of a "Latvian art" in the second half of the nineteenth century.

The ideas of the Young Latvian movement took organizational form in the visual arts with the founding of Rūķis (Gnome), the first association of Latvian student artists in St. Petersburg in the 1890s. Artists such as founding member Ādams Alksnis developed national romanticism in Latvian art, drawing extensively from the imagined pagan past of the Baltic and from contemporary Latvian peasants' life. These two themes emerged as the dominant foundations of much of Latvian cultural development. The most successful and most talented of the artists that emerged from this movement were Jānis Rozentāls and Vilhelms Purvītis. Rozentāls's two paintings, *From the Church* (*No baznīcas*) and *From the Cemetery* (*No kapsētas*), became icons of early Latvian art. Both take rural Latvia as their subject matter and present Latvians in a predominantly romantic-realistic style. Much of the pieces' sophistication lies in the careful attention to the differentiation among Latvian peasants, each treated as a distinctive individual. As a visual snapshot of Latvian rural life in the second half of the nineteenth century, these works by Rozentāls are the visual equivalents of the Kaudzītis brothers' novel. Vilhelms Purvītis, on the other hand, was predominantly a landscape painter who introduced impressionism to Latvian art. Purvītis was internationally known before World War I in the Russian art world, but the majority of his landscapes were of the Latvian countryside. After Latvia's independence, Purvītis presided over the formal side of Latvian art (as rector of the Academy of Art and as the commissioner general of Latvian exhibits abroad).

Cultural development in the second half of the nineteenth century rediscovered the Latvian past, concurrent with literary and artistic developments centered on the rural

Midsummer Eve: Līgo svētki

The most traditional, popular, and ancient festival in Latvia is Midsummer Eve (Līgo svētki, or Jāņi), marking the summer solstice. The festival's roots lie in the pagan past, and the day is one of the solar calendar turning points. Other festivals marked other solstices and equinoxes, and they are still observed, but Midsummer Eve is the most universally celebrated and is now recognized as a national holiday, celebrated on June 23. In preparation for the festival, women weave crowns from wildflowers and men, particularly those named Jānis, or John, wear crowns of oak leaves. Adorned with these garlands people roam from house to house singing traditional midsummer folk songs. The house in return provides cheese specifically made for the event (Jāņu siers) and beer. After eating, drinking, and singing, the members of the household join the procession, which ultimately arrives at a hilltop or clearing decorated with a tall signal fire and bonfire. Singing, eating, drinking, and traditional games continue all night. Young couples wander off into the woods looking for the "fern blossoms" that will only show themselves to true love. Tradition and ritual claim a host of bad omens (from sleeping all summer to poor harvests) will befall those that sleep during midsummer night. As dawn approaches and the bonfire dies down, celebrants jump over the fire for good fortune.

The history of these celebrations is complex. The celebration remained remarkably tenacious in the face of frequent attempts by Christian clergy to curtail it due to its pagan connections and profligate celebrations. By the middle of the nineteenth century, the festival gained new credibility with Latvian nationalism's glorification of the rural and the traditional. Soviet rule initially tried to ban the event (substituting a more class-conscious fishermen's festival) and monitored its tenacity with alarm. Through the 1950s and 1960s, the festival met with alternating official proscription, acceptance, proscription, and ultimate toleration. Newly independent Latvia has seen a resurgence in the festival in many different shapes—from extreme ethnographic replications of tradition to large, commercialized outdoor festivals. The Soviet contribution to the ritual and tradition around the festival comes from an unlikely source, film. The 1981 film *Limousine in the color of St. John's Night* (*Limuzīns Jāņu nakts krāsā*) has become a modern classic, and the showing of the film on television in June is similar to the showing of *It's a Wonderful Life* near Christmas in the United States. In the film, an old woman wins a car and long lost family members plot, scheme, and maneuver to inherit it. Although not specifically about Midsummer Eve, parts of the film take place during the celebrations, and if Midsummer Eve is at heart a celebration of the core of Latvian identity, the film captures archetypes of Latvians themselves.

nature of Latvian identity (and fitting these explorations into larger European trends and patterns). Again, Baltic Germans had pioneered much of this work in the early nineteenth century, but the scope of collecting expanded considerably. Peasant proverbs, customs, stories, riddles, tales, and costumes were all collected and recorded (sometimes with creative artistic license).

The history of Latvian folk costumes, for example, illustrates the changing relationship to the peasant past. At mid-century, many Latvians abandoned traditional dress to appear more German, while the Baltic German elite tried to use sumptuary pressures to keep them in peasant dress. Less than a half century later, peasant dress was considered a noble folk costume.

Collecting folk songs *(dainas)*, however, became the supreme symbol of the Latvian nationalists' new awareness of their elusive past. Krišjānis Barons became the ultimate symbol of the move to collect the dainas. Barons began his career as an early activist among the Young Latvians and a contributor to the *Petersburg Newspaper*. Barons, however, made the collection and publication of the dainas his life's work. He oversaw the work of many who scoured the countryside and collated the growing collection into a six-volume, eight-book tome *(Latvju dainas)*. Barons organized the collection around life events (birth, work, death) and collected 217,966 songs (plus variations). The work has continued to this day and now numbers more than one million songs (not including variations). The universal acclaim given Barons among Latvians suggests how central the idea of identity and its nature had become by his death in the first years of the independent state (a very different relationship to the past than at Barons's birth).

By 1900, a backlash to the efforts of the Young Latvians on the political scene led to the growing strength of the New Current and the introduction of socialist thought. Cultural developments showed a similar change in tone, but in many ways artistic change was less pronounced, and subject matter remained similar. The arrival of socialism, primarily through the periodical *Daily Pages,* introduced the idea of class struggle as central to history. Furthermore, most socialists believed that art should play an instructional role and used it to further their cause. Jānis Pliekšāns and his wife Elza Rozenberga (better known by their pseudonyms Rainis and Aspazija) were important political activists in this movement (and were forced into exile for their political activities), but became more widely known (and remembered) for literary work. Their drama became immediately acclaimed, but their socialist art continued to have a rural setting and to reflect Latvia's past. Self-sacrifice and an emphasis on women's rights were far more prevalent themes than industrial workers and valiant strikes. One of Rainis's masterpieces, *Fire and Night* (*Uguns un Nakts*), is a theatrical version of the Lāčplēsis epic partially created by Pumpurs a generation earlier. Rainis's artistic skill towers over that of Pumpurs, and he gives much more attention to a female witch who ultimately sides with Lāčplēsis; the drama and character development are far more sophisticated. Rainis's skill is in the ambiguity of the struggle; nationalists could understand the play as national commentary, while workers could see the play as a symbol of class struggle.

Other turn-of-the-century authors remained close to the themes of rural Latvian identity. Even the first long urban novel (appropriately titled *Riga* by Augusts Deglavs) revolved around rural Latvians moving to the city. If in *Mērnieku laiki* the Latvian attempting to be German is a buffoon with mangled German language and manners, by the time of *Riga*, such characters have managed to transform themselves into successful Germans, while others refuse to follow this path, but struggle for Latvian rights.

An essentially urban art did not emerge until after World War I. Other authors, from Rudolfs Blaumanis to the poet Eduārds Veidenbaums, expanded Latvian literary output in many directions (melodramatic tragedies were particularly popular), often with hints of new European trends such as Darwinism, Marxism, and realism, but the rural countryside remained the dominant setting for literature. In the visual arts, a new generation of bohemian artists made a contribution, though rather by changing the image of the artist in Latvian society than by introducing urban art and so making real innovations in their artwork.

The shock and transformation of World War I shook the settled traditions of Latvian cultural development as fundamentally as it did European art generally. Jāzeps Grosvalds and Jēkabs Kazaks both drew artistic inspiration from the war itself. They painted powerful expressionist paintings of soldiers (often wounded) and refugees. After the war and the emergence of an independent Republic of Latvia, the Latvian Academy of Art was founded (along with a plethora of artists' societies and salons). Reflecting the wide array of political beliefs, Latvian cultural development quickly took many new directions. The most innovative was the advent of modernism in Latvia, pioneered by the Skulme family (Oto Skulme, Marta Liepiņa-Skulme, Niklāvs Strunke, and Romans Suta). All of these artists (and many of their contemporaries) borrowed heavily from cubism. Strunke and Suta were particularly successful in expanding the mediums of their work to include porcelains, furniture, and glass. Striking and successful modernist influences could also be seen in graphic design, stage design, and sculpture.

The avant-garde in the arts did not become the mainstream of cultural development, but was a vibrant force that rapidly assimilated the latest art movements in Western Europe (with about a ten- to fifteen-year lag) while adding unique Latvian elements. Kārlis Padegs, a promising and extravagant young artist, showed considerable potential as a stylistic urban painter. Padegs's sketches are reminiscent of the work of Otto Dix or George Groz, but with less of their gruesomeness and more flair and style. Padegs's *Madonna with Machine-Gun (Madonna ar ložmetēju)* is a brilliant synthesis of art styles and local Baltic influences. Padegs, like several other promising interwar artists, died young.

Aleksandrs Čaks provided a similar literary phenomenon. Čaks is one of the originators of an almost purely urban Latvian literature. His subjects, like those of Padegs, were often prostitutes, criminals, and the street poor (Marijas Street, often the central location in Čaks's work, was later partially renamed Čaks Street); another kind of urban novel was created by Pāvils Rozītis in his *Ceplis* (Brick-kiln), which brilliantly lambasted the hectic and often corrupt politics and business of a newly independent Latvia. These many strands of modernism went too far for some Latvian artists, and not far enough for others.

As modernism took root among many of independent Latvia's artists, a renewed embrace of traditionalism gained ground more generally. These cultural forms of traditionalism returned to the well-worn themes of rural Latvian identity and the semimythic pagan past. Jānis Jaunsudrabiņš, a successful artist and author, continued his childhood memoirs (begun with *Baltā grāmata* [The White Book], just prior to the war) with *Zaļā grāmata* (The Green Book). These books captured the naive wonder of a child growing up in the countryside and became instant Latvian classics. Jaunsudrabiņš, although describing the world through the eyes of a child, clearly depicted the poverty and hardship in his childhood as well as youthful pranks and daily life.

Whereas the focus of Jaunsudrabiņš on the countryside was complex and multifaceted, a more simplistic, glorifying art developed in the late 1920s and into the 1930s. These artists, who could be lumped together as neotraditional stylists, turned increasingly to Latvia's mythological past as well as the more well-worn idylls of the countryside. Artists such as Ansis Cīrulis, Jēkabs Bīne, and Hilda Vīka painted Latvian gods and goddesses and extremely romanticized and stylized scenes of ancient Latvian traditions. Their work was increasingly adopted as the unofficial art of the nationalist, conservative authoritarian regime of Kārlis Ulmanis. The extreme extension of worshipping stylized images of the past as an expression of Latvian identity was re-creating an "authentic" pagan religion. Many of these artists participated in the pagan revival *(Dievturība)* invented by Ernests Brastiņš and others. The foundation of this movement was a return to a bygone era and, by extension, a refutation of the present and the social, political, and economic forces of the twentieth century.

Even as art and culture in independent Latvia tended to become more narrowly defined around the standard concepts of rural identity and a glorious pagan past, a different alternative embraced the present and the future. Latvian artists who embraced the socialist revolution in Russia and sided with the Bolsheviks continued the experiment of modern art in Soviet Russia in the experimental 1920s.

Many artists created revolutionary people's art (with at best a lukewarm reception from the people) for the short-lived Soviet Republic of Latvia in 1919. As this republic was defeated, many Latvian artists retreated to Moscow and Leningrad (the renamed St. Petersburg) to participate in the ferment of the cultural world of 1920s Soviet Russia. Artists such as Aleksandrs Drēviņš participated in constructivism and suprematism, forms of abstract art, but the most innovative cultural developments came in new media. Gustavs Klucis captured the aspirations of the Soviet elite to use technology to build a new industrial future in his innovative development of photo montage. By the late 1920s, Klucis was using his talent and medium to praise Stalin, but ultimately this did not save him from the purges of the 1930s. Interestingly, his final works of art abandoned the vibrant industrial images of progress in his early photo montage and were haunting landscapes of isolation done in oils and watercolours. Klucis was executed in 1938.

Sergei Eisenstein survived Stalin's purges of the late 1930s, but even had he not, he had already cemented his place in the history of filmmaking. His *Battleship Potemkin* is regularly picked as one of the ten most important films in film history; it uses important innovations such as montage and careful editing. Like Klucis, Eisenstein's work also embodies the belief that artistic value and accomplishment can coexist with propaganda. Eisenstein, however, also drew attention to one of the dominant theses in the cultural development of Latvia. Eisenstein was the son of the successful Baltic German architect who designed many of Riga's *Jugendstil* treasures, and not ethnically Latvian. The themes of his artwork do not suggest anything instrinsically connected to Latvia, yet he often referred to himself as a "boy from Riga."

Those who try to define Latvia's cultural tradition are equally challenged by artists such as Phillipe Halsmann, the renowned Jewish surrealist photographer, and Mark Rothko, known as an American abstract expressionist. Halsmann was born and lived in Riga, while Rothko, born in Daugavpils, emigrated to the United States while still a child. (Museums are equally unsure how to categorize Rothko, variously describing his place of birth as Russia or Latvia.) These artists and many others do not fit neatly into the standard Latvian cultural world, and their works seem far removed from Latvian influences (although Rothko did paint some of his tricolor canvases with the colors of Latvia's flag). Latvians still struggle with whether to accept and incorporate these artists into their long cultural tradition or to ignore them altogether. The debate is likely to continue and intensify with Latvia's accession to the European Union in 2004.

With the end of Latvia's independence in World War II, most of Latvia's artistic and cultural production became tied to the propaganda of the two combatants. With the end of war, Latvia's cultural development again underwent a schism. Many Latvians (and most of the elite of the interwar years) fled westward and eventually settled in countries such as the United States, Canada, Australia, and the United Kingdom. Dozens of artists and authors could be found among this wave of refugees, and many other emigrants attempted to make sense of this great upheaval through artistic and cultural expression.

Émigré Latvian art focused almost entirely on independence lost and the horror of Soviet rule. Promising young painters such as Jānis Tīdemanis and Jānis Kalmīte, or the graphic artist Sigismunds Vidbergs, essentially remained artistically tied to a sentimental nostalgia. As more and more time progressed, émigré artists either remained in the cultural milieu of the 1930s or distanced themselves from specifically Latvian motifs. By the 1970s and 1980s, the most gifted and accomplished Latvian cultural figures in the West were ethnically Latvian, but artistically within the art worlds of their countries of residence. Artists such as the painter Vija Celmins and the pianist Arturs Ozoliņš are excellent examples of this phenomenon. Incorporating their achievement into Latvia's cultural tradition after independence was restored has been as challenging as placing the production of non-Latvians in Latvia.

If Latvian émigré artists struggled to find new and innovative approaches to their native culture from exile, artists suffered more severely in Soviet-occupied Latvia due to state control of art. Artists were organized into "creative organizations," and the state determined remuneraton, production, and theme. Party circulars defined what could and could not be depicted, and all art was to serve the state as an instructional medium for Soviet citizens. Socialist realism became the dominant style (and the only permitted style in the 1940s and through much of the 1950s). Some interwar artists accepted the new dictates and produced work acceptable to the new state. Aleksandrs Čaks, for example, wrote paeans to Stalin and received high Soviet distinction (criticism of some of his later works and the burden of working in narrow constraints may have contributed to his death by alcoholism). The popular interwar novelist, Vilis Lācis (whose wildly successful novel, *Zvējnieka dēls* [Fisherman's Son], became Latvia's first full-length sound film in 1939), moved from the cultural world to become Soviet Latvia's first commissar of the interior and eventually first secretary. Painters such as Francisks Varslavāns turned from painting sorrowful countrysides and their inhabitants in the 1930s to triumphant kolkhoz farmers at the end of his life.

Not only were art and culture minutely managed and controlled by the Communist Party, but considerable efforts were made to destroy the cultural heritage of the past. Books were banned, artists were deported, churches were demolished or converted to other uses, and even traditional festivities such as the Midsummer Eve were outlawed. A cultural revival did not begin until after the death of Josef Stalin in 1953.

By the late 1950s, Nikita Khrushchev's thaw in the Soviet Union also affected the cultural production that was tolerated in Latvia. Ojārs Vācietis, a successful poet, pushed for art beyond purely propaganda purposes, and many Latvian classics from the nineteenth century and even the interwar years were rehabilitated. Soviet Latvian cinema, for example, produced adaptations of tsarist-era works by Rūdolfs Blaumanis, although these adaptations did mean recasting the originals in light of class conflict themes. By the 1970s, films based on the work of popular interwar writers, such as Pāvils Rozītis's *Ceplis,* depicted an independent Latvia (mostly in a negative light, but not entirely).

Essentially, non-propaganda art that did not criticize the regime or embrace Western values was tolerated (though often unofficially punished with limited editions). Poets such as Imants Ziedonis returned to the cultural tradition of examining Latvians' rural cultural roots. The painter Auseklis Bauškenieks painted critiques of social problems such as alcoholism, giving his work an irreverent veneer of socialist realist style. Maija Tabaka excelled at psychologically loaded portaits and a style that departed from the dogma of socialist realism. By the end of the 1960s and into the early 1970s, an apolitical hippie community in Rīga was tolerated, though kept under intense surveillance.

By the mid-1970s, the cultural world of Soviet Latvia was in crisis, but the crisis was not of the artists' doing. Communist authorities struggled with balancing lavish rewards for artists close to the regime and its prescriptions for culture and appropriate punishments for artists who pushed the envelope of what was tolerated. The authorities had to contend with the ambiguous Bolshevik mantra that culture should be national in form, but socialist in content. The song festivals that had been such an important part of Latvia's culture ever since the national awakening of the nineteenth century, as a result,

became massive state productions; they still included a celebration of the rural component of Latvian identity, but they also included socialist components and elements that demonstrated the brotherhood of Soviet nations. A defining socialist realist style receded, but not compeletely, and its replacement was ambiguous. As a result, authorities defining the cultural world would on occasion crack down on national or Western manifestations, but just as frequently tolerated them.

Soviet popular music serves as a particularly good example of this ambiguity. On the one hand, Soviet authorities restricted rock and roll and worried about its effect on Soviet youth; on the other hand, they failed to keep Western recordings from seeping into the USSR and Latvian bands from experimenting with the genre. Not surprisingly, when the currents of political reform and change began in the mid to late 1980s, the artists and cultural figures who had pushed the limits of the system played an early, central part in organizing the mass movements against Soviet rule. The poet Jānis Peters, for example, steered the Writers' Union into the forefront of the Latvian Popular Front. Popular cultural figures such as Imants Ziedonis and the composer Raimonds Pauls lent their cultural and artistic authority to the cause of an independent Latvia.

Independent Latvia's cultural world since 1991 has struggled in two different ways, one material and one more

Song Festivals

Latvia's first song festival occurred in Riga in 1873 and was organized to a large degree by the Riga Latvian Society (Rīgas latviešu biedrība) as a crowning jewel in the cultural work of the Young Latvian generation of activists. Earlier small festivals occurred in Dikļi in 1864 and Dobele in 1870. Initially the festival brought together forty-five choirs and one orchestra from across Latvia and contributed considerably to the standardization of Latvian folk songs and their arrangement in choral patterns as opposed to their initial call and response and droning song style. The second festival in Jelgava, largely organized and financed by Jānis Čakste, was the only song festival to take place outside of Riga. By the 1920s and 1930s, the song festivals, held every four years, found a home in the Esplanāde park near the Orthodox Cathedral in Riga. Construction began on Victory Square (Uzvaras laukums), which would have hosted the song festival and many other government parades, but the work was interrupted by war and occupation.

During the period of Soviet occupation, the song festivals continued as an element of Soviet nationality policy that stipulated that Soviet culture was national in form, but socialist in content. Songs of labor (and songs in Russian), together with visiting troupes from other Soviet republics, became standards of the mass Soviet song festivals. In the West, émigré communities continued to hold their own song festivals at different intervals from 1946 to the present. The 1990 song festival in Riga took on an air of reconciliation and Latvian unity in the struggle against Soviet rule. This song festival included the mass participation of choirs and dance troupes from the West.

Over the years, the Song Festival has expanded to include folk dancing—first in 1948—(with a standardizing influence and rise of strict choreography as with the transformation of folk singing to choral music), marching bands, and theater productions. The twin highlights of the festival are the parade of participants (where tens of thousands march through the streets of Riga to the cheers of hundreds of thousands) and the final concert, which seems to unite the nation in song. The Song Festivals are almost universally regarded as the unifying cultural symbol of the Latvian nation and underline the dominant themes of rural roots, tradition, and a pagan past. The XXIII Song Festival and XII Dance Festival took place in Riga at the beginning of July 2003.

abstract. The overriding concern in the arts following independence was the sudden loss of considerable state subsidies. The Soviet regime may have dictated subject matter and rewarded sycophantism over talent, but the art world was relatively lavishly supported. The tight budgetary constraints of the 1990s led to the loss of most of these subsidies. Slowly, cultural institutions such as the Opera House and the major drama theaters have raised a mix of private and public support, but the first years were exceedingly difficult. The public is ambivalent about the loss of state sponsorship of the arts. On the one hand, the public is shocked to learn of fundamental disrepair of facilities or the depths of poverty that once adored cultural figures have sunk to, but on the other hand, there is a public sense that state-sponsored art is unresponsive art. Latvia's citizenry has yet to reach a consensus on the arts and the public purse. The more abstract dilemma for most Latvians concerns what art to support and why.

The cultural world of independent Latvia at the turn of a new millennium wrestles with the same great, general questions about the nature of Latvian art and the status of art in Latvia that is not obviously a part of Latvian cultural tradition. The state does continue to support some cultural pursuits, and with relatively better economic performance in the late 1990s, it was more generous in that support. What remains problematic is the question of what culture the state should support. The song festivals are nearly universally recognized as a cornerstone of the Latvian cultural world and so deserving of public assistance. Whether or not a Russian-language cultural festival in Daugavpils is equally deserving is still very contentious. This argument is a return to the question of the legitimacy of the art of Baltic Germans and Jews in the 1920s and 1930s.

Additionally, the question has been raised whether Latvian artists who push the creative limits and merge with larger, international postmodern art currents are producing Latvian art. As late as 1995, professors of the Latvian Art Academy criticized a diploma piece that looked somewhat Latin American as not being essentially Latvian. Similarly the public was shocked in the same year to see a young artist, Miķelis Fišers, show homoerotic artwork involving human beings and extraterrestrial aliens. Both of these examples seem far from the traditional consensus that Latvian identity is rural and that true Latvian culture represents this element. The recording company Upe has successfully (commercially and artistically) returned to folk roots in a series of recordings of traditional folk songs. The series' cultural innovation is an attempt to remove the nineteenth-century Latvian elite's moral patina from earthy peasant songs and present "more authentic" variations. Of course a twenty-first century's nostalgic recreation of this past is equally flawed, but still it presents a significant reinterpretation of Latvian cultural mainstays. The ongoing question is how often the old themes can be reexamined, and whether cultural products that go beyond the old themes will be accepted as part of the new Latvia's cultural heritage. Layered over these age-old debates is a new struggle with the increasing commercialization of the arts, making profit the sole measure of success and value.

Folk musicians performing. Leva Pakalnina of Riga, wearing an outfit typical of Western Latvia, performs at the Open-Air Ethnographic Museum. The museum is a collection of several preserved wooden buildings where folklorists and craftspeople gather to recreate Latvian traditions. (Steve Raymer/Corbis)

ECONOMIC DEVELOPMENT

The economic transformations of Latvia over the centuries have been as stunning as Latvia's political history has been tumultuous. Early Latvians practiced simple agriculture, supplemented by fishing, hunting, foraging, and beekeeping. Long-distance trade has always crossed through Latvia (the Dauagava River, for example, is part of the great river system that connected the Scandinavian world with the Mediterannean through the Black Sea), and although the earliest inhabitants of Latvia played some part in this trade, they do not seem to have traveled great distances or built wealth and power principally on trade. The Teutonic conquest of the eastern Baltic was economically motivated by the desire to control trade, just as morally it was fueled by religious crusade. The German conquerors initially did little to alter the foundations of local economies, but they did tax goods and services from the conquered. More importantly, they built the first true towns and cities and introduced urban life into Latvia.

For centuries, the towns and cities of Latvia were small and supplied by local estates. The mercantile activity of these towns continued the previous pattern of servicing the long-distance trade (now of Europe, particularly Northern Europe, with the Russian interior). As Baltic German lords acquired serfs, some directed agricultural production for trade. Latvia in the Middle Ages provided timber for ship building (paticularly masts), linen for ships' sails, and wheat. Many lords, however, neglected their estates to a considerable degree, and much of Latvian agriculture was relatively primitive and mostly concerned with subsistence. Agricultural innovations such as the use of the three-field system and the introduction of new crops did not take hold in Latvia until relatively late, compared to European norms. Towns continued to be small, with limited numbers of artisans and craftsmen (often organized on guild lines) and had few cosmopolitan features. Riga was the exception.

In the eighteenth and particularly the nineteenth centuries, the economy began to transform radically (coterminous with equally radical political and demographic transformations). A variety of economic reasons pushed lords to demand more from their serfs (in service and in kind). Some lords actively improved the agriculture of their estates, introduced innovations, and produced specifically for the market. As markets grew, town populations increased, and money use grew. All of these developments further reinforced each other. Still, structural obstacles limited this economic transformation until emancipation and the later reforms that gave peasants free mobility and the right to own land also created hundreds of thousands of independent economic actors. If at the beginning of the nineteenth century some of these changes could be anticipated, by the 1890s, Latvia's rural economy was transformed into a differentiated countryside of aristocratic estates, Latvian smallholders, sharecroppers, landless agriculture laborers, and more and more members of professions (from school teachers to coopers and porters). The industrialization that began in the last decade and a half of the nineteenth century completely altered the nature of Latvia's economy.

Latvia's industrialization was part and parcel of the industrialization of imperial Russia. By the 1880s, a lack of industrial power clearly weakened Russia relative to the United Kingdom, Germany, France, and even Austria-Hungary. Emancipation and the other "Great Reforms" of the 1860s were an important first step, but without a powerful entrepreneurial class the state had to act to spur initial industrialization. Sergei Witte, a minister of finance and later prime minister for Tsar Nicholas II, was most associated with the rapid, state-sponsored industrialization of the last decades of the nineteenth century and the first of the twentieth. Witte's plan revolved around railroad construction paid for with state subsidies, foreign investment, and an increase in the sale of agricultural goods on the world market. Latvia played a natural part in almost every facet of this plan.

Wealthy Baltic German merchants had connections to Western European finance, and the port of Riga (and later Liepāja and Ventspils) became one of Russia's most important import-export harbors (rivalling Odessa). Likewise, some of the earliest railroads linked Riga to Moscow and St. Petersburg and eventually Warsaw. As Witte had hoped, railroad construction served as a catalyst for an increasingly complex and differentiated industrial economy. Riga moved quickly from being an important port city to being one of the empire's most important industrial centers with textile mills, rail wagon manufactures, a developing chemicals industry, and many secondary industries as well (from breweries to meat processing). Peasants flooded into the city for the job opportunities this industrial boom offered, and city populations mushroomed. Eventually, smaller towns such as Liepāja, Ventspils, Jelgava, Sloka, and Limbāži all developed industrial characteristics.

The relative small size of the Baltic Provinces meant that improvements in transportation infrastructure had a quick and profound effect on the countryside. The many economic and demographic changes determined the changing politics and culture of the Baltic Provinces as well. On the eve of World War I, Riga was a booming, industrial city with several hundred thousand workers in a great many industries. Industrial wealth made possible a rapid modernization of the city's services, from hospitals to street lights and from trolleys to telephones and telegraphs. Industrial Latvia, however, was a part of the industrialization of the Russian Empire. Raw materials (and workers) came to Riga from the Russian interior and manufactured goods moved on to Europe or into the empire itself. This degree of industrialization was far more than was needed to serve the Baltic Provinces alone. This fact, coupled with the devastation of World War I, radically diminished the industrial character of the independent Republic of Latvia in the interwar years.

World War I brought an almost immediate cessation of trade from Riga and Latvia's other ports. Port traffic did not resume until 1919 and even later. International merchant traffic became a thing of the prewar past. The bulk of Latvia's industrial equipment (and much of its workforce as well) was evacuated to the interior of Russia in the summer of 1915; essentially none of it returned. Even its return, however, could not have resuscitated Latvia's industrial sector. Industrialization had come as a part of imperial Russia's industrialization; without access to the abundant raw materials (including energy supplies) of Russia and capital on a huge scale, Latvia's industrial sector could not be rebuilt. The war more generally consumed Latvia's national wealth, and reconstruction demanded enormous expenditures. More damaging still was the loss of hundreds of thousands of lives from the most economically productive sectors of the economy (men between the ages of twenty and forty-five). The magnitude of World War I, coupled with the emergence of Latvia as an independent state, guaranteed fundamental economic transformations.

Latvia again became a predominantly agricultural country. Even at the outbreak of war, the majority of Latvia's inhabitants lived in the countryside, and most were occupied with agriculture. Still, from 1880 to 1914 Latvia had witnessed fundamental urbanization and industrialization. The war reversed this trend, and the new state's crowning economic policy, agrarian reform, reinforced a return to agriculture. Land hunger among Latvia's landless agricultural workers provoked unrest, such as the Revolution of 1905, and provided the migrants to the growing towns and cities. The sentiment of land hunger was still strong in 1920, and Latvia's Constituent Assembly responded by expropriating land from the Baltic German aristocracy and distributing it to the landless. Land reform created tens of thousands of smallholders with an average of roughly twenty hectares of land. These farmers (and farmers who already owned land) became the backbone of the interwar Latvian economy.

The relative small size of their holdings pushed most of these farmers into dairy and pork production (wheat production dropped considerably). Latvia's interwar prosperity (and occasional sluggishness) was a result of international demand for bacon, butter, and flax (the products that came to signify Latvia). Although agricultual efficiency may have suffered as a result of the division of holdings into many small family farms, the reform did give these farmers a stake in the new state. Land shortages did remain; there was simply not enough land for everyone. Nevertheless, the majority of those who lived in the country did receive land, and they received it as private property.

Cities and towns, chief among them Riga, went through equally profound transformations. They became less important as industrial and mercantile centers; instead they emerged as administrative centers of a new state. Populations as a whole declined, but the percentage of blue-collar workers fell drastically, whereas there was a substantial increase in white-collar fields. Riga was transformed from an important port and industrial center of the Russian Empire to the national capital of a small, independent, primarily agricultural country. The political economy of the newly independent state initially maintained the general investment in agriculture, in the form of credits to the new farmers for construction and later in the form of the needed infrastructure for dairy and pork processing. A Social Democratic government attempted to reestablish industry and trade with the USSR in 1927 and 1928 (in part due to a desire to reinvigorate their core constituency, the industrial workforce), but the policy was short-lived and bore few results. In the second half of the 1930s a new effort to build up the industrial sectors of the economy began as part of a state plan for reducing imports and making the country more self-sufficient. The building of a substantial hydroelectric dam at Ķemeri supplied needed electrical power, but agriculture remained dominant until World War II.

From the very beginning of Soviet occupation in June 1940, the foundations of independent Latvia's economy were dismantled in a manner analagous to the destruction of its statehood. Within a month, the eight hundred largest industrial enterprises were nationalized, and the banking system was quickly merged with the Soviet State Bank. The Lats (Latvia's currency) was taken out of circulation and replaced with the Soviet ruble on a one-for-one exchange (before occupation the exchange rate was one Lats for three rubles). By January 1941, all property exceeding 220 square meters (including apartments and houses) was expropriated, and a further agricultural reform redistributed land into economically unviable 10-hectare plots.

The German army invaded the USSR (in 1941) before more of the Latvian economy could be standardized into the Soviet centrally planned command economy, but German occupation proved just as destructive as Soviet occupation had. The Nazi government had a long-term policy for occupied Latvia that included German colonization, extermination of "ethnically undesirable" Latvians, and assimilation of more Nordic individuals. The immediate policy, however, was driven by the exigencies of war. Roughly 25,000 German officials entered Latvia as administrators (while 35,000 Latvians were deported to the Reich for manual labor) and ruled Latvia with two goals: to establish and maintain complete Nazi control and to appropriate every resource for the war effort. A Latvian Self-Administration was created to aid in the day-to-day operations of administration. After the disastrous year of Soviet occupation, many Latvians hoped the Germans would reverse some of the Soviet economic decrees. Instead, food rationing and the Reichsmark were introduced (at an exchange of ten to one, a step that, combined with the Soviet monetary reform, decimated the real value of most life savings). Any further economic reforms remained on the drawing board for the duration of the war.

With the Soviet victory over the Nazis in 1945, the rapid Sovietization of Latvia's economy and its assimilation into the Soviet Union resumed. The return of Soviet rule economically meant socialist construction through accelerated industrialization and the collectivization of agriculture. The human cost was exorbitant, with more than 43,000 deported from 25 to 28 March 1949 to force farmers to join collective farms. By 1952, more than ninety-eight percent of Latvia's farmers lived and worked on collective farms (kolkhozes) or state farms (sovkhozes).

The plans for rapid industrialization, considering this loss of labor and the loss of life due to war, necessitated the arrival of hundreds of thousands of industrial workers from the Soviet Union at large. The rapid heavy industrialization also relied on the importation of raw materials from other parts of the USSR. Most finished goods were distributed primarily to other Soviet republics. As with tsarist industrialization at the end of the nineteenth century, the Latvian industrial sector (and with collectivization, agriculture as well) became an integral component of the larger Soviet planned economy. Over the next forty years, a constant tug of war developed between union-level ministries and republic ministries for control over economic sectors, but fundamentally Latvia was a cog within the Soviet economy.

As a part of the Soviet economy for more than forty years, Latvia's economic performance mirrored the more general trends of the Soviet Union's five-year plans. After the 1950s, more attention was devoted to light industries and meeting basic consumer demands, but heavy and military industry took precedence. Growth rates according to official statistics (often inflated) were often impressive, and Latvia transformed itself into a modernized, industrial economy. The centrally planned economy, however, was excessively rigid and unresponsive. Resources were routinely misused or exhausted, and by the 1980s these economc infrastructural weaknesses produced general crisis. Massive military expenditures, endemic corruption, and declining productivity across the entire economy generated an economic crisis, which Mikhail Gorbachev hoped to address with perestroika (restructuring), allowing industrial managers to tinker with relying on market forces and other reforms to revive the economy. During the late 1980s, as a result of these reforms, republic-level planning grew in importance. This jurisdictional shift meant little initially, but with the sudden collapse of the Soviet Union and the reemergence of an independent Latvia in 1991, the majority of the commanding heights of Latvia were in the hands of the republic-level Communist Party apparatus.

During this same time period (and into the early 1990s), a shady coalition of organized crime elements (or individuals on the margins of legality) and former Communist Party officials seemed to be dismantling the Latvian economy for their own benefit. Clearly, cases of such corruption, graft, and theft (particularly in the selling of metal scrap) were common, but economic and industrial collapse had other fundamental causes. Independent Latvia lost its subsidized energy and raw materials and lost established markets for its finished goods. Poor quality control, together with lack of marketing and distribution, precluded widespread export to Western countries. Similar economic crises throughout Eastern Europe and the states of the former Soviet Union meant that these old clients could no longer affford Latvian goods. Furthermore, the cost of upgrading equipment seemed prohibitive because Latvia had so little homegrown capital. Independent Latvia started from scratch (often from less than scratch), with little more than a sense that a market economy would produce affluence; how to create that economy was another question. It was a massive undertaking.

Initially, some Western economists advised the Latvian government (still the Supreme Council led by the Godmanis cabinet) to remain in the so-called ruble zone to preserve economic ties. Instead, the Bank of Latvia, led by a relative novice to economic matters, Einārs Repše, opted to reintroduce the currency of interwar Latvia, the Lats. The introduction of the Lats succeeded in cushioning Latvia from the effects of Russian monetary turmoil in the 1990s, and thus the move turned out to be so fortunate that it seemed based on prophetic foreknowledge. The Bank of Latvia guarded the value of the Lats (introduced after a transitionary Latvian ruble) almost religiously, and it has been one of the most stable currencies in Eastern Europe.

The bank's tight control of monetary supply forced Latvia's governments through the different coalitions and

Riga Central Market in 1995. (Courtesy of Aldis Purs)

elections to stay within the parameters of the macroeconomic reforms suggested by the International Monetary Fund (IMF). These reforms have been defined by drastically limiting government (cutting subsidies and deregulating economic activity) and leaving economic development to market forces. The process seems simple on paper, but has involved considerable disruption and compromise. Tight control of monetary supply meant that governments were forced to operate with budgets with little or no deficits. With little economic activity, this meant that "nonessential" ministries (such as the Ministry of Culture, in 1993) were cut. The very low wages of government employees also succeeded in driving many out of government service (and contributed to the rise of corruption as well). As a result, the rate of inflation fell from triple digits in the first half of the 1990s to roughly 13 percent in 1997 and below 5 percent by 1999.

The planned transition to a market economy also required private property and the legal definition of its rights, privileges, and responsibilities. The Soviet economy essentially did not recognize private property (excepting small-scale individual possessions). The distribution of state-controlled property proved as difficult as any other economic reform. Complicating matters was the historical record of nationalization of property following Soviet occupation. The original owners of buildings and land (or their descendants) demanded the return of their property, and the Godmanis government declared its intent to return property to its "rightful" owners. The intent however proved far easier than the act.

Restitution created a myriad of problems, including multiple applicants for the same property, difficulty in obtaining legal documentation, and the challenge of determining the legal status of enterprises built after occupation on several peoples' property. It was not uncommon to have separate ownership of a building and the land underneath it. Working out these problems required considerable time and legal procedure, which tied up judicial procedures and the status of land under question. Furthermore, restitution had adverse economic side effects. The property owner, for example, might be destitute and unable to renovate or improve the property. Likewise, the uncertainty (increased by the Saeima's reluctance to allow foreign ownership of land) about legal rights to property handicapped the emergence of a real estate market and militated against capital improvements unless land claims were guaranteed. The state also privatized collective and state farms and sold state land concurrently. The privatization of large apartment buildings, often in various states of disrepair aproaching the catastrophic, further complicated the creation of private property.

Privatization of industry and economic enterprises (all owned by the state during Soviet occupation) presented similar problems. In some cases restitution was also called for, but more pressing was the politics of privatization. In order to build popular emotional investment in the state, the government decided to issue all citizens privatization certificates, or vouchers. These vouchers would then be used at state auctions of economic concerns as they became quasi joint stock enterprises. The creation of the legal side of the voucher sys-

tem demanded nearly three years, further discouraging long-term economic planning, and the actual process of divestiture was often influenced directly by government. The tortuous path toward privatizing potentially lucrative enterprises, from shipping to communications to port facilities, helped cement the close connection between specific business interests and political parties. Not surprisingly, this close connection in turn reinforced the general public's sense that privatization, intended to give indviduals a share of the state's wealth, had instead been hijacked by a new oligarchy of politicians and their wealthy business supporters.

The low point of economic reform was the bank crisis of 1995. Latvia's largest private bank, with one-fifth of all deposits (and considerable political clout), Banka Baltija, closed its doors. The ensuing crisis, caused by poor banking regulations, interbank loans, dependence on Russian oil capital, and the bank's belief that the currency would be devalued, resulted in a 10 percent drop in Latvia's gross domestic product (GDP) for the year. Many other banks closed, and popular confidence in the financial system and the direction of economic reform was seriously affected. The financial sector, however, regrouped. More stringent international auditing, consolidation around Latvia's five largest private banks, and the incursion of Western banks (primarily Swedish and Norwegian) allowed the Latvian financial system to weather the collapse of the Russian ruble in 1998. Rigas komercbanka, Latvia's fifth-largest private bank, did close its doors as result of heavy involvement with Russia, but was able to restructure and reopen as Pirmābanka in late 1999.

Industry and agriculture in Latvia also gradually reoriented itself during the 1990s, with varying degrees of success. The general problems associated with the collapse of the USSR (loss of cheap resources and markets) initially subsided. In the first half of the 1990s many industrial concerns struggled along, using barter with old suppliers and keeping old networks afloat. Breaking into Western markets seemed too difficult. The Russian crisis of 1998, however, exposed these struggling industries to increased financial pressures. Industries as varied as fish products and pharmaceuticals that continued to export primarily to Russian markets had orders frozen and defaults on debts. Those companies, however, that struggled to reorient their products for domestic consumption or to Central and Western Europe fared better. The most effective individual industries have been those that attracted foreign direct investment and used it to modernize equipment and retrain workers. Biotechnology, computer software, fiberglass, pharmaceuticals, processed foods, wood, and wood products have all shown considerable vitality. The export of wood and wood products is representative of the success in these sectors. Initially, Latvia exported primarily raw timber (considerable forest lands are one of Latvia's few natural resources), but entrepreneurs have reinvested some of these profits to sell finished and treated lumber, to find markets for by-products, and increasingly to sell furniture and other manufactured wood products.

Agriculture has followed a similar pattern. Grain, sugar beets, potatoes, vegetables, milk, eggs, and poultry account for most agricultural production, but the entire sector lacks investment and has difficulty in competing in Western markets (let alone in domestic markets against attractive Western goods). The number of people employed in agriculture has dropped substantially in the last decade. Much of this drop, despite the considerable economic misery for many farmers, is a macroeconomic trend toward Western norms. Immediately after independence, 20 percent of the population worked in agriculture. Modernized, heavily mechanized agriculture, however, can produce more, more profitably, and employ fewer people. By 2000 less than 10 percent of the population worked in agriculture, and the number is likely to decline further.

The transition in industry and agriculture is ongoing, but the shift from east to west is already accomplished. By 1998, the majority of Latvia's exports and imports went to countries of the European Union, with less than 20 percent going or coming from countries of the Commonwealth of Independent States (CIS; a loose territorial designation for much of the former Soviet Union). The continuing importance of Latvia as a transit country for Russian goods, however, influences Latvia's larger trade interests. The port of Ventspils is particularly important in this respect. Ventspils was developed by the Soviet Union for the export of oil and oil products and is the terminal of a long gas pipeline and rail network. Ventspils's mayor, Aivars Lembergs, parlayed the transit of Russian resources into wealth for the city and political importance. "Ventspils interests" has become synonomous with the foreign policy view that believes that guaranteeing the continued transit of Russian oil should be Latvia's economic and political priority. By 2002, the extension of port facilities in Lithuania and the construction of a Russian port, Primorsk, near St. Petersburg cut into Ventspils's monopoly on Russian oil and simultaneously allowed Russian oil companies to demand concessions, control, and ownership of some of the transport network. Although the issue is unresolved, Latvia's economy has diversified enough, and trade has developed sufficiently in other directions (including the construction of the Via Baltica, a road link from Helsinki to Warsaw) that the issue is no longer central or dominant in political discussions or in national economic performance.

Latvia has also modernized much of its transportation and communications infrastructure. During the Soviet era, Latvia had a relatively extensive communications network, and the State Electronics Factory produced many of the telephones and much of the telephone equipment for all of the USSR. The technology, by Western standards, was outmoded, and with independence the state contracted a British-Finnish consortium to modernize the entire system. Initially, the government hoped that the State Electronic Factory would play some role, but it was soon largely abandoned. Newly installed cable and a satellite earth station in Riga have allowed direct international connections for most calls as of 1998. The domestic network is currently under construction and still generates unsatisfied subscribers, who frequently opt out of the ground-based system for Latvia's relatively strong and sophisticated cellular phone network. Similarly, Latvia's Internet usage has grown

considerably in size and sophistication. (Latvia's Internet country code is .lv.)

The transportation network has also received considerable investment (especially in the above mentioned Via Baltica), much of it through Phare (Poland and Hungary Assistance for the Restructuring of the Economy) program of the European Union, but as in all sectors the amount of work to be done is daunting. Rural roads and bridges, for example, continue to need repair and in many places paving; more than half of Latvia's rural roads are unpaved. A similar pattern holds for repair and construction of Latvia's port facilities. The port of Ventspils is a modern, bustling facility, but the smaller Liepāja port to the south still struggles with the legacy of its Soviet submarine base. Riga's port facilities are a prime example of how so much of Latvia's economic reform is still an incomplete process. The import-export facilities are able to handle an increasing amount of trade (the amount of timber exported from facilities north of Riga is staggering), but the passenger port is poorly developed and unable to accommodate many luxury cruise ships. As a result most Baltic tourist crossings to Stockholm or Helsinki use the Tallinn port in Estonia. Municipal and national political interference, difficulties in privatization, and frequent allegations of corruption handicap the port's continued growth.

The same formula also holds for Latvia's airports. Although there are many small rural fields (many with unpaved runways), the Riga International Airport (RIX) is the primary airlink for the country. A combination of state and foreign direct investment has repaved and lengthened the runways to accommodate more and larger passenger jets, and the arrival and departure terminals have been upgraded considerably. The airport still feels small, however, and for a variety of reasons has not developed as a hub for regional travel. An expanded cargo terminal is also clearly needed with the rise in air cargo. A major Latvian airline, Latavio, has gone bankrupt, but Air Baltic (majority-owned by Scandinavian Airlines) has been relatively successful and flies direct flights to many international destinations.

The growth of tourism in Latvia is directly connected to the extension of the transportation network. Tourism began developing in the last few decades of the nineteenth century with trips to the beaches of the Bay of Riga (referred to then as the Strand, but now the city of Jūrmala) and to the town of Sigulda west of Riga (home to a Livonian Order castle and the impressive Gauja River valley). In the 1930s the Latvian government launched a domestic tourism campaign ("Travel your native land" [Apceļo savu dzimto zemi]), but its development was cut short by World War II. Under Soviet occupation, the Riga-Jūrmala became a favored tourist destination for hundreds of thousands of Soviet citizens and a preferred retirement location for many Soviet army officers and party personnel. A considerable tourist industry developed, including spas, hotels, and restaurants.

With the collapse of the USSR, most of these tourists initially stopped travelling to Latvia, and much of the state-run tourist infrastructure was of inferior quality for most Western tourists. Private initiative and foreign investment, however, responded by developing parts of this economic

Cargo ship at port of Riga. (Steve Raymer/Corbis)

sector. The growth of the service sector and the infusion of foreign currency helped cushion the worst of the economic crisis in the middle of the 1990s. A substantial percentage of tourists are vacationing émigrés and others with Baltic ancestory, but Latvia has also succeeded in carving out a niche in the competitive European tourist market. Riga's extensive Jugendstil neighborhoods, medieval churches, and old town, as well as Latvia's beaches, castles, and parks have all developed a vibrant industry with the range of affiliated services (from international hotels to private bed-and-breakfasts). The tourist sector is, however, limited by Latvia's northern climate with its short summers and is unlikely to be a driving force in Latvia's economic development.

An overview of Latvia's economic performance from 1991 into the twenty-first century shows surprising accomplishments. The collapse of the USSR and the transition from a centrally planned command economy to a free market system would have been impossible without crises, depressions, and considerable disruptions. Latvia has had its share of each of these and continues to struggle with great regional disparities and the fact that the standard of living of most people declined through the decade. The macroeconomic indicators, however, show that the transition is over. The economy has restructured around service industries, export, and skill-based industries. Agriculture has declined considerably in impor-

tance, but the outline of a small, specialized agricultural sector is taking shape.

After depression and high inflation in the first half of the 1990s, by the second half these indicators reversed. Inflation is not an immediate concern, government deficits and debts are within the Maastricht criteria for European Union members, and the GDP has begun to surge. By 2000, GDP growth was roughly 5 percent, 6 percent in 2001, and most recently in the first quarter of 2003, a vibrant 8 percent growth. Some economists optimistically forecast 10 percent growth for 2003 as a whole. The most recent upsurge, more importantly, is across all economic sectors. GDP per capita is over $7,000, as economic growth begins to have a real effect across the population. Latvia is still far behind European Union averages, but with continued rapid growth in Latvia, slow growth in the EU, and the addition of EU investment after full membership, Latvia can expect to become European in economic terms within twenty or thirty years. With the exception of the other Baltic states, Estonia and Lithuania, no other former republic of the USSR can claim such an impressive economic performance.

CONTEMPORARY CHALLENGES

The idea of an independent Latvia has been central to Latvians throughout the twentieth century and into the twenty-first, yet there have been fewer than thirty-five years of actual independence during this long century. Instead, occupation or administration within a larger political entity has been the norm throughout the twentieth century. The consequences of decades of foreign rule affect every facet of Latvian government, economy, society, and life. Overcoming these consequences will preoccupy Latvia for a considerable time. Contemporary politics and opinion are such that the debate over citizenship and minority rights is one of these consequences.

Defining citizenship is a litmus test for democratic ideals and a reflection of antecedent circumstances. Latvia was forcibly annexed and occupied by the Soviet Union during World War II. The war was a demographic catastrophe: tens of thousands of ethnic Latvians died, tens of thousands fled, the historic Baltic German community was "repatriated" to Germany, and almost all of the historic Jewish community was murdered in the Holocaust, as well as many Roma (Gypsies). After the war, tens of thousands more ethnic Latvians were deported in the violent effort to establish Soviet order. Concomitantly, tens of thousands of predominantly Russian families moved to a rapidly industrializing Latvia.

Through most of Soviet rule, changes in demography could not be questioned (the exception was by the "national communists" in the 1950s, who failed and paid with their careers). Demographic trends threatened the titular ethnic nation (Latvians) with minority status within the Latvian Soviet Socialist Republic. Mikhail Gorbachev's reforms in the 1980s unleashed popular participation in politics, and the overwhelming majority of ethnic Latvians struggled to reclaim independence; many of the non-Latvians in Latvia also shared these aspirations, although with apprehension about resurgent nationalism and their place in a national Latvia. With independence achieved in 1991, and with citizenship based on the body of citizens of June 1940, more than 700,000 inhabitants of Latvia found themselves disenfranchised. The nature of their rights, path toward citizenship, and very future in an independent Latvia was ambiguous. At the beginning of a new, democratic experiment, the Latvian state and political world was confronted with a fundamental dilemma: how to balance a sense of historical justice for the "Latvian nation" with democracy and human rights for all in Latvia.

Successful democratic politics revolves around consensus building and compromise. From the outset, the political extremes refused to compromise and presented radical options. Latvian nationalist extremists labelled all people who arrived after 1940 as occupiers and hoped that they would leave the state. At first, these extremists even called for deportations, but have since softened their demands, seeking

Giant memorial sculptures stand on the site of a Nazi concentration camp in Salaspils. The Nazis and Latvian collaborators murdered more than 100,000 Jews, prisoners of war, Roma (Gypsies), and opponents of Nazi rule between 1941 and 1944. (Steve Raymer/Corbis)

Table 1: Ethnic Composition of Latvia by Percentage, 1897–2000

	1897	1925	1935	1959	1989	2000
Population	1,929,387	1,845,000	1,905,000	2,079,900	2,666,600	2,375,300
Latvian	68	73.4	77	62	52	57.6
Russian	7.9	12.6	8.8 p	26	34	29.6
German	6.2	3.9	3.3 p	1.6	0.1	0.2
Jewish	7.4	5.2	4.9	1.7	0.9	0.4
Belarusian	4.1	n.a.	1.4	2.9	4.5	4.1
Ukrainian	n.a.	n.a.	0.1	1.4 p	3.5	2.7
Other	4.4	4.9	4.5	4.4	5	5.5

rather to deny citizenship to these people and to create a naturalization process that keeps most of the disenfranchised from Latvian citizenship. Extremists on the other end of the spectrum favor citizenship for all and the official recognition of Latvia as a multiethnic state. Through the middle of the 1990s to the end of the century, Latvia tortuously worked out the politics of a compromise between the interests of the international community, an electorate dominated by ethnic Latvians, and the noncitizens of Latvia.

The 1998 referendum and revised citizenship law has the hallmark of a successful compromise; no group is entirely pleased, but most have accepted it as the basis for citizenship and naturalization. There are still hundreds of thousands of residents of Latvia who do not have citizenship, but the naturalization path is now more clear and accessible. Some people will never assume Latvian citizenship for a variety of reasons (from young men avoiding military service to pensioners unable to learn a new language so late in life, to those apathetic toward the state), but with a long demographic view, the problem will fade progressively year by year. At the beginning of 2004, according to statistics compiled by the Naturalization Board of Latvia, there were still just over 481,000 noncitizens, which accounted for 20 percent of the population. Eventually Latvia will not have a substantial number of noncitizens, but there will always be considerable minority communities. The rights of members of those communities, particularly concerning language, have become and will continue to be the new arena for ethnic politics in Latvia.

Table 2: Ethnic Composition of Latvia and Citizenship by Percentage, 1 January 2002

	Inhabitants	Percentage who are citizens	Percent of population
Latvians	1,363,449	99.7	58.3
Russians	682,145	46	29.1
Belarusians	24,386	26	4
Ukrainians	8,900	14.5	2.6
Poles	39,825	68	2.5
Jews	5,705	59.8	0.4
Total	2,339,928	76.3	100

Although citizenship and language are interrelated, the concerns are different. The nature of reestablishing independence disenfranchised 60 percent of the Russians, 80 percent of the Belarusians, and 96 percent of Ukrainians almost overnight. Since 1998, these predominantly Russian-speakers have known the rules for naturalization. The strict language policy of the country, on the other hand, which mandates the official use of Latvian for all purposes, regulates where and how communities live their daily lives. Most Russians live in Riga (constituting almost 44 percent of the population of Riga), the other large cities, or the eastern province of Latgale. In Daugavpils and Rēzekne, Russians constitute a majority of the cities' populations. In three of the four regions of Latgale (Rēzekne, Daugavpils, and Ludza), Russians account for more than 35 percent of the population. In all of these regions, the current language policy is seen as exclusionary by a considerable portion of the inhabitants.

Daugavpils, for example, has roughly 112,000 inhabitants, 69 percent of whom are citizens, according to government statistics. Nevertheless, Daugavpils is primarily a Russian city, with ethnic Latvians making up less than 16 percent of the population, and less than 45 percent of the population speaks Latvian. This city of Russian citizens of Latvia demands equal legal status for the Russian language. Latvian nationalists fear that such status would be a serious blow to Latvian culture. They argue that Russians have a vibrant Russia that supports and produces Russian media and culture. Latvians, on the other hand, only have Latvia. Although more and more of Latvia's minorities speak Latvian (78 percent of the entire population in 2000, according to the Central Statistical Bureau), ethnic Latvians are adamant in using the state to preserve and guarantee Latvian identity. To Russian-speakers, however, the force of the state and a strict Latvian language law has serious short- and long-term consequences. Daily life is uncomfortable and artificial when most people in a city like Daugavpils are predominantly Russian, but everything from street signs to advertising is primarily (although not exclusively) in Latvian. Their argument is that a predominantly Russian community should have full legal rights for the Russian language. They fear state-orchestrated assimilation as a long-term result of strict language policies.

The ethnic dimension of Latvian politics and concerns about minority rights will not go away. As demographics and naturalization proceed, Latvia will be a state with a clear ethnic Latvian majority (already near 59 percent, it may settle between 60 and 65 percent) and a considerable Russian (currently just under 29 percent of the population) and Russian-speaking minority, according to government figures; all will be voting citizens. Either politics will coalesce around ethnicity, with both Latvians and Russians putting aside internal differences to defend collective, ethnic rights, or ethnic compromise will pave the way for parties based on general socioeconomic demands. This outcome will determine how integrated and whole Latvia's society is, a pressing question for the strength of the state, as well as of the European Union (EU), since Latvia became a full member. Latvian nationalists worry that their control over national issues and ability to support Latvian culture and language will erode. There is an undercurrent in popular opinion that simplifies this dilemma by claiming that after fifty years of struggle against one union with rule from a foreign capital, Latvia should be wary of joining a new union. The EU also worries that many from Latvia's Russian and Russian-speaking populations will migrate to the more prosperous western states of the EU because there is so little integration of their communities into Latvia's society. The EU does not want this for its own reasons, but it would also be a potentially debilitating outcome to Latvia. The challenge, beyond laws and regulations, is creating a state identity that both protects ethnic Latvians and welcomes non-Latvians.

The consolidation of ethnic identity and its application to political nationalism is less than 150 years old in the area of modern Latvia. During that time, however, ethnic composition has changed radically, often, and artificially. Latvia continues to struggle with the balance between Latvian nationalists' dreams of a nation-state and Russians' (and Russian speakers') hope for some firmer recognition of the multiethnic reality of that state. A new, pressing challenge, however, faces all of Latvia's inhabitants: a general demographic crisis. For several decades, the simplest demographic crisis has gripped Latvia; more people die each year than are born. Population is declining at an alarming rate, and the population is aging. In 1989 (the year of the last census of the USSR) there were 2,666,600 people living in the Latvian SSR. Independent Latvia's census took place in 2000, and there were 2,375,000 people, for a net loss of 291,000 people, or 10.9 percent of the entire 1989 population. The urban population has dropped by 13.5 percent and the rural population by 5.1 percent. In Liepāja, Riga, and Jelgava, the urban population has declined even more precipitously (by 22, 16, and 15 percent respectively). Some of the loss is due to emigration, the collapse of the USSR, and the removal of Soviet military bases, but the remaining demographics point to a continuing sharp decline in population.

Latvia's basic demographic breakdown has severe imbalances by age and sex. In figures compiled by the government, the middle of the age pyramid, 15 to 59 year olds, has not changed appreciably, from 61.2 percent of the population in 1989 to 61 percent in 2000. The percentages of young and old, however, have changed dramatically. In 1989 there were just over 463,000 people over 60 years of age, or 17.4 percent of the population. By 2000 the number had

risen to more than 500,000, or twenty-one percent of the population, and this percentage continues to rise. Young people, on the other hand, have seen an equally serious decline, from almost 571,000 in 1989 (21.4 percent of the population) to 424,000 in 2000 (17.9 percent). These stark changes mean that the number of people younger than fifteen has dropped by 26 percent, while the number over sixty has risen by 9 percent.

As with the more general demographic statistics, the aging of Latvia is most evident in its cities. In Liepāja, for example, the number of children has dropped by 36 percent in eleven years. In regions dominated by cities, both trends are clear; in the Riga region the number of children has dropped by more than 20 percent, and the number over 60 has risen by almost 30 percent.

An equally troubling imbalance regards the composition by sex. Women make up 54 percent of the overall population, but the imbalance is far more extreme among older people. Under fifteen years of age, the sex ratio is in favor of males at 1.05 (this seems to be a biological average). Between the ages of fifteen and sixty-five, this ration has sunk to .91 males per female. Over sixty-five years of age, the

Satellite dish at the International Radioastronomy Center in Irbene. (Courtesy of Aldis Purs)

ratio drops to a shocking .48 males per female. Latvia shows crisis numbers across the board of standard demographic indicators. There are roughly eight births per one thousand people, but almost fifteen deaths per one thousand as well. There is a net loss due to migration, and infant mortality rates are relatively high for a modern, industrial state, at over fifteen per thousand. There are more registered abortions per year than births. Latvia's overall rate of population growth is minus 0.81 percent.

The demographic crisis has two fundamental causes. First and foremost, the fertility rate declined throughout the twentieth century. Fewer and fewer children born generation after generation begins to have profound accumulative effects. Secondly, Latvia's population is unhealthy, and health problems are worse for men. Tuberculosis is a serious medical problem, and many of the cases are multi-drug resistant strains of tuberculosis. HIV/AIDS rates are relatively low (1,250 people estimated in 1999), but the widespread rise in prostitution and intravenous drug use could easily turn HIV/AIDS into an epidemic. Perhaps the most serious medical problem, however, is chronic alcoholism. Men particularly die from alcohol-related maladies, and this fact alone accounts for the sharp drop in male life expectancy compared to women (less than sixty-three years versus almost sixty-nine years). Although difficult to quantify, much of the demographic crisis is a reflection of the economic and political turmoil of the past twenty years. Poverty contributes to respiratory diseases, despair to alcoholism and suicide. These demographic crises affect all of Latvia's inhabitants (Russian-speakers slightly disproportionately), and adequately addressing them will be difficult, particularly considering the government's limited resources for health care.

The limited resources earmarked for health care are a result of the general economic collapse of the last years of the Soviet Union and the first years of independence, and of the devotion of Latvia's government to pursuing the "shock therapy" of rapid transformation to a market economy (particularly the strict monetary supply's limitations on government budgets). Shock therapy was famously advocated by the Harvard economist Jeffrey Sachs for postsocialist Poland. A similar "500-day plan" was proposed to the Yeltsin government for radical economic transformation in post-Soviet Russia. Generally speaking, as economists considered the best path for introducing market economics to centrally planned economies, there were two schools of thought. Gradualists feared the social pain that market reform would unleash and hoped to dull its severity by a slow, steady transformation. "Shock therapists," on the other hand, believed that a slow pace of reform would limit reform's effectiveness and prolong social pains. Both groups of economists worried that in the new democracies of Eastern Europe and the former Soviet Union, the social pain caused by transformation (slow or fast) could bring antireform politicians to office who would derail the process. The worst-case scenario, to market reformers, would be a populist politician who played to the lowest common denominators of poverty, misery, and inequities to gain power and then abandoned economic reform.

Belarus (under Alexander Lukashenko) seems close to this scenario, but more generally the electorates of Eastern Europe seem convinced of the merits of economic reform in spite of any immediate difficulties. In this regard, Latvia is no different, and has aggressively followed economic market reform, political liberalization and democratization, and a general reorientation from East to West for more than ten years. Latvia has undergone a fundamental reversal in orientation since 1986, from a component of the USSR to a member of the European Union, as of 2004.

The shift in orientation is often characterized as a return to Europe or the West. It is, however, more than just a return. Latvia was not completely assimilated into a European or Western standard in the 1920s or 1930s, a fact that makes its shift in orientation even more remarkable. The scope of the reorientation is complete, involving everything from politics and military alliances to cultural perceptions and economic policies. As this process of reorientation nears completion, Latvia is faced with many unanswered questions. Does reorientation demand a certain type of treatment of ethic minorities (as well as other minorities)? Does a Western bias or a consumer bias threaten traditional Latvian identity as much as the heavy-handed rule of Moscow? In the new millennium, what is Latvian identity in all of its guises?

These very questions, however, reveal much about what has happened in Latvia. In 1985 Latvia shared with the other republics of the USSR a hostility toward central rule, apprehensions about Russian dominance, and antipathy toward aspects of the Communist Party. With many of the other republics, Latvia shared a desire to not be a part of the USSR. Twenty-first century Latvia's debate about what it means to be European, to be in the EU, to be in NATO, to be a modernized industrial market economy, is shared with most of the other countries of Europe. This fact alone reveals how complete Latvia's transformation has been.

SELECTIVE BIBLIOGRAPHY

Central Election Commission of Latvia. http://web.cvk.lv/pub/?doc_id=28170 (accessed 17 July 2004).

Central Statistical Bureau of Latvia. http://www.csb.lv (accessed 17 July 2004).

Clemens, W. C. *Baltic Independence and Russian Empire.* Basingstoke, UK: Macmillan, 1991.

Dreifelds, Juris. *Latvia in Transition.* Cambridge: Cambridge University Press, 1996.

Duhanovs, M. I. Feldmanis, and A. Stranga. *1939. Latvia and the Year of Fateful Decisions.* Riga: University of Latvia, 1994.

Eksteins, Modris. *Walking since Daybreak: A Story of Eastern Europe, World War II, and the Heart of Our Century.* Toronto: Key Porter Books, 1999.

Ezergailis, Andrievs. *The Holocaust in Latvia: The Missing Center.* Riga: Historical Institute of Latvia, 1996.

———. *The Latvian Impact of the Bolshevik Revolution.* Boulder, CO: East European Monographs, 1983.

————. *The 1917 Revolution in Latvia.* Boulder, CO: East European Monographs, 1974.

Gordon, Frank. *Latvians and Jews between Germany and Russia.* Stockholm: Memento, 1990.

Haberer, Erich E. "Economic Modernization and Nationality in the Russian Baltic Provinces, 1850–1900." *Canadian Review of Studies in Nationalism* 12, no. 1 (1985): 161–175.

Hansen, Birthe, and Bertel Heurlin, eds. *The Baltic States in World Politics.* Richmond, UK: Curzon Press, 1998.

Henriksson, Anders. *The Tsar's Loyal Germans: The Riga German Community: Social Change and the Nationality Question, 1855–1905.* Boulder, CO: East European Monographs, 1983.

Hiden, J. W. *The Baltic States and Weimar Ostpolitik.* Cambridge: Cambridge University Press, 1987.

Hiden, John, ed. *The Baltic and the Outbreak of the Second World War.* Cambridge: Cambridge University Press, 1992.

Hiden, John, and Thomas Lane. *The Baltic Nations and Europe: Estonia, Latvia, and Lithuania in the Twentieth Century.* New York: Longman, 1991.

Kangeris, Karlis. "The Former Soviet Union, Fascism, and the Baltic Question. The Problem of Collaboration and War Criminals in the Baltic Countries." In *Modern Europe after Fascism, 1943–1980,* edited by Stein Ugelvik Larsen. Boulder, CO: Social Science Monographs, 1998.

Kirby, David. *The Baltic World, 1772–1993: Europe's Northern Periphery in an Age of Change.* London: Longman, 1995.

Latvian Institute. http://www.latinst.lv/ (accessed 17 July 2004).

Lieven, Anatol. *The Baltic Revolution: Latvia, Lithuania, Estonia, and the Path to Independence.* New Haven, CT: Yale University Press, 1993.

Loit, Aleksander, and John Hiden, eds. *The Baltic in International Relations between the Two World Wars.* Stockholm: University of Stockholm, 1988.

Misiunas, R., and R. Taagepera. *The Baltic States: Years of Dependence, 1940–1990.* Rev. ed. London: Hurst, 1993.

Muiznieks, N. "Latvia: Origins, Evolution and Triumph." In *Nation and Politics in the Soviet Successor States,* edited by J. Bremer and R. Taras. Cambridge: Cambridge University Press, 1993.

Naturalisation Board of Latvia. http://www.np.gov.lv (accessed 17 July 2004).

Nissinen, Marja. *Latvia's Transition to a Market Economy: Political Determinants of Economic Reform Policy.* London: Macmillan Press, 1999.

Pabriks, A. *From Nationalism to Ethnic Policy: The Latvian Nation in the Present and the Past.* Aarhus, Denmark: University of Aarhus: Department of Political Science, 1996.

Pabriks, Artis, and Aldis Purs. *Latvia: The Challenges of Change.* London: Routledge, 2001.

Page, Stanley W. *The Formation of the Baltic States: A Study of the Effects of Great Power Policies on the Emergence of Lithuania, Latvia, Estonia.* Cambridge: Harvard University Press, 1959; New York: Howard Fertig, 1970.

Plakans, Andrejs. *The Latvians: A Short History.* Stanford: Hoover Institution Press, 1996.

Purs, Aldis. "Creating the State from Above and Below: Local Government in Inter-War Latvia." Ph.D. diss., University of Toronto, 1998.

Rauch, Georg von. *The Baltic States: The Years of Independence, 1917–1940.* Berkeley: University of California Press, 1974.

Saeima. http://www.saeima.lv/index_eng.html (accessed 17 July 2004).

Skujeneeks, M. *Latvija: Zeme un eedzīvotaji.* Riga: Valsts statistikskās pārvaldes izdevums, 1922.

Smith, David J., Artis Pabriks, Aldis Purs, and Thomas Lane. *The Baltic States: Estonia, Latvia and Lithuania.* Routledge, 2002.

Society Integration Fund. http://www.lsif.lv/lv (accessed 17 July 2004).

Suny, Ronald Grigor. *The Revenge of the Past: Nationalism, Revolution and the Collapse of the Soviet Union.* Stanford: Stanford University Press, 1993.

Thaden, Edward C., ed. *Russification in the Baltic Provinces and Finland, 1855–1914.* Princeton: Princeton University Press, 1981.

Zagars, E. *Socialist Transformation in Latvia, 1940–1941.* Riga: Zinatne, 1978.

CHRONOLOGY

9000 B.C.E.	First permanent human settlement in territory of modern Latvia.
2000–1000 B.C.E.	Early Balts arrive in territory of modern Latvia.
100–300 C.E.	Existence of recognizable subpopulations within the Balt peoples.
1000	Kin-based societies (Couronians, Livs, Selonians, Semigallians, and Lettgallians) with strong leaders and hill forts throughout the territory of modern Latvia.
1160s	German merchants and Father Meinhard settle at Ikšķile on the Daugava River.
1198	Pope Innocent III proclaims a crusade in the eastern Baltic area.
1198	Bishop Berthold killed in a battle trying to convert Livs.
1200	Bishop Albert arrives at Ikšķile.
1201	Albert founds Riga.
1202	Albert founds the knightly Order of the Swordbrothers.
1207	Albert and Swordbrothers complete conquest of the Livs.
1209	Albert completes the conquest of the Selonians and their leader Visvaldis.
1216–1227	Years of warfare involving Swordbrothers, Lettgalians, Danes, Estonians, and Russians.
1231	The conquest and Christianization of the Couronians and their leader Lamekin is completed.

1236	Swordbrothers decimated at the Battle of Saule by a Semigallian and Lithuanian army.
1237–1267	Revolts by Couronians and Semigallians.
1267	Couronians surrender to Livonian Order.
1282	Riga joins Hanseatic League.
1290	Semigallians' final defeat and complete conquest of area of modern Latvia by Livonian Order.
1419	Creation of Livonian Diet in Riga.
1520s	Protestant Reformation arrives.
1558	Livonian Wars begin.
1562	Gotthard Kettler, last master of the Livonian Order, becomes the duke of Courland and Semigallia.
1561–1629	King of Poland-Lithuania becomes ultimate sovereign of area of modern Latvia.
1585–1587	First Catholic and Lutheran catechisms in a Latvian language.
1600–1629	Polish-Swedish War over control of the eastern Baltic.
1629	Treaty of Altmark ends Polish control over much of the territory, except for Latgale.
1642–1682	Reign of Duke Jacob, Courland and Semigallia's most active ruler.
1688–1694	Full translation of Bible in Latvian by Ernst Glück.
1700	Great Northern War begins between Poland, Sweden, and Russia for Baltic area dominance.
1710	Russian army captures Riga.
1721	Treaty of Nystadt establishes Russian dominance in the region.
1738–1743	Active wave of Moravianism in Livland.
1772	First partition of Poland brings Lettgalia under Russian control.
1795	All of Latvia within Russian Empire as a result of the third partition of Poland.
1802	Peasant unrest near Kauguri.
1817, 1819	Serfs emancipated in Baltic Provinces.
1817–1834	Scholarly German societies publish Latvian folklore and newspapers.
1840–1852	Mass peasant conversions to Orthodoxy in Livland.
1850–1880	Young Latvians begin Latvian National Awakening.
1861	Serfs emancipated in Latgale.
1880–1900	Beginning of industrialization in Russian Empire.
1882	Senator Nikolai Manasein proposes a general program of Russification after reviewing peasant grievances.
1890s	New Current movement introduces progressive theories and Marxism.
1890s	National awakening among Lettgalians.
1897–1904	Tsarist repression against workers' movements in Riga.
1904	Latvian Social Democratic Workers Party founded.
1905–1907	Revolution particularly pronounced in cities and countryside of Baltic provinces.
1914–1918	World War I.
Autumn 1915	At least 700,000 refugees flee approaching German army.
Spring 1916	Eight separate Latvian infantry battalions begin defending part of Daugava front.
1917	Revolutions begin in Russian Empire.
18 November 1918	Republic of Latvia declared, with Kārlis Ulmanis as minister president.
1918–1920	War of Independence.
January–May 1919	Latvian Soviet Socialist Republic, headed by Pēteris Stučka in Riga.
April–June 1919	Pro-German Government of Andrievs Niedra.
June–November 1919	Armies loyal to the Ulmanis government defeat German forces.
January 1920	Pro-Ulmanis armies allied with Polish forces push Bolshevik forces from Latgale.
11 August 1920	Peace Treaty with Soviet Russia.
1 May 1920	National Constitutional Convention convenes in Riga and elects Jānis Čakste state president and Kārlis Ulmanis minister president.
16 September 1920	Constitutional Convention passes Radical Agrarian Reform.
15 February 1922	Constitutional Convention ratifies constitution.
1922–1934	Era of rule by parliament (Saeima).
15 May 1934	Ulmanis's coup d'état ends parliamentary rule.
23 August 1939	Molotov-Ribbentrop Pact.
5 October 1939	Treaty stations Soviet troops in Latvia.
1939–1940	Baltic Germans "repatriated."
16 June 1940	Soviet troops enter Latvia.
14–15 July 1940	"Elections" to the "People's Saeima" recognize only the communist-backed list of delegates.
5 August 1940	Latvia "admitted" into the USSR.
14 June 1941	First mass deportation.
21 June 1941	Germany invades USSR.
July–December 1941	Holocaust of Latvia's Jews.
8 May 1945	Nazi surrender ends WWII in Europe.
1945–1953	Latvian partisan war against Soviet power.
24–30 March 1949	Mass deportation of kulaks.
1953–1959	National Communists attempt to assert local control of affairs in Latvian SSR.
1966–1984	Augusts Voss as first secretary of Latvia's Communist Party mimics the rule of Leonid Brezhnev in the larger USSR.
October 1986	Environmental movement inspired by Dainis Īvans and Arturs Snīps successfully

	contests plans to build a hydroelectric dam.
1987	Beginning of "calendar demonstrations" by dissident group Helsinki–86.
8–9 October 1988	Latvian Popular Front founded.
23 August 1989	Three Baltic Popular Fronts link 2 million people in Baltic Way human chain from Tallinn, Estonia, to Vilnius, Lithuania.
4 May 1990	Supreme Council votes to renew independence.
January 1991	Soviet attacks on Latvian government buildings kill four people.
19 August 1991	Hard-line communists attempt coup against Gorbachev in USSR.
21 August 1991	Latvia renews independence.
September 1991	Latvia seated at the United Nations.
5–6 June 1993	Elections for the Fifth Saeima.
7 July 1993	Guntis Ulmanis elected state president.
30 September–1 October 1995	Elections to Sixth Saeima.
3 October 1998	Elections to Seventh Saeima and national referendum on citizenship.
17 June 1999	Vaira Viķe-Freiberga elected state president.
October 2002	Elections to Eighth Saeima.
November 2002	A NATO summit in Prague, Czech Republic, formally invites Latvia to join the military alliance.
December 2002	An EU summit in Copenhagen, Denmark, formally invites Latvia to join the EU in 2004.
September 2003	Referendum strongly supports Latvian membership in the EU.
March 2004	Latvia joins NATO.
1 May 2004	Latvia joins the EU.

LITHUANIA

TERRY D. CLARK

LAND AND PEOPLE

Lithuania is the largest of the three Baltic states, located in East Central Europe at roughly the same latitude as Moscow, Northern Ireland, and the southern part of Hudson Bay in Canada. Its 1,747 kilometer–long border is shared with Belarus to the east and southeast (724 kilometers), Poland to the south (110 kilometers), Russia's Kaliningrad region to the southwest (303 kilometers), and Latvia to the north (610 kilometers). Its 99 kilometer–long western border is bounded by the Baltic Sea. With a total landmass of 65,300 square kilometers, the country is slightly smaller than Ireland and a little larger than the state of West Virginia. The greatest distance is 276 kilometers from north to south and 372 kilometers from east to west.

The Baltic Sea coast is low-lying, with wide sand beaches. The area on the Courland Spit extending south from Klaipėda to the town of Nida, just north of the border with Russia's Kaliningrad region, is one of the most unique areas in the world and a favored vacation spot for well-to-do Lithuanians. The narrow spit (0.4 kilometers wide), bounded on the west by the Baltic Sea and on the east by a large lagoon, is known for its sand dune formations and narrow sand beaches.

Most of the country is close to sea level, with the capital of Vilnius at 213 meters above sea level. The country's western, northern, southern, and central districts are dominated by a lowland plain. The eastern region is largely hilly upland. As one moves eastward from the Baltic Sea, the land gently increases in elevation before falling again in the central regions. From the central regions, altitudes gently increase until one reaches the highest elevations in the country's eastern regions.

Lithuania's river network is dense. There are 722 rivers and more than 2,800 lakes in the country. Lakes occupy 1.5 percent of the country's territory and are most numerous in the northeast. The river network is densest in the central regions and sparsest in the southeast. The country's two largest rivers are the Neris and the Nemunas. The Neris River flows through Vilnius to Kaunas, where it joins with the Nemunas. The Nemunas flows west along the border with the Kaliningrad region and empties into the Baltic Sea. Lithuania's rivers are frozen for three months in most winters.

Possessing a cool, wet climate, Lithuania is located in the transition zone from a maritime to a continental climate. The average daily temperature is 43 degrees Fahrenheit (6.1 degrees Celsius). The coldest month is January, with an average temperature of 23 degrees Fahrenheit (minus 5 degrees Celsius), and the warmest month is July, when temperatures average 80 degrees Fahrenheit (23 degrees Celsius). The first frost generally occurs on or

Rooftops of Vilnius, ca. 2002. (Tibor Bognar/Corbis)

about 5 October, the last in early May. There are relatively few hours of sunlight in winter, when days are quite short owing to the northern latitude. Most of the sunlight hours occur during the long days of summer.

Average annual rainfall reaches 42 inches in some parts of the country. The greater part falls in the west in winter and in the east in summer. There are from 40 to 100 foggy days a year and 15 to 30 thunderstorms a year. The growing season varies from 169 days in the east to 202 days in the west.

Approximately 17 percent of the country is dominated by grasslands and 3.3 percent by wetlands. Seventy percent of Lithuania's national territory is arable land, and 27.6 percent is forested. Pine forests account for 37.2 percent of the forested lands, spruce forests comprise 18.5 percent, birch forests 23.0 percent, white alder forests 7.5 percent, black alder forests 5.7 percent, aspen forests 4.8 percent, oak forests 1.4 percent, and ash forests 1.4 percent of the total forested area. The southeast is the most wooded; approximately half of its area is covered with forests. Forty-five percent of the land is under cultivation. The best agricultural land, comprising 7 percent of the total available land, is located in the north central and central regions, particularly along the rivers in these regions. Land suitable for farming can also be found in the southwest. The lands of the west and east are marginal, the former composed largely of sandy

soils and the latter stony. The southeast is also largely made up of sandy soils. Twenty-five percent of agriculture is conducted on sandy soils.

Wildlife is abundant, particularly in the forested areas. The most common mammals are fox, badger, elk, deer, wild boar, beaver, squirrel, muskrat, and rabbit. Among birds, ducks are present in particularly large numbers, as are pheasants, coots, and partridges. Storks are also present in significant numbers and play an important role in the folklore of the peasants.

The major sectors of the Lithuanian economy are agriculture, industry, and energy. The major agricultural products produced for the domestic market are potatoes, beef, pork, milk, eggs, vegetables, and flax. Major export crops are grains (for the eastern market) and sugar beets (for the western market). Industry is dominated by food products, textiles, apparel, electronics, chemicals, and fertilizers. Oil refining also contributes a large share of the country's gross domestic product (GDP). The energy sector is equally important to the economy, the total production of indigenous energy sources making up 43 percent of energy consumed in the republic. Natural gas and oil must be imported; however, the country is self-sufficient in electrical energy, some of which it exports to Belarus. The nuclear power plant at Ignalina is a Soviet-designed reactor of the type that exploded north of

Kiev in Ukraine in the town of Chernobyl in 1996 (which rendered large tracts of Belarus unfit to this day for habitation or raising crops). Located 119 kilometers northeast of Vilnius, the power station supplies the country with 73.1 percent of its energy, making Lithuania the second most nuclear-dependent country in the world, after France.

POPULATION

Lithuania has 3.7 million citizens with a population density of 147.4 people per square mile (56.9 people per square kilometer), making it a relatively sparsely populated country by European standards, but quite dense in comparison with the nearby countries of Scandinavia. The population is decreasing at a rate of 0.27 percent per year, a consequence of more citizens dying than being born. Sixty-eight percent of the country's citizens live in urban areas. The largest cities are the capital of Vilnius (578,000 inhabitants), Kaunas (414,500 inhabitants), the port city of Klaipėda located on the Baltic Sea (202,000 inhabitants), Šiauliai (147,000 inhabitants), and Panevėžys (133,500 inhabitants).

There are 1.6 million Lithuanian citizens in the work force. The country's labor costs are among the lowest in Central Europe, with the average gross monthly income the equivalent of U.S.$264. The official unemployment rate is 12.9 percent.

Among those with jobs, two-thirds are employed in the private sector. Some 20.3 percent of Lithuanians possess a university education, and another 24.4 percent have a technical education. Of the labor force, 20 percent are involved in agriculture, 30 percent in industry, and 50 percent in the service sector. The majority of persons in the agriculture sector are engaged in traditional peasant agriculture. Most own 3 hectares of land or less, not enough to permit profitable farming. This part of the economy is the poorest and represents a significant demand for state subsidies and social welfare transfers. An estimated 5 percent are operating farms large enough to permit efficient and profitable farming.

The official state language is Lithuanian, a member of the Baltic family of Indo-European languages. The only other languages in this family are Latvian and Prussian. The latter is a dead language no longer spoken in the modern world. One of the oldest spoken languages in Europe, Lithuanian is closely related to Sanskrit, a fact of which Lithuanians are quite proud. During the national reawakening in the nineteenth century, the Lithuanian language came to occupy a crucial position in the national identity and culture. It retains this position today.

Most Lithuanians are Roman Catholics; however, a significant minority of ethnic Lithuanians are Lutherans, particularly those living in the region surrounding the port of

Hill of crosses near Šiauliai, Lithuania. (Corel Corporation)

The Lithuanian Language

The Lithuanian language is spoken primarily in Lithuania. It is also used in some parts of Poland and Belarus, as well as among the Lithuanian diaspora, in the United States, Canada, Western Europe, Latin America, Australia, and Siberia.

The Lithuanian language, together with Latvian, belongs to the Baltic group of Indo-European languages. It has two major dialects: highlander (or High Lithuanian) and lowlander (or Low Lithuanian). Lithuanian is characterized by an abundance of diverse word formations and synonyms. Of all of the living Indo-European languages, it has best preserved archaic sound systems and lexical features. Indeed, it is considered the most archaic Indo-European language still spoken. For this reason, researchers wishing to fully comprehend Indo-European languages study Lithuanian. Many consider that Sanskrit and the Baltic languages constitute the two closest descendants of Proto-Indo-European, allowing researchers to deduce most accurately the nature of that original language.

The written language evolved relatively late, mostly because of the late adoption of Christianity. The history of the written language began in Lithuania Minor in the middle of the sixteenth century. The earliest documents were translations of Christian prayers in 1525. The first book written in Lithuanian was *Catechismus* by Martynas Mažvydas (1547). The Lithuanian language of the sixteenth century was used mostly for religious writings and differs in many significant respects from modern Lithuanian.

Modern Standard Lithuanian did not develop fully until just before the first period of Lithuanian political independence (1918—1940), when it became the country's official language. The modern language, written in a 32-letter Latin alphabet, is based on the West High Lithuanian dialect. In 1988 Lithuanian was declared the official language of Lithuania.

The Lithuanians are a Baltic people related to the Latvians. They constitute 80 percent of the country's population. Another 9.4 percent are Russians, 7 percent are Poles, and 3.6 percent of the population is composed of other peoples: Belarusians, Ukrainians, Latvians, Tatars, and Jews. Poles are concentrated in the eastern regions, particularly those surrounding Vilnius. Russians are usually found in the largest cities and the town of Visaginas, located near the Ignalina nuclear power station. The most ethnically diverse city is Vilnius, the capital. Of the capital's population, 52.8 percent are ethnically Lithuanian, 19.2 percent Poles, 19.2 percent Russians, 4.8 percent Belarusians, 0.7 percent Jews, and 3.3 percent other nationalities. Klaipėda's population is the next most diverse (63 percent Lithuanians, 28.2 percent Russians, 3.9 percent Ukrainians, 2.7 percent Belarusians, 0.5 percent Poles, and 1.7 percent other nationalities). Kaunas is the least diverse city; 88 percent of the city's inhabitants are ethnic Lithuanians, 8.8 percent Russians, 0.7 percent Belarusians, 0.7 percent Ukrainians, 0.6 percent Poles, 0.1 percent Latvians, and 1.5 percent other nationalities.

The Lithuanians, who are indigenous to the country, took shape as a nation by the sixth century C.E. However, they were not able to consolidate the Lithuanian state until the beginning of the fifteenth century, after a long and bitter struggle against crusading knights of the Teutonic Order. By then, the Grand Duchy of Lithuania, a feudal medieval state, stretched from the Baltic Sea to the Black Sea, encompassing most of the area of modern Belarus and Ukraine and the westernmost regions of Russia.

The Poles came to Lithuania following the marriage of the grand duke with the Queen of Poland, which ultimately led to the merger of the two crowns in the Treaty of Lublin in 1569. Poles are concentrated in the Vilnius region, which Poland occupied in the period between World War I and World War II.

Russians are predominantly urban. They first came to Lithuania during the height of the Grand Duchy. Another wave came when Lithuania was incorporated into the Russian Empire following the third partition of the Polish Republic at the end of the eighteenth century. A final wave of Russian immigrants arrived after the Soviet Union forcibly incorporated the country. However, thanks to the policies of the leadership of the Lithuanian Communist Party, which de-emphasized industrialization, far fewer Russians came to Lithuania than to their Baltic neighbors, whose Russian populations are substantially larger.

Jews live almost exclusively in the cities. They arrived in Lithuania for the first time in the twelfth century seeking refuge from the eastward expansion of the Roman Catholic Church, against which the Lithuanians, a pagan nation, were struggling. Grand Duke Vytautas recognized them as a class of artisans and merchants and freed them from serving the landed nobility, placing them under his direct rule. By the end of the nineteenth century, they were the country's second largest ethnic group, comprising 39.6 percent of the urban population. Vilnius was then one of the three centers of Jewish culture in the world, boasting a major rabbinical school. It also became the home of the first Jewish socialist

Klaipėda. Furthermore, almost all Poles are Catholics as well. Hence, religion does not play the same role in the national identity that language does. Moreover, loyalty to Catholicism tends to be dampened among Lithuanians by the continued influence of pagan traditions and celebrations. Of the country's citizens, 70 percent profess a faith in Roman Catholicism, 4 percent are Russian Orthodox, and 17 percent are Lutheran, Evangelical Christian Baptist, adherents of other Protestant denominations, Jews, and Muslims. The latter are mostly Tatars.

labor movement. While they became the third largest ethnic group with the arrival of large numbers of Poles during the Polish occupation of the Vilnius regions in the interwar period, they continued to thrive culturally, socially, and economically. All of this was destroyed during the German occupation of World War II, when the Nazis exterminated over 96 percent of the Jewish community. It has not since recovered. Jews today remain a very small minority in Lithuania.

HISTORY
THE ANCIENT BALTS

Lithuania is first mentioned in written records in the Latin chronicle *Annales Quedinburgenses* of 1009, when Bruno of Querful traveled from Prussia to baptize a Lithuanian tribal chief. No less developed than other regions of Central and Northern Europe at the time, it is not mentioned in historical records for another 200 years. Despite the relatively infrequent mention of the Lithuanians in historical records, they are among the oldest peoples of Europe, having been settled adjacent to the Baltic Sea for at least 4,000 years. Their ancestors migrated to the Baltic Sea from the Volga region of central Russia about 3000 B.C.E. These proto-Baltic tribes ultimately established themselves on what is presently known as Lithuanian territory during the seventh through the second centuries B.C.E. However, their identity as Balts did not develop until the first through the sixth centuries C.E., an era of cultural development and rapid expansion of trade with the Roman Empire and Germanic tribes to their west.

By the first century C.E., the territory inhabited by the Balts stretched from the Baltic Sea to the Dnieper and Oka Rivers. The expanse of their domains brought them into conflict with the Scandinavians to the north and later the Slavs to the east. The latter, whose territorial expansion began in the fifth century, succeeded in assimilating the easternmost Balts. The most serious threat to the early Balts, however, came from the west. At the beginning of the thirteenth century, Catholic orders of knights seeking to Christianize the Baltic region began a series of crusades. The first of these crusading orders, the Order of the Brothers of the Sword, was defeated by the Lithuanians at the Battle of Saulė in 1236. Following that defeat, the Roman Catholic pope called for a renewed campaign to conquer and Christianize the pagan Lithuanians. The call was answered by a succession of crusading knights, the most formidable of which were the members of the Teutonic Order.

Lithuanians had yet to form a unified nation-state. The political organization consisted of a nobility composed of feudal dukes and princes ruling over fiefdoms and tribes. Had they chosen to fight the Teutonic Order separately, they would have been easily defeated. Therefore, the nobility formed an alliance, led by a noble called Mindaugas, to engage in the struggle. Despite the alliance, however, the united Lithuanian duchies were not able to stem the continued advances of the Teutonic Order. Recognizing the inevitability of defeat, Mindaugas submitted to the pope in 1251 and accepted Christianity. As a consequence he was crowned the king of Lithuania in 1253 by the pope, an act establishing the first Lithuanian state.

THE FIRST LITHUANIAN STATE

Mindaugas's decision was not popular among the Lithuanian nobility, many of whom refused to be baptized. The population as well remained overwhelmingly pagan. Hence, the new state was a pagan one with a Christian king. The opposition of the population to Christianity led to the murder of King Mindaugas in 1263 and the renewal of the struggle against the Christian crusaders. Following the murder of Mindaugas, rule of Lithuania reverted to the various dukes and princes. However, in order to fight the Teutonic Order, they submitted to a grand duke, who ruled as first among equals. Thanks to their unity, this time they were able to establish Lithuanian dominance in the Baltic Sea region by the end of the thirteenth century. Nonetheless, the struggle against the Teutonic Order continued throughout most of the fourteenth century, forcing the country to allocate virtually all of its resources to defense; consequently, the country's political system of the time is referred to by some as a military monarchy.

The concentration of resources permitted the Lithuanian state to become one of the greatest empires in Europe over the course of the next 150 years—the Grand Duchy of Lithuania. Grand Duke Gediminas (1316–1341) began the long-term eastward expansion of the Lithuanians, assimilating Slavic territories, many of which willingly submitted to the Grand Duchy in order to escape having to pay tribute to the Mongols, who ruled most of the Russian lands in that era (having destroyed the Kievan state in the thirteenth century). Gediminas also sought to break out of the international isolation thrust upon the country by the continued struggle against the Catholic Church and the Teutonic Order. He established formal contacts between the Grand Duchy of Lithuania and the countries of Western Europe, engaged in regular correspondence with their rulers, and began a dynasty that intermarried with many of the ruling families of Europe. Much of this was done in an effort to create rifts within the Catholic Church and between the ruling houses of Europe. To further this strategy, Gediminas also invited Western merchants, artisans, and academics to the new capital that he founded at Vilnius. Among those responding were many Jews, who took advantage of the remarkable degree of religious tolerance that marked the Grand Duchy and established one of the great centers of Judaism in Vilnius.

During the mid-fourteenth century, Grand Duke Algirdas (1345–1377) continued the eastern expansion begun by Gediminas. Under his rule, the Grand Duchy's Lithuanian subjects were gradually outnumbered by newly assimilated peoples. Algirdas was followed by Grand Duke Jogaila, who is much maligned in Lithuanian history for his decision in 1386 to marry the queen of Poland, thereby entering into an alliance with that state. Jogaila's decision was motivated by a desire to ensure Lithuanian preeminence in an emerging contest with Moscow for the loyalties of eastern Slavic princes. While still under the Mongol yoke, Moscow was laying claim to the Russian lands, many of which had been assimilated into the Grand Duchy of Lithuania. In addition, Moscow had been recognized by Byzantium as the seat of religious authority for Orthodox Christianity in the Slavic lands. The recognition brought with it significant legitimacy for the Russian claims over these lands. Given Lithuania's status as the last pagan nation in Europe, it found itself isolated between a Catholic West and an Orthodox East, both of which claimed the divine right to rule over the territories of the Grand Duchy. A marriage with Poland thus offered the means to both reduce the threat from the West and lay claim to a religious title (that of representing Catholic Slavs, a title that Poland had acquired) competing for the loyalties of Slavic princes. Hence, Lithuania was baptized in 1387, and the last pagan state in Europe became Christian.

As a consequence of the marriage, the Grand Duchy entered a long period of decline, even though this would not be readily apparent for several centuries. By entering into marriage with the queen of Poland, Jogaila became the king of Poland, retaining his title as the Grand Duke of Lithuania. While in the short term this appeared highly beneficial to Lithuania, it meant that the Lithuanians faced the disadvantage of being far fewer in number than the Poles. In the long term, as Lithuania's territorial holdings were reduced (in the face of continuing Russian expansion), it became the lesser of the two states in the union. However, the advantages of the marriage uniting the two countries appeared to outweigh any disadvantages at the time. Therefore, unlike the first christening, this one was not reversed.

The subsequent grand duke, Vytautas the Great, who ruled at the beginning of the fifteenth century, not only retained Lithuania's commitment to Christianity, he took full advantage of the union with Poland to further the prosperity of the country. In fact, the reign of Vytautas the Great marks the zenith of Lithuania's military and political fortunes. In one of the most significant battles of the Middle Ages, Vytautas, leading a joint Lithuanian-Polish army, decisively defeated the Teutonic Order at the Battle of Grünwald (1410; the battle is known as the Battle of Žalgiris in Lithuania), bringing the final defeat of the order and ending the centuries-long threat from the west. In the east, Vytautas pursued a successful policy, annexing further territories in Belarus, Russia, and Ukraine, expanding the borders of the Grand Duchy from the Baltic Sea to the Black Sea, and blocking Moscow's further expansion westward into Europe.

Vytautas also took advantage of the union with Poland to lay the foundations for Lithuania's full integration into Central Europe, something that its pagan identity had prevented it from achieving. In the 150 years after his death, Lithuania assimilated the political and cultural heritage of Western civilization. The country adopted the crop rotation system, adapted its social system to monarchism, experienced the rise of craft guilds, adopted a written language, and built a university system. Reflecting these changes, Lithuania's first publishing house was founded in Vilnius in 1522; in addition, a legal code was written in 1529 and subsequently redrafted in 1566 and 1588. The 1588 code remained in force until the middle of the nineteenth century.

Vytautas the Great

Vytautas the Great (r. 1392–1430) is the most famous political figure in Lithuanian history. During his reign, the Grand Duchy of Lithuania achieved the height of its political and military power and economic prosperity. Vytautas annexed many Belarusian, Russian, and Ukrainian territories, and extended Lithuania's border all the way to the shores of the Black Sea. It was Vytautas who led the Polish-Lithuanian army against the Teutonic Knights on 15 July 1410 in the Battle of Grünwald (Tannenberg). The German order never recovered from its defeat in this battle. As a consequence, German supremacy in the Baltic area was broken, and Poland-Lithuania ultimately came to be regarded as a great power.

Perhaps most importantly, Vytautas laid the foundations for the country's orientation toward Central Europe. Over a period of approximately 150 years following Vytautas, Lithuania assimilated the institutions and intellectual heritage of Western Europe, including the institutions of crop rotation, feudalism, craft guilds, Christianity, an education system, and a written language. Since the time of Vytautas the Great, Lithuania has identified itself politically and culturally with the West. For this reason, the Soviet occupation was seen by many as a forced break with the country's historical and cultural roots, and only the end of the Soviet period could restore Lithuania to those roots.

THE POLISH-LITHUANIAN COMMONWEALTH

The same period, however, saw the gradual loss of the eastern territories to the expansion of the Grand Duchy of Moscow (a process often referred to as the "regathering of the Russian lands"). By 1569, thanks to Jogaila's marriage, the Lithuanians were at best a tiny minority in a small feudal state in comparison with its much larger and more numerous Polish ally. In that year, the two states signed the Treaty of Lublin, which merged what had been separate political and social institutions into one. The most important institutional change was that the positions of king of Poland and grand duke of Lithuania were henceforth to be vested in the same person. Although relations between the two states in the Polish-Lithuanian Commonwealth were initially based on no more than the fact that they were under the same ruler, the nobility of the two states rapidly fused, sharing the ideal of two peoples with an inseparable past and future. This convergence ultimately meant that the Poles would dominate the less numerous Lithuanians politically and culturally, a reality that found expression in the

The Battle of Žalgiris

The Battle of Žalgiris (also known as the Battle of Grünwald, or Tannenberg), in which the joint military forces of the Grand Duchy of Lithuania and the Kingdom of Poland defeated the Teutonic Order, was one of the greatest battles of the Middle Ages, let alone in East Central Europe. The defeat of the Teutonic Order, an order of crusaders of the Catholic Church, on 15 July 1410, marked the end of the order's expansion along the southeastern coast of the Baltic Sea eastward and the beginning of the decline of the order's power.

The first German crusading orders came to Poland and the Baltic region in the thirteenth century. Two hundred years later, they had conquered most of the Baltic coastal region, including Latvia and Estonia. It is doubtless the case that they were intent on controlling Lithuania, Poland, and Russia as well. Had they succeeded, the Roman Catholic Church would have dominated the whole of Central and Eastern Europe.

Hoping to forcibly spread Christianity and acquire more territory, the focus of the Teutonic Order's military activities in the fourteenth century was the pagan Lithuanian state. Even after Lithuania accepted Christianity in 1387, the Knights of the Teutonic Order did not cease their aggression against the country. It was obvious that diplomatic efforts would not be able to avert war with the Knights. Therefore, the only hope of defeating the order was if Lithuania and Poland united their military forces.

Hence, on 15 July 1410, a joint Lithuanian-Polish army, joined by Tatar, Bohemian, Russian, Moravian, and Moldavian soldiers, met the Teutonic Knights on the field of Žalgiris (located in the northeast of present-day Poland). The allied army was led by the grand duke of Lithuania, Vytautas the Great, and the king of Poland, Jogaila. Although outnumbered (the Knights numbered 32,000, compared to more than 50,000 Poles, Lithuanians, and allies), the order enjoyed superiority in weaponry, experience, and battlefield leadership. Nonetheless, at the end of an entire day of fighting, the Teutonic Knights were defeated, a defeat from which they never recovered. On 1 February 1411, both sides signed a peace treaty, after which the Teutonic Order never again threatened Lithuania.

The Battle of Grünwald is the most important battle in the history of both Lithuania and Poland. As a consequence of the defeat of the Teutonic Order, Eastern Europe was not Germanized, and the emerging nations of Lithuania and Poland were able to develop their own cultures. For that reason, Vytautas the Great is honored in Lithuanian history as the savior of not only the nation of Lithuania, but all of Eastern Europe. Jogaila is awarded that position in Polish history.

---

fact that only one-third of the seats in the Seimas, a parliament of nobles, were allotted to the Lithuanian nobility.

The first king of Poland following the Union of Lublin was Zygimantas Augustus (Sigismund II Augustus; r. 1548–1572), a descendant of Grand Dukes Gediminas and Jogaila. Thanks to intermarriage, this same dynasty ruled the Czech lands and Hungary, uniting these realms with the Polish-Lithuanian Commonwealth to rival the Habsburgs for influence. However, the Jogiellonian dynasty, or as it was known in Poland, the Jagiellonian dynasty, ended with the death of Zygimantas Augustus. With his passing, the Commonwealth became the first republic in Europe, the Seimas electing the successor, Henry Valois of the House of Bourbon (in France), in 1573. The titles of king of Poland and grand duke of Lithuania were transferred to the Poles with the election of King Steponas Batoras (known in Poland as Stephen Batory and in Hungary as Stephen Báthory) in 1576. A Lithuanian never again achieved the title of grand duke of Lithuania.

With the dominance of Poland, Lithuania's history is intertwined with that of Poland from 1576 until its incorporation into the Russian Empire in 1795. The period was marked by the Polonization of the country's culture. By

1698, Polish culture had become so dominant that Polish was declared the official state language for the entire Commonwealth. Lithuanian had been largely relegated to the status of a language spoken by the illiterate peasant population of the Polish-Lithuanian Commonwealth's eastern regions. The language of cultural, political, and economic discourse was Polish. Courses offered at Vilnius University, founded by the Jesuit Order in 1579 as part of the Counter-Reformation, were in Polish. Even the Lithuanian city of Vilnius itself became a center of Polish and later Jewish culture. Lithuanian was spoken only in the countryside and smaller towns by common folk and peasants. The first literary work written in Lithuanian did not appear until 1775, when Kristijonas Donelaitis wrote the poem *Metai* (The Seasons).

The era was also marked by the waning of the Polish-Lithuanian Commonwealth, which by the end of the period was referred to as simply the Polish Republic. The checks placed by the nobility on the power of the king rendered the Republic increasingly less able to deal effectively with the expanding empires of Eastern and Central Europe that bordered the Polish Republic. As a consequence, Lithuania was invaded by the Swedes and Russians during a period that came to be known as the Flood (from 1654 to 1667); at one point, Vilnius was occupied by a foreign army for the first time in the city's history. The country also became the battleground for the Great Northern War (1700–1721) between Sweden (under its young king, Charles XII) and a coalition comprised of Russia (led by Peter the Great), Poland, and Denmark.

By the latter half of the eighteenth century, the Polish Republic had become so weak that it was subjected to three successive partitions by Russia, Prussia, and Austria (the first in 1772, the second in 1793, and the third in 1795). In between the second and third partitions, an uprising in the Lithuanian and Polish territories against the loss of Polish sovereignty, led by Tadeusz Kościuszko (a hero of the American Revolutionary War), was crushed by the Russian army. Following the third and final partition, Lithuania found itself part of the Russian Empire. Lithuania was to remain a part of the Russian Empire from 1795 to 1918.

THE RUSSIAN EMPIRE

The country's forcible incorporation into its larger neighbor meant that it was involuntarily subjected to foreign rule for the first time in its history. Furthermore, Lithuanians found themselves cut off from their traditional ties to Central Europe (with which they shared cultural affinities). The political, social, and cultural effects of the incorporation were mostly felt by the nobility and townspeople. For most of the Lithuanian peasantry, little of consequence changed; peasant obligations (including serfdom) remained burdensome. Napoleon's occupation in 1812 was welcomed by many of the nobles as well as some city dwellers. His defeat and the subsequent reimposition of Russian rule left a bitter taste in their mouths. Their feelings were reflected in intense resistance to Russian rule, a resistance that culminated in the Insurrection of 1831.

The insurrection, the aim of which was to restore the Polish-Lithuanian Commonwealth, was confined to the largely Polonized upper class and residents of towns. The insurrection was quickly and brutally crushed by Tsar Nicholas I, a reactionary ruler who greatly feared the influence of the liberal ideals of the French Revolution. To guard against such influences, as well as to reduce the likelihood of their reoccurrence, he undertook a series of reprisals against the Lithuanian lands, which included executions and deportations of the nobility, land seizures, and the closing of Vilnius University, which had served as a center for the maintenance and spread of Polish culture. He also abolished the 1588 legal code nine years later (in 1840) and imposed the substantially more restrictive Russian legal code on the country. In general, however, the reprisals had little impact on the Lithuanian-speaking peasant population, which had taken little part in the nationalist yearnings that had provoked the insurrection.

Tsar Alexander II assumed the Russian throne upon the death of Nicholas I in 1855 and, owing to the defeat suffered by Russia during the Crimean War (1853–1856), engaged in a number of internal reforms, the most significant of which were the abolition of serfdom in 1861, the opening of the educational system to the lower classes, the enactment of judicial reforms, and the creation of local governments with substantial powers and responsibilities.

The abolition of serfdom in 1861 changed the relative passivity of the Lithuanian lower classes. The attendant social and educational reforms had the further unintended consequence of fueling a Lithuanian national reawakening, something seen in much of Central Europe during the nineteenth century. Taking advantage of the new freedoms and opportunities offered by the reforms, a significant proportion of the Lithuanian-speaking lower classes experienced rapid upward social mobility, entering the ranks of the professions and educated elite. Unlike the Lithuanian nobility and gentry, they rejected both Polish and Russian culture. Many of them quickly formed the vanguard of an independence movement, which resulted in another uprising in 1863. Unlike the earlier revolt, the Insurrection of 1863 sought an independent Lithuanian state. Indeed, these new intellectuals and professionals rejected the Polish-Lithuanian Commonwealth and its claim to represent the inseparable interests of the Polish and Lithuanian peoples. Hence, the Insurrection of 1863 can properly be viewed as the start of the Lithuanian national reawakening.

The tsarist response to the Insurrection of 1863 was harsh. In addition to executions and deportations, the use of the Latin alphabet was banned. In essence, no publication in the Lithuanian language was permitted. This policy remained in force from 1864 to 1904.

The effect of the crackdown was twofold. First, it helped to identify the Lithuanian language as central to the national identity of the people. This emphasis on language paralleled similar movements throughout Central and Southeastern Europe. The increased education level of the general population now created a groundswell of desire to "discover" Lithuanian culture. A unique movement, the so-called book-bearers, emerged, in which Lithuanian books were printed in the Latin script in areas under German rule and illegally smuggled into Lithuania. Second, it consolidated support for an independent Lithuanian nation-state (distinct from the old Polish-Lithuanian Commonwealth) among virtually the entire population.

During the period, several illegal Lithuanian language periodicals emerged, urging national resistance to assimilation and rejecting reunification with Poland. At the forefront of these publications was *Aušra* (Dawn), founded by Dr. Jonas Basanavičius in 1883. The intensity of the resistance to the Russian Empire is most evidenced, however, in the willingness of many to school their children in the Lithuanian language despite serious punishments for doing so. The Russian government's harsh attempts to repress these illegal activities helped to swell the numbers of those emigrating abroad. Almost one-third of the population left the country in the latter half of the nineteenth century. Nevertheless, the national awakening continued apace, fostering ever increasing popular support for Lithuanian independence.

The lifting of the ban on publishing in the Lithuanian language was part of a package of concessions made by the tsar in the wake of the disastrous defeat in the Russo-

Japanese War of 1904–1905 and the resulting Revolution of 1905. In response, the independence movement formally organized and continued to press for an independent and national Lithuanian state in which Lithuanian would be the only official language. A committee declaring itself a national Seimas (legislature) representing the will of the Lithuanian people passed a resolution demanding full autonomy within the Russian Empire. It also urged the population not to pay taxes, send their children to the Russian schools, or even treat Russian state institutions as legitimate.

Caught off balance by the strength of the upsurge sweeping across the length of the empire, the tsar (Nicholas II) acceded to many of the demands and permitted greater local self-rule. However, over the course of the next five years, as St. Petersburg regained firm control over the empire, these concessions were rescinded. Nevertheless, the experience was a positive one for political activists who supported national independence. The experience would especially prove to be invaluable near the end of World War I, in the wake of the Bolshevik Revolution that brought the Communist Party to power in Russia and brought an abrupt end to the Russian Empire. Many of these same activists took advantage of the ensuing political vacuum and declared the restoration of an independent Lithuanian state on 16 February 1918. The Germans, who had occupied Lithuania since 1915, recognized Lithuanian independence. However, the country's international status remained uncertain until the German defeat in November 1918.

THE RESTORATION OF STATEHOOD

The withdrawal of German troops at the end of World War I did not end the problem of foreign intervention. From 1918 to 1920, the newly declared Lithuanian Republic had to struggle against several foreign invasions, among them that of the Bermondt-Avalov army, a German-sponsored group seeking to preserve German influence in the Baltic states. Moreover, the new state had to contend with an effort by the Bolshevik Red Army in November 1918 to reimpose Russian rule on Lithuania. Nevertheless, the Bolshevik invasion was defeated in July 1920, and a peace treaty was signed recognizing Lithuanian independence. The most disturbing military intervention occurred at the end of the same year, when Polish troops forcibly annexed the capital city of Vilnius (which was called Wilno in Polish) and the regions surrounding it. They continued to occupy the city until World War II. As a consequence, the country's relations with its western neighbor were seriously strained throughout the interwar period.

Much of the country's energies were focused on foreign policy from 1920 to 1940. The effort to regain the capital of Vilnius dominated much of the country's attention and informed many of the country's actions in the League of Nations, which Lithuania joined in 1921. Problems also emerged with Germany over the port of Memel on the Baltic Sea coast. Originally inhabited by Lithuanians, the city had been under German rule for 700 years (since the time of the Teutonic Order). The Treaty of Versailles at the end of World War I placed the city under French administration. In 1923 the Lithuanian government secretly organized a successful local uprising, which resulted in the annexation of the city (renamed Klaipėda) and the surrounding area.

Deep divisions concerning relations with Poland plagued domestic politics in the interwar period. The Polish seizure of the capital city of Vilnius had the support of many of the Polish and Jewish landowners and townspeople of the region. Hence, ethnic minorities as well as those political parties associated with them came under deep suspicion from many ethnic Lithuanians. Left-wing political parties, particularly the Social Democratic Party and Communist Party, had been active in organizing ethnic minorities prior to independence. The Social Democratic Party of Lithuania, which was founded in 1895, focused almost exclusively upon the Polish and Jewish working-class communities of Vilnius in its early years. While the party's leadership was decimated by the repression of political activity in the Russian Empire from 1897 to 1899, the party managed to resurface in 1900, changing its focus from a primary concern with defending workers' interests to one that advocated independence from Russia. This shift permitted it to broaden its political base to include peasants. Nonetheless, the party's members continued to be drawn primarily from non-Lithuanians.

The Bolshevik seizure of power in Russia ultimately led to a split among social democrats in Lithuania. Those remaining in the Social Democratic Party of Lithuania argued that socialism could best be achieved incrementally and within an independent Lithuanian state. Others, following the example of the Bolsheviks, declared the necessity of a violent revolution, the elimination of private property, and the creation of a workers' state uniting the peoples of the former Russian Empire. The disagreement ultimately ended in the formation of two parties, the pro-independence (and gradualist) Lithuanian Social Democratic Party and the pro-Bolshevik Lithuanian Communist Party. The former became the forerunner of today's Lithuanian Social Democratic Party (LSDP), while the latter was the predecessor of the Lithuanian Democratic Labor Party (LDLP), as it was renamed in 1990.

The Lithuanian Communist Party, which maintained close ties with the Bolshevik regime in Moscow, fared poorly in comparison to the Social Democratic Party in the first years of independence. While it managed to gain five seats in the elections to the first national legislature (the Seimas), it lost those seats in the next election. In contrast, the Lithuanian Social Democratic Party was a major political party, gaining between 10 and 18 percent of the vote in elections. It reached its zenith in 1926, when it entered into a coalition government with the Populists. However, the party's ties with Poles and Jews—in light of those communities' support for Polish rule in Vilnius—created great distrust among many Lithuanian nationalist parties. These parties led a military coup late the same year, forcibly deposing the left-wing government and dissolving the Seimas.

The coup installed the leader of the Union of Nationalists (Tautininkai), Antanas Smetona, who, as president until 1940, governed Lithuania with near dictatorial powers. The

Vilna, Poland: A street scene in the disputed city of Vilna (Vilnius) during the 1920s, where a technical state of war existed. Vilna, the historic capital of Lithuania, was awarded to Poland by the League of Nations in 1923. Lithuania, however, wanted to regain its old capital. The problem was left to the League to resolve, which sought to prevent war between the two states. (Underwood & Underwood/Corbis)

national legislature, the Seimas, was eventually reconstituted, but the scope of its responsibilities was severely reduced. The government, which had previously been elected by the Seimas, was now appointed by the president, thereby reducing the powers of the legislature to performing a largely formalistic advisory role. All of these institutional changes became part of the Constitution of 1938. Finally, leftist parties were virtually denied the right to political participation for the remainder of the interwar period. The Lithuanian Communist Party was officially outlawed, and the Social Democratic Party was subjected to harassment and arrests.

Despite the collapse of democratic rule in Lithuania, the interwar period was marked by a revival of Lithuanian culture, which was reflected as well in the patriotism that led to the coup installing a nationalist president. A symbol of this nationalism was the heroism of two Lithuanian-American pilots, Steponas Darius and Stasys Girėnas, who achieved worldwide acclaim in 1936 by crossing the Atlantic Ocean in a single-engine aircraft. Their fame was further heightened in Lithuania by the fact that the two pilots

perished in a mysterious crash in Germany after crossing the Atlantic. The country also won international recognition in sports, highlighted by the national men's basketball team winning the European championship in 1937 and repeating in 1939.

WORLD WAR II

The rise of Adolf Hitler in Germany and the consolidation of power by Josef Stalin in the Soviet Union ultimately emerged as a much greater threat to Lithuanian security and independence than the continued Polish occupation of the Vilnius region. Lithuania's problems with these two dictatorships began in earnest in 1939. Early in that year, Germany issued an ultimatum for the return of Klaipėda (Memel), to which Lithuania had no choice but to accede. In secret, however, the Germans were at the same time engaging in a prolonged negotiation with the Soviet Union over the division of Eastern Europe between them. The agreement, the Molotov-Ribbentrop Pact, was signed in August 1939. The pact's secret protocol (not made public in the USSR until decades later) initially assigned Lithuania to the German sphere of influence. However, when Lithuania refused to attack Poland as a German ally in September 1939, the country was reassigned to the Soviet sphere in a second secret protocol signed on September 27.

The invasion and division of Poland by the forces of the German *Wehrmacht* (armed forces) and the Soviet Red Army, which marked the beginning of World War II, resulted in the return of the Vilnius region to the Lithuanian Republic. However, the country was also forced to permit the stationing of Soviet troops on its territory. In a treaty of mutual assistance signed by both countries at the insistence of the Soviet Union, Lithuania agreed to "host" 20,000 Soviet troops. In the summer of 1940, with the German Army about to take Paris, the Soviet Union, suddenly wary of its German ally and Berlin's future designs, accused the Lithuanian government of violating the agreement and presented it with an ultimatum to permit the Soviet Army to enter and operate within the country freely. The Lithuanian government acceded to the demands, and President Smetona fled the country on 15 June 1940.

The Soviet Army occupied Lithuania and seized control of the government on the same day. A puppet government was established, and elections to a new legislature were organized. On 21 July, the deputies to the new legislature, many of whose elections had been rigged, voted unanimously to request formal incorporation into the Soviet Union. A few weeks later, Lithuania became the fourteenth republic of the Soviet Union, on 3 August 1940.

The Soviet regime immediately set about integrating Lithuania's largely free market into the Soviet politically managed economic system. Banks, industrial enterprises, retail shops, and land were nationalized, peasants were organized into collective farms, and culture was Sovietized. Those capable of organizing any form of resistance to these efforts, no matter how small, as well as those who were suspect by virtue of being from the former upper class or middle class (including anyone who owned property or possessed a higher education), were subject to arrest and deportation to Siberia. On the night of 11 July 1940, two thousand Lithuanian statesmen and party leaders were arrested. Thirty-four thousand subsequently were rounded up and deported almost a year later in the mass arrests of 14–18 June 1941. Tens of thousands of others were arrested randomly throughout the period.

These purges were brought to a halt by the German invasion of the Soviet Union, which began in June 1941. The German advance through Lithuania was rapid. Within a few days the entire country was occupied. The Soviets, however, executed thousands of those whom they had detained before leaving the country; the most notorious of these atrocities was the mass execution of thousands of prisoners at Červenė on 24 and 25 June 1941.

Lithuanians were divided in their reaction to the German occupation (which lasted until 1944). Some welcomed the Germans with open arms, but were troubled by the Nazi campaign to liquidate the Jews. Others, however, appear to have collaborated in the Nazi attempt to eradicate Europe's Jews, Hitler's Final Solution.

Before the war, Vilnius was home to one of the most thriving Jewish communities in the world. Ninety-six percent of that community was liquidated in the Holocaust. While some deny any Lithuanian complicity in the Holocaust, it is difficult to imagine that it could have occurred without the active involvement, or passive acquiescence, of at least some part of the Lithuanian community. Countercharges that some Jews were implicated in what Lithuanians believe to have been the Soviet genocide of their nation during the occupation in no way excuses the actions of those involved. Fortunately, not all Lithuanians supported the German occupation. In fact, the Front of Lithuanian Activists (FLA), formed by Lithuanians who had fled to Germany during the Soviet occupation, declared the formation of a provisional Lithuanian government when the Germans invaded the Soviet Union. However, the Germans did not recognize the FLA government and banned the organization itself. This action, along with other factors, convinced many in the country that the German occupation was no better than that of the Soviet Union. As a result, a substantial resistance movement operated in the country throughout the entire period of Nazi occupation. Many of these organizations had formed during the Soviet occupation as well and continued the effort to restore Lithuanian independence by now combating the Germans. Among these organizations were the Lithuanian Front, the Union of Lithuanian Fighters for Freedom, the Lithuanian Freedom Army, the Lithuanian National Party, and the Lithuanian Solidarity Movement. Some published underground newspapers, while others were involved in illegal political efforts; still others fought an on-going guerrilla war against the German Army. As the Soviet Army advanced toward Lithuania in late 1943, these organizations united into the General Lithuanian Liberation Committee.

THE SOVIET ERA

After Lithuania was reincorporated into the Soviet Union in 1944, the Lithuanian Communist Party (LCP) became an arm of the Communist Party of the Soviet Union (CPSU). It was declared the only legal political party in the country; all other parties were banned and actively suppressed by the Soviet authorities. Communist Party members staffed all social, economic, and political positions of importance. Reincorporation into the Soviet Union as well as the Soviet system also resulted in the forced collectivization of agriculture, nationalization of all businesses and property that had been returned to their owners by the Germans, and organized repression of the Lithuanian people. In response, Lithuanians continued the armed independence struggle under the umbrella of many of the same organizations that had led the effort during the German occupation. The armed resistance movement lasted for eight years (1945–1953) and covered the entire country. Almost 100,000 persons were involved in the resistance, which was highly organized and so effective that the Soviets were confined to the major towns and cities at night.

The Soviet response to continued resistance, Lithuanian nationalism, and the independence of native institutions was further deportations and executions. There were eight large-scale deportations to Siberia during the period of the resistance: September 1945, 18 February 1946, 17 December 1947, 22 May 1948, 24–27 March 1949, 27–28 May 1949, March 1950, and 2 October 1953. The largest of them occurred on 22 May 1948, when approximately 80,000 people were sent to Siberia. As a consequence of deportations, mass executions, the resistance struggle, the Jewish Holocaust, forced labor sent to Germany, and emigration, Lithuania lost an estimated one-third of its population from 1941 to 1951.

Even after the decision was made by Lithuanian partisans, also known as the Forest Boys *(Broliai Miško),* to end the armed resistance and return to civilian life, resistance to Soviet rule continued in one form or another throughout the Soviet period. The 1968 Soviet invasion of Czechoslovakia did much to strengthen opposition to the Soviet occupation, as did the intensified efforts to force the Russian language and culture on the population from 1970 to 1982, during the Brezhnev era. Romas Kalanta, a young student, became a symbol of national resistance to these efforts when he set himself on fire publicly in the city of Kaunas in 1972. The act sparked spontaneous student protests that had to be forcibly suppressed by the Soviet secret police, the KGB. The most durable and longest lasting form of resistance was the illegal publication of the *Chronicles of the Catholic Church,* which appeared for the first time in 1973, a defiant act in a system that constitutionally permitted religious freedom but actively suppressed it. The *Chronicles* were later joined by secular publications of illegal human rights groups that formed following the 1976 signing of the Human Rights agreements by the United States, the Soviet Union, and the European countries in Helsinki, Finland.

This prolonged resistance to Soviet rule helped Lithuanians to define their national identity more precisely. More than for most nations, language is central to that identity. Nothing else served as well to unite those identifying themselves as Lithuanians as did the language. Different regions of the country demonstrate wide variation in traditions and even symbols. Even religion does not unite the nation. While a plurality are professing Catholics, a large part of the nation is Protestant or even pagan, holding to the earliest traditions of the Grand Duchy of Lithuania as the last pagan state in Europe. Indeed, the Lithuanian language serves as more than a means of transmitting culture. It is itself virtually the only way of identifying that one is or is not culturally Lithuanian.

The centrality of the Lithuanian language to the national identity is not surprising, given the forty-year long effort by the Russian Empire to abolish the language in its written form as well as the fifty-year Soviet occupation, during which Russian was the language of political and economic discourse. During the independence struggle of 1988–1991, language played an important role in helping to define Lithuanian identity and shape the struggle against outsiders.

THE RESTORATION OF INDEPENDENCE

With the coming to power of Mikhail Gorbachev in the 1980s in Moscow and the launching of his policy of glasnost (openness) and perestroika (restructuring), it became easier for people to engage in formerly prohibited forms of protest. The first such act in Lithuania occurred on 23 August 1987, when a small public meeting was held near a monument to a national poet to commemorate the Molotov-Ribbentrop Pact, which had led to the forcible incorporation of the country within the Soviet empire. The official Soviet position had been that Lithuania had voluntarily entered the Soviet Union and that no secret protocols of the pact existed. A year later, a group of intellectuals, drawn from discussion clubs, the Lithuanian Writer's Union, and a number of small groups concerned with the protection of the environment and historical buildings, declared the creation of the Lithuanian Reform Movement, Sąjūdis, also known as the Lithuanian Movement for Perestroika. The movement's initial goals were largely concerned with the protection of Lithuanian culture, particularly the language. This was reflected in the very first platform, which called for proclaiming the Lithuanian language as an official state language of the republic, strengthening the teaching of Lithuanian in schools, establishing language schools for national minorities, and correcting misrepresentations of Lithuanian history.

These and other demands were adopted at Sąjūdis's founding congress in October 1988, an event of enormous importance in the movement toward restoring independence. Aired on television and on radio, the congress stirred the Lithuanian nation and resulted in a dramatic change in the movement's membership. Almost overnight, Sąjūdis was transformed from an intellectual movement to a mass one. Within a short time, previously prohibited national myths and symbols were once again being displayed throughout the republic. The movement's changing demographics radicalized Sąjūdis. In response, many of the movement's initial founders became some of its harshest critics. The centrality of the cultural concerns that had united the intellectuals of the initiative group now gave way to the politicization of nationalism. Within a year, initial demands for economic sovereignty within the Soviet Union were replaced by insistence on the restoration of the country's prewar independence, reflecting a tidal wave of nationalism that was taking place throughout the crumbling Soviet Union.

Such political activity outside of official party channels signaled the emergence of a de facto multiparty system and threw the Lithuanian Communist Party (LCP) into a state of crisis. Particularly troubling was the popular groundswell that formed behind Sąjūdis. Popular support for the movement was so high that a number of its candidates were successfully elected to the highest legislative institution in the Soviet Union, the Congress of People's Deputies. Hoping to moderate the movement's demands for full independence, the congress proclaimed Lithuania's sovereignty within the Soviet Union. This did little, however, to quell the rising tide of public sentiment in favor of full independence. In August 1989 over two million people linked hands in a human chain stretching 650 kilometers from Vilnius to the capital city of Estonia, Tallinn, in protest of the Molotov-Ribbentrop Pact.

Concerned that it would be decimated in the upcoming elections to the newly created republican-level Supreme Council, the Lithuanian Communist Party held an extraordinary congress in December 1989, at which it debated whether to formally split from the Communist Party of the Soviet Union (CPSU). A majority voted for the split and formed an independent Lithuanian Communist Party. Those who opposed the breakup with Moscow formed their own party, which retained formal ties with the CPSU, the LCP(CPSU). Despite these efforts, the independent Lithuanian Communist Party (LCP) was dealt a severe blow in the 1990 elections to the Supreme Council. Sąjūdis candidates won an absolute majority in the legislature. The newly elected assembly elected Vytautas Landsbergis, Sąjūdis's leader, as its chair and declared the formal restoration of independence for Lithuania. Within a month, Gorbachev issued an ultimatum, demanding that the republic's legislature recant its declaration. When it refused to do so, the Soviet leader ordered that Lithuania be subjected to an economic blockade.

Despite the party's minority status in the Supreme Council, the legislature elected an LCP government. Renaming themselves the Lithuanian Democratic Labor Party (LDLP) at a congress in December 1990, the former communists were unable to sustain their government for long. After securing the concurrence of the Supreme Council for a moratorium on the act of the restoration of independence as a precondition for getting the Soviets to the bargaining table, the LDLP government found itself subjected to attempts at micromanagement by the legislative majority. The situation came to a head in January 1991, in the wake of public protests over proposed government increases in food prices. When Prime Minister Kazimiera Prunskienė flew to Moscow to hold talks with Gorbachev, she was accused of plotting to reestablish Soviet rule. Upon her return, her government was displaced by a Sąjūdis government, headed by Albertas Šimėnas.

The subsequent annulment of the government's planned price increases should have ended the crisis; however, Moscow's actions over the next several days continued to inflame the situation. Citing calls by Communist Party front groups (which included an organization calling itself the National Salvation Committee) for the imposition of direct presidential rule in the republic, Soviet president Mikhail Gorbachev issued an open demand for the immediate revocation of the acts restoring the republic's independence. He further stated that he was considering dissolving the republic's legislature and imposing direct presidential rule. The next day (11 January 1990) the National Salvation Committee announced that it was assuming all political authority in the republic. Simultaneously, the Soviet Army surrounded the press center and radio and TV tower and threatened to seize the Supreme Council building itself.

The public response to the Soviet actions was immediate. Tens of thousands of citizens surrounded the legislature in an act of defiance that may have dissuaded the military from an assault. Crowds surrounding the radio and TV tower, however, failed to deter its seizure; fourteen people lost their lives in the effort. The Soviet Army also seized the press center.

At the peak of the crisis, on the night of the assault on the radio and TV tower, Prime Minister Šimėnas mysteriously disappeared. Not to be found in the parliament, he later claimed that he had been working at another location to ensure the proper functioning of the government. Whether his story is true or whether he panicked, the Supreme Council voted only a few days after his confirmation as prime minister to replace him with Gediminas Vagnorius.

The following month, Lithuania's citizens voted overwhelmingly in favor of independence in a popular referendum. Nevertheless, the standoff with Moscow continued, as both sides claimed control over the country. A "war of laws" ensued, creating confusion as to whether the laws of Lithuania or those of the Soviet Union were to take precedence. Making the situation even more tense was the presence on the streets of both Lithuanian and Soviet armed police and military patrols, whose paths often crossed. Indeed, the potential for violence was underscored in July (1991) when several Lithuanian border guards were murdered at their post at Medininkai.

Further complicating the situation were the concerns within the country's minority populations about reemerging Lithuanian nationalism. The articulation of the Lithuanian national idea, requiring as it did the rejection of Polish and Russian culture, combined with the insistence that the Lithuanian language should become the primary vehicle for political and economic discourse, gave rise to anxieties among the republic's national minorities. The politicization of the national idea within Sąjūdis led to nationalist exclusivity that further exacerbated their concerns. The movement's demands that an independent Lithuania be a national state, with priority given to the Lithuanian culture and language, appeared to be a clear threat of oppression or perhaps even forcible assimilation for minorities, particularly those of Polish or Russian origin or descent. This threat was reflected in the fact that Sąjūdis was almost totally a Lithuanian movement. At the 1988 Constituent Congress, 980 of the 1021 deputies were Lithuanian; only nine were Poles and eight were Russians.

The response was predictable. Many Russians and smaller Russian-speaking minority groups—including Belarusians, Ukrainians, Jews, and Tatars—formed Edinstvo. This movement, formed with the encouragement of Moscow (indeed, almost certainly at the instigation of the KGB, to help undermine political stability in the breakaway republic), stood in open opposition to Sąjūdis, and in particular to the demands to make Lithuanian the official state language. But Edinstvo never succeeded in fully organizing the Russian-speaking community. While this was partially due to the organization's open support of the Soviet regime, it also reflected the highly fragmented nature of the Russian community itself. Hardly a community with a common interest, it was divided both socioeconomically and by varying degrees of integration into Lithuanian society. Large numbers of Russians, particularly those living in Vilnius, were descended from families that had lived in the region for centuries. Others were relatively new arrivals, who had been brought to the republic to provide a labor force in Soviet

The Two Bookends of Lithuanian Politics

Vytautas Landsbergis and Algirdas Brazauskas tower above all other Lithuanian politicians in leading Lithuania during the transition from being one of fifteen republics in the former Soviet Union to independence. Although they were allies in the struggle to free Lithuania from Soviet rule, they personified different approaches to achieving that goal. The competition between the two continued in the post-independence era, as they led opposing parties with conflicting visions of the country's economic and political future. Whereas in the West Landsbergis is seen as the main symbol of the Lithuanian struggle for independence, Brazauskas is more popular among the Lithuanian population.

Brazauskas, the son of a state official and a farmer in the first Republic of Lithuania, had a long and successful career in the Communist Party. He became the leader of the Communist Party of Lithuania (the General Secretary) in 1988 and remained in that position until the party renamed itself the Democratic Labor Party in December 1990.

Landsbergis was born into a family of intellectuals that had been actively involved in the Lithuanian national movement since the nineteenth century. He was a professor of music and an expert on the most famous Lithuanian painter and composer, Čiurlionis.

Landsbergis demonstrated a strong sense of patriotism, personal courage, and nerve in leading the Lithuanian people in their struggle with the Soviet Union. Believing that the Soviet Union was in decline, he called for a quick break with Moscow, which he believed would be successful. His view proved to be more accurate than that of Brazauskas, who believed that the Soviet Union remained internally strong and capable of quashing a rebellion. As a consequence, Brazauskas was much more cautious in his approach, advocating a policy of slow steps toward independence in order to avoid a direct conflict with Moscow, whose power he feared.

Landsbergis and Brazauskas had radically different visions of an independent Lithuania. Landsbergis held romantic notions about restoring the country to its pre-Soviet status. His vision was that of an idealized Lithuania whose culture, values, Catholic traditions, and symbols would occupy center stage, uniting the country and informing its politics. His preoccupation with the defense of the national identity de-emphasized the importance of social and economic development. A strategic thinker, he is noted for his lack of interest in and unwillingness to deal with administrative, financial, and legal details.

Brazauskas's character stands in stark contrast to that of Landsbergis. He rarely speaks about culture or national identity, preferring to focus instead on economic matters. For Brazauskas, the state's first responsibility is to be an efficient administrator. His sober, down-to-earth positions were attractive to the Lithuanian population during the years of economic crisis that followed independence, when personal financial considerations, not national survival, occupied people's minds.

The two are also distinguished by their different political styles. Landsbergis is famous for his rhetorical, complicated, sarcastic way of speaking. He makes frequent indirect and ironic remarks about looming international threats to Lithuania, his speeches often referring to the threat from Russia, domestic enemies, and invidious Western cultural influence. This, together with his demagogic and vicious verbal attacks on political opponents, has seriously eroded his public support and undermined his claim to being the Father of the Nation since independence. As a consequence, he has thus far failed to achieve his personal goal of being elected president.

Brazauskas, on the other hand, avoids personal attacks on his political opponents, in particular Landsbergis. His uncomplicated speech is far more appealing to the public than the academic style of Landsbergis. Furthermore, his speech and mannerisms reflect a deeper understanding of the public mood as well as a greater concern for the plight of the average Lithuanian. Elected president in 1993, he has retained the public's trust. As a consequence, following four years of retirement, he returned to politics in 2002, becoming prime minister.

In general, it is fair to say that Brazauskas remains one of the most popular politicians in Lithuania. As for Landsbergis, his political influence has waned significantly, and he is struggling to regain his symbolic status as the leader of the Lithuanian independence movement.

factories and projects, including the nuclear power station in the Ignalina region.

Poles, on the other hand, were a good deal more socio-economically and historically united. Unlike the Russians, who were spread across many of the urban centers of the republic, Poles were largely concentrated in the regions in and around Vilnius that had been forcibly seized and occupied by Poland during the interwar period. The community's major weakness was the lack of an intelligentsia; most of its members were peasants with low levels of education. The Polish intelligentsia had fled during and after World War II. Those who had not were in many cases liquidated. Lacking an intelligentsia, and subjected to the Russification efforts of the Soviet era, the language spoken by Lithuanian Poles was a dialect of Polish with strong Russian and Belarusian influence. In this context, Sąjūdis's demands that Lithuanian be the state language appeared to many to be an effort to assimilate the Polish minority. As a consequence, they formed the Union of Poles in Lithuania to counter these efforts and came into direct conflict with Sąjūdis.

The demands of the Union of Poles contributed to fears among Lithuanian nationalists within Sąjūdis of a reemergence of Polish cultural dominance or, worse, the loss once again of the Vilnius region. Their demands included increasing the quality of Polish language instruction in schools, creating a Polish university, and forming an autonomous Polish region in the area around Vilnius where the Polish population was in the majority. In pursuit of these goals, the political leadership of the Polish regions openly opposed Lithuanian independence and negotiated with Moscow for greater autonomy from Vilnius.

Despite opposition from Moscow and from within its borders, Lithuania nevertheless achieved its independence in the wake of the abortive coup in the Soviet Union in August 1991. Hard-liners, hoping to arrest the disintegration of Communist Party rule (as well as the disintegration of the empire), had arrested Mikhail Gorbachev in his Crimean retreat and declared emergency rule throughout the Soviet Union. However, the coup collapsed three days later, as the Soviet Army refused to back the putschists. Soviet Army units that had occupied the Lithuanian press center and television and radio tower since January now abandoned their occupation. In September 1991 Gorbachev, who had opposed any territorial change in the Baltic region, now recognized Lithuania's independence. International recognition immediately followed. The United States recognized Lithuania on 11 September, and the country was admitted to the United Nations on 17 September.

INDEPENDENT LITHUANIA

Having obtained the goals uniting most of the country and the restoration of independence, Prime Minister Vagnorius directed his government's attention to two highly contentious social and economic issues: de-Sovietization and privatization. These two issues, as it turned out, quickly led to the collapse of his government, by mid-1992. In the immediate aftermath of the collapse of Soviet rule in the country, the Vagnorius government launched a campaign to nationalize the property and assets of the former communists, to include those of the LDLP (previously the LCP). Among the assets seized were two newspapers. The LDLP protests drew support from much of the republic's independent press, which feared that the confiscations could ultimately be directed against all opposition media.

At the urging of the government, the legislature also considered broadening a law that banned former informants and employees of the Soviet KGB from government service for a period of five years so that the law would include former members of the Communist Party who had held positions of responsibility at virtually any level. This not only threatened members of the LDLP, but also affected the members of almost every political party, since many of them had been members of the Communist Party (either through belief in the system or as a means of advancement). The proposal resulted in significant opposition to the new government.

The opposition was further increased by the privatization of state-owned property. Although legislation to return land and property to prewar ownership had been passed in the summer of 1991, formal opposition did not emerge until after the government began implementing the law in the fall (following independence). By November, the LDLP formally declared itself in opposition to the government's program, arguing that the legislation encouraged land speculation and that only those farming the land should be permitted to own it. By spring, the Sąjūdis coalition had seriously fragmented over both the de-Sovietization and privatization efforts, and the Supreme Council moved to severely curtail government efforts to undertake both.

Fragmentation of the Sąjūdis movement was further exacerbated by the government's strained relations with the country's national minorities, particularly the Poles. Governors of the Polish districts of Vilnius and Šalčininkai had aligned themselves with the Soviet authorities during the independence struggle, going so far as to support the effort by Communist Party hard-liners in the August 1991 coup to reestablish Soviet rule in the republic. Many of these same governors were also either making overtures toward Warsaw or demanding autonomy following independence. The fear was that these regions would ultimately sue for independence or union with Poland. Concerns were openly expressed that Warsaw might even raise the "Vilnius question," with the grave repercussions that a struggle over territory might bring. In response to this threat, the Lithuanian government introduced direct rule in these regions in September 1991.

This action led to serious strains in relations with Poland, which despite its renunciation of any territorial claims on Vilnius or the Polish regions, found itself unable to reduce Lithuanian fears. The Lithuanian government further poisoned the atmosphere between the two countries by insisting on a Polish apology for and condemnation of the interwar seizure of Vilnius. Although the demand was motivated by Lithuanian concerns that their own claims to the capital were questionable (given that they had regained the city as a "gift" from the Soviet authorities), nationalist

Gediminas Vagnorius. (Reuters/Rich Clement/Archive Photos/Getty)

yearnings to "correct" the historical record by establishing Polish guilt and Lithuanian innocence were just as apparent. Whatever the motives on the part of the Lithuanian government, the Poles would not agree to the demands, fearing that in doing so they might provide the pretext for further repression of the Polish minority in Lithuania. When Vilnius reneged on its promise to restore self-rule in the Polish regions, Poland was left with no other option than to engage in formal protest, an action that led to Lithuanian charges that Warsaw was interfering in Lithuania's internal affairs.

The introduction of direct rule in the Vilnius and Šalčininkai regions heightened tensions between the Lithuanian government and the country's Polish population, leading to fears that the new state was bent on assimilating them. These fears were increased by statements from nationalist leaders—among them the head of the Independence Party, a close personal confidant of Sąjūdis chair Vytautas Landsbergis—that the country's Poles were in reality Polonized Lithuanians who had been deprived of their true

identity and culture by centuries of Polish rule, particularly in the regions in which they lived.

Those supporting the actions of the government in dealing with the internal threat posed by "disloyal" Poles stayed with the Sąjūdis parliamentary group. Others who wanted even more resolute action gravitated toward several smaller nationalist parties, including the Union of Lithuanian Nationalists, the Union of Political Prisoners and Deportees, the Independence Party, and the Christian Democrats. Those opposed to the government action left Sąjūdis to join parties taking more moderate positions on the national issue (the Center Union, the Liberal Union, the Social-Democrats, and even the Democratic Labor Party).

By May 1992, the political situation reached crisis proportions: the legislature was deadlocked for several weeks, during which time the government's supporters and those in opposition refused to sit together in joint session, each holding separate plenary sessions. The impasse was overcome only after a referendum to establish a strong presidency failed. All parties agreed to hold elections to a new assembly (renamed the Seimas) in October, and it was later agreed that a referendum on a strong presidency would be held at the same time as the elections; the referendum passed in October. Vagnorius resigned, and Aleksandras Abišala became prime minister in July 1992, after the opposition refused to form a government until the fall elections. Essentially a provisional government lacking majority coalition support in the Supreme Council, the Abišala cabinet avoided any new initiatives and attempted to defend the Vagnorius economic reforms against legislative cutbacks until the promised fall elections.

The 1992 elections were a stunning victory for the former Communist Party, renamed the Democratic Labor Party (LDLP). The LDLP won an absolute majority in the Seimas. This victory was followed in early 1993 by the election of the LDLP's leader, Algirdas Brazauskas, as the first president of the republic (an office created by the Constitution of 1992, which was approved in the referendum of fall 1992).

The electoral victory of the Democratic Labor Party, which was owed in part to the support the party enjoyed with the overwhelming majority of the country's national minorities, helped to greatly reduce ethnic tensions in Lithuania. Entering office at the same time as direct rule was being lifted in the Polish regions, the leftist government made economic matters its first priority and de-emphasized national issues.

This in turn permitted the president to achieve several foreign policy successes during his term in office. (The

Vytautas Landsbergis. (Hulton Archive/Getty Images)

Lithuanian constitution assigns primary responsibility for the country's foreign policy to the president.) Lithuania was admitted to the European Council in May 1993. Soviet military forces withdrew from the country in August of the same year. Finally, relations with Poland were normalized, and a treaty between the two countries was signed in 1995. Furthermore, by the end of his presidential term, Brazauskas had established the three priorities of Lithuanian foreign policy: membership in NATO, membership in the European Union, and good relations with its neighbors.

The LDLP government, headed by Prime Minister Šleževičius, did not, however, fare as well. Although it continued privatization of the country's economy, it did so over the opposition of parliamentary deputies from its own party. As the economy worsened, an "Initiative Group" formed within the LDLP faction calling for abandonment of the commitment to free market reforms. The opposition, for its part, accused the government of carrying out privatization in a manner that most directly served the economic interests of LDLP members. The charge was a particularly difficult one for the LDLP to deny, given the enterprises that many of its members acquired; among those members was former prime minister Bronislavas Lubys, a personal friend of President Brazauskas who headed the government from the fall 1992 legislative elections until the presidential elections of 1993.

Even more damaging for the LDLP, however, were the scandals that plagued the government. Among them were the resignation of the head of the Central Bank on charges of corruption, the dramatic rise in Mafia-related crime, and a scandal arising over the government's participation in a conference of former Soviet states on investment and access to Russian energy resources. (The Lithuanian constitution prohibits the country from entering into any collective agreements with countries of the former Soviet Union.) The most pressing crisis, however, was the series of bank failures that occurred in 1995. Šleževičius was accused of withdrawing personal savings from one of these banks prior to its collapse, benefiting from insider information on its financial situation. Ultimately, the prime minister was forced to resign under pressure from the president, owing to this scandal.

As a consequence of the continuing economic crisis and the scandals associated with the LDLP, the Homeland Union (the political party emerging out of the right-wing remnants of Sąjūdis) won the 1996 legislative elections. Hence, President Brazauskas during his last year and a half in office was faced with an opposition government, once again headed by Prime Minister Gediminas Vagnorius. The latter pursued an economic program that mixed a free market with a considerable degree of state regulation. Of greater concern to the International Monetary Fund was the fact that the government consistently overspent. As a result, the country's businesses became increasingly monopolistic and less competitive.

Valdas Adamkus, a Lithuanian-American, was elected president in the 1998 elections. Brazauskas chose not to run and threw his support behind the former prosecutor general, Artūras Paulauskas, who barely lost in the final vote count. Assuming office amid doubts that he knew Lithuania's political situation well enough to serve effectively as president, Adamkus moved quickly to dispel such concerns. Employing his enormous public popularity, he was able to successfully pursue a number of major initiatives early in his term. Collectively these initiatives had a significant impact on the further development and interpretation of the Lithuanian constitution, redefining not only the role of the presidency but executive-legislative relations as well.

Despite a Constitutional Court decision denying him the right to appoint a prime minister, Adamkus succeeded in requiring the entire cabinet to retake the oath of office. (The Constitutional Court had ruled that a newly elected president was required to resubmit a sitting prime minister's name for a renewed vote of confidence from the Seimas; in the event that the Seimas refused to reaffirm its confidence in the government, the president could then appoint a new prime minister.) Shortly thereafter, the president successfully pursued rationalization of the government, reducing the number of ministries from seventeen to eleven. He also promised to continue Lithuania's commitment to "rejoining Europe" (NATO membership, European Union membership, and good relations with the country's neighbors) and to clean up government corruption. The latter promise resulted in a large number of high-level government resignations in 1998. Among them were the minister of health, the minister of internal affairs, the minister of communications, the general director of the Security Department, the chief of the Special Investigations Division, the chief of the tax inspectorate, and the chief of customs. Several of these resignations involved scandals related to the personal use of government property, as in the case of the minister of communications. Others occurred over alleged incompetence, as was the case with the chief of customs.

Ultimately, however, the president had to deal with Prime Minister Vagnorius himself. Although early in his term the president seemed to be working in tandem with the head of the government, by late 1998, it was increasingly evident that there were significant policy differences between the two, particularly regarding the economy. With the support of his economic and political advisers, the president called for cuts in government spending, while Prime Minister Vagnorius and his staff favored spending as a means to get the economy going in the wake of the downturn caused by the Russian ruble crisis. (The Russian ruble rapidly lost value in fall of 1998, making Lithuanian products unaffordable for Russian consumers and thereby reducing Lithuanian exports.) In pursuit of this objective, the government provided loans and direct assistance to Lithuanian industries hurt by the loss of the Russian market. This caused a growing budget deficit and ultimately drew the criticism of the European Union, which was concerned that the government was propping up inefficient businesses.

Convinced that part of the problem was a lack of accountability and transparency in government expenditures, the president nominated Kęstutis Lapinskas for the post of state controller, an office charged with responsibility for checking the government's financial activities. Lapinskas, who was not a member of the ruling coalition, ran into fierce opposition from the prime minister and was ultimately rejected by the parliamentary majority. Despite this, the president submitted Lapinskas's candidacy yet a second time, again unsuccessfully. The political conflict created a breach between the president and the prime minister, one that was further widened when the president criticized the government's economic program in his annual report to the Seimas.

The rift between the two carried over into spring of 1999, as they continued to publicly disagree over how best to deal with the economic crisis in the face of a growing government revenue loss. Further adding to the difficulties between the two was the political storm that emerged when it was revealed that Belarus was not paying its bill for imported Lithuanian electrical power. As the crisis unfolded, news surfaced that the government was selling the electrical power through a third party. Numerous rumors spread concerning personal interests related to the third party; however, it never became clear how that third party had come to be involved or whether it indeed was involved in the sale of electrical power to Belarus.

The rift between the president and the prime minister came to a head in April 1999, when Adamkus officially expressed a lack of confidence in Vagnorius and asked him to resign. In a press release, Vagnorius agreed to withdraw from the post of prime minister to prevent further escalation of political tensions; however, the Seimas announced its official support for the prime minister by a vote of 77 in favor and 46 opposed. Seimas Chairman Vytautas Landsbergis stated the resolution was an independent assessment of the prime minister, indicating the parliament's desire for Vagnorius to maintain his position. According to Lithuania's constitution, only the Seimas can remove a prime minister. Hence, the president found himself faced with the prospect that the prime minister might continue to serve. The crisis was resolved, however, on 30 April 1999, when Prime Minister Vagnorius resigned of his own accord.

Adamkus's efforts to force the resignation of the prime minister, together with his earlier heavy-handedness in trying to appoint Lapinskas as state controller, irritated many in the Seimas ruling coalition, particularly within the key party of the parliamentary majority, the Homeland Union (Conservatives of Lithuania). As a consequence, the Conservatives initially refused to enter a new government and called upon Adamkus to ask another party to form a governing coalition within the Seimas. Ultimately, however, the Conservatives agreed to the appointment of the popular Conservative mayor of Vilnius, Rolandas Paksas. In June 1999, Paksas received widespread support from the Seimas, where his appointment was confirmed on a vote of 105 to 1, with 31 abstentions.

Upon assuming his responsibilities as the prime minister, Paksas committed his government to reduced spending along the lines supported by the president. This in turn created a rift within the Conservative majority in the Seimas, as former prime minister Vagnorius publicly criticized the new government's spending priorities. Paksas's position was further undermined by the fact that almost

Rolandas Paksas after announcing his resignation as prime minister in Lithuania's capital, Vilnius, on 20 June 2001. (AFP/Getty Images)

half of the Vagnorius cabinet retained their ministerial portfolios. With his legislative support tenuous, the new prime minister was dependent upon presidential support to remain in office. Hence, when he went on national television on 18 October, to announce his unwillingness to sign the agreements with Williams International permitting the American company to purchase a management stake in Mažeikiai Nafta (the country's oil industry), an agreement recently approved by the Seimas majority and supported by the president, the fate of his government was sealed. After only four months in office, Paksas tendered his resignation at the request of President Adamkus on 27 October 1999.

The country's third government in 1999 was confirmed in a Seimas vote on 3 November. Andrius Kubilius, a member of the Homeland Union (Conservatives of Lithuania) received 82 votes. Twenty deputies voted in opposition to his confirmation, and 36 abstained. Kubilius pledged himself to continue a policy of reduced government expenditures as the best strategy for resolving the economic crisis. He further called for measures to promote foreign investment and indicated his support for the Williams deal. The latter had created the greatest political storm in the entire post-Soviet era, as political leaders, particularly those on the left, and numerous public demonstrations demanded that the agreement be abrogated. At the end of the year the gov-

ernment was still in office, but there were growing calls for early parliamentary elections in 2000.

The political turmoil of 1999 carried over into 2000, as the economy continued to suffer from the prolonged recession brought on by the devaluation of the Russian ruble and the consequent loss of the eastern market to Lithuanian goods and produce. Public frustration with the economic situation found expression in continued opposition to the Williams deal and was reflected in falling trust in political institutions and a major realignment of the country's party system. As the ruling Homeland Union's popularity fell precipitously, parties on the political left, particularly the Democratic Labor Party, were able to capitalize on the public's growing discontent by championing populist platforms eschewing further privatization of state enterprises, demanding reconsideration of the pace of entry into the European Union and NATO, and questioning budget priorities.

The political turmoil gave rise to some troubling phenomena, not the least of which was the election of Vytautas Šustauskas, a poorly educated man prone to anti-Semitic and anti-Western rhetoric, as mayor of Kaunas, the republic's second largest city. This, together with the emergence of former prosecutor Arturas Paulauskas as a major political figure (whom many on the political right suspected of having family ties to Soviet-era security structures), led to concerns in some corners that a Red-Brown Coalition (that is, a communist-fascist coalition) was threatening to come to power in the country. Despite these concerns, the country's commitment to democratic norms remained steadfast. Indeed, prior to the October 2000 elections to the national legislature, the Organization for Security and Cooperation in Europe (OSCE) announced that it would not be sending observers.

By the end of the millennium, the Baltic country was continuing its commitment to full global and regional integration. In 2001 it became the 141st member of the World Trade Organization (WTO); and, in 2004, the country gained membership in both NATO and the European Union (EU). More importantly, the country's political systems had endured ten years of reforms without any significant threat of turning back from its commitment to democratic norms. The ability of Lithuanian political institutions to weather these political storms says much about the degree to which democracy and democratic institutions are consolidated.

POLITICAL DEVELOPMENTS

The Constitution of the Republic of Lithuania, adopted in a national referendum in October 1992, makes it abundantly clear that the new state is a national state. The preamble makes the unambiguous claim that the state is the creation of the Lithuanian nation and that the Lithuanian language is the state language. Further, the national identity of the Lithuanian people as it had emerged during the independence period is laid out. The Lithuanian people, having "established the State of Lithuania many centuries ago" and having "defended its freedom and independence and

Mažeikiai Nafta

The Lithuanian oil refinery at Mažeikiai is the only oil refinery in the Baltic States. It supplies the majority of Lithuania's gasoline and much of that used in Estonia and Latvia as well. Nafta (Mažeikiai Oil) consists of the Mažeikiai oil refinery, capable of refining 300,000 barrels of crude oil a day; the Naftotiekis pipeline; and the Butinge oil terminal, with a capacity of 160,000 barrels of oil a day, according to the Department of Statistics of the government of Lithuania.

In 1998 the government of Lithuania merged the Mažeikiai oil refinery with the mostly state-owned pipeline and terminal companies into a single entity, AB Mažeikiai Nafta. Owing to extensive debt and poor management, the government decided to seek an investor to manage the enterprise. The privatization process that had been undertaken following the collapse of Soviet rule and the return to independence was charged with political emotions and had led to the collapse of two governments in one year. At the center of the public debate was the question of which side—Russia or the West—should be allowed to have managing control of Lithuania's most important industry. One view in the debate held that selling shares to a Russian investor would deepen the country's economic dependence on Russia. The alternative view questioned the transparency of the negotiations with American investors.

In the fall of 1999 an American company, Williams International, acquired 33 percent of the shares of Mažeikiai Nafta, as well as control over management decisions, for $150 million, according to Lithuania's Ministry of Economics. An additional 7.4 percent of the company was sold to various Lithuanian and foreign investors. Owing to the economic and political importance of the company, the government decided to retain the remaining 59.6 percent of the shares in the enterprise.

Despite hopes that new management would help Mažeikiai Nafta to resolve its financial difficulties, the Lithuanian company is still struggling. In January 2002, the company announced an unaudited loss of 277.2 million Litai ($69.3 million) for the year 2001, according to the Department of Statistics. In the first quarter of 2002 revenues from refining were about $30 million less than had been projected. The most important factors accounting for these losses were a sharp decline in crude oil and oil product prices and a drop in sales in Lithuania. The company also struggled with oil supply problems. Its primary oil suppliers are Russian companies, which did not provide the enterprise with a consistent, uninterrupted supply of crude. In an effort to resolve this problem, Mažeikiai Nafta signed a deal with Yukos permitting the Russian oil supplier to purchase a 26.85 percent stake in the Lithuanian enterprise for $75 million. In return Yukos was obligated to supply 4.8 million tons of crude oil per year. The deal reduced the government's stake to 40.66 percent. Williams's stake was also lowered to 26.85 percent, but it remained the chief operator of the plant, with Yukos having advisory input. However, in 2002 Williams sold its management stake to Yukos.

Mažeikiai Nafta is one of the largest taxpayers in the country, and its economic performance is of enormous importance to the overall economy. It is the primary determinant of gas prices in Lithuania, with its performance influencing the prices of all oil products and services on the Lithuanian market. The future development and economic performance of Mažeikiai Nafta will have much to say about the success of market reform in Lithuania.

preserved its spirit, native language, writing, and customs," are nevertheless a tolerant people desiring to foster "national accord" and a "harmonious civil society."

Lithuania has a premier-presidential system similar in design to the French political system. The key institutions established by the 1992 constitution are a legislature (the Seimas), a split executive comprising a popularly elected president and a prime minister nominated by the president and confirmed by the Seimas, and a split court system. The Supreme Court serves as the last court of appeal, and the Constitutional Court rules on issues of constitutionality (judicial review). The major differences from the French political system are that the Seimas is a unicameral legislature

and the president is somewhat weaker. Nonetheless, in contrast to a parliamentary system based on the British Westminster model, the president as the head of state has substantial de jure powers in both the policy-making and government-forming processes.

The legislature, the Seimas, is composed of 141 deputies. Until the summer of 2000, 71 of them were elected in majority fashion in single-mandate districts. If no one candidate received more than 50 percent of the vote in the first round, a second round was required between the two top vote getters. In the hopes of gaining a larger number of seats in the upcoming elections, the former legislative majority changed the system to the first-past-the post (plurality)

The Constitution of the Republic of Lithuania

The Constitution of the Republic of Lithuania was approved in a referendum on 25 October 1992. The document was a compromise between a parliamentary system, in which the legislative branch would dominate a figurehead president, and a presidential system, in which the legislature would be coequal with the president. This mixed system, similar in design to that of France, is often referred to as a semipresidential system.

The constitution states that Lithuania is a unitary state, no part of which may become independent. Lithuania's constitution includes the Act on the Non-Alignment of the Republic of Lithuania to Post-Soviet Eastern Alliances, which is intended to prohibit the country from entering into any alliances or multilateral forums uniting the country with the former Soviet Union. The constitution further establishes that Lithuania is a democratic republic with sovereignty vested in the people. Fundamental human rights and democratic values, including freedom of speech, religion, and conscience are guaranteed. Certain social guarantees are also provided, among them free medical care, retirement pensions, unemployment compensation, and state support for families and children.

Governmental powers are divided between the legislature, executive, and judiciary. The legislative powers are vested in a parliament called the Seimas. Elected every four years, the Seimas comprises 141 members, 70 of whom are elected from party lists on the basis of proportional representation. The remaining 71 are elected in winner-take-all contests in single-member districts. The Seimas exercises a significant degree of control over the government. Not only does it pass the laws that the government implements, it must confirm the head of government, the prime minister, and the prime minister's program. It can also vote the prime minister and the cabinet out of office.

The executive consists of a president, the head of state, and a prime minister, the head of government. The government, with its constituent ministries, exercises broad authority over day-to-day affairs, particularly in the economic realm. The prime minister is appointed by the president with the approval of the Seimas and can be removed by the Seimas.

As the head of state, the president is concerned with broad policy questions, particularly in the security and foreign affairs fields. The president also selects the prime minister (with the approval of the Seimas), approves ministerial candidates, and appoints the commander in chief of the armed forces (with the approval of the Seimas). The president is elected directly by the people for a five-year term and a maximum of two consecutive terms. Candidates must be at least forty years old. For a candidate to be elected in the first round, 50 percent of the voters must participate, and the candidate must receive more than half of the total votes cast. If the first round does not produce a president, a second round is held between the two top candidates, and a plurality vote is sufficient to win.

The judiciary is composed of the Supreme Court and subordinate courts, which decides on cases in law, and a Constitutional Court, which decides on the constitutionality of acts of the Seimas, the president, and the government.

---

rules, used in the American and British system to elect members to the lower house. The remaining 70 seats in the Seimas are decided on the basis of a party-list vote, with parties achieving the 5 percent threshold (7 percent in the event of party blocs) being allotted a proportion of the deputies roughly equivalent to the percentage of the vote they receive. (The actual proportion of deputies is almost always greater, given the large number of voters who cast their ballots for parties and blocs that do not achieve the minimum threshold.)

The government is responsible for the day-to-day running of the country. The head of the government is the prime minister, who is nominated by the president but elected by the Seimas. Upon confirmation, the prime minister selects his cabinet and presents a program to the Seimas. The government program must be approved by the Seimas. Although the president may ask for the resignation of the prime minister, only the Seimas is constitutionally empowered to remove a prime minister in a vote of no confidence.

The government comprises the prime minister and his cabinet, who collectively serve as the political masters of the bureaucracy of the government's ministries. The bureaucracy remains one of the political problems facing the country. Although much has been done to consolidate the political institutions of state power (the legislature, the prime minister, and the president), little if any reform of state administrative institutions has been effected. This neglect owes largely to both the lack of a coherent strategy for reform and the persistence of Soviet era bureaucratic operating patterns. The high turnover rate of Lithuania's governments (there were eight governments from the implementation of the 1992 constitution to the turn of the century) has not given elected politicians the time to plan and execute a comprehensive reform of the bureaucracy. Only the government of Andrius Kubilius, which served for one year from the end of 1999 to the elections in fall of 2000, attempted to do so. Subsequent governments have not yet been able to fully implement these reforms.

The most meaningful reforms undertaken thus far that have in any measurable way contributed to better performance and greater coordination within and between the ministries have been those mandated by the European Union in anticipation of Lithuania's entry into the organization. However, many of these reforms have been adopted without any proper understanding of how they actually operate.

The office of the president was created in the 1992 constitution to resolve the paralysis that gripped the legislature in the summer of 1992. The introduction of the presidency has done much to ensure against a repeat of this situation. (It is significant to note in this regard that of the three governments removed by majority vote of the Seimas, two were removed at the initiative and request of the president.) Nevertheless, although the president has substantial powers, which include the right of veto, initiation of legislation, and appointment of the prime minister, all of these powers are limited in scope, so that the president has no guaranteed check over either the legislature or the government. Although the president can veto legislation, an absolute majority of the Seimas can override that veto. (A simple majority of legislators present for a quorum is all that is required to initially pass most bills.)

Just as importantly, the government is ultimately responsible to the Seimas. Although the president alone has the right to nominate a prime minister, only the Seimas can confirm or remove the prime minister in a majority vote. The vote to remove a prime minister triggers a choice for the president. The president can either abide by the decision of the Seimas and agree to the removal of the prime minister or instead call for early elections to the Seimas. There are only two other conditions under which the president may dissolve the legislature prior to its serving out its elected term: if the Seimas fails to confirm a government program two times in succession within a sixty-day period or is not able to reach a decision on a nomination to prime minister within thirty days. This power is, however, subject to important qualifications based on the time remaining of the president's term and the amount of time served by the Seimas since it was elected to office.

As is the case for the bureaucracy, the primary problem facing the country's court system is the persistence of Soviet attitudes and work methods. There is a dearth of judges and lawyers trained in the rules and procedures of the new court system; like most areas of public life in Lithuania (as well as throughout Eastern Central Europe), the ideological nature of communist rule created atrophy within institutions and a body of professionals whose first duty was to the state. A professional code of ethics has been drafted, but one still needs to be written for lawyers and other legal professionals. The independence of the courts is also not yet fully established. The Ministry of Justice continues to intervene in court decisions, and both judges and lawyers often look to central ministries and political authorities for clues on how to resolve cases.

Despite these problems, the courts have played an important role in habituating political elites and the public to the rule of law and democratic values. Although the public remains cautious in its evaluation of the courts, it is significant that most would nonetheless refer disputes with state authorities to these same courts. The Constitutional Court in particular has issued important decisions contributing to the strengthening of the rule of law as well as the independence of the judiciary. Its most important challenge thus far involved a series of rulings that eventually led to the impeachment and removal of the country's president, Rolandas Paksas, in 2004. (Paksas had been accused of violating his authority by interceding in the privatization process on behalf of businessmen and leaking classified information to businessmen.)

Lithuania has a multiparty system. In the early stages of development from 1989 to 1992, parties were concerned with the issue of the restoration of the country's independence. Reflecting this unidimensional concern, the party system was divided into two highly polarized blocs, one (the Sąjūdis bloc) supporting a radical and rapid break with Moscow, the other (members of the Communist Party who had broken with Moscow and formed an independent party) a more gradual and rational one.

The achievement of independence led to divisions within each of the two blocs (particularly the Sąjūdis bloc) as other issues became more salient. These divisions in turn resulted in the formation of new parties and the emergence of a multiparty system, beginning in 1992. However, the Lithuanian public has yet to fully identify with parties and has demonstrated a significant degree of disillusionment with the party system.

Despite the presence of a multiparty system, most of the first decade of independence has been marked by the continued dominance of the two core parties of the pre-independence struggle. There were three legislative elections in the first decade after the restoration of the republic. The Democratic Labor Party (LDLP) won a majority in the 1992 elections. The right-wing remnants of Sąjūdis, the Homeland Union (Conservatives) won a plurality in the elections to the second Seimas in 1996. They formed a government with their allies, the Christian Democratic Party. Although in both the first and second Seimas the ruling parties (and their coalition allies) served out a full term, each experienced problems with governmental stability. The Democratic Labor Party majority in the first Seimas elected the governments of Bronislavas Lubys (1992–1993), Adolfas Šleževičius (1993–1996), and Mindaugas Stankevičius (1996). The coalition led by the Homeland Union in the second Seimas elected the governments of Gediminas Vagnorius (1996–1999), Rolandas Paksas (1999), and Andrius Kubilius (1999–2000).

The rise and fall of governments in the first two Seimases was not, however, related to coalition instability in the Seimas. Rather, the primary cause was scandal revolving around economic crises. The Šleževičius LDLP government fell as a consequence of the prime minister having transferred bank deposits using insider information in the midst of a bank crisis. The Vagnorius Conservative–Christian Democratic government resigned when the prime minister was not able to adequately explain his personal financial interests in the sale of energy to Belarus in the midst of a continuing economic crisis brought on by the collapse of the Russian ruble. Of the remaining four governments, two were care-taker LDLP governments—the Lubys government led by a prime minister who was pledged to resign once a new president was elected, and the Stankevičius government, which served until the end of the term of the Seimas. A third was the Paksas Conservative–Christian Democratic government, which resigned over policy differences with the parliamentary majority concerning the privatization of the country's oil industry. The fourth was the caretaker Kubilius Conservative–Christian Democratic government of 1999–2000.

The October 2000 elections to the third Seimas marked the first time in the post-Soviet era that one party did not capture a majority or overwhelming plurality (as in the case of the Homeland Union, which won 69 of 141, 2 seats short of an absolute majority) in the legislature. This departure has ushered in a new era of coalition politics, in which agreements between two or more parties are essential to the formation and maintenance of governments. The first government elected by the third Seimas was led by Rolandas Paksas and was backed by the right-wing Liberal Union, the left-of-center New Union (Social Liberals), and a consortium of smaller parties, none of which was rewarded with any positions in the new government. The Paksas government (the second one he had headed) lasted only a few short months, from 2000 to mid-2001. The coalition behind it was simply too ideologically diverse. The government of Algirdas Brazauskas (the country's first president) was elected in mid-2001, and was backed by a left-wing coalition uniting the Social Democratic Party and the Social Liberals. It should be noted that the old Social Democratic Party merged with the Democratic Labor Party (the former Communist Party) to form the new Social Democratic Party in late 2001. The new party is dominated by the core of the Democratic Labor Party, as attested to by the fact that Brazauskas is the party's leader.

To be sure there are problems, as reflected in the inability of the state bureaucracy to deal effectively with the economic crisis brought on by the collapse of the Russian markets in late 1998. Overall, however, Lithuania's political institutions have achieved a substantial degree of stability. This stability was demonstrated in the 2004 impeachment of President Paksas, the country's third president. Despite the trauma associated with an impeachment, the Seimas and the Constitutional Court successfully led the country through the process. There is nonetheless much that remains to be accomplished. The party system is still forming and the courts are still transitioning to Western ethical standards and practices. The most important goal, however, is to increase public trust in state institutions.

CULTURAL DEVELOPMENT

The Lithuanian state was the last pagan state in Europe, resisting conversion to Christianity for many centuries. Even when the country's rulers were finally Christianized at the end of the fourteenth century, the peasantry remained pagan for several centuries afterward. Even today, Lithuanian culture is heavily influenced by pagan mythology. This is particularly evident in folk art and music. Wood carvings, sculptures, and wooden masks date back to pagan times. The images of demons, trolls, and gods that provide the themes for these wood carvings all have pagan origins. The wooden poles that are found alongside many of the country's roads in the rural areas were familiar in pagan times as well. Christian symbols such as crosses were merely added to them. Musical instruments, particularly wind flutes, as well as the folk songs of Lithuania, possess the haunting quality familiar to those who have participated in Scandinavian nature festivals.

Many supposedly Christian holidays celebrated in the country are marked with pagan symbols and traditions. For example, the arrangements made of dyed meadow grasses, forest flowers, berry leaves, moss, and corn ears used to celebrate Palm Sunday in the Vilnius region have their origin in pagan festivals. Indeed, paganism has worked to transform some of the core themes of Christianity in the country. The image of the mourning Christ that is so much a part of folk

Statuette in the town of Stripeikiai. (Corel Corporation)

art transforms Jesus from an all-powerful savior with the power to change lives to a grieving deity unable to bear the sufferings of the Lithuanian people. The devil as well is little more than a bumbling, humorous character who is more to be pitied for his ineptness than feared for any evil power.

Pagans worship nature. (Their gods are gods of fire, thunder, water, and the forest, among other natural objects.) This nature worship is reflected in the strong attachment that Lithuanians have to nature. During the Soviet era, Lithuanians would spend their summers looking for the remains of those deported to Siberia in order to return them to Lithuania where they could rest in peace in their own soil. It is therefore not at all surprising that environmental concerns were among the key issues that led to the initial formation of the Sąjūdis movement, which ultimately led the country to regain its independence from the Soviet Union.

LITHUANIAN NATIONAL IDENTITY

Lithuanians are also extremely proud of their language. Believed to be one of the oldest extant languages in Europe, it is considered by scholars to have retained with the least changes most of the elements of Proto-Indo-European, the original language from which all of the languages spoken in Europe have evolved. (For that reason it is studied in many linguistics programs across the globe.) Nationalistic pride in their language has formed within the Lithuanians a strong attachment to it and determination to protect it. The nation and culture survived a two-hundred year-long union with the more numerous Poles (the Polish-Lithuanian state), repeated efforts by the Russian tsars to assimilate Lithuania in the eighteenth and nineteenth centuries, and Soviet repression during and after World War II. Since the restoration of statehood in 1991, the Lithuanian state has funneled substantial resources into the preservation of the national language and culture, in order to sustain them against Polish cultural domination and Russian influence. Commissions have been established at all levels of governance charged with surveying government documents for grammatical errors or the use of foreign words in place of Lithuanian words. To avoid using foreign loan words when their own language does not have a suitable term (as frequently occurs when new ideas and concepts emerge from technological innovation), the Ministry of Culture has even gone so far as to create a Lithuanian word to replace the foreign one.

Such efforts suggest that the Lithuanians are a stubborn people, a characteristic noted by more than one observer. This stubbornness may indeed account for their having been the first people within the Soviet Union to have demanded full independence, against what could have only have been viewed as impossible odds at the time. The independence drive was further fueled by a strong sense of moral superiority vis-à-vis the country's neighbors. Lithuanians view themselves as having first been invaded by crusaders intent on forcing a religion upon them that they did not want, then subjected to Polonization of their culture and society by the more numerous Poles, and finally humiliated on two occasions by prolonged Russian occupations

(first occupation by the Russian Empire beginning in the late eighteenth century, then occupation by the Soviet Union in the latter half of the twentieth century). In contrast, Lithuanians point to their own tolerance of others. Indeed, Jews settled in Lithuania in the twelfth century seeking safe harbor from the crusading knights of Europe. There they built one of the great centers of Judaism. Tatars also came to the country and freely practiced Islam.

This focus on the oppression they have suffered and their own virtue has fueled a national myth that Lithuanians are a nation of "innocent sufferers." The Lithuanian self-image as a nation of innocent sufferers manifests itself in the form of a distinct distrust of outsiders. While not resulting in overt hostility—indeed Lithuanians are outwardly quite tolerant—this distinctive form of xenophobia is more than mere national pride. It is informed by a sense that all foreigners, not just representatives of historically repressive nations such as the Poles or Russians, have little to contribute to Lithuania. Indeed, there is a pervasive belief that the Lithuanian nation is so unique that it defies understanding by outsiders. Hence, there is a decided resistance to advice or assistance proffered by foreigners. This resistance is all the more pronounced when Lithuanians believe that the outsider has engaged in what they consider immoral conduct against them. For example, many Lithuanians feel intense moral disdain for the United States on two counts. First, the United States never came to the assistance of the Forest Boys, who carried out an eight-year armed struggle against Soviet occupation at the end of World War II, despite repeated promises to do so. Second, the official U.S. position throughout the Cold War was that Lithuania had been illegally incorporated into the Soviet Union. Yet when the country declared its independence in 1990, the United States did not recognize it. In fact, the United States actively encouraged the country to remain within the Soviet Union in order not to undermine Mikhail Gorbachev's legitimacy or endanger his rule. In other words, at the moment of truth, the United States, in the minds of Lithuanian nationalists, forsook its decades-long stance, simply because it did not fit the larger geopolitical reality of the moment.

None of this is to suggest that Lithuanians are anti-American. Nothing could be further from the truth, all the more so given the country's desire to enter NATO and strong U.S. support of that goal. Younger generations in particular admire American material wealth and popular culture, especially music and films. But it does perhaps help to account for the fact that Lithuanians can appear to the outsider to be cool, haughty, and indifferent.

A HISTORY OF CULTURAL ACHIEVEMENTS

Given their rich history, it is not surprising that the Lithuanian people are credited with many achievements in education and the sciences. The development of science began in Lithuania with the establishment of Vilnius University in 1579 by the Society of Jesus (the Jesuits). The university gave prominence to scholasticism, a theological and philosophical system of education based on the authority of the church fathers and the traditions of the Roman

Catholic Church. An order of the Catholic Church, the Jesuits were established as part of the Counter-Reformation to fight the rise of Protestantism among the educated classes of Europe. Their presence in Lithuania did much to deepen the faith of both the nobility and the peasantry in Catholicism, a faith that had never been very strong. (As discussed above, paganism had persisted among the Lithuanians long after their supposed Christianization.) It also accomplished its intended purpose. The country rejected the Protestant Reformation. The only Lithuanian Protestants in the modern era are those from the westernmost regions around the port of Klaipėda, which was founded by the Livonian Order, an order of crusading knights.

Despite the openly religious purpose of the university, by the seventeenth century, much of the scholarship was increasingly informed by the classical humanism of the Renaissance, and the classical ideas of the Greeks and Romans began to become more prominent in Lithuanian cultural life. The first works by Lithuanians on mathematics and the sciences occurred about the same time. In the latter half of the eighteenth century the Enlightenment came to be the main influence on Lithuanian ideas. The influence of scholasticism among Lithuanian scholars and intellectuals had waned considerably by then. When the Jesuit Order was disbanded in 1773, Vilnius University became a state university (it was known as the Highest School of Vilnius until 1803, after which it once again became known as Vilnius University), and scholasticism was no longer in evidence.

By the beginning of the nineteenth century, faculties in physics, medicine, mechanics, probability theory, statistics, and agronomy were added, as science became increasingly more prominent in the curriculum. Influenced by the ideals of the French Revolution, scholars were also in the forefront of the national reawakening. They undertook to write a history for the Lithuanian people, study its language, and identify its culture. This activity helped to arouse a sense of nationalism among the population. Among the more important scholars involved in this effort was Simonas Daukantas (a student of Zegota Ignac Onacewicz, the first to lecture on Lithuanian history), who was the first to write about the history of Lithuania in Lithuanian. Joachim Lelewel was another important figure. He paid less attention to the role of kings and the nobility in history and focused instead on social movements and society as a whole. All of this fostered a sense of social and political activism on the part of the university's students, which led them to participate in the unsuccessful 1830 November Uprising against Russian rule.

After the insurrection was suppressed, Vilnius University was closed by order of Nicholas I, and Lithuanian scholars had to continue their work abroad or illegally within the country; despite this, they kept alive the dream of an independent Lithuanian state. Their efforts to develop the Lithuanian language, history, and culture were also important during a time of intense Russification (the promotion of Russian language and culture among the ethnic population of the Russian Empire, particularly in the western regions). Noteworthy in this regard was the work of Motiejus Valančius, a Catholic bishop who had been a student at Vilnius University. He helped resist Russification by writing a critical history of Lithuania and educating his parishioners on the history of the country and its people.

In the wake of the January Uprising of 1863 (another failed revolt), the use of the Latin alphabet was prohibited, and only the Cyrillic alphabet, in which Russian was written, was allowed. All courses in schools also had to be taught in Russian. These decrees were intended to reduce the amount of literature available on Lithuanian history and culture, in the hope of ending any threat of yet another nationalist popular uprising against the rule of the Russian tsar. However, the population steadfastly resisted the Cyrillic alphabet, which they came to hate. In many cases, they continued to use old textbooks written in Lithuanian, rather than accept the newer texts provided by the tsarist government. Lithuanians even refused to purchase prayer books written in Cyrillic, making their publication unprofitable. They relied instead upon books printed in Prussia and illegally smuggled into the country.

Bishop Valančius remained active in the years after the 1863 uprising. He urged parishioners to hide books from the police, to organize secret meetings to study the Lithuanian language, to refuse to learn the Russian alphabet or read books in Russian, and to burn the Russian books. He was also instrumental in organizing the publication and smuggling of books into Lithuania. The bishop's actions did much to bring about a broad-based resistance to Russification and Russian rule.

While Valančius was important in keeping Lithuanian nationalism alive, others continued to further its development. In 1883 Jonas Basanavičius began a monthly newsletter, *Aušra,* which he published in Prussia. The newsletter, which was written in Lithuanian, contained poems, literature, historical notes, and commentaries on current events. Other newsletters followed the example of *Aušra.* Illegal political organizing was spurred by these publications, as many political parties, among them the Social Democratic, were secretly founded. Faced with the failure of the decree against the use of the Lithuanian language, the Russian government lifted the ban in 1904. The changes that came in the wake of the general strike following the disastrous Russian defeat in the Russo-Japanese War of 1904–1905 and of the Revolution of 1905 ended censorship and permitted the use of the Lithuanian language in the schools and in public discourse.

Lithuanian culture blossomed during the period of relative freedom from 1905 to the declaration of independence on 16 February 1918. It was during this period that the country's most celebrated painter and composer, Mikalojus Konstantinas Čiurlionis, produced his works. A romantic, he wrote a musical score interpreting his paintings of nature, which were infused with a strong pantheistic sentiment, emphasizing the pagan elements of Lithuanian culture. It was not, however, until independence in 1918 and the creation of a Lithuanian republic that the country was left to develop its arts and culture without foreign interference.

The greatest challenge to the new state was the high level of illiteracy. Moreover, there was no university in which Lithuanian was the primary language of instruction. While

Mikalojus Konstantinas Čiurlionis (1875–1911)

M.K. Čiurlionis (1875–1911) is considered the founder of Lithuanian symphonic music. In addition, his paintings are the most significant Lithuanian contribution to European culture. Indeed, his work is so extraordinary that it has no parallel in Lithuanian art.

Čiurlionis's paintings, embracing the symbolism and romanticism of the late nineteenth and early twentieth century, constitute the core of his artistic contribution. His early works deal with religious, philosophical, and psychological issues related to the origins and development of the universe. Most are imaginary or allegorical landscapes. His later works show a diversity of themes and artistic images, touching on existentialism and occult aspects of nature. By the end of his short thirty-six-year life, Čiurlionis had developed a style that unmistakably distinguishes him from any other artist.

Čiurlionis introduced many new themes and original images to Lithuanian art. His work is marked by silhouettes, symbolic figures, and graceful waves. Particularly noteworthy is his ability to represent ideas that transcend the physical universe, elevating the viewer to a position beyond the temporal.

Čiurlionis is also the founder of modern Lithuanian music. His work consists of symphonic music, compositions for piano, and choral compositions (primarily harmonized Lithuanian folk songs). Given his short life, his having written more than three hundred musical scores is truly impressive. What is even more remarkable, however, is the originality of these works. For example, *The Sea,* the greatest symphonic work by Čiurlionis, is rich in dramatic effect, expression, and fantasy. Reflecting the artist's search for the meaning of life, it is noteworthy for its depth of emotion and loftiness of purpose.

Both Čiurlionis's paintings and music aroused much controversy in his day. While their originality was appreciated by some, both were rejected as too modern by the greater part of the public of the time. These same works are now considered to be the greatest that Lithuanian art has yet produced.

significant progress was made in establishing a system of mandatory primary and secondary education, a national university was not established until 1922. The original intent had been to reopen Vilnius University; however, the seizure of Vilnius by Poland forced Lithuania to establish the university at the new capital of Kaunas. A teachers' college was also established in Klaipėda in 1935, but a few years later it had to relocate to Panevėžys, following the German occupation of the city.

Independence did much for the development of Lithuanian art, theater, and music as well. A state opera company was established in 1920, the number of choirs grew, national music festivals were instituted, and several new theaters came into existence. Literature also experienced a revival, fueled by the increase in the literacy rate.

Although the Soviet era was one of general repression, it was also a period in which the state provided massive subsidies to the arts. Hence, Lithuanians continued to excel in education, science, and the arts. Marija Alkekaitė-Gimbutienė, for example, was a renowned archaeologist who was instrumental in the development of theories concerning the early origins of the Baltic peoples. Her theorizing about the Goddess, influenced by her upbringing in a still half-pagan Lithuania, has made her well known (under the name of Marija Gimbutas) far beyond the academic world of archaeology.

Further, many took advantage of state largesse to advance the cause of maintaining and further developing the Lithuanian national consciousness. This was particularly the case for Jonas Kubilius, the rector of Vilnius University from 1958 to 1991. Resisting intense pressure to Russify the university's curriculum, he managed to restore the Lithuanian language and culture to a place of preeminence at the university (which had been returned to Lithuania by the Soviets). Kubilius was also an accomplished mathematician, noted for his significant mathematical discoveries (the Lemma of Kubilius and the Inequality of Kubilius), as well as his work in the theory of probability.

Artists also did much to further the cause of Lithuanian nationalism. Muza Rubačkytė was an internationally known pianist who was prohibited from traveling abroad due to her intense nationalist views, and Justinas Marcinkevičius was a renowned poet and writer whose works helped to develop Lithuanian national consciousness. In theater, the work of Juozas Miltinis gained international recognition. In film, Vytautas Žalakevičius achieved fame as a director. His best-known film, *Nobody Wanted to Die,* filmed in 1965, is still widely considered to be the best example of Lithuanian cinematography. The film explores the post–World War II conflict between communists and the anticommunist resistance in a Lithuanian village, celebrating the struggle of Lithuanians against the Soviet occupation.

Post-Soviet Lithuania has been able to build on the achievements of the past. Indeed, many of those trained in the Soviet era continue to perform today. For example, the conductor and violinist Eglė Spokaitė has continued to perform as a ballet soloist, winning numerous international awards, and Šarūnas Bartas continues his work as a film di-

Juozas Miltinis

Juozas Miltinis (1907–1994) is considered the patriarch of Lithuanian theater. Miltinis received his education in the arts in Western Europe. Disillusioned by the repressive control of the Soviet state in the arts, he left for France in 1932. Returning to Lithuania in the fall of 1940, he founded the Panevežys Drama Theater, the first theater in Lithuania. His plays were so out of line with the sterile and overly formalistic style of the Soviet theater that he was dismissed from the theater in 1954. However, he was reinstated in 1959 and remained at the theater until 1983.

Despite his rebellious ideas, Miltinis was named a National Artist of the Soviet Union in 1973. In 1977 he received the Order of National Peace and in 1995 the French government awarded Miltinis the Order of Knight for his achievements in art and literature. After his death, the Panevežys Drama Theatre was renamed in his honor.

In violation of the general dictates of the Soviet theater, with its focus on socialist realism (ideologically based art glorifying Soviet life), Miltinis concentrated on portraying life as it was. Although his style of directing was considered somewhat dictatorial, it meant that he demanded of his artists their maximum effort physically, emotionally, and intellectually. By sheer determination, he managed to stage many Western plays despite official opposition, thanks to which his theater was visited by audiences from all parts of the Soviet Union as well as the West. Indeed, the Panevežys Drama Theater was famous outside of the Soviet Union and was permitted to tour in Western Europe during the Cold War.

rector. Among well-known playwrights of the Soviet era who have continued their work in the aftermath of the restoration of independence are Oskaras Koršunovas and Eimuntas Nekrošius. Koršunovas is famous for his original staging of the production of *There to Be Here*. Known for blending expressionism and surrealism, he was recognized as the country's best young artist in 1994. He has won numerous awards for his directing of performances at international theater festivals in Europe. Nekrošius became famous in the mid-1980s. In 1994 he was awarded the New European Theater Realities prize by the European Theater Union. In the same year, he was named the best stage manager of the year in Lithuania; and in 1998, his production of *Hamlet* won an award as the best performance of the year. He has performed his plays throughout Europe and the United States.

The restoration of Lithuanian independence has not only brought with it a renewed emphasis on folk art, it has been marked by the flourishing of traditional art forms that had formerly been subsidized by the Soviet state. Many of the institutions organized during the Soviet era or funded by the Soviet government also continue to operate in present-day Lithuania. The country has eighty-five museums, the most famous of which are the National Gallery, the Vilnius Picture Gallery, the M. K. Čiurlionis Art Museum, the Radvila Palace Museum, the Trakai Historical Museum, and the Museum of the Devil. The numerous churches and other architectural treasures of Vilnius's Old Town caused the whole area to be placed on the World Heritage list by UNESCO in 1994. In the arts and entertainment, the country boasts a national symphony orchestra (conducted by Gintaras Rinkevičius), a national opera and ballet, and a national theater.

Finally, one would be remiss if consideration were not given to Lithuania's achievements in sports. The country is one of the great basketball powers in international competition. Indeed, basketball is the most popular sport in the country, followed by soccer and hockey. Lithuania's basketball team won the bronze medal in the 1992 and 1996 Olympic Games. During the Soviet era, Lithuanian basketball players provided the best players for the Soviet Union's Olympic basketball teams. One of the country's most celebrated players, Arvydas Sabonis, was on the 1982 Soviet basketball team that was the first in Olympic history to take the gold medal away from the United States. He has played for the Portland Trailblazers in the NBA since 1996. Another player on that same Olympic team was Šarūnas Marčiulionis. Marčiulionis also played in the NBA from 1994 to 1997. He is now the president of the Lithuanian Basketball League.

Other celebrated sports figures include Virgilijus Alekna, the 2000 Olympic gold medal winner in discus, Diana Žiliutė, the 1998 world champion cyclist, and Vidmantas Urbonas, five time runner-up in world triathlon competition. Vladas Vitkauskas is a renowned mountain climber, who climbed and raised the Lithuanian flag on the highest peak on each continent of the globe from 1993 to 1996.

Finally, one must also note the country's passion for flying. Virtually every town of any size in the country has a flying field and sport club. Since Steponas Darius and Stasys Girėnas's ill-fated single-engine trans-Atlantic flight in 1936, flying has been among the country's most popular pastimes. Many of the Soviet Union's best pilots were Lithuanians. The current world champion in high altitude flying is Jurgis Kairys.

ECONOMIC DEVELOPMENT

Throughout its history, the Lithuanian economy was often deeply affected by foreign occupiers. The partitions of Poland in the eighteenth century, which resulted in the country falling under tsarist rule, tied Lithuania to the most backward economy of any of the great powers. Although a reorientation toward the West began to develop during the interwar period, the end of World War II brought the communists to power. The imposition of the Soviet command

Lithuania's Šarūnas Jasikevičius (2nd L) puts the ball under his shirt as he celebrates with teammates after beating Australia in the men's bronze medal match at the Olympic Games in Sydney, 1 October 2000. Lithuania won 89–71. (Reuters/Corbis)

economy not only retarded economic development, it also left the country facing difficult economic times following the collapse of the Soviet empire.

Following the restoration of the republic's independence, Lithuania was faced with two enormous challenges: constructing a political democracy and creating a market economy. Neither had existed in the Soviet Union, which was defined by the political and economic dominance of the Communist Party. All property was owned and operated by the government bureaucracy under the direction of the Party.

Serious reform of the Lithuanian economy was discussed as early as 1988. While still a constituent republic of the Soviet Union, the government of the Lithuanian Soviet Socialist Republic (LSSR) prepared a plan for severing Lithuania's economy from Moscow. The key element in the plan was the privatization of state property. However, enabling legislation was not passed until May 1990, two months after the newly installed Sąjūdis-led legislature had declared its intent to reestablish Lithuania's full prewar independence. The new legislation, the Law on Enterprises, legalized private and collective ownership of enterprises. In June 1991, subsequent legislation was adopted returning lands nationalized by the Soviet Union to their former owners. Together these two laws created the legal basis for the privatization of the economy.

Privatization begin in earnest following the August Coup in Moscow (in which communist hard-liners temporarily seized control of Moscow and placed Mikhail Gorbachev under house arrest) and international recognition of Lithuania's independence in fall 1991. The process proceeded with citizens receiving vouchers with which to purchase shares in state-owned property. The intent was to make it possible for all citizens to become owners of private property and thereby reduce the likelihood of the economy being dominated by a small class of wealthy enterprise owners. The approach further recommended itself as a precaution against the former communist ruling elites seizing control of much of the private economy.

Despite this measure, capital tended to accumulate in the hands of a small business elite, comprised in large part of Soviet-era enterprise directors. This occurred for two reasons. First, the majority of the population, having no experience with the concept of share holding, sold their vouchers for next to nothing. Second, following the elections to the national legislature at the end of 1992, the Democratic Labor Party (the former Communist Party) used its majority to substantially modify the privatization process. The initial privatization law gave employees of the enterprise in question the right to purchase up to 10 percent of shares on favorable terms. Amendments to the law increased this to 50 percent. Furthermore, the auction of shares was limited in some cases by the administrative fiat of central government ministries. These changes had the effect of severely limiting competition in the bidding process and weighting the process strongly in favor of the previous enterprise directors.

At the same time, foreign investment, critical for the reorientation and rejuvenation of the economy, was minimal. Unlike Latvia and Estonia, which moved quickly to permit foreign capital to purchase land, Lithuania had as part of the constitution adopted in a popular referendum in October 1992 an article, Article 47, that limited ownership of land to Lithuanian citizens. This article was eventually changed in the summer of 1995 under pressure from the European Union, but the change was not implemented until the country was admitted to the EU. In addition, foreign banks were not permitted to operate in the country until the summer of 1996. Even so, the banking crisis of that year greatly reduced both foreign investment and banking operations.

As a consequence, the privatization process introduced numerous distortions in the Lithuanian economy. Not only did substantial social inequality result, but the country's economic development lagged significantly in comparison to the other Baltic states, a fact that contributed to the overall economic stress felt by the population. The former enterprise directors, now owners, were for the most part unable to make the transition to the realities of a competitive market. This problem, coupled with the loss of markets in the former Soviet Union, resulted in large-scale layoffs and the widespread threat of bankruptcy. Furthermore, the fact that enterprises had been auctioned off at bargain prices for vouchers instead of cash, and that foreign investment had been largely barred from participating in the process, meant there had been no infusion of new capital. Hence, little money was available for those seeking to start new business ventures that might potentially provide jobs for the growing number of unemployed and underemployed.

Nevertheless, a significant portion of state-owned assets were privatized in the first round from 1991 to 1995, and the basis for a middle class had been laid. During this initial phase, 92.8 percent of industrial enterprises, 85.1 percent of the construction sector, and 83 percent of the agriculture sector were turned over to private owners. Also during that span of time, most Soviet-era collective farms were turned over to individuals, in accordance with the Law on Privatization of Agricultural Enterprises. As a consequence, almost 71 percent of state-owned assets were privatized, and 6,000 new farms were created, leading to the emergence of a private sector that dominated the economy by 1996. The legal basis for the second phase of privatization was contained in the Law on the Privatization of State-Owned and Municipal Property passed by the legislature in July 1995. Properties to be privatized under this law differed from those sold in the first round in that they constituted higher-value property. The rules for their privatization were also different. According to the law, this kind of property was to be sold to the highest bidder for cash. Further, foreign investors were permitted to engage in the auction. This second round of privatization began in 1996 and continues to the present.

Thus far, a significant number of the 3,135 state enterprises to be privatized have been auctioned off in phase two, enticing a substantial degree of foreign investment. The two most important enterprises sold have been Lietuvos Telekomas, the national communications monopoly, and Mažeikiai Nafta, the oil industry. Yet to be privatized are Lietuvos Avialinijos, the national airline; the national passenger rail system; the national energy system; Lietuvos Dujos, the natural gas monopoly; state-owned banks, including the Lithuanian Agricultural Bank, the Lithuanian Savings Bank, and the Lithuanian Development Bank; and LISCO, the Lithuanian Shipping Company. The list also contains real estate properties. The intent is to sell the land as well as the buildings on it, the first time this has been done.

The launching of the second phase of privatization has been attended by a significant increase in direct foreign investment. Although the free economic zones that have been established have generally failed to attract any significant investment, such major international corporations as Phillip Morris International, Kraft Foods International, Williams International, the Coca-Cola Company, Shell Overseas Holdings Limited, and Siemens AG have invested in the Lithuanian economy. Sweden accounted for 21.6 percent of all foreign direct investments, Denmark for 15.9 percent, Finland for 11.8 percent, the United States for 8.5 percent, and Germany for 6.4 percent, according to figures compiled by the Department of Statistics of the Government of Lithuania.

One of the reasons that Lithuania has been relatively attractive to foreign investors is that the country has a well-trained, low-cost labor force. The proportion of university graduates in the labor pool is one of the highest in Central Europe. All five major cities have universities. The average monthly wage is one-tenth that of industrialized countries, and the cost of living is low by Western standards. The normal workweek is forty hours, and employees are entitled by law to twenty-eight days of paid vacation time each year (plus national holidays). The law also requires employers to permit paid maternity and childcare leave (up to the age of three years). A disincentive to foreign investment has been the relatively early retirement age. The retirement age for women is fifty-five years and four months, for men sixty years and two months. Another disincentive is the requirement for employers to contribute 31 percent of an employee's salary toward social security, health insurance, and disability insurance. (On the other hand, these employer contributions are tax deductible.)

The country has a well-developed transportation system that is also increasingly attractive to potential investors. The EU Transport Commission has designated the country as the hub for the region. Two of the ten priority European corridors intersect in Lithuania, and European-standard four-lane highways link the country's industrial centers. The country also has a well-developed rail network (although the rail passenger system is currently not operating at a profit), four airports, and an ice-free seaport (Klaipėda). All are slowly being modernized, as is the communications system.

With the private sector now accounting for most of the country's GDP, Lithuania has one of the fastest growing economies in East Central Europe. From 1995 to 1998, the average annual growth rate was 5.1 percent. Owing to the economic crisis at the end of 1998 in Russia, which substantially reduced Lithuanian exports to that country, the growth rate slowed in 1999, the GDP falling 3.9 percent, according to government statistics. By 2000, the government had succeeded in stabilizing the financial markets, and the country's economy was reorienting toward Western markets. Economic growth rebounded to 3.8 percent in that year. The growth rate in 2001 was 5.9 percent.

Part of the reason for the country's strong economic growth is its stable monetary policy. Until 2002, the Lithuanian currency, the Litas, was fixed to the U.S. dollar at a rate of four Litai to one U.S. dollar. In preparation for entry into the European Union, the Litas was instead fixed to the euro. Thanks to the successful operation of the fixed currency rate, managed by a currency board, the inflation rate has been brought under control. Inflation in the immediate post-Soviet period was quite high (189 percent in 1993, 45 percent in 1994, and 36 percent in 1997), but by 1996 government statistics showed that the inflation rate had been reduced to 13.1 percent. In 1998 it had dropped to 2.4 percent from a rate of 8.4 percent in 1997. It was at 0.3 percent in 1999, 1.4 percent in 2000, and 2.0 percent in 2001. The government hopes to abandon the currency board and permit the value of the Litas to float on international currency exchange markets at some point in the next several years.

Given the small size of its domestic market, Lithuania is dependent on foreign trade to maintain economic stability and growth. The country exports electrical power, but must import oil and natural gas. Major agricultural exports include sugar beets and grain. Based on customs declarations over the period from January to September 2002 (as compared to the same period in 2001), compiled by the Department of Statistics, exports increased by 3.5 percent, while imports increased by 12.3 percent, thus representing a negative trade balance. Lithuania's exports were to the United Kingdom (15.7 percent), Latvia (9.5 percent), Germany (10.8 percent), and Russia (13.6 percent). It imported most of its goods from Russia (21.4 percent), Germany (17.7 percent), Poland (4.8 percent), and Italy (4.4 percent). Overall, 50.1 percent of its exports were to European Union (EU) member states in 2002, while 21.3 percent were to the states of the former Soviet Union. Lithuanian exports to the United States constituted only 3 percent of its total exports. As for imports, 46.2 percent of its imports trade were from EU states, 25.9 percent from the former Soviet Union, and 3.1 percent from the United States.

The industrial sector includes electronics, chemicals, machine tooling, metal processing, construction materials, food processing, textiles, clothing, furniture, household appliances, petroleum products, and fertilizers. The most dynamic sectors are light industry, food products, beverages, and oil refining. More recently, gains have been registered in the manufacture of electronics and communications equipment, textiles, and beer production. The increased purchasing power of the country's citizens, combined with greater consumer confidence in Lithuanian goods, has resulted in

Ignalina nuclear power station in Lithuania. (Dan Vander Zwalm / Corbis Sygma)

an increased share of the domestic market going to Lithuanian enterprises in recent years.

The country is self-sufficient in agriculture, but a very large portion of the rural population is engaged in little more than subsistence-level farming. No more than 5 percent of the population is engaged in profitable farming. These farmers own the largest farms and best equipment. In most cases, they are the former directors and agricultural specialists on the Soviet collective farms. The return of land to prewar owners has also resulted in the return of some of these farm families to agricultural activity as well.

Petroleum products, nuclear energy, and natural gas account for the majority of the energy sector. The absence of long-term contracts with Russian oil suppliers plagued Williams International's operations at Mažeikiai Nafta. Many believe that the Russians were attempting to convince Williams to abandon its investment in the country. If so, they succeeded. Williams sold its shares to a Russian oil company in 2002. The main source of electrical power for the country is generated at the nuclear power station at Ignalina. Lithuania has had problems settling accounts with

Belarus and Russia for electrical energy provided to those two countries. Citing concerns with the safe operation of the Chernobyl-style reactor, the European Union has also demanded that Lithuania decommission the power plant as a precondition for membership. The inexpensive power that Ignalina provides the country has led many politicians, including the president, to insist on keeping one of the reactors in operation until at least 2009. Some politicians have even called for the station to operate until 2020.

CONTEMPORARY CHALLENGES

Lithuania considers the prolonged period of tsarist rule followed by the Soviet occupation as periods of isolation from Europe, with which the country shares a common set of political and social values. Not surprisingly, therefore, Lithuanian foreign policy has been dominated since the restoration of independence by a concern to "return to Europe." The primary indicator that the country has indeed broken out of its isolation and returned to its natural place in the international arena is its membership in the two primary institutions of Europe: the North Atlantic Treaty Organization (NATO) and the European Union (EU). It achieved both goals in 2004.

Although there is broad consensus among Lithuania's political elites that the country will best be served by membership in NATO, there is disagreement over why. The political right insists that Russia remains the greatest threat to the country's security; therefore, Lithuania must seek security within the European defense organization. Reflecting this view, the Constitution of 1992 declared that the country may not enter into any multilateral forums uniting the post–Soviet states. This has kept Lithuania out of the Commonwealth of Independent States (the successor to the Soviet state after its breakup) and its many arenas of interaction even when participation would have been beneficial, as would be the case with access to cheap Russian energy resources. For its part, although the political left worries that NATO membership might irritate Russia and thereby deny Lithuania access to its markets, they believe that the security organization offers the best means for securing critical Western investments in the country by raising confidence in the stability of its economic and political institutions. Hence it was Algirdas Brazauskas, a left-wing politician, who formally requested membership in NATO in 1994 during his term as president.

Paradoxically, the campaign for NATO membership had to be conducted by way of Poland. Given the troubled

During the ceremony of hoisting the NATO flag in front of the parliament building on the celebration of Lithuania's entry into NATO. (Petras Malukas / Itar-Tass / Corbis)

interwar relations between the two countries owing to Poland's seizure of Vilnius, relations between the two remained less than friendly in the early years following the restoration of independence. Relations were also aggravated by the imposition of direct rule by the central government over the country's Polish-dominated regions, as well as by Lithuania's insistence on a formal apology for the interwar annexation of the Vilnius region. Given that Poland was likely to be among the first postcommunist countries to be invited to join NATO, however, President Brazauskas succeeded in normalizing relations between the two countries in a formal treaty signed in 1995. This treaty both opened the door for Lithuania's bid for membership and gained Poland as an ally for that bid.

Lithuania's second president, Valdas Adamkus, affirmed his commitment to seek NATO membership in his inaugural speech in 1998. As a demonstration of that commitment, he announced that Lithuania would commit 2 percent of its gross domestic product to defense spending, the standard established by NATO for its members. Despite the economic hardships that this has entailed, Lithuania has maintained that commitment. Adamkus's former career in the U.S. Environmental Protection Agency (EPA) provided him with many contacts in the U.S. executive branch. Moreover, his former status as an American citizen (which he surrendered in order to campaign for president of Lithuania) removed some of the concerns that the West had had about Lithuania when under the leadership of President Brazauskas, the former leader of the Communist Party. Several high-level discussions during 1998 helped raise the visibility of the country's campaign for NATO membership. In July of that year, NATO Secretary General Javier Solana visited Vilnius and reaffirmed that all countries wanting membership in the security organization would eventually be granted entry. In October, Adamkus visited with President Bill Clinton to discuss the country's accession to NATO, reminding him that there was "unfinished business" in Europe as long as Lithuania remained outside of European security structures. The country also participated in the Baltic Challenge naval exercises with eleven member and candidate-member states of NATO. However, the election of Social Democrat Gerhard Schroeder as chancellor in Germany resulted in a notable diminution in German support for NATO expansion eastward. The newly elected German chancellor called for the full integration of Poland, Hungary, and the Czech Republic into the alliance before any new invitations were made.

In mid-1999 President Adamkus announced that Lithuania was making progress in its bid for NATO membership. He cited Lithuania's commitment to democratic principles and good relations with the country's neighbors as critical examples of Lithuania's preparedness for NATO membership. On the other hand, Adamkus criticized lingering psychological barriers as the main force impeding full NATO membership. The president contended that the East fears NATO because of its Cold War roots, while the West fears expansion because of possible adverse effects on Russian relations. He urged swift Lithuanian entrance into NATO, arguing that such a move would strengthen stability and positively affect the development of NATO-Russia rela-

tions, and declared 2002 as the year in which Lithuania aimed to achieve full NATO membership.

Despite the economic recession of 2000–2001, which began in late 1999 and was brought on by the loss of the Russian markets in the wake of the devalued Russian ruble, Lithuania's preparations for entry to NATO continued unabated. Ties with Western militaries increased. The country received 100 armored personnel carriers from Germany and 40,000 rifles from the United States, and in September 2000 joint military training exercises were conducted with Italy. Furthermore, the newly elected government confirmed the commitment of the previous Conservative-led government to devote 2 percent of the GDP to the military, this despite campaign promises by key elements of the new ruling coalition to reduce that commitment. The decision was all the more noteworthy as the New Union had led an effort earlier in the year to collect the signatures necessary to force consideration of a legislative bill transferring $37 million from defense to education.

The country received several assurances during the course of 2000 concerning its prospects for becoming a NATO member. The most important came in February, when U.S. Deputy Secretary of State Strobe Talbott announced that the Baltic states' integration into Western structures served the national interest of the United States. Then the results of the U.S. presidential elections of 2000 put the question of NATO accession into question by the end of the year. The country was unsure of the new Bush administration's position on the issue.

These concerns were overcome in 2001, as the new American administration made it clear that Lithuania would be among the countries invited to join NATO in the next round of expansion. In response, in a remarkable show of unity, the country's ten largest parties, covering the political spectrum from left to right, signed a statement in May emphasizing the country's commitment to entering NATO and its willingness to boost the defense budget as much as needed. Solid majorities on both sides of the aisle in the national legislature voted in April 2001 to extend Lithuania's participation in peacekeeping operations in both Bosnia and Kosovo. Lithuania also sent contingents to support U.S. operations in Iraq. These efforts were continued by the country's third president, Rolandas Paksas, who accepted NATO's invitation to membership in 2004.

Along with the successful effort to gain membership in NATO, integration into the European Union (EU) was one of the most important foreign policy goals of Lithuania. The country sought EU membership for both symbolic and economic reasons. In the symbolical sense it would mark the country's return to Europe and its legitimation as part of Western Europe. During his first term in office, President Valdas Adamkus occasionally referred to Lithuania as a bridge connecting East and West Europe. In economic terms, membership would provide the country with the benefits of the European free trade area, including greater product availability, lower prices, increased trade, greater efficiency, and more competition.

Lithuania declared its intent to become part of the EU (at the time it was referred to as the European Community) almost immediately following the declaration of independence in 1990. The European Community recognized the independence of Lithuania on 27 August 1991. On 18 July 1994, a free trade agreement between the EU and Lithuania was signed. The Europe (Association) Agreement was signed on 12 June 1995, and came into force on 1 February 1998. The Europe Agreement recognized Lithuania's aspiration to become a member of the European Union. An official membership application was submitted on 8 December 1995, and on 15 February 2000, Lithuania started negotiations for EU membership.

Every year the European Commission rendered a report on Lithuania's progress toward fulfilling the requirements for EU membership. The commission's regular report in November 2001 noted that Lithuania had continued to implement the Europe Agreement and had contributed to the smooth functioning of various joint institutions. Lithuania met all the political criteria for membership, which included the establishment of democratic institutions, the rule of law, support for human rights, and respect for the rights of minorities. On the other hand, Lithuania encountered some problems related to the restructuring of its agricultural and energy sectors, setting up appropriate administrative structures for financial control and regional policy, and the protection of intellectual property rights.

The only major obstacle to EU membership was the continued disagreement over the date of the decommissioning of the nuclear power station at Ignalina. The EU insisted that the Chernobyl-style nuclear reactor at Ignalina be closed by 2009. That demand generated considerable debate within Lithuania. Many worried that closing the country's primary energy source would leave Lithuania overly dependent on others for energy. Others questioned whether Lithuania could survive economically were it to replace the cheap energy provided by Ignalina with expensive electricity generated in other parts of Europe. President Adamkus stated publicly that he favored continued operation of the plant until 2014. However, all EU member states continued to press Lithuania to decommission the last reactor in 2009. In the end, Lithuania acceded to the EU's demands and ultimately won full membership in the union in 2004.

THE RUSSIAN QUESTION

Given Russia's opposition to NATO expansion, relations between the two countries have been strained for the last several years and are likely to remain so. Russia has avoided the use of military threats, which would only serve to underscore Lithuanian security concerns. However, many believe that the Russian government is behind the use of what appear to be a set of economic sanctions meant to punish the country. The most serious of these has been the exploitation of Lithuania's energy dependence. While there have been no overt threats of formal sanctions, the continued disruption of oil supplies to Mažeikiai Nafta seems to be the strongest evidence of this policy. Further substantiating these concerns is the fact that Russia has impeded Kazakhstan from selling crude oil to Mažeikiai Nafta by imposing prohibitive transit tariffs. Although oil supplies have become less of a problem since Williams sold its shares in Mažeikiai Nafta to a Russian oil company, Yukos, the Russian government's subsequent legal proceedings against Yukos continue to raise concerns in Lithuania regarding Russian intentions.

Since 11 September 2001, however, improved relations between the United States and Russia have led to a relaxation in relations between Lithuania and Russia as well. In October 2001 Russian foreign minister Igor Ivanov signaled a new Russian position on Lithuania's possible NATO membership when he said Russia was "open to any form of cooperation" that strengthened security and stability in the Baltic.

One remaining concern between the two countries is what to do with the Russian enclave of Kaliningrad. A small piece of land to the west of Lithuania separated from Russia, the region was given to the Soviet Union following World War II. Given its western location, Kaliningrad is a heavily militarized zone. Russian concerns for the region have as much to do with the EU as NATO. Should all the countries surrounding Kaliningrad become members of the EU, as it appears will be the case, the region could be denied important economic trade ties. Russia has asked for special consideration for the region's citizens and economy. In particular, it desires that Kaliningrad's residents be granted visa-free travel rights. This request, together with Russian demands for unimpeded transit across Lithuanian territory, complicated Lithuania's bid for entry to the EU. The EU thus took responsibility for negotiating the outstanding issues with Russia following Lithuania's entry into the union in 2004.

THE TRIPLE TRANSITION

The greatest challenge facing Lithuania, however, remains what the scholar Claus Offe has called "the triple transition." The country is faced with simultaneously creating a functioning market, democratizing, and building an integrated state. The latter two have proven to be the easiest challenges to meet. Owing largely to its relatively homogeneous population (over 80 percent of the country's citizens are ethnically Lithuanian), Lithuania has not been faced with impediments to creating a unified, integrated state to the degree that Latvia and Estonia, the two other Baltic states, have. The only major difficulty it has faced has been in the regions surrounding Vilnius (in which the country's Polish citizens are concentrated). In many districts near Vilnius they comprise an absolute majority. While these districts demanded full autonomy in the wake of the collapse of the Soviet Union in 1991, the demands soon died out, owing to a lack of support from Poland. Indeed, improving relations between Vilnius and Warsaw have put an end to any such demands.

Lithuania's progress toward democracy has been equally successful. Democracy can even be said to have consolidated in the country, as there is no evidence of the existence of opposition to democratic rules and procedures on the part of either the political elites or the general public. The party system, while still forming, is moving away from polarization and has avoided extremism. There is no broad support for either a communist party calling for a return to the past or a fascist party. The presidency (instituted in the 1992 Constitution) has played a particularly important role in the development of the country's democratic system. Manipulating the powers of appointment, dissolution, and veto, Lithuania's presidents have been active in sustaining and removing governments in response to the changing economic and social environment. In so doing, they have contributed significantly to stabilizing both the constitutional and political order.

The primary political institution in which there has been insufficient progress is the state bureaucracy. Essentially outside of the reach of most of the reforms, it possesses too much autonomy and is largely unaccountable to political authorities. Hence, the Lithuanian government has been severely limited in its capacity to effectively manage economic change. Indeed, conversion to a free market economy is the one challenge that Lithuania has yet to sufficiently address. This problem was most evident in the haphazard response to the crisis in Russia and the economic recession that that crisis produced in Lithuania's market from 1998 to 2000. Lithuania has been slower than the rest of the Baltic states in carrying out market reform in general. While continued economic difficulties could ultimately undermine faith in democracy, at present Lithuania's prospects appear hopeful. Reform of the state bureaucracy has begun; and more important, entry into EU will open the economy to greater investment and competition.

The resiliency and stability of Lithuania's democracy is evidenced by the impeachment of the country's third president in the post-Soviet era, Rolandas Paksas. Although there is likely to be some fallout from the impeachment for some years to come, the essential strength of the country's democratic institutions, particularly the parliament and the Constitutional Court, is not in doubt. Lithuania is the first country in East Central Europe to impeach a head of state. Paksas had narrowly defeated the incumbent, Valdas Adamkus, in 2003. However, Paksas, whose two terms as prime minister had been marked by political conflict, found himself embroiled in political scandal by the end of the year. During a speech before the parliament, the outgoing head of the State Security Department (SSD) spoke of direct attempts by the Russian structures to influence politics in Lithuania. A few days later, a secret memorandum prepared by the SSD was leaked to the Lithuanian mass media, exposing information that the president's adviser on national security matters had links with the criminal world. Subsequent parliamentary investigations charged with looking into whether Paksas himself might be implicated determined that the president was vulnerable, due to the influence over him exercised by a Russian businessman known to have ties to criminal organizations. Further, the president was charged with leaking classified information when he informed the businessman that his telephone conversations were being taped by the SSD. Finally, he was accused of overstepping his authority by attempting to influence the privatization process in favor of the same businessman. Following these findings, parliament voted to initiate impeachment proceedings. Throughout the proceedings, Lithuania's political elite increasingly pressed the president to resign; however, Paksas stubbornly refused to do so, insisting on his innocence. He was ultimately removed from office in the spring of 2004.

SELECTIVE BIBLIOGRAPHY

Buracas, A. ed. *Lithuanian Economic Reforms: Practice and Perspective,* Vilnius, Lithuania: Margi Rastai, 1997.

Clark, Terry D. *Beyond Post-Communist Studies: Political Science and the New Democracies of Europe.* Armonk, NY: M. E. Sharpe, 2002.

———. "Coalition Realignment in the Supreme Council of the Republic of Lithuania and the Fall of the Vagnorius Government." *Journal of Baltic Studies,* vol. 24, no. 1 (spring 1993): 53–66.

———. "Coalitional Behavior in the Lithuanian Parliament: The First Four Years." *Demokratizatsiya: The Journal of Post-Soviet Democratization,* vol. 3, no. 1 (winter 1995): 61–75.

———. "Nationalism in Independent Lithuania: New Approaches for the Nation of 'Innocent Sufferers.'" In *After Independence: Nationalism in Post-Colonial and Post-Communist States,* edited by Lowell W. Barrington. Ann Arbor: University of Michigan Press, forthcoming.

———. "Privatization and Democratization in Lithuania: A Case Study of Who Benefits in Siauliai." *Policy Studies Journal,* vol. 28, no. 1 (2000): 134–151.

———. "The Democratic Consolidation of Lithuania's State Institutions." Special issue. *Journal of Baltic Studies,* vol. 32, no. 2 (2001): 125–192.

———. "The Lithuanian Political Party System: A Case Study of Democratic Consolidation." *EEPS: Eastern European Politics and Societies,* vol. 9, no. 1 (winter 1995): 41–62.

———. "The 1996 Elections to the Lithuanian Seimas and Their Aftermath." *Journal of Baltic Studies,* vol. 29, no. 2 (summer 1998): 135–148.

———. "Who Rules Siauliai? A Case Study of an Emerging Urban Regime." *Slavic Review,* vol. 56, no. 1 (spring 1997): 101–122.

Clark, Terry D., and Andrea Adams. "The Year of the President." In *Holding the Course: Annual Survey of Eastern Europe and the Former Soviet Union, 1998,* edited by Peter Rutland. Armonk, NY: M. E. Sharpe, 2000, 123–129.

Clark, Terry D., with Brian Bartels. "A Year of Political Turmoil." *Transitions Online.* Country Files: Lithuania: Annual Report 1999. http://www.tol.cz/countries/litar99.html. Posted 1 May 2000.

Clark, Terry D., Stacy J. Holscher, and Lisa Hyland. "The LDLP Faction in the Lithuanian Seimas, 1992–1996." *Nationalities Papers,* vol. 27, no. 2 (1999): 227–246.

Clark, Terry D., and Nerijus Prekevičius. "The Durability of Lithuania's Ruling Coalition." *Tiltas,* vol. 2, no. 2 (September 2001): 28–33.

———. "The Effect of Changes to the Electoral Law in Premier-Presidential Systems: The Lithuanian Case." In

Lithuanian Political Science Yearbook 2000, edited by Algimantas Jankauskas. Vilnius: Institute of International Relations and Political Science, 2001, 124–137.

———. "Explaining the 2000 Lithuanian Parliamentary Elections: An Application of Contextual and New Institutional Approaches." *Slavic Review,* vol. 62, no. 3 (2003): 548–569.

Clark, Terry D., and Gražvydas Jasūtis. "Lithuanian Politics: Implications of the Parliamentary Elections." *Analysis of Current Events,* vol. 13, no. 1 (February 2001): 1, 3–5.

Clark, Terry D., and Robin M. Tucker. "Lithuania beyond the Return of the 'Left.'" In *Beyond the Return of the Left in Post-Communist States,* edited by Charles Bukowski and Barnabas Racz. Cheltenham, UK: Edward Elgar, 1999, 35–58.

Dobrynin, Alexander, and Bronius Kuzmickas, eds. *Personal Freedom and National Resurgence: Lithuanian Philosophical Studies I.* Washington, DC: Paideia Press and The Council for Research in Values and Philosophy, 1994.

Eidintas, Alfonsas. "The Nation Creates Its State." In *Lithuania in European Politics: The Years of the First Republic, 1918–1940,* edited by Edvardas Tuškenis. New York: St. Martin's Press, 1997, 33–58.

———. "The Presidential Republic." In *Lithuania in European Politics: The Years of the First Republic, 1918–1940,* edited by Edvardas Tuškenis. New York: St. Martin's Press, 1997, 111–138.

Juozaitis, Arvydas. "The Lithuanian Independence Movement and National Minorities." *Peace Research Reports.* Frankfurt, Germany: Peace Research Institute, December 1992.

Linz, Juan J. "Transitions to Democracy." *Washington Quarterly,* vol. 13, no. 13 (summer 1990): 143–164.

Linz, Juan J., and Alfred Stepan. *Problems of Democratic Transition and Consolidation: Southern Europe, South America, and Post-Communist Europe.* Baltimore: Johns Hopkins University Press, 1996.

Nakrošis, Vitalis. "Lithuanian Public Administration: A Usable State Bureaucracy." *Journal of Baltic Studies,* vol. 32, no. 2 (2001), 170–181.

Offe, Claus. "Capitalism by Democratic Design? Democratic Theory Facing the Triple Transition in East Central Europe." *Social Research,* vol. 58 (1991): 864–902.

Popovski, Vesna. "Citizenship and Ethno-Politics in Lithuania." *International Politics,* vol. 33 (1996): 45–55.

Sabaliūnas, Leonas. *Lithuanian Social Democracy in Perspective, 1893–1914.* Durham, NC: Duke University Press, 1990.

Senn, Alfred Erich. *Gorbachev's Failure in Lithuania.* New York: St. Martin's Press, 1995.

———. *Lithuania Awakening.* Berkeley: University of California Press, 1990.

Šimenas, Albertas. "Formation of the Market Economy in Lithuania." In *Lithuanian Economic Reforms: Practice and Perspective,* edited by A. Buracas. Vilnius, Lithuania: Margi Rastai, 1997, 17–62.

———. "Lithuania's Economy during the Period of Reforms." In *Lithuanian Economic Reforms: Practice and Perspective,* edited by A. Buracas. Vilnius, Lithuania: Margi Rastai, 1997, 63–74.

Snyder, Tim. "National Myths and International Relations: Poland and Lithuania, 1989–1994." *East European Politics and Societies,* vol. 9, no. 2 (1995): 317–343.

Stukas, Jack J. *Awakening Lithuania: A Study on the Rise of Modern Lithuanian Nationalism.* Madison, NJ: Florham Park Press, 1966.

Tuškenis, Edvardas, ed. *Lithuania in European Politics: The Years of the First Republic, 1918–1940.* New York: St. Martin's, 1997.

Vardys, V. Stanley, and Judity B. Sedaitis. *Lithuania: The Rebel Nation,* Boulder, CO: Westview, 1997.

CHRONOLOGY

700–600 B.C.E.	Finno-Ugric people settled in the area of modern Lithuania.
1–100 C.E.	Baltic cultural identity begins to emerge.
100–500 C.E.	Expansion and conflict with Scandinavians and Slavs.
1009	Lithuania is first mentioned in written records in the Latin chronicle *Annales Quedinburgenses.*
1236	The Teutonic Order expands into the Baltics to forcibly Christianize the pagan peoples of the region.
1251	Mindaugas accepts Christianity.
1253	Mindaugas is crowned king of Lithuania by the Catholic pope.
1263	Assassination of King Mindaugas and renewal of the struggle against Christianity.
1266	The Lithuanians defeat the Knights of the Sword.
1316–1377	Expansion of the Grand Duchy of Lithuania.
1386	Grand Duke Jogaila marries the Queen of Poland.
1387	Lithuania, the last remaining pagan state in Europe, is baptized into the Christian faith.
1392–1430	The Grand Duchy of Lithuania reaches the zenith of its power under Grand Duke Vytautas the Great.
15 July 1410	Lithuania and Poland defeat the Teutonic Knights at the Battle of Grünwald.
1 February 1411	The Grand Duchy of Lithuania and the Teutonic Knights sign a treaty, ending the threat that the order had posed to the Grand Duchy for almost two centuries.
1522	The first publishing house is founded in Vilnius.
1529	The country's first legal code is adopted.
1566	Lithuania's legal code is redrafted.
1569	The Grand Duchy of Lithuania and Poland sign the Treaty of Lublin vesting the titles of king of Poland and grand duke of Lithuania in the same person.

1573	The Polish-Lithuanian Commonwealth becomes the first republic in Europe.	1920	The Constitution of the Republic of Lithuania is adopted.
1576	The titles "king of Poland" and "grand duke of Lithuania" are transferred to the Poles.	1920–1940	Poland occupies Vilnius and the surrounding regions.
1576–1795	Polish political, economic, social, and cultural domination of Lithuania.	1921	Lithuania joins the League of Nations.
		1923	Lithuania annexes the port of Memel.
1579	The Jesuit Order founds Vilnius University.	1926	The Social Democrats and Populists gain an electoral victory and form a coalition government.
1588	Lithuania's legal code is redrafted.	1926	A military coup deposes the government.
1654–1667	Lithuania is invaded on successive occasions by the Swedes and the Russians.	1926–1940	Antanas Smetona rules as president with dictatorial powers.
1698	Polish is declared the official language of the Polish-Lithuanian Commonwealth, which becomes the Polish Republic, of which Lithuania is a constituent part.	1938	A new constitution is written, granting virtually all political powers to the president.
1700–1721	The Great Northern War is fought in Lithuania between Russia and Sweden.	1939	Germany issues an ultimatum for the return of the port of Memel.
1772	The first partition of the Polish Republic.	1939	The Molotov-Ribbentrop Pact is signed; subsequent changes to the Secret Protocols assign Lithuania to the Soviet Union.
1775	The first literary work written in Lithuanian is published, Kristijonas Donelaitis's poem *Metai* (The Seasons).	1940	Poland is occupied by Germany and the Soviet Union, and Vilnius is returned to Lithuania.
1793	The second partition of the Polish Republic.	15 June 1940	The Soviet Union occupies Lithuania.
		11–12 July 1940	The First Deportation.
1795	The third partition of the Polish Republic; Lithuania becomes part of the Russian Empire.	21 July 1940	The People's Seimas requests formal incorporation into the Soviet Union.
1812	Napoleon is greeted as a liberator in Lithuania.	3 August 1940	Lithuania is formally incorporated into the Soviet Union.
1831	Insurrection against tsarist rule. Vilnius University is closed, and the legal code of 1588 is replaced with the Russian legal code as part of the suppression of the insurrection.	14–18 June 1941	The Second Deportation.
		Summer 1941–1944	The German Third Reich occupies Lithuania.
		1944	Lithuania is reincorporated into the Soviet Union.
1861	The emancipation of the serfs.	1945–1948	Soviet repression of Lithuanian nationalism.
1863	Second insurrection against tsarist rule. The use of the Latin alphabet is banned.	1945–1953	The Miško Broliai (Forest Boys) resist Soviet rule.
1864–1904	The period of national awakening.	1968	Lithuanian nationalism is reignited by the Prague Spring and the Soviet suppression of Czechoslovakia.
1904–1905	The Russo-Japanese War.		
1905	The National Seimas forms and demands full autonomy within the Russian Empire.	1970–1982	The Soviet Russification campaign in Lithuania.
1905	The tsar accedes to demands for Lithuanian autonomy.	1972	The public self-immolation of Romas Kalanta in Kaunas sparks student protests.
1914–1918	World War I.	1973	The *Chronicles of the Catholic Church* begin illegal publication of human rights abuses in Lithuania under Soviet occupation.
1915	Germany occupies Lithuania.		
16 February 1918	Lithuania declares the restoration of its independence.		
November 1918	Germany withdraws from Lithuania following its defeat in World War I, leaving Lithuania de facto independent.	1985	Mikhail Gorbachev becomes general secretary of the Communist Party of the Soviet Union.
1918–1920	The military struggle to defend the independence of the Lithuanian state.	1986	The Soviet Union embarks upon the perestroika reforms.
July 1920	Lithuania defeats the Bolshevik Army and signs a treaty with the Russian Bolshevik regime recognizing Lithuanian independence.	23 August 1987	A small public meeting is held to mark the Molotov-Ribbentrop Pact and Lithuania's forced incorporation into the Soviet Union.

October 1988	The Lithuanian Movement for Perestroika, Sąjūdis, holds its founding congress.	May 1992	The legislature reaches deadlock, immobilizing the government.
1988–1990	Sąjūdis radicalizes, its demands evolving from autonomy within the Soviet Union to the full restoration of Lithuania's independence.	Summer 1992	Agreement is reached over a new constitution.
		October 1992	The new constitution is approved in a public referendum. The Democratic Labor Party wins elections to the newly constituted legislature.
August 1989	Hands across the Baltic protests the forcible incorporation of the Baltic States into the Soviet Union.	February 1993	Brazauskas is elected president.
		1993	Direct rule is lifted in the Polish regions.
December 1989	The Communist Party of Lithuania declares its independence from the Communist Party of the Soviet Union.	May 1993	Lithuania is admitted to the European Council.
March 1990	Sąjūdis supported deputies win 100 of the 140 seats in the newly established republican legislature.	August 1993	Soviet troops leave Lithuania.
		1995	Relations are normalized with Poland.
		1995	The banking crisis and public scandals lead to the collapse of the Šleževičius government.
11 March 1990	The newly elected Supreme Council declares the restoration of Lithuania's independence and appoints a communist government.	October 1996	The Homeland Union wins the legislative elections.
		1998	Adamkus is elected president; the government is reorganized.
May 1990	The Soviet Union initiates an economic blockade against Lithuania, demanding that the legislature recant the declaration of the restoration of independence.	April 1999	Conflict with the president and an economic recession related to the Russian ruble crisis leads to the resignation of the Vagnorius government.
December 1990	The Communist Party of Lithuania renames itself the Democratic Labor Party.	Summer 1999	A public storm erupts over the oil privatization deal with an American firm.
January 1991	The Democratic Labor Party government is replaced by a Sąjūdis government in the wake of mounting public protests over increases in food prices.	October 1999	The Paksas government refuses to sign the oil privatization deal. Paksas resigns.
		November 1999	The Kubilius government signs the oil privatization deal. Public protests continue unabated.
11 January 1991	The National Salvation Front announces it is assuming all political authority in Lithuania, and the Soviet Army forcibly occupies the TV tower and press center in Vilnius.	October 2000	For the first time legislative elections do not return a majority party. A coalition of parties forms a government headed by Paksas.
February 1991	A public referendum votes overwhelmingly for independence.	Spring 2001	The Paksas government resigns and is replaced by a new coalition government headed by Brazauskas.
July 1991	Lithuanian border guards are murdered at Medininkai.	2001	Lithuania joins the World Trade Organization.
August 1991	A conservative coup fails in Moscow.	2002	Lithuania is extended invitations to membership in NATO and the European Union (EU).
September 1991	The Soviet Union and the United States recognize Lithuanian independence.		
17 September 1991	Lithuania is formally admitted to the United Nations.	2003	Paksas is elected president.
		December 2003	Impeachment proceedings are initiated against President Paksas.
September 1991	Direct rule is introduced in the ethnically Polish regions surrounding Vilnius.	2004	Paksas is removed as president.
		2004	Lithuania joins NATO and the EU.